Greenberg's GUIDES ®

LIONEL® TRAINS
POCKET PRICE GUIDE

Editor: Kent J. Johnson
with assistance from Roger Carp

KALMBACH BOOKS

Twenty-fifth Edition

For more information, visit our website at
www.kalmbachbooks.com

Cover design: Kristi Ludwig
Book layout: Lesley Weiss

Cover photo: Provided by Joe Algozzini, model no. 2345 Western
Pacific F3 AA units was produced in 1952.

We constantly strive to improve *Greenberg's Pocket Price Guides*.]
you find missing items or detect misinformation, please, by all
means, write to us. If you have recommendations for improving
listing, we would like to hear from you. Send your comments, ne
information, or corrections to:

Editor—Lionel Pocket Guide (10-8705)
Books Division
Kalmbach Publishing Co.
21027 Crossroads Circle
P.O. Box 1612
Waukesha, WI 53187-1612

Or via e-mail: books@kalmbach.com

*This edition involved the participation of many people who
generously gave of their time and knowledge. Although we apprecic
the contributions of everyone involved with this publication, we ar
especially indebted to Ken Meehan for the diligent effort he put fort
this year.*
                                                        —Kent J. Johns

CONTENTS

This handy reference is divided into seven major sections: Prewar 1901–1942, Postwar 1945–1969, Modern Era (MPC/LTI/Lionel LLC) 1970–2005, Modern Tinplate, Large Scale, Special Production, and Catalogs. In the first five sections and in the Large Scale section, production is listed numerically, using the item's catalog number. In the Prewar section, equipment is further described by gauge—Standard, O, OO, or 2⅞. The gauge type is within the parentheses.

    Steam locomotives in all sections include value with tender, even if tenders are not listed in detail. Be advised that the value of steam locomotives, particularly those of the Prewar period, may be significantly affected by the type of tender the item came with. For detailed information on tenders, consult the relevant comprehensive guides.

INTRODUCTION

What Products Are Listed

This Pocket Price Guide lists nearly every Lionel toy train product produced between the years 1901–1942 and 1945–2004 (there was no Lionel production during World War II). This list of items also includes Lionel products tentatively planned for production in 2005, but not yet released at the time of publication. Subsequent additions and deletions to the 2005 product line will be reported in the next edition of this pocket guide.

How Products Are Listed

This guide is divided into seven major sections, each representing a significant era or type of production: Prewar, 1901–1942; Postwar, 1945–1969; Modern Era, 1970–2005 (including MPC, LTI, and Lionel LLC production); Modern Tinplate; Large Scale; Special Production; and Catalogs.

In the first five sections and in the Large Scale section, production is listed **numerically**, using the item's catalog number. In some cases, Lionel numbered products with a number different from the catalog number. In these cases we also list this number, enclosed in parentheses, and refer the reader to the published catalog number for the full product description.

In the Prewar section, equipment is further described by gauge—Standard, O, OO, or 2⅞. The gauge type is within the parentheses. Steam locomotives in all sections include value with tender, even if tenders are not listed in detail. Be advised that the value of steam locomotives, particularly those of the Prewar period, may be significantly affected by the type of tender the item came with. For detailed information on tenders, consult the relevant comprehensive guides.

Dates cited in this guide are cataloged dates. If there is no catalog date, production dates are listed, if known. While many products are frequently marked with "Built" or "New" dates, these dates often reflect the dates that company artists picked up from prototype photographs or the date when the artists prepared their drawings. These dates may or may not have any relation to catalog dates or actual production dates.

How Product Values Are Listed

We have provided three columns for items listed in Sections 1 through 5. The first two columns give the current market values for each piece. In the Prewar and Postwar sections, values are denoted for items in Good and Excellent condition. In the Modern Era sections, the Large Scale section, and the Catalog section, values are given for items in Excellent and New condition. The "Cond/$" column is for noting the condition and cost of items you acquire.

How Product Values Are Determined

The values presented in this Pocket Price Guide are meant to serve only as a guide to collectors. They are an averaged reflection of prices for items bought and sold across the country, and are intended to assist the collector in making informed decisions concerning purchases and sales.

Values listed herein are based on values obtained at train meets held throughout the nation during the Spring and Summer of 2003, and from private transactions reported by members of our nationwide review panel. Values in your area may be consistent with values published in this guide, or higher or lower, depending upon the relative availability, scarcity, or desirability of a particular item. General economic conditions in your area may also affect values. Even regional preferences for specific roadnames may be a factor.

If you are selling a train to an individual who is planning to resell it—a retailer, for example—you will NOT obtain the values reported in this book. Rather, you may expect to receive about 50 percent of these prices. For your item to be of interest to such a buyer, it must be purchased for considerably less than the price listed here. But if you are dealing one-to-one with another private collector, values may be expected to be more consistent with this guide.

Our studies of train values indicate that mail order and retail store prices are generally higher than prices found at train meets because of the cost and effort of running a retail establishment or producing and distributing a price list, as well as packing and shipping trains.

The values quoted in this guide are for the most common variety of each item. Some rare variations are worth considerably more, and a few of the more significant ones are cited. For more detailed information about variations, please refer to our comprehensive line of collector guides described at the back of this guide.

Note that new products usually enter the list at their suggested retail price, since most have yet to sell regularly on the secondary market.

WE STRONGLY RECOMMEND THAT NOVICE COLLECTORS SEEK THE ADVICE AND ASSISTANCE OF FRIENDS OR ASSOCIATES WHO HAVE EXPERIENCE IN BUYING, SELLING, AND TRADING TRAINS.

PRODUCT NUMBER
- **(#)** Numbers that have been put in parentheses by us do not appear on the actual items.
- **[#]** means decorations which make this item unique were not done by Lionel.
- **No Number** means item may have lettering, but lacks an item number.
- **(no letters)** means no lettering or number appears on the item.
- * means excellent reproductions have been made.

2343 Santa Fe F-3 AA Units, *50–52*
2343C Santa Fe F-3 B Unit, *50–55*
　　　　(A) Screen roof vents
　　　　(B) Louver roof vents
2344 NYC F-3 AA Units, *50–52*
2344C NYC F-3 B Unit, *50–55*
2345 Western Pacific F-3 AA Units, *52*
2346 B&M GP-9, *65–66*

DESCRIPTION
The text description for most items identifies the road (railroad) name, equipment type, equipment number (indicated in quotes), notable color or lettering data, and the year the item was first cataloged or produced (those dates followed by a "u" denote uncataloged items).

CONDITION

Trains and related items are usually classified by condition relating to appearance. The following definitions apply for this guide:

- **FAIR**—well-scratched, chipped, dented, rusted, or warped condition.
- **GOOD**—scratched, small dents, and dirty.
- **VERY GOOD**—few scratches, no dents, rust or warpage; very clean.
- **EXCELLENT**—minute scratches or nicks; no dents or rust; exceptionally clean.
- **LIKE NEW**—free of blemishes, nicks or scratches; original condition throughout, with vibrant colors; only faint signs of handling or use; price includes original box.
- **NEW**—brand new, absolutely unmarred, all original and unused, in original packaging with all paperwork provided by the manufacturer.
- **CP (Current Production)** means that the item is now being advertised, manufactured, or is currently available from retail stores.
- **NRS (No Recorded Sales)** means that we do not know the current market value of the item. The item may be very scarce and bring a substantial premium over items in its general class, or it may be relatively common but unnoticed. Usually NRS listings occur when an older and previously unknown item is first reported, although we are still discovering relatively common variations that have not been previously reported. If you have confirmable information about the value of an NRS item, please write to us.
- **NM (Not Manufactured)** means that the item may have been cataloged or otherwise advertised, but it was not produced.

● Good	Exc		
175	350	___	3
100	215	___	1
115	220	___	1
205	570	___	3
130	275	___	2
620	1250	___	2
190	315	___	1 ●

ACTIVE TRADING INDEX

The Active Trading Index is a measurement of how often a particular train is offered for sale on the open market. The Greenberg's Toy Train Active Trading Index is based on a five-point scale: an Active Trading Index value of "5" indicates that a train has appeared for sale in various advertisements, lists, and at shows/auctions with a frequency that places it in the top 20% of all toy trains. (To borrow a little terminology from the stock and bond markets, we can say that pieces with an Active Trading Index of "5" are among the most actively traded among collectors.) An Active Trading Index value of "4" indicates that the piece was offered for sale less frequently (i.e., in the next 20%), and so on, down to an Active Trading Index of "1."

7

TOY TRAIN COLLECTING

Excerpted from the Kalmbach Book *Toy Train Collecting and Operating: An Introduction to the Hobby.*

How to Start Collecting Toy Trains

Who collects toy trains? Most of today's toy train collectors have simply retained their love of trains from youth and continued to build upon it, going through various stages, changes, or specializations along the way. Others have experienced a rekindling of their childhood enthusiasm later in life, when they had children or grandchildren to share in the hobby.

Few hobbyists can afford to purchase everything produced by a particular manufacturer. Most collectors, therefore, choose a specific concentration of toy trains to collect. Collectors often narrow their focus to:

- One particular gauge or scale
- A specific manufacturer's products
- A certain era of toy train production
- One class of locomotive, rolling stock, accessory, or an individual road name

Where to Buy and Sell Toy Trains

The following suggested sources of old toy trains are tried and true. They are presented as starting points as you enter this fascinating and engrossing hobby.

- Private homes, garage sales, estate sales
- Classified ads in newspapers and magazines
- Mail order
- Hobby shops
- Swap meets and train shows
- Auctions
- Antique shops
- Trades with other collectors

How to Buy Toy Trains

While geared to the basic circumstances of swap meets, these guidelines will serve the uninitiated train buyer in other places and situations as well. Although they resemble flea markets and gypsy camps on the surface, these train events usually have rules governing them. Most are sponsored by groups or organizations that have a vested interest in promoting the hobby, and they are concerned about scam artists bilking their customer-guests.

Most regular dealers are fairly honest or at least try to be fair. Many are there primarily because they enjoy the hobby, too. Don't expect trade-ins, unlimited return privileges, layaways, or gift wrap. Few dealers are equipped to handle credit card purchases. And don't be surprised if they refuse to take your check. The first rule of the swap meet game: CASH AND CARRY.

What you see is what you get. All swap meet merchandise is sold as-is. While flaws and malfunctions should be noted, don't assume anything. Look over the merchandise carefully. Note the flaws. Ask questions about it before you start negotiating. Is it all original or does it include reproduced or remanufactured parts? Does it come with an original box? Does it work? Ask to take it to the test track so you can check the performance. Your best assurance is to buy from a dealer who has a good reputation or attends the meets regularly.

That brings us to the negotiation. Some dealers hold firmly to their ticket prices, considering them to be fair appraisals of market value. Others believe that dickering is part of the process of selling. A third group doesn't believe in ticket prices at all and will give you oral quotes if you ask. Give these dealers a wide berth unless you really know what you are doing.

The key to successful bargaining is to make a reasonable offer. Chiseling 10 to 15 percent from the ticket price in good-faith negotiation will probably be acceptable to most dealers. Some will consider larger discounts, but that is hard to predict. Package deals are good. Volume buying will often get you a few more total percentage points.

A dealer's willingness to negotiate on price can be contingent on many variables. Here's a list of the more common ones:

- Price of the item
- Rarity of the item
- Length of time the dealer has carried the item
- Volume of traffic at the meet
- Length of time into the meet
- Season of the year

One final bit of advice: Don't walk around a swap meet thumbing through your pocket price guide. That's a sure sign you're either ripe for picking or looking for an argument. The most vulnerable buyer is a neophyte with a book in his hand.

Preserving Toy Trains

As your collection grows, you will undoubtedly take more interest in maintaining its condition and value. How you choose to deal with this issue may well be one of the most important decisions you make regarding your collection.

Many would have you believe that toy trains should be kept only in a temperature- and humidity-controlled environment, free of dust and pollution, and away from direct sunlight. These trains were produced as toys. Although not indestructible, they are inherently tough.

High humidity can cause rust, but it is easily controlled using a small dehumidifier. Temperature, too, is only a factor in the extreme. And as far as dust, pollution, and direct sunlight are concerned, you need only look for practical solutions such as soft brushes, cans of compressed air, or in worst cases, mild soap and water or furniture polish.

—John Grams

Is Your Collection Properly Insured?
Don't make assumptions—talk to your agent!

There are many reasons why your model trains are special to you. Perhaps some trains are from childhood, others were acquired, still others were gifts...all have sentimental value, and some have substantial dollar value as well. Have you ever thought about what your collection is worth...and conveyed this information to your insurance agent?

If not, it's time to get educated! Many model train collectors (as well as collectors of vintage toys, automotive memorabilia, animation art, and other types of collectibles) assume—often wrongly—that their homeowner's insurance will adequately cover any loss or damage to their collection.

Test your knowledge and take this insurance quiz:

1. Your layout and some of your new in-box trains are in the basement and there is a flood. The water damages the layout and destroys some of the boxes—but luckily the trains are okay. Your homeowner's insurance company will:
   A) Ask you how much money you want to compensate for the damage
   B) Compensate you for damage to the layout, as well as for the value that the boxes had added to the trains, less a $100 deductible
   C) Not pay you a dime because flood coverage is excluded by your policy

2. A minor earthquake occurs in your area; the vibrations cause a shelf displaying your trains to be knocked loose. The loaded shelf falls on top of another shelf, and in the ensuing "domino effect," several trains sustain irreparable damage; there is minor damage to quite a few others. Your homeowner's insurance company will:
   A) Ask you how much money you want to compensate for the damage
   B) Pay full value for the trains that have been irreparably damaged and also pay to repair the trains that have sustained minor damage, less a $100 deductible
   C) Not pay you a dime because earthquake damage is excluded by your policy

3. Heavy winds cause a large tree to uproot and crash into your house. The insurance company will pay for debris removal, roof repair, and window replacement. You report that several of your pre- and postwar Lionel pieces were also destroyed. Your homeowner's insurance company will:
   A) Ask you how much money you want to compensate for the loss of the trains
   B) Pay you the collector market value of the trains ($950, less a $100 deductible)
   C) Ask the adjuster to investigate (he tells you he's never worked a "train claim" before)

4. Your American Flyer S Gauge trains were damaged in a house fire. The good news is, they can be fixed. The bad news is, it will cost $500 to repair them properly. Your homeowner's insurance company will:
   A) Ask how much money you want to get the trains repaired
   B) Pay for the professional repair, less a $100 deductible
   C) Not contribute towards the repair because your homeowner's deductible is $500 (or greater)

You didn't answer "A" for any of those, did you? (That's not how the insurance industry works!) Unfortunately, the correct answers to the quiz are all "C"—unless you happen to have a stand-alone policy for your collectibles or a very specific addendum to your homeowner's policy that covers your collection for "all perils" (e.g., earthquake, flood, etc.).

At the very least after reading this article, you should call your insurance agent and let him or her know that you have a collection and provide its approximate worth. Have a conversation about what types of losses would be covered—and what wouldn't. You can go one step further and ask your agent to investigate stand-alone collectibles coverage. This would be a policy that is separate from your homeowner's policy, and would provide primary coverage for your trains (and perhaps other collections in the household) in the event of damage or loss.

There are several big advantages to purchasing a stand-alone policy. The first advantage is that collectibles insurance provides "Agreed Value" coverage—meaning that the collector market value of your collectibles is recognized (and the full insured value of scheduled items is guaranteed) in the event of total loss. By contrast, most homeowner's policies pay claims based on "Actual Cash Value," defined as "replacement cost minus depreciation."

Second, collectibles insurance typically provides broad, "all risk" coverage, meaning that all perils (causes of loss) are insured against except for those specifically excluded by the policy (such as war, normal wear & tear, mechanical breakdown, and fraudulent acts). Homeowner's insurance policies typically list the perils insured against—such as fire and theft—but coverage is excluded for perils not named (such as flood and earthquake).

Third, homeowner's insurance is designed to protect your dwelling and its contents (furniture, carpeting, appliances, and so forth), and usually does not contain any language specific to collectibles. With homeowner's insurance, in the event of a claim, your collectibles get lumped in with personal property (unless a "rider" is attached, specifically addressing collectibles coverage).

Collectibles insurance is specifically for your collection(s) and can be surprisingly affordable. One specialty insurance provider by the name of American Collectors Insurance (Cherry Hill, NJ) offers $10,000 of blanket coverage for under $100 a year. If your collection is worth more than $10,000, American Collectors offers additional blanket coverage per $1000 of value. By the way, I used American Collectors as my benchmark for collectibles insurance (so if you have a policy with American Collectors, "B" becomes the answer to all the quiz questions above).

Here are some contact names/phone numbers of collectibles insurance providers, in case you want to check them out or pass them on to your agent:

1. American Collectors Insurance, www.AmericanCollectors.com,
   1 (800) 360-2277
2. AXA Art Insurance, www.axa-art.com, 1 (877) AXA-4ART
3. Chamberlin & Reinheimer (specializes in sports memorabilia),
   www.insuranceagency.com/sports/, 1 (800) 246-3740
4. Chubb Insurance (the sponsor of PBS's "Antiques Road Show"),
   www.chubb.com/personal/collectors.jsp, 1 (866) 324-8222
5. Hugh Wood, Inc. (specializes in stamp collections),
   www.hwint.com, (212) 509-3777

—Terry Kohl

Terry Kohl is a freelance writer and publicist for a number of national companies. She specializes in writing about collectibles, collector automobiles, and the automotive marketplace.

Years of Lionel Trains Timeline

1900 — 1901—Lionel trains are born with the 2⅞-inch scale train no. 200 Electric Express.

1905 — 1907—Standard gauge trains running on 3-rail tubular track replace 2⅞-inch scale trains.

1910

1915 — 1915—The no. 700, based on New York Central electric prototype, debuts as the first O gauge Lionel locomotive.

1920 — 1920 to 1930—Lionel rises to the top during the Classic Period of Standard gauge trains.

1925

1930 — 1934—The $1 Mickey Mouse handcar helps Lionel stay afloat during the Great Depression.

1935 — 1937—Lionel creates a masterpiece: the magnificent 700E scale Hudson steam locomotive.

1940

1945 — 1948—Lionel, in conjunction with General Motors, the Santa Fe Railway, and the New York Central Railroad, produces its landmark no. 2333 F3 diesels.

1950 — 1957—Lionel introduces its last and largest new steam locomotive of the Postwar era, the no. 746 Norfolk and Western J-class 4-8-4.

1955

1960 — 1969—The Postwar era ends. Lionel Corp. sells its train line to General Mills.

1965 — 1970—General Mills sets up train production in Michigan, and then briefly shifts production to Mexico in the early 1980s.

1970

1975 — 1974—Fundimensions issues the GE U36B, its first new locomotive that is not a Postwar reissue.

1980 — 1986—Richard Kughn buys Lionel from General Mills, forming Lionel Trains Inc.

1985

1990 — 1994—Lionel announces its high-tech TrainMaster wireless control system.

1995 — 1995—Richard Kughn sells Lionel to Wellspring Associates, an investment firm that creates Lionel LLC.

2001 — 2001—A century after it started, American production of Lionel electric trains moves offshore to China.

ANNUAL MARKET REPORT

In this report you'll find a number of features we've devised to help you gather an accurate assessment of the current market for Lionel Trains.

The **ATI® Top Ten** lists rank the ten products (within each production era) most regularly offered for sale on the open market. Whether you're buying or selling, these lists will help you see what items hold the most competitive positions. Additionally, the **ATI Composite**, a chart indicating the annual conglomerate value of a selected set of common and actively traded items, helps you evaluate the direction of product values in the overall market.

With the growing popularity of on-line auctions, you'll certainly want to read through the **CTT Market Basket Recap** for review and analysis of both conventional and on-line auction prices. And to wrap up the report, we've included **The Lionel Marketplace** segment to bring you dealer's feedback and comments regarding the latest product offerings and announcements.

ATI Top Ten lists

Lionel Prewar			Good	Exc
1.	2817	Caboose (O), *36–42*		
		(A) Light red body and roof	90	145
		(B) Flat red, tuscan roof	140	225
2.	58	Lamp Post, 7⅜" high, *22–42*	34	48
3.	92	Floodlight Tower, *31–42**	120	265
4.	700E	Steam 4-6-4, Scale Hudson, 5344 (O), *37–42**	1400	2550
5.	513	Cattle Car (Std.), *27–38*		
		(A) Olive green	70	145
		(B) Orange	70	110
		(C) Cream, maroon roof	70	135
6.	253	Electric 0-4-0 (O), *24–32*		
		(A) Maroon	180	430
		(B) Dark green	105	195
		(C) Mohave	105	235
		(D) Terra-cotta	180	430
		(E) Peacock	95	195
		(F) Red	210	475
7.	654	Tank Car (O), *34–42*		
		(A) Orange of aluminum finish	35	60
		(B) Gray	42	75
8.	814	Boxcar (O), *26–42*		
		(A) Cream, orange roof	46	105
		(B) Cream, maroon roof	115	140
		(C) Yellow, brown roof	115	120
9.	514	Refrigerator Car (Std.), *29–40*	170	225
10.	97	Coal Elevator, *38–42*	150	225

Lionel Postwar

			Good	Exc
1.	**3927**	Lionel Lines Track Cleaner, *56-60*	60	85
2.	**ZW**	Transformer, 275 watts, *50-66*	140	230
3.	**736**	Steam 2-8-4, 2671WX/2046W/736W Tender, *50-66*	235	390
4.	**50**	Lionel Gang Car, *54-64*	45	70
5.	**KW**	Transformer, 190 watts, *50-65*	90	125
6.	**364**	Conveyor Lumber Loader, *48-57*	85	115
(Tie)				
	2321	Lackawanna Train Master, *54-56*	350	415
	2332	Pennsylvania GG-1, *47-49*	355	850
9.	**60**	Lionelville Rapid Transit Trolley, *55-58*	95	155
(Tie)				
	3360	Operating Burro Crane, *56-57*	140	215

Lionel Modern Era

			Exc	New
1.	**(11711)**	Santa Fe F3 ABA set "8100," "8101," "8102," *91*	450	550
2.	**(28052)**	N&W Class A 2-6-6-4 Articulated Steam Locomotive "1218," *00*	—	1100
3.	**(8606)**	B&A 4-6-4 "784," *86 u*	800	900
4.	**(18303)**	Amtrak GG-1 "8303," *89*	360	440
5.	**(18045)**	"777" Commodore Vanderbilt, *96*	—	780
6.	**(18007)**	Southern Pacific 4-8-4 "4410," *91*	590	620
7.	**(29294)**	Hellgate Bridge Boxcar "1900-2000," *99 u*	—	90
8.	**(18000)**	PRR 0-6-0 "8977" *89, 91*	420	475
9.	**(18205)**	Union Pacific Dash 8-40C "9100," *89*	190	230
10.	**(28029)**	UP Big Boy 4-8-8-4 Articulated Steam Locomotive "4006," *99-00*	—	1350

ATI Composite Trading Ticker

`Catalog No.•Description•Current price`

```
Prewar 116 Station •$1,450 . . . . . .Prewar 400E Steam
Postwar 455 Operating Oil Derrick •$170 . . . . . .Postwar
. . . . Postwar 2344 NYC F-3 AA units $570 . . . . .
6907 NYC Wood-sided Caboose •$90 . . . . . . Modern 11711
Steam Turbine Locomotive •$1,350 . . . . . . . . . . .
```

ATI Composite Value

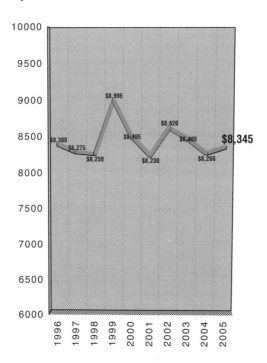

ATI Composite Summary

	Current Value	2004	1996	MSRP
			Percentage change from	
2004 Composite	$8,345	1.0%	0.4%	407.8%
Prewar	$3,600	0.0%	5.9%	6445.5%
Postwar	$2,755	3.2%	4.8%	1890.6%
Modern	$1,990	0.0%	-15.3%	37.2%

Locomotive •$2,150 . . . . . . Postwar ZW •$230. . . . .
773 LL 4-6-4 Steam Locomotive w/ 2426W Tender •$1,700 . .
Postwar 3927 Track Cleaning Car •$85 . . . . . . .Modern
AT&SF F-3 ABA set •$550 . . . . Modern 18010 PRR 6-8-6
. . . .

CTT MARKET BASKET RECAP

What looks good in the catalogs?

Picking which Lionel products will be hot can be dangerous to your mental health. For example, I would have guessed that Lionel's no. 38056 rendering of the Pennsylvania Railroad's M1-class 4-8-2 would have been a high-demand item, but by the end of 2003 it was being blown out under $700, down from an MSRP of $1,200. Another notable blow-out was the 31704 Alton Limited passenger set originally priced at $1,400, selling for $850; and the no. 21797 Southern Pacific Daylight set, listed for $1,000 and being sold for $650. The clear plastic 38150 Lionel Lines F3 A-A set was retailing at one shop for $295. Ouch.

This just reminds us all to buy trains because we like them, not because they'll hold their original value!

In 2003 Lionel representatives stated that the firm would slow-down production to help reduce retailer-level problems with an over-saturated market. While that has happened, it doesn't mean that any of the recent Lionel dream books have been light on interesting goodies.

High-end contenders

The no. 31714 Amtrak *Acela* is special in many ways. The first thing any fan noticed was the price: $2,000. This sets a new high for a modern-era Lionel product's retail price. Targeting a niche within the hobby (both Amtrak and electric railway enthusiasts) a unique order deadline was instituted and promotional material on the internet drew attention to the product to ensure that Lionel would have the required minimum order number in hand before initiating production.

The model itself could be either Lionel's greatest triumph, or it's most colossal blunder if it fails to live up to the technological promises. Promising uncompromising detail, opening doors, controllable pantographs, and even a tilt function, it will need to deliver a lot. Some will say "It has a lot of features," while others will retort "It has a lot to go wrong with it."
The proof will be in the pudding. With a sticker price of $2,000 it will need to be done right, or it will kill potential sales for any future super-premium trains.

The no. 51008 *Pioneer Zephyr*, with its die-cast metal shells could a major hit with enthusiasts of Retroville streamline passenger gear. The prewar-styling coupled with modern control and sound systems should be a winner for operators and collectors alike.

Mid-range goodies

Lionel's new scale F3 is now cataloged in two body styles (raised and lowered fans) and at least five road names. Packed with loads of detail, it is priced at $699.99 for an A-A set, $299.99 for a powered B unit and $199.99 for an unpowered B unit. The first run of Santa Fe is tough, if not impossible to find. The second Santa Fe run may satisfy demand for this beauty.

The Lionel E6 continues to be one of the sharpest looking diesels out there. Now available in Southern, Milwaukee Road, and Santa Fe, this is a slick addition to any layout focusing on the steam/diesel transition years. This diesel may appeal to the same hobbyists who set out to snag the Zephyr.

Low-end contenders

The coup of the year might be Lionel's landing the license for the upcoming animated movie "Polar Express," based on the children's book of the same name. If the movie is a hit (with either kids, or perhaps more importantly, the parents and grandparents who buy their kids' toys) it could be a large asset to the hobby, simply by planting a seed that will bear fruit in 20 years when today's kids reach middle age and need a family oriented hobby.

Lionel is offering up a new 0-6-0 switcher for under $100. The firm's new small Berkshire is a superb buy at $229.99, and the firm's assortment of track speeders, ballast tampers, and other motorized units let operators buy equipment for a change of pace, that has the side benefit of not breaking the bank.

Lionel continues to develop superb rolling stock. While I'm not much for gondolas, the new PS-5 gon with a flat top and opening access hatch stands out amid 50 years of gondola production. The series of Lionel steel- and wood-sided refrigerator cars may well become as hot a collectors item as similar reefers made by Atlas O. Combine production quality with superb, bright, creative graphics and you've got a winner.

Auction action

There is far less of a distinction between electronic auctions and conventional auctions these days, simply because in many cases, bidders have the chance to follow and bid on the auction electronically. The major difference is that "long distance" bidders in a "brick-and-mortar" auction house don't have the chance to visually scope out the competition and receive the satisfaction you get when you can see on their faces that you've topped their bid!

The saying "Top quality goods will receive top dollar prices," is now pretty much a cliché. So rather than track the astronomical "one-of-a-kind" sales that have a lot of "wow" but very little bearing on most operators or collectors, this year I tried to focus on trains that they typical hobbyist might try to get on-line or waving his paddle in the auction gallery. I've also tossed in a curiosity or two, like empty boxes and smoke pellets.

PREWAR:
Prewar trains are far from dead. There seem to be quite a few major collections that have been broken up recently, and a lot of quality goods are getting into the hands to of the next generation of tinplate aficionado.

No. 1 Trolley $6,700; No. 54 locomotive $2,829; No. 400E (black) locomotive $2,225; No. 203 armored locomotive $1,658; No. 230 B6 switcher $995; No. 840 power station $968; No. 752W *City of Salina* set $910; No. 300 Hell Gate bridge $776; No. 763E locomotive $676; No. 217 orange standard gauge caboose $572; No. 512

Lionel City station $512; No. 442 diner w/OB $510; No. 115 station $475; No. 214 standard gauge Terra-Cotta boxcar $461; No. 16 standard gauge ballast car $455; No. 438 switch tower $395; No. 752W set $382; No. 134 station $306

POSTWAR: *Accessories*

A lot of great accessories are on the market right now. Everything from coal loaders to little blister packs with untouched 40 year-old merchandise. Collectors can score the boxed operating accessory of their dreams, and the operator can find a good deal on those lamp posts and crossing gates they to complete the vintage look.

No. 460P platform in sealed box $5,200; No. 455 oil derrick apple green and red w/OB and inserts $1,950; No. 448 missile firing range w/OB $1,000; No. 968 Lionel Plasticville TV transmitter w/OB and inserts $750; No. 123 lamp assortment in original box $425; No. KW transformer w/OB $400; No. B925 blister pack of Lionel lubricant $375; No. B151 automatic semaphore blister pack $375; No. 334 dispatch board w/OB $375; No. 348 manual culvert unloader w/OB and inserts $325; No. 497 coal loader w/OB and inserts $325; No. 415 diesel service station w/OB $300; No. 164 lumber loader w/OB $300; ZW 275 watt transformer $271; 342 Culvert loader w/OB $252; No. 352 Icing station w/OB $250; No. 193 control tower $213; No. 362 barrel loader $168; No. 30 water tower w/OB $160; No. 397 coal loader w/OB $152; No. 465 dispatch station w/OB $144; No. 394 operating beacon $102;

POSTWAR and MODERN: *Locomotives*

These two eras don't normally appear together. I thought it was fun to compile a listing that allows you to get a good perspective in where motive power of the two eras fall in the hearts, minds, and pocketbooks of today's hobbyists.

No., 212T USMC dummy Alco A unit w/OB $4,100; No. 729 Burlington center cab w/OB $2,200; No. 2431 Jersey Central Train Master $1,580; No. 2378 Milwaukee Road F3 A-A set $1,525; No. 773 w/2426W tender $1,500; No. 21786 Santa Fe F3 A-B-B-A $1,425; No. 773 (1964 version) w/OB $1,400; No. 2373 Canadian Pacific F3 A-A $1,332; No. 28062 100th Anniversary Gold Hudson $1,200; No. 28063 PRR T1 4-4-4-4 $711; No. 28064 Challenger $1,450; No. 28028 Virginian 2-6-6-6 $1,200; No. 38024 PRR S1 6-4-4-6 $935-$1,275; No. 14536 Santa Fe F3 A-B-A prices from $900-$1,250; No. 2031 Rock island A-A w/OB $1,000; No. 28052 N&W 2-6-6-4 $796; No. 18058 Century Club 4-6-4 Hudson $788; No. 28069 Century Club 4-8-4 Mohawk $750; No. 671RR Turbine w/OB $700; No. 28022 Westside Lumber shay $697; No. 44 Missile launcher w/OB $600; No. 2367 Wabash F3 A-B $599; No. 58 Great Northern motorized unit $550; No. 24520 Alaska F3 set $529; No. 746 Norfolk & Western J class 4-8-4 $450; No. 18002 gray Hudson prices from $325-$417; No. 18005 Scale Hudson, prices from $400 to $850; No. 18006 Reading T1 4-8-4 $355 to $400; No. 18131 Northern Pacific F3 set $465; No. 682 Turbine with 2046W-50 tender $225; No. 226E w/2426W tender $225; No. 18007 Daylight 4-8-4 w/OB $225; No. 726 Berkshire w/2426W tender (1946) $200; No. 681 Turbine $175; No. 2321 maroon-top Lackawanna Train master

$175; No. 205 Missouri Pacific Alco A-A $160; No. 1065 Union Pacific Alco A unit $145; No. 211 Texas special Alco A-A $100

BOXED SETS

Boxed sets have always had a certain mystique for me, simply because so few kid's kept everything together. The hobbyists of today salute the Mom's and Dad's of yesteryear for ensuring that their kid's toys were well cared for. Today we find that many sets in all grades and quality ranges are coming out of collections and offer even stingy collectors the chance to add a few intact outfits to their collections.

No. 707W steam freight set $16,358; No. 2551W EP5 electric freight set $11,000; No. 2253W GG1 freight set $7,250; No. 1805 USMC Land and Air set $4,100; No. 381E Lionel Classics State set $2,199; No. 21787 Lionel Classics *Blue Comet* set $1,695; No. 1587S "Lady Lionel" steam freight set $1,950; No. 1517 Texas Special diesel freight $1,700; No. 21786 Santa Fe anniversary set $1,524; No. 9820 Sears Allstate military set $1,508; No. 1615 diesel freight set $1,500; No. 2190W diesel passenger set $1,426; No. 2190W diesel passenger set $950; No. 29122 Erie-Lackawanna F3 *Phoebe Snow* set $535; No. 1542/X150 (electric freight) $475; No. 19440 diesel freight set $450; No. 1702E diesel passenger set $443; No. 1509WS steam freight set $425; No. 296 prewar passenger set $400; No. 1513S steam freight set $360; No. 1503WS steam freight set $325; No. 1867 Milwaukee Limited diesel freight set $250; No. 1585 75th Anniversary set $200; No. 1868 Minneapolis & St. Louis Service Station Set $150

LIONEL BOXES

Pieces of old cardboard continue to show their worth. Whenever someone asks "Are the old boxes worth anything," I always say "Yes." Their next question is always "How much?" To which I always say "I don't know." Depending on the item or the scarcity of the box, the box could be worth a lot more than the item it contained. There are also a lot of fairly common postwar boxes, so an old box doesn't always mean you'll be able to super-size that new swimming pool!

Set box for 4209WS Electronic outfit $2,600; Master carton for CTC lock-ons $2,000; Master carton for no. 2020LTS set $1,500; Box for no. 400E-72 locomotive with insert $455; Set box for no. 42 standard gauge outfit $404; Box for no. 6464-825 Alaskan boxcar $400; Set box for no. 267W Flying Yankee outfit $305; Box for no. 2023 w/center insert $250; Master carton for set no. 2161W $175; Box for no. 1872 General $170; Box for no. 746 steam locomotive $133; Box for no. 2322 Virginian Train Master $132; Box for no. 2353 Santa Fe powered A unit $125

—Bob Keller, associate editor of *Classic Toy Trains*

Products of Distinction

No. 28628 Virginian Berkshire

The Virginian only had a handful of 2-8-4's, but they delivered did as good a job on coal drags as they did moving fast freight.
Lionel's no. 38077 Berkshire offers upgraded tooling and a robust sound system that will make you cry for joy.

No. 28628 small L&N Berkshire

Lionel's small Berkshire is a gem. The no. 28628 features excellent performance, Lionel RailSounds, and O-27 operation for under $230. You can't ask for much more than that in an entry-level locomotive.

No. 28817 Reading GP30

Lionel's no. 28817 Reading GP30 is a superb
model of a locomotive that might be easy to for-
get in the years between the F3 and the GP40.
The gentle curves were most "un-diesel-like" and
make this possible the mosr graceful hood unit
ever fielded.

No. 21788 missile launch set

Lionel's re-creations of classic postwar train sets
now gives every vintage train guy or gal the
chance to purchase brand new versions of the
outfits that "got away" from them as children.
The no. 21788 missile launch set offered great
value and modern production methods.

No. 38045 Hudson

Lionel's no. 38045 added something to the mix
we hadn't seen before. A small O-31 Hudson with
tons of scale detail. This locomotive sets the bar
for quality for Lionel's tight-radius fleet.

No. 38058 C&O 2-8-8-2

The no. 38058 Chesapeake & Ohio H7-class 2-8-8-2 illustrated Lionel's committment to build unique, scale models of historic loco-motion. Priced at $1,649.99, it also raised expectations among hobbyists that seem to have been satisfied.

No. 38083 N&W Y3 2-8-8-2

The no. 38083 Norfolk & western Y3 2-8-8-2 is one prime example of the massive steam giants that once served the coal railways. The locomotive packs every feature available along with a new synchronized smoke func-tion. Priced at $1,499.99 it is also available in the no. 38082 Pennsylvania road name.

No. 21791 American Freedom Train

Lionel's rendering of the original, Alco PA-powered Freedom Train does the historic train proud. Both in detail and (gasp) opera-tion, this is one collector's item that will see plenty of track time. The no. 21791 looks stunning and runs like a top.

Nos. 38079 and 38080 4-8-4s

Lionel's latest salute to West coast railroading are the nos. 38079 Southern Pacific GS-2 4-8-4 and the 38080 Western Pacific GS-64. Not just a slight variation of the same model tooling, both feature specific details such as unique tenders, to help re-create the look of these sleek beauties. The locomotive is priced at $1,199.99.

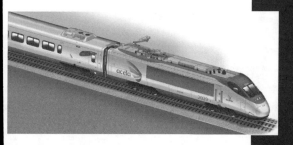

No. 31714 Acela

As previous eras of Lionel were known for the Blue Comet, scale Hudson, or F3, the Lionel of the 21st Century may be known by the no. 31714 Acela. Lionel promises close coupling, car tilt, engraved control panels with illuminated gauges, operating pantograph, and opening doors. Succeed or fail, this model will be a milestone in Lionel's history.

No. 24147 sawmill

Lionel's re-introduction (and improvement) of venerable accessories from both the Lionel and American Flyer product lines has made many an operator happy. Priced to be competitive with original issue products, rigs like this no. 24147 Lionel sawmill ($129.99) are finding homes on traditional layouts who's owners prefer new to elderly operating gear.

No. 17181 center flow hopper

Lionel's designers are working hard to eliminate the toy-like and implement the scale-like throughout all their new rolling stock releases, such as the no. 17181 New York Central ACF four-bay Center Flow aluminum hopper is available for grain service. The car operates on O-31 or wider curves and costs $64.99.

Visit classictoytrains.com

No. 14166 train order building

Lionel has reworked it's Mountie accessory and produced an item that makes operational sense on any O gauge pike: The no.14166 train order building on which, an O scale employee runs out to pass train orders to a passing locomotive crew, Big, realistic O gauge fun for $69.99.

Flyer talking station

"Train 7, now leaving for Barstow, San Diego, Sacramento, and Kookamonga...." Record the announcements of your choice with the no. 49812 talking station. with some careful placement, this american Flyer S gauge product can nestle right in and be at home on any traditional O gauge pike. The 49812 costs $199.99.

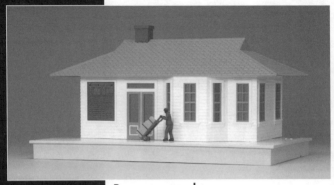

Baggage smasher

Don't let the heritage of the no. 49813 baggage smasher dissuade you from checking it out. Come'on, don't those pesky passengers who force you to run those money-losing passenger trains really deserve some grief? The no. 49813 costs $129.99.

No. 38079 Daylight

Lionel may not exactly "own" the Southern Pacific Daylight 4-8-4 design in O gauge, but it has offered a number of excellent examples of this colorful prototype. The latest is the no. 38079 Southern Pacific GS-2. Featuring specific details such as a unique tender, it re-creates the look of this orange marvel, rather than evoking the image of a re-worked Norfolk & Western "J." The locomotive is priced at $1,199.99.

Section 1
PREWAR 1901–1942

		Good	Exc	Cond/$
001	Steam 4-6-4 (OO), *38-42*	195	395	__1
1	Bild-A-Motor, *28-31*	60	140	__1
1	Trolley (Std.), *06-14*			
	(A) Cream body, orange band/roof	1900	4750	__1
	(B) White body, blue band/roof	1750	4750	__1
	(C) Cream body, blue band/roof	1300	3150	__1
	(D) Cream body, blue band/roof	2150	5550	__1
	(E) Blue, cream band, blue roof	1450	3150	__1
1/111	Trolley Trailer (Std.), *06-14*	1000	2700	__1
002	Steam 4-6-4 (OO), *39-42*	160	315	__1
2	Bild-A-Motor, *28-31*	100	180	__1
2	Countershafting, *04-11*		NRS	__
2	Trolley (Std.), *06-16**			
	(A) Yellow, red band	1200	2250	__1
	(B) Red, yellow band	1200	2250	__1
2/200	Trolley Trailer (Std.), *06-16*	1000	1800	__1
003	Steam 4-6-4 (OO), *39-42*			
	(A) With 003W whistling tender	190	395	__1
	(B) With 003T non-whistling tender	175	355	__1
3	Trolley (Std.), *06-13*			
	(A) Cream, orange band	1400	3100	__1
	(B) Cream, dark olive green band	1400	3100	__1
	(C) Orange, dark olive green band	1400	3100	__1
	(D) Dark green, cream windows	1400	3100	__1
	(E) Green, cream window, "BAY SHORE"	1650	3700	__1
3/300	Trolley Trailer (Std.), *06-13*	1500	3500	__1
004	Steam 4-6-4 (OO), *39-42*			
	(A) With 004W whistling tender	210	350	__1
	(B) With 004T non-whistling tender	190	310	__1
4	Electric 0-4-0 (O), *28-32**			
	(A) Orange, black frame	550	900	__1
	(B) Gray, apple green stripe	580	1050	__1
4	Trolley (Std.), *06-12*			
	(A) Cream, dark olive green band	3000	4950	__1
	(B) Green or olive green, cream roof	3000	4950	__1
4U	#4 Kit form (O), *28-29*	1150	1600	__1
5	Electric ($2\frac{7}{8}$") (See 100)			
5	Steam 0-4-0, no tender, Early (Std.), *06-07*			
	(A) "N.Y.C. & H.R.R."	1000	1450	__1
	(B) "PENNSYLVANIA"	1400	2300	__1
	(C) "N.Y.C. & H.R.R.R." (3 Rs)	1250	2050	__1

		Good	Exc	Cond/$
	(D) "B. & O. R.R."	1500	2400	__1
5	Steam 0-4-0, w/ tender, Early Special (Std.), *06-09*	1150	1500	__1
5	Steam 0-4-0, no tender, Later (Std.), *10-11*	750	1150	__1
5	Steam 0-4-0, w/ tender, Later Special (Std.), *10-11*	830	1400	__1
5/51	Steam 0-4-0, w/ tender, Latest (Std.), *12-23*	800	1100	__1
6	Steam 4-4-0 (Std.), *06-23*	750	1100	__1
6	Steam 0-4-0 Special (Std.), *08-09*	2050	2950	__1
7	Steam 4-4-0 (Std.), *10-23**	1850	2300	__1
8	Electric 0-4-0 (Std.), *25-32*			
	(A) Maroon, brass windows/trim	235	250	__1
	(B) Olive green or mojave w/ brass	155	205	__1
	(C) Red, brass or cream window	195	250	__1
	(D) Peacock, orange windows	520	750	__1
8	Trolley (Std.), *08-14**			
	(A) Cream, orange band and roof	3000	5400	__1
	(B) Dark green, cream windows	3000	5400	__1
8E	Electric 0-4-0 (Std.), *26-32*			
	(A) Mojave, brass windows/trim	175	240	__1
	(B) Red, brass or cream window	130	205	__1
	(C) Peacock, orange windows	370	590	__1
	(D) Pea green, cream stripe	465	670	__1
9	Electric 0-4-0 (Std.), *29**	1200	2150	__1
9	Trolley (Std.), *09*	3000	5400	__1
9E	Electric 0-4-0 (Std.), *28-35**			
	(A) 0-4-0	700	1250	__1
	(B) 2-4-2, two-tone green	880	1600	__1
	(C) 2-4-2, gun-metal gray	820	1300	__1
9U	Electric 0-4-0 Kit (Std.), *28-29*	1050	2050	__2
9	Motor Car (Std.), *09-12*		NRS	___
10	Electric 0-4-0 (Std.), *25-29**			
	(A) Mojave, brass trim	150	215	__1
	(B) Gray, brass trim	125	205	__1
	(C) Peacock, brass inserts	145	205	__1
	(D) Red, cream stripe	580	880	__1
10	Interurban (Std.), *10-16*			
	(A) Maroon	3000	5750	__1
	(B) Dark olive green	1200	2150	__1
10E	Electric 0-4-0 (Std.), *26-30*			
	(A) Olive green, black frame		NRS	___
	(B) Peacock, dark green or black frame	345	470	__1
	(C) State brown, dark green frame	435	630	__1
	(D) Gray, black frame	165	220	__1
	(E) Red, cream stripe	620	890	__1
011	Switches, pair (O), *33-37*	17	35	__1

		Good	Exc	Cond/$
11	Flatcar, Early (Std.), *06-11*	150	360	__1
11	Flatcar, Later (Std.), *11-16*	50	90	__1
11	Flatcar, Latest (Std.), *16-18*	50	90	__1
11	Flatcar, Lionel Corp. (Std.), *18-26*	50	80	__1
012	Switches, pair (O), *27-33*	21	38	__1
12	Gondola, Early (Std.), *06-11*	600	720	__1
12	Gondola, Later(Std) *11-16*	50	90	__1
12	Gondola, Latest (Std.), *16-18*	45	70	__1
12	Gondola, Lionel Corp. (Std.), *18-26*	50	70	__1
013	(2) 012 Switches and 439 Panel Board, *27-33*	120	190	__1
13	Cattle Car, Early (Std.), *06-11*	300	450	__1
13	Cattle Car, Later (Std.), *11-16*	150	225	__1
13	Cattle Car, Latest (Std.), *16-18*	65	115	__1
13	Cattle Car, Lionel Corp. (Std.), *18-26*	65	115	__1
0014	Boxcar (OO), *38-42*			
	(A) Yellow, "Lionel Lines"	80	155	__1
	(B) Tuscan body, "PENNSYLVANIA"	50	75	__1
14	Boxcar, Early (Std.), *06-11*	195	435	__1
14	Boxcar, Later (Std.), *11-16*	80	105	__1
14	Boxcar, Latest (Std.), *16-18*	80	105	__1
14	Boxcar, Lionel Corp. (Std.), *18-26*	80	105	__1
0015	Tank Car (OO), *38-42*			
	(A) Silver, "SUN OIL"	40	80	__1
	(B) Black, "SHELL"	40	75	__1
15	Oil Car, Early (Std.), *06-11*	200	360	__1
15	Oil Car, Later (Std.), *11-16*	75	115	__1
15	Oil Car, Latest (Std.), *16-18*	75	115	__1
15	Oil Car, Lionel Corp. (Std.), *18-26*	75	115	__1
0016	Hopper Car (OO), *38-42*			
	(A) Gray	75	145	__1
	(B) Black	75	105	__1
16	Ballast (Dump) Car, Early (Std.), *06-26*	245	395	__1
16	Ballast (Dump) Car, Later (Std.), *11-16*	95	175	__1
16	Ballast (Dump) Car, Latest (Std.), *16-18*	95	175	__1
16	Ballast (Dump) Car, Lionel Corp. (Std.), *18-26*	95	175	__1
0017	Caboose (OO), *38-42*	50	90	__1
17	Caboose, Early (Std.), *06-11*	220	440	__1
17	Caboose, Later (Std.), *11-16*	70	135	__1
17	Caboose, Latest (Std.), *16-18*	70	135	__1
17	Caboose, Lionel Corp. (Std.), *18-26*	50	90	__1
18	Pullman (Std.), *08*			
	(A) Dark olive green, unremovable roof	700	2150	__1
	(B) Dark olive green, removable roof	90	195	__1
	(C) Yellow-orange, removable roof	275	870	__1
	(D) Orange, removable roof	80	180	__1

		Good	Exc	Cond/$
	(E) Mojave, removable roof	275	870	__1
18	Pullman (Std.), *11-13*		NRS	__
18	Pullman (Std.), *13-15*	150	270	__1
18	Pullman (Std.), *15-18*	150	270	__1
18	Pullman (Std.), *18-22*	80	135	__1
18	Pullman (Std.), *23-26*	270	530	__1
19	Combine (Std.), *08*			
	(A) Dark olive green, unremovable roof	1100	2600	__1
	(B) Dark olive green, removable roof	80	125	__1
	(C) Yellow-orange, removable roof	225	375	__1
	(D) Orange, removable roof	100	180	__1
	(E) Mojave, removable roof	275	870	__1
19	Combine (Std.), *11-13*		NRS	__
19	Combine (Std.), *13-15*	200	270	__1
19	Combine (Std.), *15-18*	200	270	__1
19	Combine (Std.), *18-22*	80	135	__1
19	Combine (Std.), *23-26*	265	520	__1
020	90° Crossover (O), *15-42*	2	5	__1
020	90° Crossover (O), *15-42*	2	5	__1
020X	45° Crossover (O), *17-42*	2.50	7	__1
20	90° Crossover (Std.), *09-32*	4	9	__1
20	Direct Current Reducer, *06*	—	195	__1
20X	45° Crossover (Std.), *28-32*	5	9	__1
021	Switches, pair (O), *15-37*	20	46	__1
21	Switches, pair (Std.), *15-25*	40	70	__2
21	90° Crossover (Std.), *06*	10	18	__1
022	Switches, pair, Remote (O), *38-42*	38	70	__1
22	Switches, pair (Std.), *06-25*	47	75	__1
023	Bumper (O), *15-33*	15	37	__1
23	Bumper (Std.), *06-23*	19	39	__1
0024	PRR Boxcar (OO), *39-42*	45	75	__1
24	Railway Station (Std.), *06*		NRS	__
025	Bumper (O), *28-42*	22	31	__1
0025	Tank Car (OO), *39-42*			
	(A) Black, "SHELL"	40	90	__1
	(B) Silver, "SUNOCO"	40	80	__1
25	Open Station (Std.), *06*		NRS	__
25	Bumper (Std.), *27-42*	30	44	__1
26	Passenger Bridge (Std.), *06*	—	40	__1
0027	Caboose (OO), *39-42*	40	70	__1
27	Lighting set, *11-23*	15	41	__1
27	Station (Std.), *09-12*		NRS	__
28	Double Station w/ dome, *09-12*		NRS	__
29	Day Coach (Std.), *07-22*			
	(A) Dark olive green, 9-window	1500	3000	__2
	(B) Maroon, 10-window body	1200	1500	__2

		Good	Exc	Cond/$
	(C) Dark green, 10-window body	3000	4500	__2
	(D) Dark olive green, 10-window	680	1000	__2
	(E) Dark green, 10-window body	500	900	__2
29	(See #3 Trolley)			
31	Combine (Std.), *21-25*			
	(A) Maroon	70	90	__1
	(B) Orange	115	170	__1
	(C) Dark olive green	70	90	__1
	(D) Brown	75	95	__1
32	Mail Car (Std.), *21-25*			
	(A) Maroon	85	125	__1
	(B) Orange	105	160	__1
	(C) Dark olive green	65	85	__1
	(D) Brown	70	90	__1
32	Miniature Figures, *09-18*	75	135	__1
33	Electric 0-6-0, Early (Std.), *13*			
	(A) Dark olive green, NYC in oval	90	175	__1
	(B) Black, NYC LINES in oval	440	950	__1
	(C) Dark olive green, NYC	440	950	__1
	(D) "PENNSYLVANIA RAILROAD"	580	1250	__1
33	Electric 0-4-0, Later (Std.), *13-24*			
	(A) Dark olive green or black, NYC	90	150	__1
	(B) Black, lettered "C & O"	395	720	__1
	(C) Maroon, red, or peacock	340	620	__1
34	Electric 0-6-0, Early (Std.), *12*	450	810	__1
34	Electric 0-4-0 (Std.), *13*	200	385	__1
35	Blvd. Lamp, 6⅛" high, *40-42*	23	45	__1
35	Pullman (Std.), *12-13*			
	(A) Dark blue	470	900	__1
	(B) Dark olive green	150	205	__1
35	Pullman (Std.), *14-16*			
	(A) Dark olive green, maroon windows	50	70	__1
	(B) Maroon, green windows	85	105	__1
	(C) Orange, maroon windows	125	170	__1
35	Pullman (Std.), *15-18*	50	70	__1
35	Pullman (Std.), *18-23*			
	(A) Dark olive green, maroon windows	36	50	__1
	(B) Maroon, green windows	30	45	__1
	(C) Orange, maroon windows	110	195	__1
	(D) Brown, green windows	36	50	__1
35	Pullman (Std.), *24*	40	55	__1
35	Pullman (Std.), *25-26*	40	55	__1
36	Observation (Std.), *12-13*			
	(A) Dark blue	315	810	__1
	(B) Dark olive green	125	180	__1

		Good	Exc	Cond/$
36	Observation (Std.), *14-16*			
	(A) Dark olive green, maroon windows	70	95	__1
	(B) Maroon, green windows	50	70	__1
	(C) Orange, maroon windows	180	290	__1
	(D) Brown, green windows	60	75	__1
36	Observation (Std.), *15-18*	60	80	__1
36	Observation (Std.), *18-23*			
	(A) Dark olive green, maroon windows	40	55	__1
	(B) Maroon, green windows	40	55	__1
	(C) Orange, maroon windows	120	205	__1
	(D) Brown, green windows	40	55	__1
36	Observation (Std.), *24*	40	55	__1
36	Observation (Std.), *25-26*	40	55	__1
38	Electric 0-4-0 (Std.), *13-24*			
	(A) Black	100	120	__1
	(B) Red	475	680	__1
	(C) Mojave or pea green	405	540	__1
	(D) Dark green	270	360	__1
	(E) Brown	270	315	__1
	(F) Red, cream trim	405	540	__1
	(G) Maroon	170	270	__1
	(H) Gray	110	125	__1
40	(See #4 Trolley)			
41	Accessory Contactor, *37-42*	1	3	__1
042	Switches, pair (O), *38-42*	17	39	__1
42	Electric 0-4-4-0, square hood, Early (Std.), *12**	660	1450	__1
42	Electric 0-4-4-0, round hood, Later (Std.), *13-23*			
	(A) Black or gray	280	475	__1
	(B) Maroon	1250	2050	__1
	(C) Dark gray	375	600	__1
	(D) Dark green or mojave	500	800	__1
	(E) Peacock	1100	1800	__1
	(F) Olive or dark olive green	750	1200	__1
043/43	Bild-A-Motor Gear set, *29*		85	__1
43	Boat, Runabout, *33-36, 39-41*	435	640	__1
0044	Boxcar (OO), *39-42*	37	70	__1
0044K	Boxcar Kit (OO), *39-42*	75	120	__1
44	Boat, Speedster, *35-36*	510	780	__1
0045	Tank Car (OO), *39-42*			
	(A) Black, "SHELL"	40	90	__1
	(B) Silver, "SUNOCO"	40	80	__1
0045K	Tank Car Kit (OO), *39-42*	75	120	__1
45/045/45N	Automatic Gateman, *35-42*	40	70	__1
0046	Hopper Car (OO), *39-42*	45	80	__1
0046K	Hopper Car Kit (OO), *39-42*			

		Good	Exc	Cond/$
	(A) "SOUTHERN PACIFIC"	75	135	__1
	(B) "READING"		NRS	___
46	Crossing Gate, *39-42*	75	120	__1
0047	Caboose (OO), *39-42*	31	60	__1
0047K	Caboose Kit (OO), *39-42*	75	135	__1
47	Crossing Gate, *39-42*	70	140	__2
48W	Whistle Station, *37-42*	30	65	__1
49	Lionel Airport, *37-39*	160	410	__1
50	Airplane, *36-39*	120	280	__1
50	Electric 0-4-0 (Std.), *24*			
	(A) Dark green or dark gray	125	225	__1
	(B) Maroon	315	600	__1
	(C) Mojave	155	300	__1
50	Cardboard Train, Cars, Accessory (O), *43**	200	360	__1
51	Steam 0-4-0, 5 Late eight-wheel (Std.), *12-23*	800	1150	__1
51	Lionel Airport, *36, 38*	155	395	__1
52	Lamp Post, *33-41*	40	75	__1
53	Electric 0-4-4-0, Early (Std.), *12-14*	1200	2450	__1
53	Electric 0-4-0, Later (Std.), *15-19*			
	(A) Maroon	500	900	__1
	(B) Mojave	670	1350	__1
	(C) Dark olive green	560	1150	__1
53	Electric 0-4-0, Latest (Std.), *20-21*	200	450	__1
53	Lamp Post, *31-42*	30	43	__1
53	Electric 0-6-6-0, Early (Std.), *11*		NRS	___
54	Electric 0-4-4-0, Early (Std.), *12**	2500	4050	__1
54	Electric 0-4-4-0, Late (Std.), *13-23*	1800	2700	__1
54	Lamp Post, *29-35*	45	80	__1
55	Airplane w/ stand, *37-39*	165	450	__1
56	Lamp Post, removable lens and cap, *24-42*	39	60	__3
57	Lamp Post w/ street names, *22-42*	38	85	__1
58	Lamp Post, 7⅜" high, *22-42*	36	55	__4
59	Lamp Post, 8¾" high, *20-36*	36	75	__2
60/060	Telegraph Post (Std./O), *29-42*	11	23	__1
60	Electric 0-4-0, F.A.O.S. (Std.), *15 u*		NRS	___
61	Electric 0-4-4-0, F.A.O.S. (Std.), *15 u*		NRS	___
61	Lamp Post, one globe, *14-36*	40	65	__2
62	Electric 0-4-0, F.A.O.S. (Std.), *24-32 u*		NRS	___
62	Semaphore, *20-32*	25	50	__1
63	Lamp Post, two globes, *33-42*	135	230	__1
63	Semaphore, *15-21*	25	50	__1
64	Lamp Post, *40-42*	33	65	__2
64	Semaphore, 6¾" high, *15-21*	30	60	__1

		Good	Exc	Cond/$
65	Semaphore, one-arm, *15-26*	30	60	__1
65	Whistle Controller, *35*	5	7	__1
66	Semaphore, two-arm, *15-26*	35	70	__1
66	Whistle Controller, *36-39*	9	10	__1
67	Lamp Post, *15-32*	85	145	__1
67	Whistle Controller, *36-39*	4	8	__1
68/068	Crossing Sign, *25-42*	11	17	__1
69/069/69N	Electric Warning Signal, *21-42*	33	70	__1
70	Outfit: (2) 62s (1) 59 (1) 68, *21-32*	60	130	__1
071	(6) 060 Telegraph Poles (Std.), *24-42*	70	160	__1
71	(6) 60 Telegraph Poles (Std.), *29-42*	70	160	__1
0072	Switches, pair (OO), *38-42*	225	355	__1
0074	Boxcar (OO), *39-42*	36	70	__1
0075	Tank Car (OO), *39-42*	48	90	__1
076/76	Block Signal, *23-28*	25	75	__1
76	Warning Bell and Shack, *39-42*	70	285	__1
0077	Caboose (OO), *39-42*	34	60	__1
77/077/77N	Automatic Crossing Gate, *23-39*	28	55	__1
78/078	Train Signal (Std.), *24-32*	40	100	__1
79	Flashing Signal, *28-40*	115	140	__1
80	Automobile, *12-16*	440	770	__1
80/080/80N	Semaphore (Std), *26-42*	48	125	__1
81	Automobile, *12-16*	720	1450	__1
81	Controlling Rheostat, *27-33*	2	5	__1
82/082/82N	Semaphore, *27-42*	55	110	__1
83	Flashing Traffic Signal, *27-42*	65	200	__1
084	Semaphore, *28-32*	60	100	__1
84	Semaphore, *27-32*	55	85	__1
84	(2) Automobiles, *12-16*	1400	2900	__1
85	Telegraph Pole (Std.), *29-42*	15	27	__1
85	(2) Automobiles, *12-16*	1400	2900	__1
86	(6) Telegraph Poles, *29-42*	60	120	__1
87	Flashing Crossing Signal, *27-42*	85	165	__1
88	Battery Rheostat, *15-27*	3	7	__1
88	Rheostat Controller, *33-42*	3	5	__1
89	Flag Pole, *23-34*	38	75	__1
90	Flag Pole, *27-42*	39	85	__1
91	Circuit Breaker, *30-42*	34	60	__2
092	Signal Tower, *23-27*	120	190	__1
92	Floodlight Tower, *31-42**	155	305	__4
93	Water Tower, *31-42*	75	135	__1
94	High Tension Tower, *32-42**	145	270	__1
95	Controlling Rheostat, *34-42*	2.50	6	__1
96	Coal Elevator, manual, *38-40*	170	230	__1
097	Telegraph set (O)	50	75	__1
97	Coal Elevator, *38-42*	150	270	__3

		Good	Exc	Cond/$
98	Coal Bunker, *38-40*	190	440	__1
99/099/99N	Train Control, *32-42*	44	145	__1
100	Electric Loco (2⅞"), *03-05* *	2900	5200	__1
100	Trolley (Std.), *10-16*			
	(A) Blue, white windows	1300	2700	__1
	(B) Blue, cream windows	1850	3600	__1
	(C) Red, cream windows	1300	2700	__1
100	(2) Bridge Approaches (Std.), *20-31*	20	36	__1
100	Wooden Gondola (2⅞"), *01*		NRS	___
101	Bridge Span (2) Approaches (Std.), *20-31*	60	115	__1
101	Summer Trolley (Std.), *10-13*	1300	2700	__1
102	(2) Bridge Spans (2) Approaches (Std.), *20-31*	70	175	__1
103	Bridge (Std.), *13-16*	50	70	__1
103	(3) Bridge Spans (2) Approaches (Std.), *20-31*	60	145	__1
104	Bridge Span (Std.), *20-31*	20	41	__1
104	Tunnel (Std.), *09-14*	50	135	__1
105	Bridge (Std.), *11-14*	40	70	__1
105	(2) Bridge Approaches (O), *20-31*	50	70	__1
106	Bridge Span, (2) Approaches (O), *20-31*	30	65	__1
107	DC Reducer, 110V, *23-32*		NRS	___
108	(2) Bridge Spans, (2) Approaches (O), *20-31*	50	90	__1
109	(3) Bridge Spans, (2) Approaches (O), *20-32*	50	115	__1
109	Tunnel (Std.), *13-14*	30	70	__1
110	Bridge Span (O), *20-31*	12	23	__1
111	Box of 50 Bulbs, *20-31*	50	90	__1
112	Gondola, Early (Std.), *10-12*	195	350	__1
112	Gondola, Later (Std.), *12-16*	40	65	__1
112	Gondola, Latest (Std.), *16-18*	40	65	__1
112	Gondola, Lionel Corp. (Std.), *18-26*	40	65	__1
112	Station, *31-35*	155	285	__1
113	Cattle Car, Later (Std.), *12-16*	50	70	__1
113	Cattle Car, Latest (Std.), *16-18*	50	70	__1
113	Cattle Car, Lionel Corp. (Std.), *18-26*	40	55	__1
113	Station, *31-34*	150	295	__1
114	Boxcar, Later (Std.), *12-16*	50	90	__1
114	Boxcar, Latest (Std.), *16-18*	40	70	__1
114	Boxcar, Lionel Corp. (Std.), *18-26*	40	70	__1
114	Station, *31-34*	530	1200	__1
115	Station, *35-42* *	245	440	__1
116	Station, *35-42* *	640	1450	__2
116	Ballast Car, Early and Later (Std.), *10-16*	75	100	__1
116	Ballast Car, Latest (Std.), *16-18*	55	95	__1
116	Ballast Car, Lionel Corp. (Std.), *18-26*	55	95	__1
117	Caboose, Early (Std.), *12*	60	70	__1
117	Caboose, Later (Std.), *12-16*	50	70	__1

		Good	Exc	Cond/$
117	Caboose, Latest (Std.), *16-18*	50	70	__1
117	Caboose, Lionel Corp. (Std.), *18-26*	43	70	__1
117	Station, *36-42*	110	285	__1
118	Tunnel, 8" long (O), *22-32*	20	55	__1
118L	Tunnel, 8" long, *27*	20	55	__1
119	Tunnel, 12" long, *20-42*	22	60	__1
119L	Tunnel, 12" long, *27-33*	20	55	__1
120	Tunnel, 17" long, *22-27*	27	75	__1
120L	Tunnel, *27-42*	70	130	__1
121	Station (Std.), *09-16*			
	(A) 14" x 10" x 9"		NRS	__
	(B) 13" x 9" x 13"	150	300	__1
121	Station (Std.), *20-26*	75	150	__1
121X	Station (Std.), *17-19*	110	255	__1
122	Station (Std.), *20-30*	85	165	__2
123	Station (Std.), *20-23*	75	205	__1
123	Tunnel, 18½" long (O), *33-42*	90	205	__1
124	Station, "Lionel City," *20-36**			
	(A) Tan or gray base, pea green	90	180	__1
	(B) Pea green base, red roof	200	360	__1
125	Station, "Lionelville," *23-25*	85	195	__1
125	Track Template, *38*	1	4	__1
126	Station, "Lionelville," *23-36*	75	160	__1
127	Station, "Lionel Town," *23-36*	90	160	__1
128	124 Station & Terrace, *31-34**	900	1900	__1
128	115 Station & Terrace, *35-42**	900	1900	__1
129	Terrace, *28-42**	600	1100	__1
130	Tunnel, 26" long, *20-36*	100	450	__1
130L	Tunnel, 26" long, *27-33*	150	450	__1
131	Corner Display, *24-28*	125	295	__1
132	Corner Grass Plot, *24-28*	125	295	__1
133	Heart Shaped Plot, *24-28*	125	295	__1
134	Oval Shaped Plot, *24-28*	125	300	__1
134	Station, "Lionel City," w/ stop, *37-42*	200	340	__1
135	Circular Plot, *24-28*	125	295	__1
136	Large Elevation, *24-28*		NRS	__
136	Station, "Lionelville," w/ stop, *37-42*	75	180	__1
140L	Tunnel, 37" long, *27-32*	460	1050	__1
150	Electric 0-4-0, Early (O), *17*	90	160	__1
150	Electric 0-4-0, Late (O), *18-25*			
	(A) Brown, brown or olive windows	95	150	__1
	(B) Maroon, dark olive windows	90	135	__1
152	Electric 0-4-0 (O), *17-27*			
	(A) Dark green	90	135	__1
	(B) Gray	115	160	__1
	(C) Mojave	340	680	__1

		Good	Exc	Cond/$
	(D) Peacock	340	680	__1
152	Crossing Gate, *40-42*	21	45	__2
153	Block Signal, *40-42*	23	45	__2
153	Electric 0-4-0 (O), *24-25*			
	(A) Dark green	100	160	__1
	(B) Gray	100	160	__1
	(C) Mojave	100	160	__1
154	Electric 0-4-0 (O), *17-23*	100	180	__1
154	Highway Signal, *40-42*	21	47	__1
	(A) Black Base	21	47	__1
	(B) Orange base	35	90	__1
155	Freight Shed, *30-42**			
	(A) Yellow base, orange floor	180	320	__2
	(B) White base, terra-cotta floor	240	400	__2
156	Electric 4-4-4 (O), *17-23*			
	(A) Dark green	475	810	__1
	(B) Maroon	540	890	__1
	(C) Olive green	600	1050	__1
	(D) Gray	670	1200	__1
156	Electric 0-4-0 (O), *17-23*	400	720	__1
156	Station Platform, *39-42*	85	135	__2
156X	Electric 0-4-0 (O), *23-24*			
	(A) Maroon	380	495	__1
	(B) Olive green	440	550	__1
	(C) Gray	530	710	__1
	(D) Brown	470	600	__1
157	Hand Truck, *30-32*	25	41	__1
158	Electric 0-4-0 (O), *19-23*			
	(A) Gray, red windows	75	205	__1
	(B) Black	95	250	__1
158	(2) 156s and (1) 136, *40-42*	120	280	__1
159	Block Actuator, *40*	10	27	__1
161	Baggage Truck, *30-32**	44	85	__1
162	Dump Truck, *30-32**	40	75	__1
163	(2) 157 (1) 162 (1) 161, boxed, *30-42**	220	310	__1
164	Log Loader, *40-42*	145	225	__3
165	Magnetic Crane, *40-42*	175	305	__3
166	Whistle Controller, *40-42*	3	7	__1
167	Whistle Controller, *40-42*	6	13	__2
167X	Whistle Controller (OO), *40-42*	5	12	__1
169	Controller, *40-42*	3	7	__1
170	DC Reducer, 220V, *14-38*	3	7	__1
171	DC to AC Inverter, 110V, *36-42*	3	15	__1
172	DC to AC Inverter, 229V, *39-42*	3	7	__1
180	Pullman (Std.), *11-13*			
	(A) Maroon body and roof	125	180	__1

		Good	Exc	Cond/$
	(B) Brown body and roof	125	235	__1
180	Pullman (Std.), *13-15*	80	160	__1
180	Pullman (Std.), *15-18*	80	160	__1
180	Pullman (Std.), *18-22*	80	135	__1
181	Combine (Std.), *11-13*			
	(A) Maroon, dark olive doors	125	180	__1
	(B) Brown, dark olive doors	125	180	__1
	(C) Yellow-orange, orange door	350	495	__1
181	Combine (Std.), *13-15*	80	160	__1
181	Combine (Std.), *15-18*	80	160	__1
181	Combine (Std.), *18-22*	80	135	__1
182	Observation (Std.), *11-13*			
	(A) Maroon, dark olive doors	125	180	__1
	(B) Brown, dark olive doors	125	180	__1
	(C) Yellow-orange, orange door	350	495	__1
182	Observation (Std.), *13-15*	80	160	__1
182	Observation (Std.), *15-18*	80	160	__1
182	Observation (Std.), *18-22*	80	135	__1
183	Pullman (Std.)		NM	__
184	Bungalow, Illuminated, *23-32**	65	110	__1
184	Combine (Std.), *11*		NM	__
185	Bungalow, *23-24*	50	115	__1
185	Observation (Std.), *11*		NM	__
186	(5) 184 Bungalows, *23-32*	195	610	__1
186	Log Loader Outfit, *40-41*	130	340	__1
187	(5) 185 Bungalows, *23-24*	170	590	__1
188	Elevator and Car set, *38-41*	115	370	__1
189	Villa, Illuminated, *23-32**	165	195	__1
190	Observation (Std.), *08*			
	(A) Dark olive green, unremovable roof	1150	2600	__1
	(B) Dark olive green, removable roof	100	180	__1
	(C) Yellow-orange, removable roof	280	540	__1
	(D) Orange, removable roof	100	180	__1
	(E) Mojave, removable roof	345	870	__1
190	Observation (Std.), *11-13*		NRS	__
190	Observation (Std.), *13-15*	200	295	__1
190	Observation (Std.), *15-18*	200	295	__1
190	Observation (Std.), *18-22*	80	135	__1
190	Observation (Std.), *23-26*	230	475	__1
191	Villa, Illuminated, *23-32**	165	285	__1
192	Villa set, Illuminated: (1) 189;			
	(1) 191; (2) 184, *27-32*		800	__1
193	Accessory set, boxed, *27-29*	150	325	__1
194	Accessory set, boxed, *27-29*	100	325	__1
195	Terrace, *27-30*	350	740	__1

		Good	Exc	Cond/$
196	Accessory set, *27*	200	335	__1
200	Electric Express (2⅞"), *03*	4150	5600	__1
200	Turntable, *28-33**	85	190	__1
200	Wooden Gondola (2⅞"), *01-02*		NRS	__
200	Trailer, matches #2 Trolley (Std.), *11-16*		2400	__1
200	Electric Express (2⅞"), *03-05**	4000	6300	__1
201	Steam 0-6-0 (O), *40-42*			
	(A) With 2201B tender w/ bell	375	760	__1
	(B) With 2201T tender w/o bell	345	690	__1
202	Summer Trolley (Std.), *10-13*			
	(A) "ELECTRIC RAPID TRANSIT"	1300	2700	__1
	(B) "PRESTON ST."	3250	4500	__1
203	Armored 0-4-0 (O), *17-21*	1100	1800	__1
203	Steam 0-6-0 (O), *40-42*			
	(A) With 2203B tender w/ bell	400	590	__1
	(B) With 2203T tender w/o bell	365	550	__1
204	Steam 2-4-2 (O), *40-42 u*			
	(A) Black locomotive	55	105	__1
	(B) Gun-metal gray locomotive	80	165	__1
205	(3) Merch. Containers, *30-38**	130	290	__1
206	Sack of Coal, *38-42*	5	16	__1
208	Tool set, boxed, *34-42**	65	150	__1
0209	Barrels, *34-42*	5	14	__1
209	Wooden Barrels, *34-42*	8	19	__1
210	Switches, pair (Std.), *26, 34-42*	42	75	__1
211	Flatcar (Std.), *26-40**	125	220	__1
212	Gondola (Std.), *26-40**			
	(A) Gray or green	100	205	__1
	(B) Maroon	75	135	__1
213	Cattle Car (Std.), *26-40**			
	(A) Mojave, maroon roof	180	400	__1
	(B) Terra-cotta, green or maroon roof	130	285	__1
214	Boxcar (Std.), *26-40**			
	(A) Terra-cotta, green roof	195	295	__1
	(B) Cream body, orange roof	150	270	__1
	(C) Yellow, brown roof	300	495	__1
214R	Refrigerator Car (Std.), *29-40**			
	(A) Ivory or white, peacock roof	325	495	__1
	(B) White, light blue nickel roof	435	720	__1
215	Tank Car (Std.), *26-40**			
	(A) Pea green	150	215	__1
	(B) Ivory	220	360	__1
	(C) Silver	315	720	__1
216	Hopper Car (Std.), *26-38**			
	(A) Brass plates	195	335	__1
	(B) Nickel plates	445	1100	__1

		Good	Exc	Cond/$
217	Caboose (Std.), *26-40**			
	(A) Orange, maroon roof	250	510	__1
	(B) Red, peacock roof	120	245	__1
	(C) Red body/roof, white door	150	320	__1
217	Lighting set, *14-23*		NRS	___
218	Dump Car (Std.), *26-38**	210	350	__2
219	Crane (Std.), *26-40**			
	(A) Peacock, red boom	135	240	__3
	(B) Yellow, light green boom	270	400	__3
	(C) Ivory, light green boom	270	435	__3
	(D) Cream, red boom	130	305	__3
	(E) White, green boom	300	470	__3
220	Floodlight Car (Std.), *31-40**			
	(A) Terra-cotta base	225	385	__2
	(B) Green base	340	485	__2
220	Switches, pair (Std.), *26**	25	90	__1
222	Switches, pair (Std.), *26-32*	40	100	__1
223	Switches, pair (Std.), *32-42*	29	115	__1
224/224E	Steam 2-6-2 (O), *38-42*			
	(A) Black, die-cast 2224 tender	155	290	__1
	(B) Black, plastic 2224 tender	110	195	__1
	(C) Gun-metal, die-cast 2224 tender	385	950	__1
	(D) Gun-metal, 2689 tender	120	210	__1
225	222 Switches, 439 Panel, *29-32*	105	235	__2
225/225E	Steam 2-6-2 (O), *38-42*			
	(A) Black, 2235 or 2245 tender	210	370	__1
	(B) Black, 2235 plastic tender	185	320	__1
	(C) Gun-metal, 2225 or 2265 tender	210	360	__1
	(D) Gun-metal, 2235 die-cast tender	285	730	__1
226/226E	Steam 2-6-4 (O), *38-41*	345	670	__1
227	Steam 0-6-0 (O), *39-42*			
	(A) With 2227B tender w/ bell	600	1250	__2
	(B) With 2227T tender w/o bell	600	1150	__2
228	Steam 0-6-0 (O), *39-42*			
	(A) With 2228B tender w/ bell	600	1250	__1
	(B) With 2228T tender w/o bell	600	1150	__1
229	Steam 2-4-2 (O), *39-42*			
	(A) Black or gun-metal w/ 2689W	155	280	__2
	(B) Black or gun-metal w/ 2689T	120	200	__2
	(C) Black w/ 2666W whistle tender	155	280	__2
	(D) Black w/ 2666T non-whistle tender	120	200	__2
230	Steam 0-6-0 (O), *39-42*	1100	2050	__1
231	Steam 0-6-0 (O), *39*	1000	1800	__1
232	Steam 0-6-0 (O), *40-42*	1000	1800	__1
233	Steam 0-6-0 (O), *40-42*	1000	1800	__1
238	Steam 4-4-2 (O), *39-40 u*	430	710	__2

		Good	Exc	Cond/$
238E	Steam 4-4-2 (O), *36-38*			
	(A) W/ 265W or 2225W whistle tender	280	365	__1
	(B) W/ 265 or 2225T non-whistling tender	275	360	__1
248	Electric 0-4-0 (O), *27-32*	145	240	__1
249/249E	Steam 2-4-2 (O), *36-39*			
	(A) Gun-metal, 265T or 265W tender	100	200	__1
	(B) Black, 265W tender	110	210	__1
250	Electric 0-4-0, Early (O), *26*	125	220	__1
250	Electric 0-4-0, Late (O), *34*			
	(A) Yellow-orange, terra-cotta frame	145	245	__1
	(B) Terra-cotta body, maroon frame	160	275	__1
250E	Steam 4-4-2 Hiawatha (O), *35-42**	400	1100	__1
251	Electric 0-4-0 (O), *25-32*			
	(A) Gray body, red windows	190	340	__1
	(B) Red body, ivory stripe	215	410	__1
	(C) Red body, w/o ivory stripe	200	380	__1
251E	Electric 0-4-0 (O), *27-32*			
	(A) Red body, ivory stripe	225	425	__1
	(B) Red body, w/o ivory stripe	215	395	__1
	(C) Gray, red trim	195	350	__1
252	Electric 0-4-0 (O), *26-32*			
	(A) Peacock or olive green	95	190	__2
	(B) Terra-cotta or yellow-orange	125	255	__2
252E	Electric 0-4-0 (O), *33-35*			
	(A) Terra-cotta	145	250	__1
	(B) Yellow-orange	125	205	__1
253	Electric 0-4-0 (O), *24-32*			
	(A) Maroon	180	430	__3
	(B) Dark green	105	195	__3
	(C) Mojave	105	235	__3
	(D) Terra-cotta	180	430	__3
	(E) Peacock	95	195	__3
	(F) Red	210	475	__3
253E	Electric 0-4-0 (O), *31-36*			
	(A) Green	150	205	__1
	(B) Terra-cotta	190	305	__1
254	Electric 0-4-0 (O), *24-32*	205	300	__1
254E	Electric 0-4-0 (O), *27-34*	155	220	__1
255E	Steam 2-4-2 (O), *35-36*	485	1000	__1
256	Electric 0-4-4-0 (O), *24-30**			
	(A) Rubber-stamped lettering	470	1250	__3
	(B) (A) w/o outline and "LIONEL..."	425	770	__3
	(C) "LIONEL" and "256" on brass	450	1050	__3
257	Steam 2-4-0 (O), *30-35 u*			
	(A) Black tender	145	305	__1
	(B) Black crackle-finish tender	240	435	__1

		Good	Exc	Cond/$
258	Steam 2-4-0, Early (O), *30-35 u*			
	(A) With 4-wheel 257 tender	85	170	__1
	(B) With 8-wheel 258 tender	100	195	__1
258	Steam 2-4-2, Late (O), *41 u*			
	(A) Black	60	90	__1
	(B) Gun-metal	85	135	__1
259	Steam 2-4-2 (O), *32*	70	135	__1
259E	Steam 2-4-2 (O), *33-42*	65	120	__2
260E	Steam 2-4-2 (O), *30-35**			
	(A) Black, green or black frame	385	520	__2
	(B) Dark gun-metal body and frame	440	640	__2
261	Steam 2-4-2 (O), *31*	130	215	__1
261E	Steam 2-4-2 (O), *35*	170	250	__1
262	Steam 2-4-2 (O), *31-32*	240	360	__2
262E	Steam 2-4-2 (O), *33-36*			
	(A) Gloss black, copper/brass trim	100	210	__2
	(B) Satin black, nickel trim	125	265	__2
263E	Steam 2-4-2 (O), *36-39**			
	(A) Gun-metal gray	315	610	__2
	(B) 2-tone blue, from Blue Comet	415	950	__2
264E	Steam 2-4-2 (O), *35-36*			
	(A) Red, "RED COMET"	150	295	__1
	(B) Black	220	380	__1
265E	Steam 2-4-2 (O), *35-40*			
	(A) Black or gun-metal	170	330	__2
	(B) Light blue, "BLUE STREAK"	460	800	__2
267E/267W	Sets: 616, (2) 617s, 618, *35-41*	560		__1
270	Bridge, 10" long (O), *31-42*	18	50	__1
270	Lighting set, *15-23*		NRS	__
271	(2) 270 Spans (O), *31-33, 35-40*	65	150	__1
271	Lighting set, *15-23*		NRS	__
272	(3) 270 Spans (O), *31-33, 35-40*	60	165	__1
280	Bridge, 14" long (Std.), *31-42*	50	115	__1
281	(2) Bridge Spans (Std.), *31-33, 35-40*	85	205	__1
282	(3) Bridge Spans (Std.), *31-33, 35-40*	105	240	__1
289E	Steam 2-4-2 (O), *37 u*	120	305	__1
300	Electric Trolley Car (2⅞"), *01-05*	2000	3600	__1
300	Hell Gate Bridge (Std.), *28-42**			
	(A) Cream towers, green trusses	800	1350	__2
	(B) Ivory towers, aluminum truss	700	1600	__2
300	(See #3 Trolley)			
301	Batteries, set of 4 (2⅞"), *03-05*		NRS	__
302	Plunge Battery (2⅞"), *01-02*		NRS	__
303	Summer Trolley, *10-13*	1500	3150	__1
303	Carbon Cylinders (2⅞"), *02*		NRS	__
304	Composite Zincs (2⅞"), *02*		NRS	__

		Good	Exc	Cond/$
306	Glass Jars (2⅞"), *02*		NRS	___
308	(5) Signs (O), *40-42*	26	70	___1
309	Electric Trolley Trailer (2⅞"), *01-05*	2500	4050	___1
309	Pullman (Std.), *26-39*			
	(A) Maroon body/roof, mojave window	100	160	___1
	(B) Mojave body/roof, maroon window	100	160	___1
	(C) Light brown body, dark brown roof	120	185	___1
	(D) Medium blue body, dark blue roof	170	260	___1
	(E) Apple green body, dark green roof	170	260	___1
	(F) Pale blue body, silver roof	100	160	___1
	(G) Maroon body, terra-cotta roof	130	185	___1
310	Baggage (Std.), *26-39*			
	(A) Maroon body/roof, mojave window	100	160	___1
	(B) Mojave body/roof, maroon window	100	160	___1
	(C) Light brown body, dark brown roof	115	185	___1
	(D) Medium blue body, dark blue roof	170	260	___1
	(E) Apple green body, dark green roof	170	260	___1
	(F) Pale blue body, silver roof	100	160	___1
310	Rails and Ties, complete section (2⅞"), *01-02*	5	14	___1
312	Observation (Std.), *24-39*			
	(A) Maroon body/roof, mojave window	100	160	___1
	(B) Mojave body/roof, maroon window	100	160	___1
	(C) Light brown body, dark brown roof	120	185	___1
	(D) Medium blue body, dark blue roof	170	260	___1
	(E) Apple green body, dark green roof	170	260	___1
	(F) Pale blue body, silver roof	100	160	___1
	(G) Maroon body, terra-cotta roof	130	185	___1
313	Bascule Bridge (O), *40-42*			
	(A) Silver bridge	235	500	___1
	(B) Gray bridge	250	590	___1
314	Girder Bridge (O), *40-42*	17	40	___1
315	Trestle Bridge (O), *40-42*	28	80	___1
316	Trestle Bridge (O), *40-42*	21	48	___1
318	Electric 0-4-0 (Std.), *24-32*			
	(A) Gray, dark gray, or mojave	150	250	___1
	(B) Pea green	150	250	___1
	(C) State brown	250	395	___1
318E	Electric 0-4-0, *26-35*			
	(A) Gray, mojave, or pea green	150	250	___1
	(B) State brown	275	440	___1
	(C) Black	550	990	___1
319	Pullman (Std.), *24-27*	105	175	___1
320	Baggage (Std.), *25-27*	100	175	___1
320	Switch and Signal (2⅞"), *02-05*		NRS	___
322	Observation (Std.), *24-27, 29-30 u*	100	175	___1
330	Crossing, 90° (2⅞"), *02-05*		NRS	___

		Good	Exc	Cond/$
332	Baggage (Std.), *26-33*			
	(A) Red body and roof, cream d	80	120	__2
	(B) Peacock body/roof, orange door	75	115	__2
	(C) Gray body/roof, maroon doors	75	115	__2
	(D) Olive green body/roof, red doors	90	145	__2
	(E) State brown body, dark brown roof	165	375	__2
337	Pullman (Std.), *25-32*			
	(A) Red body/roof, cream doors	95	190	__1
	(B) Mojave body/roof, maroon doors	95	190	__1
	(C) Olive green body/roof, red doors	105	225	__1
	(D) Olive green body/roof, maroon doors	95	190	__1
	(E) Pea green body/roof, cream doors	210	500	__1
338	Observation (Std.), *25-32*			
	(A) Red body/roof, cream doors	95	190	__1
	(B) Mojave body/roof, maroon doors	95	190	__1
	(C) Olive green body/roof, red doors	105	225	__1
	(D) Olive green body/roof, maroon doors	95	190	__1
339	Pullman (Std.), *25-33*			
	(A) Peacock body/roof, orange doors	55	100	__1
	(B) Gray body/roof, maroon doors	55	100	__1
	(C) State brown body, dark brown roof	120	330	__1
	(D) Peacock body, dark green roof	75	130	__1
	(E) Mojave body, maroon roof/doors	145	230	__1
340	Suspension Bridge (2⅞"), *02-05**		NRS	___
341	Observation (Std.), *25-33*			
	(A) Peacock body/roof, orange doors	50	70	__1
	(B) Gray body/roof, maroon doors	50	70	__1
	(C) State brown body, dark brown roof	110	240	__1
	(D) Peacock body, dark green roof	65	95	__1
	(E) Mojave body, maroon roof/doors	135	165	__1
350	Track Bumper (2⅞"), *02-05*		550	__1
370	Jars and Plates (2⅞"), *02-03*		NRS	___
380	Electric 0-4-0 (Std.), *23-27*	310	440	__1
380	Elevated Pillars (2⅞"), *04-05**	30	70	__1
380E	Electric 0-4-0 (Std.), *26-29*			
	(A) Mojave	445	630	__1
	(B) Maroon	295	400	__1
	(C) Dark green	370	460	__1
381	Electric 4-4-4 (Std.), *28-29**	1600	2100	__1
381E	Electric 4-4-4 (Std.), *28-36**			
	(A) State green, apple green sub-frame	1500	2500	__1
	(B) State green, red sub-frame	1900	2850	__1
381U	Electric 4-4-4 Kit (Std.), *28-29*	1600	3600	__1
384	Steam 2-4-0 (Std.), *30-32**	375	660	__1
384E	Steam 2-4-0 (Std.), *30-32**	400	570	__1
385E	Steam 2-4-2 (Std.), *33-39**	415	750	__1

		Good	Exc	Cond/$
390	Steam 2-4-2 (Std.), *29**	460	820	__1
390E	Steam 2-4-2 (Std.), *29-31**			
	(A) Black, w/ or w/o orange stripe	460	690	__1
	(B) 2-tone blue, cream-orange stripe	590	1200	__1
	(C) 2-tone green, orange or green stripe	990	2050	__1
392E	Steam 4-4-2 (Std.), *32-39**			
	(A) Black, 384 tender	750	1250	__1
	(B) Black, large 12-wheel tender	1050	1800	__1
	(C) Gun-metal gray	1000	1800	__1
400	Express Trail Car (2$\frac{7}{8}$"), *03-05**	3500	5850	__1
400E	Steam 4-4-4 (Std.), *31-39**			
	(A) Black or dark gun-metal	1400	2150	__2
	(B) Medium blue boiler	1550	2400	__2
	(C) Crackle black finish	1550	2450	__2
402	Electric 0-4-4-0 (Std.), *23-27*	345	570	__1
402E	Electric 0-4-4-0 (Std.), *26-29*	300	495	__1
404	Summer Trolley (Std.), *10*		NRS	__
408E	Electric 0-4-4-0 (Std.), *27-36**			
	(A) Apple green or mojave, red pilots	700	1150	__1
	(B) 2-tone brown, brown pilots	2100	2650	__1
	(C) Dark green, red pilots	1850	3400	__1
412	Pullman, "California" (Std.), *29-35**			
	(A) Light green body, dark green roof	590	1750	__1
	(B) Light brown body, dark brown roof	620	2100	__1
413	Pullman, "Colorado" (Std.), *29-35**			
	(A) Light green body, dark green roof	590	1750	__1
	(B) Light brown body, dark brown roof	620	2100	__1
414	Pullman, "Illinois" (Std.), *29-35**			
	(A) Light green body, dark green roof	590	2050	__1
	(B) Light brown body, dark brown roof	590	1750	__1
416	Observation, "New York" (Std.), *29-35**			
	(A) Light green body, dark green roof	590	1750	__1
	(B) Light brown body, dark brown roof	620	2100	__1
418	Pullman (Std.), *23-32**	225	320	__1
419	Combination (Std.), *23-32**	205	280	__1
420	Pullman, "Faye" (Std.), *30-40**	520	900	__1
421	Pullman, "Westphal" (Std.), *30-40**	550	900	__1
422	Observation, "Tempel" (Std.), *30-40**	520	900	__1
424	Pullman, "Liberty Belle" (Std.), *31-40**			
	(A) Brass trim	350	530	__1
	(B) Nickel trim	385	650	__1
425	Pullman, "Stephen Girard" (Std.), *31-40**			
	(A) Brass trim	350	530	__1
	(B) Nickel trim	385	650	__1
426	Observation, "Coral Isle" (Std.), *31-40**			
	(A) Brass trim	350	530	__1

		Good	Exc	Cond/$
	(B) Nickel trim	385	650	__1
427	Diner (Std.), *30*		NM	__
428	Pullman (Std.), *26-30**			
	(A) Dark green body and roof	250	385	__1
	(B) Orange body/roof, apple green window	390	890	__1
429	Combine (Std.), *26-30**			
	(A) Dark green body and roof	250	385	__1
	(B) Orange body/roof, apple green window	390	890	__1
430	Observation (Std.), *26-30**			
	(A) Dark green body and roof	250	385	__1
	(B) Orange body/roof, apple green window	390	890	__1
431	Diner (Std.), *27-32**			
	(A) Mojave body, screw-mounted roof	350	540	__1
	(B) Mojave body, hinged roof	465	720	__1
	(C) Dark green body, orange windows	410	720	__1
	(D) Orange body, apple green window	410	720	__1
	(E) Apple green body, red window	410	720	__1
435	Power Station, *26-38**	200	400	__1
436	Power Station, *26-37**			
	(A) "POWER STATION" plates	135	265	__1
	(B) "EDISON SERVICE" plate	270	610	__1
437	Switch/Signal Tower, *26-37**	190	370	__1
438	Signal Tower, *27-39**			
	(A) Mojave base, orange house	215	425	__1
	(B) Gray base, ivory house	325	640	__1
	(C) Black base, white house	325	640	__1
439	Panel Board, *28-42**	80	125	__1
440/0440/440N	Signal Bridge, *32-42**	180	445	__1
440C	Panel Board, *32-42*	90	145	__1
441	Weighing Station (Std.), *32-36*	495	1400	__1
442	Landscape Diner, *38-42*	220	305	__2
444	Roundhouse (Std.), *32-35**	1350	2850	__1
444-18	Roundhouse Clip, *33*		NRS	__
450	Electric 0-4-0, Macy's (O), *30 u*			
	(A) Red, black frame	295	700	__1
	(B) Apple green, dark green frame	415	880	__1
450	Set: 450; matching 605; (2) 606s, *30 u*	750	1800	__1
455	Electric Range, *30, 32-33*	355	1000	__1
490	Observation (Std.), *23-32**	195	260	__1
500	Dealer Display, *27-28*		NRS	__
500	Electric Derrick Car (2$^{7}/_{8}$"), *03-04**	5000	6750	__1
501	Dealer Display, *27-28*		NRS	__
502	Dealer Display, *27-28*		NRS	__
503	Dealer Display, *27-28*		NRS	__
504	Dealer Display, *24-28*		NRS	__
505	Dealer Display, *24-28*		NRS	__

		Good	Exc	Cond/$
506	Dealer Display, *24-28*		NRS	___
507	Dealer Display, *24-28*		NRS	___
508	Dealer Display, *24-28*		NRS	___
509	Dealer Display, *24-28*		NRS	___
510	Dealer Display, *27-28*		NRS	___
511	Flatcar (Std.), *27-40*	65	115	___2
512	Gondola (Std.), *27-39*			
	(A) Peacock	38	70	___1
	(B) Green	50	90	___1
513	Cattle Car (Std.), *27-38*			
	(A) Olive green	70	145	___3
	(B) Orange	60	110	___3
	(C) Cream, maroon roof	70	135	___3
514	Boxcar (Std.), *29-40*			
	(A) Cream yellow, orange roof	90	155	___2
	(B) Yellow, brown roof	115	270	___2
514	Refrigerator Car (Std.), *27-28*			
	(A) White, peacock roof	240	540	___3
	(B) Cream, peacock roof	215	340	___3
	(C) Ivory, peacock roof	285	800	___3
	(D) Cream, green roof	265	680	___3
514R	Refrigerator Car (Std.), *29-40*			
	(A) Ivory, peacock roof, brass plates	140	180	___3
	(B) Ivory, light blue roof, nickel plate	440	600	___3
	(C) White, light blue roof, brass plates	140	180	___3
515	Tank Car (Std.), *27-40*			
	(A) Ivory or terra-cotta	90	160	___3
	(B) Light tan	115	170	___3
	(C) Silver	90	160	___3
	(D) Orange, red "SHELL" decal	340	520	___3
516	Hopper Car (Std.), *28-40*	155	225	___3
517	Caboose (Std.), *27-40*			
	(A) Pea green, red roof	50	100	___1
	(B) Red body and roof	105	155	___1
	(C) Red, black roof, orange windows	355	610	___1
520	Floodlight Car (Std.), *31-40*			
	(A) Terra-cotta base	95	185	___1
	(B) Green base	95	215	___1
529	Pullman (O), *26-32*			
	(A) Olive green body and roof	25	45	___1
	(B) Terra-cotta body and roof	25	60	___1
530	Observation (O), *26-32*			
	(A) Olive green body and roof	25	45	___1
	(B) Terra-cotta body and roof	25	60	___1
550	Miniature Figures, boxed (Std.), *32-36* *	175	305	___1

		Good	Exc	Cond/$
551	Engineer (Std.), *32*	25	45	__1
552	Conductor (Std.), *32*	21	38	__1
553	Porter (Std.), *32*	25	38	__1
554	Male Passenger (Std.), *32*	25	45	__1
555	Female Passenger (Std.), *32*	25	45	__1
556	Red Cap Figure (Std.), *32*	25	45	__1
600	Derrick Trailer (2⅞"), *03-04**	5000	8550	__1
600	Pullman, Early (O), *15-23*			
	(A) Dark green	65	170	__1
	(B) Maroon or brown	48	85	__1
600	Pullman, Late (O), *33-42*			
	(A) Light red or gray; red roof	50	90	__1
	(B) Light blue, aluminum roof	70	120	__1
601	Observation, Late (O), *33-42*			
	(A) Light red body and roof	50	90	__1
	(B) Light gray, red roof	50	90	__1
	(C) Light blue body, aluminum roof	70	120	__1
601	Pullman, Early (O), *15-23*	50	70	__1
602	Baggage, Lionel Lines, Late (O), *33-42*			
	(A) Light red or gray; red roof	60	110	__1
	(B) Light blue body, aluminum roof	90	150	__1
602	Baggage, NYC (O), *15-23*	30	45	__1
602	Observation (O), *22 u*	30	36	__1
603	Pullman, Early (O), *22 u*	40	70	__1
603	Pullman, Later (O), *20-25*	20	45	__1
603	Pullman, Latest (O), *31-36*			
	(A) Light red body and roof	45	85	__1
	(B) Red body, black roof	35	60	__1
	(C) Stephen Girard green, dark green roof	35	60	__1
	(D) Maroon body/roof, "MACY SPCL"	60	125	__1
604	Observation, Later (O), *20-25*	35	60	__1
604	Observation, Latest (O), *31-36*			
	(A) Light red body and roof	44	85	__1
	(B) Red body, black roof	35	60	__1
	(C) Yellow-orange body, terra-cotta roof	35	60	__1
	(D) Stephen Girard green, dark green roof	35	60	__1
	(E) Maroon body and roof	70	150	__1
605	Pullman (O), *25-32*			
	(A) Gray, "LIONEL LINES"	85	170	__1
	(B) Gray, "ILLINOIS CENTRAL"	85	170	__1
	(C) Red, "LIONEL LINES"	170	255	__1
	(D) Red, "ILLINOIS CENTRAL"	255	340	__1
	(E) Orange, "LIONEL LINES"	170	255	__1
	(F) Orange, "ILLINOIS CENTRAL"	300	430	__1
	(G) Olive green, "LIONEL LINES"	255	340	__1
606	Observation (O), *25-32*			

		Good	Exc	Cond/$
	(A) Gray, "LIONEL LINES"	130	215	__1
	(B) Gray, "ILLINOIS CENTRAL"	90	170	__1
	(C) Red, "LIONEL LINES"	170	255	__1
	(D) Red, "ILLINOIS CENTRAL"	255	340	__1
	(E) Orange, "LIONEL LINES"	170	255	__1
	(F) Orange, "ILLINOIS CENTRAL"	170	255	__1
	(G) Olive green, "LIONEL LINES"	255	340	__1
607	Pullman (O), *26-27*			
	(A) Peacock, "LIONEL LINES"	50	70	__1
	(B) Peacock, "ILLINOIS CENTRAL"	75	115	__1
	(C) 2-tone green, "LIONEL LINES"	50	75	__1
	(D) Red, "LIONEL LINES"	75	110	__1
608	Observation (O), *26-37*			
	(A) Peacock, "LIONEL LINES"	50	70	__1
	(B) Peacock, "ILLINOIS CENTRAL"	75	115	__1
	(C) 2-tone green, "LIONEL LINES"	50	75	__1
	(D) Red, "LIONEL LINES"	75	110	__1
609	Pullman (O), *37*	55	75	__1
610	Pullman, Early (O), *15-25*			
	(A) Dark green body and roof	50	65	__1
	(B) Maroon body and roof	60	95	__1
	(C) Mojave body and roof	60	95	__1
610	Pullman, Late (O), *26-30*			
	(A) Olive green body and roof	65	80	__1
	(B) Mojave body and roof	55	80	__1
	(C) Terra-cotta body, maroon roof	100	155	__1
	(D) Pea green body and roof	70	115	__1
	(E) Light blue body, aluminum roof	130	260	__1
	(F) Light red, aluminum finish roof	100	155	__1
611	Observation (O), *37*	55	90	__1
612	Observation, Early (O), *15-25*			
	(A) Dark green body and roof	50	60	__1
	(B) Maroon body and roof	70	90	__1
	(C) Mojave body and roof	70	90	__1
612	Observation, Late (O), *26-30*			
	(A) Olive green body and roof	55	80	__1
	(B) Mojave body and roof	55	80	__1
	(C) Terra-cotta body, maroon roof	100	155	__1
	(D) Pea green body and roof	70	115	__1
	(E) Light blue body, aluminum roof	130	260	__1
	(F) Light red, aluminum finish roof	100	155	__1
613	Pullman (O), *31-40**			
	(A) Terra-cotta, maroon/terra-cotta roof	85	195	__1
	(B) Light red, light red/aluminum roof	175	350	__1
	(C) Blue, two-tone blue roof	115	225	__1
614	Observation (O), *31-40**			

		Good	Exc	Cond/$
	(A) Terra-cotta, maroon/terra-cotta roof	100	190	__1
	(B) Light red, light red/aluminum roof	175	350	__1
	(C) Blue, two-tone blue roof	115	225	__1
615	Baggage (O), *33-40**	150	260	__1
616E/616W	Diesel only (O), *35-41*	90	215	__1
616E/616W	Set: 616, (2) 617s, 618	310	570	__1
617	Coach (O), *35-41*			
	(A) Blue and white	55	85	__1
	(B) Chrome, gun-metal skirts	55	85	__1
	(C) Chrome, chrome skirts	55	85	__1
	(D) Silver finish	55	85	__1
618	Observation (O), *35-41*			
	(A) Blue and white	55	85	__1
	(B) Chrome, gun-metal skirts	55	85	__1
	(C) Chrome, chrome skirts	55	85	__1
	(D) Silver finish	55	85	__1
619	Combine (O), *36-38*			
	(A) Blue, white window band	100	205	__1
	(B) Chrome, chrome skirts	100	205	__1
620	Floodlight Car (O), *37-42*	50	85	__1
629	Pullman (O), *24-32*			
	(A) Dark green body and roof	30	40	__1
	(B) Orange body and roof	30	40	__1
	(C) Red body and roof	20	32	__1
	(D) Light red body and roof	40	55	__1
630	Observation, *24-32*			
	(A) Dark green body and roof	30	40	__1
	(B) Orange body and roof	30	40	__1
	(C) Red body and roof	20	32	__1
	(D) Light red body and roof	40	55	__1
636W	Diesel only (O), *36-39*	90	175	__1
636W	Set: 636W, (2) 637s, 638, *36-39*	375	640	__1
637	Coach (O), *36-39*	70	105	__1
638	Observation (O), *36-39*	70	105	__1
651	Flatcar (O), *35-40*	28	55	__2
652	Gondola (O), *35-40*	28	55	__2
653	Hopper Car (O), *34-40*	35	65	__
654	Tank Car (O), *34-42*			
	(A) Orange or aluminum finish	35	60	__
	(B) Gray	42	75	__
655	Boxcar (O), *34-42*			
	(A) Cream, maroon roof	35	60	__
	(B) Cream, tuscan roof	47	75	__
656	Cattle Car (O), *35-40*			
	(A) Light gray, vermilion roof	40	75	__
	(B) Burnt orange, tuscan roof	70	125	__

		Good	Exc	Cond/$
657	Caboose (0), *34-42*			
	(A) Red body and roof	20	34	__2
	(B) Red, tuscan roof	25	42	__2
659	Dump Car (0), *35-42*	40	75	__2
700	Electric 0-4-0 (0), *15-16*	360	690	__1
700	Window Display (2⅞"), *03-05*		NRS	__
700E	Steam 4-6-4, Scale Hudson,			
	5344 (0), *37-42**	1400	2550	__4
700K	Steam 4-6-4, unbuilt (0), *38-42*	4400	5950	__1
701	Electric 0-4-0 (0), *15-16*	390	660	__1
701	Steam 0-6-0 (See 708)		2350	__1
702	Baggage (0), *17-21*	115	305	__1
703	Electric 4-4-4 (0), *15-16*	1400	2350	__1
706	Electric 0-4-0 (0), *15-16*	375	630	__1
708	Steam 0-6-0, "8976" on boiler			
	front (0), *39-42**	1450	2850	__1
710	Pullman (0), *24-34*			
	(A) Red, "LIONEL LINES"	200	300	__2
	(B) Orange, "LIONEL LINES"	150	225	__2
	(C) Orange, "NEW YORK CENTRAL"	200	225	__2
	(D) Orange, "ILLINOIS CENTRAL"	300	450	__2
	(E) 2-tone blue, "LIONEL LINES"	300	415	__2
	(F) Orange, "NEW YORK CENTRAL"	200	260	__2
711	R.C. Switches, pair (072), *35-42*	85	170	__3
712	Observation (0), *24-34*			
	(A) Red, "LIONEL LINES"	185	355	__1
	(B) Orange, "LIONEL LINES"	140	265	__1
	(C) Orange, "NEW YORK CENTRAL"	185	310	__1
	(D) Orange, "ILLINOIS CENTRAL"	280	530	__1
	(E) 2-tone blue, "LIONEL LINES"	280	485	__1
	(F) Orange, "NEW YORK CENTRAL"	185	310	__1
714	Boxcar (0), *40-42**	390	710	__1
714K	Boxcar, unbuilt (0), *40-42*		650	__1
715	Tank Car (0), *40-42**			
	(A) "S.E.P.S. 8124" decal	340	610	__1
	(B) "S.U.N.X. 715" decal	435	880	__1
715K	Tank Car, unbuilt (0), *40-42*		530	__1
716	Hopper Car (0), *40-42**	315	570	__1
716K	Hopper, unbuilt (0), *40-42*		730	__1
717	Caboose (0), *40-42**	390	590	__1
717K	Caboose, unbuilt (0), *40-42*		590	__1
720	90° Crossing (072), *35-42*	21	40	__1
721	Manual Switches, pair (072), *35-42*	50	105	__1
730	90° Crossing (072), *35-42*	20	36	__1
731	R.C. Switches, pair, T-rail (072), *35-42*	80	135	__1
751E/751W	Set: 752; (2) 753s; 754 (0), *34-41**	640	1050	__1

		Good	Exc	Cond/$
752E	Diesel only (O), *34-41*			
	(A) Yellow and brown	190	355	__1
	(B) Aluminum finish	180	340	__1
753	Coach (O), *36-41*			
	(A) Yellow and brown	100	185	__1
	(B) Aluminum Finish	95	180	__1
754	Observation (O), *36-41*			
	(A) Yellow and brown	100	185	__1
	(B) Aluminum Finish	95	180	__1
760	16-piece Curved Track (O72), *35-42*	41	80	__1
761	Curved Track (O72), *34-42*	1	2.50	__1
762	Straight Track (O72), *34-42*	1	2.50	__1
762	Inside Straight Track (O72), *34-42*	2	5	__1
763E	Steam 4-6-4 (O), *37-42*			
	(A) Gun-metal, 263 or 2263W tender	1200	2650	__2
	(B) Gun-metal, 2226X or 2226WX	1350	2950	__2
	(C) Black, 2226WX tender	1200	2650	__2
771	Curved Track, T-rail (O72), *35-42*	3	9	__1
772	Straight Track, T-rail (O72), *35-42*	4	12	__1
773	Fishplate Outfit (O72), *36-42*	25	32	__1
782	Hiawatha Combine (O), *35-41 **	230	380	__1
783	Hiawatha Coach (O), *35-41 **	140	290	__1
784	Hiawatha Observation (O), *35-41 **	205	445	__1
792	Rail Chief Combine (O), *37-41 **	290	800	__1
793	Rail Chief Coach (O), *37-41 **	290	800	__1
794	Rail Chief Observation (O), *37-41 **	250	800	__1
800	Boxcar (O), *15-26*			
	(A) Light orange, brown-maroon roof	45	70	__1
	(B) Orange body/roof, "PENN RR"	30	50	__1
800	Boxcar (2⁷⁄₈"), *04-05 **	2500	4050	__1
801	Caboose (O), *15-26*	36	46	__1
802	Stock Car (O), *15-26*	43	60	__1
803	Hopper Car, Early (O), *23-28*	32	47	__1
803	Hopper Car, Late (O), *29-34*	35	60	__1
804	Tank Car (O), *23-28*	27	47	__1
805	Boxcar (O), *27-34*			
	(A) Pea green, terra-cotta roof	35	60	__1
	(B) Pea green, maroon roof	44	115	__1
	(C) Orange, maroon roof	44	95	__1
806	Stock Car (O), *27-34*			
	(A) Pea green, terra-cotta roof	42	75	__
	(B) Orange; various color roof	35	60	__
807	Caboose (O), *27-40*			
	(A) Peacock, dark green roof	20	35	__
	(B) Red, peacock roof	20	35	__
	(C) Light red body and roof	23	40	__

		Good	Exc	Cond/$
809	Dump Car (O), *31-41*			
	(A) Orange bin	40	75	__1
	(B) Green bin	40	85	__1
810	Crane (O), *30-42*			
	(A) Terra-cotta cab, maroon roof	190	200	__2
	(B) Cream cab, vermilion roof	125	180	__2
811	Flatcar (O), *26-40*			
	(A) Maroon	40	70	__2
	(B) Aluminum finish	47	100	__2
812	Gondola (O), *26-42*	46	95	__2
812T	Tool Set, *30-41*	40	85	___
813	Stock Car (O), *26-42*			
	(A) Orange, pea green roof	65	145	__2
	(B) Orange, maroon roof	55	135	__2
	(C) Cream, maroon roof	100	225	__2
	(D) Tuscan body and roof		1600	__2
814	Boxcar (O), *26-42*			
	(A) Cream, orange roof	46	105	__3
	(B) Cream, maroon roof	115	140	__3
	(C) Yellow, brown roof	110	120	__3
814R	Refrigerator Car (O), *29-42*			
	(A) Ivory, peacock roof	100	190	__1
	(B) White, light blue roof	120	265	__1
	(C) Flat white, brown roof	600	900	__1
815	Tank Car (O), *26-42*			
	(A) Pea green, maroon frame	250	510	__1
	(B) Pea green, black frame	70	155	__1
	(C) Aluminum, black frame	50	115	__1
	(D) Orange-yellow, black frame	150	255	__1
816	Hopper Car (O), *27-42*			
	(A) Olive green	85	155	__1
	(B) Red body	65	135	__1
	(C) Black body	370	680	__1
817	Caboose (O), *26-42*			
	(A) Peacock, dark green roof	45	80	__3
	(B) Red, peacock roof	45	80	__3
	(C) Light red body and roof	45	80	__3
820	Boxcar (O), *15-26*			
	(A) Orange, "ILLINOIS CENTRAL"	45	80	__1
	(B) Orange, "UNION PACIFIC"	65	105	__1
820	Floodlight Car (O), *31-42*			
	(A) Terra-cotta	100	175	__2
	(B) Green	100	175	__2
	(C) Light green	105	180	__2
821	Stock Car (O), *15-16, 25-26*	45	85	__1
822	Caboose (O), *15-26*	35	70	__1

		Good	Exc	Cond/$
831	Flatcar (O), *27-34*	22	41	__1
840	Industrial Power Station, *28-40**	1200	3050	__1
900	Ammunition Car (O), *17-21*	120	340	__1
900	Box Trail Car (2$\frac{7}{8}$"), *04-05**	2000	3600	__1
901	Gondola (O), *19-27*	23	50	__1
902	Gondola (O), *27-34*	23	38	__1
910	Grove of Trees, *32-42*	70	155	__1
911	Country Estate, *32-42*	195	410	__1
912	Suburban Home	300	620	__1
913	Landscaped Bungalow, *40-42*	140	285	__1
914	Park Landscape, *32-35*	90	205	__1
915	Tunnel, *32, 34-35*	160	435	__1
916	Tunnel, 29$\frac{3}{4}$" long, *35*	95	180	__1
917	Scenic Hillside, *32-36*	90	205	__1
918	Scenic Hillside, *32-36*	90	205	__1
919	Park Grass, bag, *32-42*	8	17	__1
920	Village, *32-33*	600	1600	__1
921	Scenic Park, 3 pieces, *32-33*	980	2600	__1
921C	Park Center, *32-33*	400	1050	__1
922	Terrace, *32-36*	80	155	__1
923	Tunnel, 40$\frac{1}{4}$" long, *33-42*	90	225	__1
924	Tunnel, 30" long (O72), *35-42*	50	135	__1
925	Lubricant, *35-42*	1	2.50	__1
927	Flag Plot, *37-42*	70	135	__1
1000	Passenger Car (2$\frac{7}{8}$"), *05**	4500	6750	__1
1000	Trolley Trailer (Std.), *10-16*	1400	2250	__1
1010	Electric 0-4-0, Winner (O), *31-32*	90	160	__1
1010	Interurban Trailer (Std.), *10-16*	1000	1800	__1
1011	Pullman, Winner (O), *31-32*	55	75	__1
1011	Interurban (Std.), *10*		NM	__
1012	Station, *32*	50	70	__1
1012	(See #1011 Interurban)			
1015	Steam 0-4-0 (O), *31-32*	100	205	__1
1017	Winner Station, *33*	25	70	__1
1019	Observation (O), *31-32*	50	70	__1
1020	Baggage (O), *31-32*	65	110	__1
1021	90° Crossover (O27), *32-42*	1	4	__1
1022	Tunnel, 18$\frac{3}{4}$" long (O), *35-42*	15	32	__1
1023	Tunnel, 19" long, *34-42*	20	41	__1
1024	Switches, pair (O27), *37-42*	4	15	__1
1025	Bumper (O27), *40-42*	14	25	__1
1027	Transformer, Tin Station, *34*	50	115	__1
1028	Transformer, 40 watts, *39*	3	11	__1
1030	Electric 0-4-0 (O), *32*	75	135	__1
1035	Steam 0-4-0 (O), *32*	75	115	__1
1045	Watchman, *38-42*	13	50	__2

		Good	Exc	Cond/$
1050	Passenger Car Trailer (2⅞"), *05**	5000	7200	__1
1100	Handcar, Mickey Mouse, *35-37**			
	(A) Red base	405	640	__1
	(B) Apple green base, orange shoes	500	880	__1
	(C) Orange base	600	1200	__1
1100	Summer Trolley Trailer (Std.), *10-13*		NRS	__
1103	Handcar, Peter Rabbit (O), *35-37**	330	820	__1
1105	Handcar, Santa Claus (O), *35-35**			
	(A) Red base	580	1250	__1
	(B) Green base	630	1400	__1
1107	Transformer, Tin Station, *33*	25	70	__1
1107	Handcar, Donald Duck (O), *36-37**			
	(A) White dog house w/ red roof	475	1200	__1
	(B) White dog house w/ green roof	450	1100	__1
	(C) Orange dog house w/ green roof	640	1850	__1
1121	Switches, pair (O27), *37-42*	15	34	__1
1506L	Steam 0-4-0 (O), *33-34*	95	125	__1
1506M	Steam 0-4-0 (O), *35*	250	430	__1
1508	Steam 0-4-0, Commodore Vanderbilt w/ Mickey in 1509 Stoker Tender, *35*	385	620	__1
1511	Steam 0-4-0 (O), *36-37*	110	160	__1
1512	Gondola (O), *31-33, 36-37*	29	47	__1
1514	Boxcar (O), *31-37*	25	41	__1
1515	Tank Car (O), *33-37*	25	41	__1
1517	Caboose (O), *31-37*	25	41	__1
1518	Mickey Mouse Diner (O), *35*	105	235	__1
1519	Mickey Mouse Band (O), *35*	105	235	__1
1520	Mickey Mouse Animal (O), *35*	105	235	__1
1536	Circus: 1508, 1509, 1518, 1519, 1520, *15-20*	700	1550	__1
1550	Switches, pair, windup, *33-37*	2	5	__1
1555	90° Crossover, windup, *33-37*	1	2.50	__1
1560	Station, *33-37*	15	34	__1
1569	Accessory set, 8 pieces, *33-37*	35	70	__1
1588	Steam 0-4-0 (O), *36-37*	150	250	__1
1630	Pullman (O), *38-42*			
	(A) Aluminum windows	35	70	__1
	(B) Light gray windows	47	80	__1
1631	Observation (O), *38-42*			
	(A) Aluminum windows	35	70	__1
	(B) Light gray windows	47	80	__1
1651E	Electric 0-4-0 (O), *33*	130	240	__1
1661E	Steam 2-4-0 (O), *33*	75	160	__1
1662	Steam 0-4-0 (O27), *40-42*	270	445	__1
1663	Steam 0-4-0 (O27), *40-42*	200	385	__1
1664/1664E	Steam 2-4-2 (O27), *38-42*			

		Good	Exc	Cond/$
	(A) Gun-metal	60	100	__1
	(B) Black	60	95	__1
1666/1666E	Steam 2-6-2 (027), *38-42*			
	(A) Gun-metal	115	170	__1
	(B) Black	95	145	__1
1668/1668E	Steam 2-6-2 (027), *37-41*			
	(A) Gun-metal	75	115	__1
	(B) Black	75	130	__1
1673	Coach (O), *36-37*			
	(A) Aluminum windows	35	75	__1
	(B) Light gray windows	47	90	__1
1674	Pullman (O), *36-37*	35	75	__1
1675	Observation (O), *36-37*	30	70	__1
1677	Gondola (O), *33-35, 39-42*			
	(A) "IVES/R.R. LINES," light blue	40	60	__1
	(B) "LIONEL," blue or red	21	37	__1
1679	Boxcar (O), *33-42*			
	(A) Cream, "IVES" on side	23	38	__2
	(B) Cream, "LIONEL" on side	23	38	__2
	(C) Cream or yellow, "BABY RUTH"	23	38	__2
1680	Tank Car (O), *33-42*			
	(A) Aluminum, "IVES TANK LINES"	80	95	__2
	(B) Aluminum, no "IVES" lettering	19	34	__2
1681	Steam 2-4-0 (O), *34-35*			
	(A) Black, red frame	55	120	__1
	(B) Red, red frame	110	145	__1
1681E	Steam 2-4-0 (O), *34-35*			
	(A) Black, red frame	65	130	__1
	(B) Red, red frame	130	165	__1
1682	Caboose (O), *33-42*			
	(A) Vermilion, "IVES" on side	34	70	__1
	(B) Red or tuscan, "LIONEL"	17	40	__1
1684	Steam 2-4-2 (027), *41-42*	50	80	__2
1685	Coach (O), *33-37 u*			
	(A) Gray, maroon roof	240	495	__1
	(B) Red, maroon roof	170	335	__1
	(C) Blue, silver roof	170	315	__1
1686	Baggage (O), *33-37 u*			
	(A) Gray, maroon roof	240	495	__1
	(B) Red, maroon roof	170	335	__1
	(C) Blue, silver roof	170	315	__1
1687	Observation (O), *33-37 u*			
	(A) Gray, maroon roof	170	315	__1
	(B) Red, maroon roof	180	315	__1
	(C) Blue, silver roof	170	315	__1
1688/1688E	Steam 2-4-2 (027), *36-46*	50	85	__1

		Good	Exc	Cond/$
1689E	Steam 2-4-2 (O27), *36-37*			
	(A) Gun-metal	75	115	__1
	(B) Black	60	100	__1
1690	Pullman (O), *33-40*	35	60	__1
1691	Observation (O), *33-40*	35	60	__1
1692	Pullman (O27), *39 u*	45	70	__1
1693	Observation (O27), *39 u*	45	70	__1
1700E	Diesel, power unit only (O27), *35-37*	45	70	__1
1700E	Set: 1700 (2) 1701s, 1702 (O27), *35-37 u*			
	(A) Aluminum and light red	140	250	__1
	(B) Chrome and light red	140	250	__1
	(C) Orange and gray	155	285	__1
1701	Coach (O27), *35-37*			
	(A) Chrome sides and roof	20	46	__1
	(B) Silver sides and roof	30	55	__1
	(C) Orange and gray	75	150	__1
1702	Observation (O27), *35-37*			
	(A) Chrome sides and roof	20	46	__1
	(B) Silver sides and roof	30	55	__1
	(C) Orange and gray	75	150	__1
1703	Observation w/ hooked coupler, *35-37 u*	49	110	__1
1717	Gondola (O), *33-40 u*	30	48	__1
1717X	Gondola (O), *40 u*	27	48	__1
1719	Boxcar (O), *33-40 u*	30	50	__1
1719X	Boxcar (O), *41-42 u*	30	50	__1
1722	Caboose (O), *33-42 u*	25	50	__1
1722X	Caboose (O), *39-40 u*	26	41	__1
1766	Pullman (Std.), *34-40**			
	(A) Terra-cotta, maroon roof, brass trim	300	650	__2
	(B) Red, maroon roof, nickel trim	300	540	__2
1767	Baggage Car (Std.), *34-40**			
	(A) Terra-cotta, maroon roof, brass trim	295	850	__1
	(B) Red, maroon roof, nickel trim	295	700	__1
1768	Observation (Std.), *34-40**			
	(A) Terra-cotta, maroon roof, brass trim	300	650	__1
	(B) Red, maroon roof, nickel trim	300	540	__1
1811	Pullman (O), *33-37*	32	70	__1
1812	Observation (O), *33-37*	30	65	__1
1813	Baggage Car (O), *33-37*	60	135	__1
1816/1816W	Diesel (O), *35-37*	100	240	__1
1817	Coach (O), *35-37*	22	50	__1
1818	Observation (O), *35-37*	22	50	__1
1835E	Steam 2-4-2 (Std.), *34-39*	650	1050	__1
1910	Electric 0-6-0, Early (Std.), *10-11*	800	1800	__1
1910	Electric 0-6-0, Late (Std.), *12*	550	1350	__1
1910	Pullman (Std.), *09-10 u*	1000	1800	__1

		Good	Exc	Cond/$
1911	Electric 0-4-0, Early (Std.), *10-12*	1000	2000	__1
1911	Electric 0-4-0, Late (Std.), *13*	700	1100	__1
1911	Electric 0-4-4-0, Special (Std.), *11-12*	1000	2500	__1
1912	Electric 0-4-4-0 (Std.), *10-12**			
	(A) NY, New Haven & Hartford	1800	3200	__1
	(B) "NEW YORK CENTRAL LINES"	1500	2700	__1
1912	Electric 0-4-4-0 Special (Std.), *11**	2500	4500	__1
2200	Summer Trolley Trailer (Std.), *10-13*	1100	2250	__1
2600	Pullman (O), *38-42*	80	155	__1
2601	Observation (O), *38-42*	60	115	__1
2602	Baggage Car (O), *38-42*	90	185	__1
2613	Pullman (O), *38-42**			
	(A) Blue, 2-tone blue roof	100	270	__2
	(B) State green, 2-tone green roof	200	440	__2
2614	Observation (O), *38-42**			
	(A) Blue, 2-tone blue roof	100	270	__1
	(B) State green, 2-tone green roof	200	440	__1
2615	Baggage Car (O), *38-42**			
	(A) Blue, 2-tone blue roof	115	270	__1
	(B) State green, 2-tone green roof	200	420	__1
2620	Floodlight Car (O), *38-42*	49	105	__2
2623	Pullman (O), *41-42*			
	(A) "IRVINGTON"	170	335	__2
	(B) "MANHATTAN"	155	295	__2
2624	Pullman (O), *41-42*	750	1700	__1
2630	Pullman (O), *38-42*	30	70	__1
2631	Observation (O), *38-42*	30	70	__1
2640	Pullman Illuminated (O), *38-42*			
	(A) Light blue, aluminum roof	30	70	__1
	(B) State green, dark green roof	28	70	__1
2641	Observation Illuminated (O), *38-42*			
	(A) Light blue, aluminum roof	30	70	__1
	(B) State green, dark green roof	28	70	__1
2642	Pullman (O), *41-42*	32	70	__1
2643	Observation (O), *41-42*	30	65	__1
2651	Flatcar (O), *38-42*	30	50	__1
2652	Gondola (O), *38-41*	24	50	__2
2653	Hopper Car (O), *38-42*			
	(A) Stephen Girard green	38	65	__1
	(B) Black	60	100	__1
2654	Tank Car (O), *38-42*			
	(A) Aluminum finish, "SUNOCO"	35	60	__3
	(B) Orange, "SHELL"	35	60	__3
	(C) Light gray, "SUNOCO"	41	70	__3
2655	Boxcar (O), *38-42*			
	(A) Cream, maroon roof	35	65	__1

		Good	Exc	Cond/$
	(B) Cream, tuscan roof	38	75	__1
2656	Stock Car (O), *38-41*			
	(A) Light gray, red roof	45	75	__1
	(B) Burnt orange, tuscan roof	75	115	__1
2657	Caboose (O), *40-41*	23	39	__3
2657X	Caboose (O), *40-41*	25	41	__1
2659	Dump Car (O), *38-41*	40	70	__1
2660	Crane (O), *38-42*	70	90	__1
2672	Caboose (O27), *41-42*	21	33	__1
2677	Gondola (O27), *39-41*	26	37	__1
2679	Boxcar (O27), *38-42*	18	30	__1
2680	Tank Car (O27), *38-42*			
	(A) Aluminum finish, "SUNOCO"	15	41	__1
	(B) Orange, "SHELL"	15	41	__1
2682	Caboose (O27), *38-42*	18	32	__1
2682X	Caboose (O27), *38-42*	22	35	__1
2717	Gondola (O), *38-42 u*	21	41	__1
2719	Boxcar (O), *38-42 u*	29	50	__1
2722	Caboose (O), *38-42 u*	25	50	__1
2755	Tank Car (O), *41-42*	60	115	__1
2757	Caboose (O), *41-42*	24	36	__1
2757X	Caboose (O), *41-42*	25	36	__1
2758	Automobile Boxcar (O), *41-42*	38	55	__1
2810	Crane (O), *38-42*	165	230	__2
2811	Flatcar (O), *38-42*	65	115	__1
2812	Gondola (O), *38-42*			
	(A) Green	42	90	__1
	(B) Dark orange	44	95	__1
2813	Stock Car (O), *38-42*	120	250	__1
2814	Boxcar (O), *38-42*			
	(A) Cream, maroon roof	85	210	__3
	(B) Orange, brown roof	85	205	__3
2814R	Refrigerator Car (O), *38-42*			
	(A) White, light blue roof, nickel plates	150	250	__1
	(B) White, brown roof, no plates	375	660	__1
2815	Tank Car (O), *38-42*			
	(A) Aluminum finish	85	165	__1
	(B) Orange	135	250	__1
2816	Hopper Car (O), *35-42*			
	(A) Red	100	190	__2
	(B) Black	110	205	__2
2817	Caboose (O), *36-42*			
	(A) Light red body and roof	90	145	__5
	(B) Flat red, tuscan roof	140	225	__5
2820	Floodlight Car (O), *38-42*			

		Good	Exc	Cond/$
	(A) Stamped nickel searchlight	110	235	__1
	(B) Gray die-cast searchlights	120	260	__1
2954	Boxcar (O), *40-42**	190	470	__2
2955	Sunoco Tank Car (O), *40-42**			
	(A) "SHELL" decal	225	560	__1
	(B) "SUNOCO" decal	340	780	__1
2956	Hopper Car (O), *40-42**	185	470	__1
2957	Caboose (O), *40-42**	170	440	__2
3300	Summer Trolley Trailer (Std.), *10-13*	1400	2250	__1
3651	Operating Lumber Car (O), *39-42*	24	55	__2
3652	Operating Gondola (O), *39-42*	33	75	__3
3659	Operating Dump Car (O), *39-42*	22	35	__2
3811	Operating Lumber Car (O), *39-42*	35	70	__1
3814	Operating Merchandise Car (O), *39-42*	135	260	__3
3859	Operating Dump Car (O), *38-42*	48	110	__1
4351	(See 14, 17, 117)			
4400	(See #404 Summer Trolley)			
5344	(See 700E)			
5906	(See 14, 17)			
8118	(See 14)			
8976	(See 227, 228, 229, 230, 706, 708)			
19050	(See 14)			
51906	(See 17)			
54078	(See 14, 114)			
62976	(See 114)			
65784	(See 12, 16, 112)			
76399	(See 16, 112)			
98237	(See 14, 114)			
342715	(See 17)			
A	Miniature Motor, *04*	50	95	__1
A	Transformer, 40, 60 watts, *27-37*	8	25	__1
B	New Departure Motor, *06-16*	75	135	__1
B	Transformer, 50, 75 watts, *16-38*	6	24	__1
C	New Departure Motor, *06-16*	100	180	__1
D	New Departure Motor, *06-14*	100	180	__1
E	New Departure Motor, *06-14*	100	180	__1
F	New Departure Motor, *06-14*	100	180	__1
G	Battery Fan Motor, *06-14*	100	180	__1
K	Power Motor, *05*	100	180	__1
K	Transformer, 150, 200 watts, *13-38*	26	95	__1
L	Power Motor, *05*	50	100	__1
L	Transformer, 50, 75 watts, *13-38*	8	24	__1
M	Battery Motor, *15-20*	30	80	__1
N	Transformer, 50 watts, *41-42*	7	23	__1
Q	Transformer, 50, 75 watts, *14-15*	13	32	__1

		Good	Exc	Cond/$
R	Battery Motor, *15-20*	30	75	__1
R	Transformer, 100 watts, *38-42*	27	60	__1
S	Transformer, 50, 80 watts, *14-17*	18	37	__1
T	Transformer, 75, 100,150 watts, *19-28*	10	30	__1
U	Transformer, Aladdin, *32-33*	6	16	__1
V	Transformer, 150 watts, *39-42*	65	125	__1
W	Transformer, 75 watts, *32-33*	7	22	__1
Y	Battery Motor, *15-20*	40	80	__1
Z	Transformer, 250 watts, *39-42*	110	160	__1

Other Transformers and Rheostats made by Lionel

		Good	Exc	Cond/$
106	Rheostat, *11-14*	3	9	__1
1029	25 watts, *36*	6	18	__1
1030	40 watts, *35-38*	6	23	__1
1031	Rheostat, circa 1938, *38*	2	4	__1
1036	Rheostat, circa 1941, *40*	2	5	__1
1037	Transformer, 40 watts, *40-42*	7	23	__1
1038	Rheostat, circa 1940, *40*	2	4	__1
1039	Transformer, 35 watts, *37-40*	7	18	__1
1040	Transformer, 60 watts, *37-39*	12	27	__1
1041	Transformer, 60 watts, *39-42*	13	30	__1

Track, Lockons, and Contactors

	Good	Exc	Cond/$
O Straight	0.25	0.70	__1
O Curve	0.25	0.70	__1
O72 Straight	1	2	__1
O72 Curve	1	2	__1
O27 Straight	0.10	0.50	__1
O27 Curve	0.10	0.45	__1
Standard Straight	0.70	3	__1
Standard Curve	0.60	2	__1
O Gauge Lockon	0.10	0.55	__1
Standard Gauge Lockon	0.30	1	__1
UTC Lockon	0.35	0.95	__1
145C Contactor	0.85	3	__1
153C Contactor	0.75	3	__2

Section 2
POSTWAR 1945–1969

		Good	Exc	Cond/$
011-11	Fiber Pins (O), *46-50*	0.10	0.15	__1
011-43	Insulating Pins, dz. (O), *61*	1	1.50	__1
020	90° Crossover (O), *45-61*	7	11	__1
020X	45° Crossover (O), *46-59*	7	10	__1
022	R.C. Switches, pair (O), *45-69*	33	50	__2
022-500	Adapter set (O), *57-61*	1	3	__1
022A	R.C. Switches, pair (O), *47*	75	135	__1
025	Bumper (O), *46-47*	8	19	__1
026	Bumper, *48-50*	10	17	__1
027C-1	Track Clips, dz. (027), *47, 49*	0.55	0.90	__1
30	Water Tower, *47-50*	75	115	__2
31	Curved Track (Super O), *57-66*	1	1.50	__1
31-7	Power Blade Con. (Super O), *57-61*		0.35	__1
31-15	Ground Rail Pin (Super O), *57-66*		0.60	__1
31-45	Power Blade Connection (Super O), *61-66*		0.60	__1
32	Straight Track (Super O), *57-66*	0.95	2.50	__1
32-10	Insulating Pin (Super O), *57-60*		0.35	__1
32-20	Power Blade Ins. (Super O), *57-60*		0.15	__1
32-25	Insulating Pin (Super O), *57-61*		0.15	__1
32-30	Ground Pin (Super O), *57-61*		0.15	__1
32-31	Power Pin (Super O), *57-61*		0.15	__1
32-32	Insulating Pin (Super O), *57-61*		0.15	__1
32-33	Ground Pin (Super O), *57-61*		0.15	__1
32-34	Power Pin (Super O), *57-61*		0.15	__1
32-45	Power Blade Insulators, dz. (Super O), *61-66*	0.85	1.50	__1
32-55	Insulating Pins, dz. (Super O), *61-66*	1	2	__1
33	Half Curved Track (Super O), *57-66*	1	2.50	__1
34	Half Straight Track (Super O), *57-66*	1	2.50	__1
35	Boulevard Lamp, *45-49*	15	39	__1
36	Remote Control set (Super O), *57-66*	11	16	__1
37	Uncoupling Track set (Super O), *57-66*	8	15	__1
38	Water Tower, *46-47*	180	405	__1
38	Accessory Adapter Track (Super O), *51-61*	5	11	__1
39	Operating set (Super O), *57*	4	8	__1
39-5	Operating set (Super O), *57-58*	4	8	__1
39-10	Operating set (Super O), *58*	4	8	__1
39-15	Operating set, w/ blade (Super O), *57-58*	4	8	__1
39-20	Operating set (Super O), *57-58*	4	8	__1
39-25	Operating set (Super O), *61-66*	4	9	__1
39-35	Operating set (Super O), *59*	4	9	__1
40	Hookup Wire, *50-51, 53-63*	4	32	__1

		Good	Exc	Cond/$
40-25	Conductor Wire, *56-59*	5	18	__1
40-50	Cable Reel, *60-61*	4	9	__1
41	Contactor (Super O)	0.50	1.50	__1
41	U.S. Army Switcher, *55-57*	85	125	__3
42	Picatinny Arsenal Switcher, *57*	145	300	__2
042/42	Manual Switches, pr. (O), *46-59*	16	38	__1
43	Power Track (Super O), *59-66*	4	7	__1
44	U.S. Army Mobile Launcher, *59-62*	125	225	__1
44-80	Missiles, *59-60*	11	21	__1
45	U.S. Marines Mobile Launcher, *60-62*	135	250	__1
45	Automatic Gateman, *46-49*	28	46	__1
45N	Automatic Gateman, *45*	37	65	__2
48	Insl. Straight Track (Super O), *57-66*	4	9	__1
49	Insl. Curved Track (Super O), *57-66*	4	9	__1
50	Lionel Gang Car, *54-64*	45	70	__4
51	Navy Yard Switcher, *56-57*	90	185	__2
52	Fire Car, *58-61*	95	200	__2
53	Rio Grande Snowplow, *57-60*			
	(A) Backwards "A" in Rio Grande	165	275	__2
	(B) Correctly printed "A"	375	700	__2
54	Ballast Tamper, *58-61, 66, 68-69*	95	180	__2
54-6446	(See 6446 or 6446-25), *54-55*	19	43	__1
55	Tie-jector, *57-61*	125	230	__3
55-150	Ties, *57-60*	5	15	__1
56	Lamp Post, *46-49*	23	49	__1
56	M&St L Mine Transport, *58*	250	425	__1
57	AEC Switcher, *59-60*	395	690	__1
58	Lamp Post, *46-50*	22	65	__1
58	GN Snowplow, *59-61*	295	500	__2
59	Minuteman Switcher, *62-63*	230	415	__1
60	Lionelville Rapid Transit Trolley, *55-58*	95	155	__4
61	Ground Lockon (Super O), *57-66*	0.25	0.45	__1
62	Power Lockon (Super O), *57-66*	0.25	0.45	__1
64	Street Lamp, *45-49*	28	55	__1
65	Lionel Lines Handcar, *62-66*	140	260	__1
68	Executive Inspection Car, *58-61*	190	315	__3
69	Lionel Maintenance Car, *60-62*	135	190	__1
70	Yard Light, *49-50*	25	50	__1
71	Lamp Post, *49-59*	11	21	__2
75	Goose Neck Lamp, set of 2, *61-63*	12	21	__1
76	Blvd. Street Lamp, *59-66, 68-69*	11	22	__1
80	Controller	11	20	__1
88	Controller, *46-60*	4	8	__1
89	Flagpole, *56-58*	17	47	__1
90	Controller	3	8	__1

		Good	Exc	Cond/$
91	Circuit Breaker, *57-60*	13	25	__1
92	Circuit Breaker, *59-66, 68-69*	9	16	__1
93	Water Tower, *46-49*	25	47	__1
96C	Controller	3	6	__1
97	Coal Elevator, *46-50*	100	175	__1
100	Multivolt-DC/AC, Trans., *58-66*	—	70	__1
108	Trestle set	25	36	__1
109	Partial Trestle set, *61*	—	30	__1
110	Graduated Trestle set, *55-69*	11	18	__2
111	Elevated Trestle set, *56-69*	9	17	__1
111-100	Two Elevated Trestle Piers, *60-63*	10	18	__1
112	R.C. Switches, pr. (Super O), *57-66*	60	90	__2
114	Newsstand w/ horn, *57-59*	46	105	__1
115	Passenger Station, *46-49*	165	315	__1
118	Newsstand w/ whistle, *57-58*	43	95	__1
119	Landscaped Tunnel, *57-58*		NRS	___
120	90° Crossing (Super O), *57-66*	6	10	__1
121	Landscaped Tunnel, *59-66*		NRS	___
122	Lamp Assortment		170	__1
123	Lamp Assortment, *55-59*	85	185	__1
123-60	Lamp Assortment, *60-63*		150	__1
125	Whistle Shack, *50-55*	26	46	__1
128	Animated Newsstand, *57-60*	75	160	__1
130	60° Crossing (Super O), *57-61*	7	13	__1
131	Curved Tunnel, *59-66*		NRS	___
132	Passenger Station, *49-55*	45	90	__2
133	Passenger Station, *57, 61-62, 66*	28	75	__1
137	Passenger Station (See Prewar section), *46*	75	135	__1
138	Water Tower, *53-57*	80	145	__1
140	Automatic Banjo Signal, *54-66*	22	39	__1
142	Man. Switches, pr. (Super O), *57-66*	28	55	__1
145C	Contactor, *50-60*	1	7	__1
145	Automatic Gateman, *50-66*	25	41	__3
147	Whistle Controller, *61-66*	1	4	__1
148	Dwarf Trackside Signal, *57-60*	24	55	__1
150	Telegraph Pole set, *47-50*	38	75	__1
151	Auto. Semaphore, *47-69*	24	48	__2
152	Auto. Crossing Gate, *45-49*	14	32	__1
153	Auto. Block Control, Signal, *45-59*	17	30	__2
153C	Contactor	1	7	__1
154	Auto. Highway Signal, *45-69*	19	46	__2
155	Blinking Light Signal w/ bell, *55-57*	36	70	__1
156	Station Platform, *46-49*	48	105	__2
157	Station Platform, *52-59*	29	65	__1
160	Unloading Bin, *52-57*			
	(A) Plastic	1	3	__1

		Good	Exc	Cond/$
	(B) Metal	10	50	__1
161	Mail Pickup set, *61-63*	40	95	__1
163	Single Target Block Signal, *61-69*	17	30	__1
164	Log Loader, *46-50*	90	190	__2
167	Whistle Controller, *45-46*	6	11	__1
175	Rocket Launcher, *58-60*	125	295	__1
175-50	Extra Rocket, *59-60*	5	18	__1
182	Magnetic Crane, *46-49*	125	265	__1
192	Oper. Control Tower, *59-60*	110	255	__1
193	Industrial Water Tower, *53-55*	90	105	__2
195	Floodlight Tower, *57-69*	29	65	__2
195-75	Eight-Bulb Extension, *58-60*	21	40	__1
196	Smoke Pellets, *46-47*		75	__1
197	Rotating Radar Antenna, *57-59*	50	100	__1
199	Microwave Relay Tower, *58-59*	27	65	__1
202	UP Alco A Unit, *57*	49	100	__1
204	Santa Fe Alco AA Units, *57*	115	185	__1
205	Missouri Pacific Alco AA Units, *57-58*	60	105	__1
206	Artificial Coal, large bag, *46-68*	5	10	__1
207	Artificial Coal, small bag, *46-48*	3	8	__1
208	Santa Fe Alco AA Units, *58-59*	110	240	__1
209	New Haven Alco AA Units, *58*	300	620	__1
209	Wooden Barrels, set of 4, *46-50*	8	18	__1
210	Texas Special Alco AA Units, *58*	95	140	__1
211	Texas Special Alco AA Units, *62-66*	95	165	__1
212	USMC Alco A Unit, *58-59*	95	170	__1
212	Santa Fe Alco AA Units, *64-66*	80	160	__1
212T	USMC Dummy A Units, *58-59 u*	300	550	__1
213	Railroad Lift Bridge, *50*		NM	__
213	M&St L Alco AA Units, *64*	75	160	__1
214	Plate Girder Bridge, *53-69*	10	22	__1
215	Santa Fe Alco Units, *65 u*			
	(A) AB Units	85	165	__1
	(B) Double A Units (usually w/ 212T)	80	160	__1
216	Burlington Alco A Unit, *58*	95	315	__1
216	M&StL Alco AA Units, (usually w/ 213T), *64 u*	90	180	__1
217	B&M Alco AB Units, *59*	85	190	__1
218	Santa Fe Alco Units, *59-63*			
	(A) Double A Units	70	155	__1
	(B) AB Units	70	165	__1
219	Missouri Pacific Alco AA Units, *59 u*	75	140	__1
220	Santa Fe Alco Units, *60-61*			
	(A) A Unit only	75	115	__1
	(B) AA Units	100	205	__1
221	2-6-4, 221T/221W Tender, *46-47*			
	(A) Gray die-cast body	80	165	__1

		Good	Exc	Cond/$
	(B) Black die-cast body	80	155	__1
221	Rio Grande Alco A Unit, *63-64*	55	90	__1
221	USMC Alco A Unit, *63-64 u*	145	345	__1
221	Santa Fe Alco A Unit, *63-64 u*	180	400	__1
222	Rio Grande Alco A Unit (adv. cat.), *62*	38	75	__1
223	218C Santa Fe Alco AB Units, *63*	85	165	__1
224	Steam 2-6-2, 2466T/2466W Tender, *45-46*	85	115	__1
224	U.S. Navy Alco AB Units, *60*	140	250	__1
225	C&O Alco A Unit, *60*	70	105	__1
226	B&M Alco AB Units, *60 u*	85	185	__1
227	CN Alco A Unit, *60 u*	85	155	__1
228	CN Alco A Unit, *61 u*	80	145	__1
229	M&St L Alco Units, *61-62*			
	(A) A unit only, *61*	65	110	__1
	(B) AB units, *62*	95	205	__1
230	C&O Alco A Unit, *61*	70	120	__1
231	Rock Island Alco A Unit, *61-63*	75	130	__1
232	New Haven Alco A Unit, *62*	60	115	__1
233	Steam 2-4-2, 233W Tender, *61-62*	55	95	__1
235	Steam 2-4-2, 1130T/1060T Tender, *60 u*	70	165	__1
236	Steam 2-4-2, 1130T/1050T Tender, *61-62*			
	(A) 1050T slope-back tender	18	41	__1
	(B) 1130T tender	18	41	__1
237	Steam 2-4-2, *63-66*			
	(A) w/ 1060T Tender	25	55	__1
	(B) w/ 234W Tender	45	90	__1
238	Steam 2-4-2, 234W Tender, *63-64*	55	115	__1
239	Steam 2-4-2, 234W Tender, *65-66*	48	75	__1
240	Steam 2-4-2, 242T, *64 u*	140	235	__1
241	Steam 2-4-2 w/ 234W Tender, *65 u*	70	135	__1
242	Steam 2-4-2 w/ 1060T Tender or			
	1062T Tender, *62-66*	20	46	__1
243	Steam 2-4-2, 243W Tender, *60*	70	115	__1
244	Steam 2-4-2, 244T/1130T Tender, *60-61*	25	36	__1
245	Steam 2-4-2, w/ 1060T Tender, *59-60 u*	55	110	__1
246	Steam 2-4-2, 244T/1130T Tender, *59-61*	22	36	__1
247	Steam 2-4-2, 247T Tender, *59*	30	50	__1
248	Steam 2-4-2, 1130T Tender, *58*	34	100	__1
249	Steam 2-4-2, 250T Tender, *58*	20	45	__1
250	Steam 2-4-2, 250T Tender, *57*	21	48	__1
251	Steam 2-4-2, 1062T Tender, *66 u*			
	(A) Slope-back tender	160	305	__1
	(B) 250T-type tender	145	280	__1
252	Crossing Gate, *50-62*	24	40	__2
253	Block Control Signal, *56-59*	17	31	__1
256	Illuminated Freight Station, *50-53*	25	47	__2

		Good	Exc	Cond/$
257	Freight Station w/ diesel horn, *56-57*	41	95	__1
260	Bumper, *51-69*			
	(A) Die-cast	9	16	__1
	(B) Black plastic	22	39	__1
262	Highway Crossing Gate, *62-69*	22	60	__1
264	Operating Forklift Platform w/ 6264, *57-60*	170	350	__2
270	Metal Bridge (O), *46*	19	38	__1
282	Gantry Crane, *54-57*	130	205	__2
282R	Gantry Crane, *56-57*	125	210	__1
299	Code Transmitter Beacon set, *61-63*	85	175	__1
308	Railroad Sign set, die-cast, *45-49*	22	38	__1
309	Yard Sign set, plastic, *50-59*	15	28	__2
310	Billboard set, *50-68*	13	27	__1
313	Bascule Bridge, *46-49*	250	430	__2
313-82	Fiber Pins, *46-60*		0.05	__1
313-121	Fiber Pins, dozen, *61*		1.50	__1
314	Scale Model Girder Bridge, *45-50*	12	25	__1
315	Trestle Bridge, *46-48*	55	105	__1
316	Trestle Bridge, *49*	17	41	__1
317	Trestle Bridge, *50-56*	17	37	__1
321	Trestle Bridge, *58-64*	13	37	__1
332	Arch-Under Bridge, *59-66*	17	38	__1
334	Operating Dispatching Board, *57-60*	140	255	__1
342	Culvert Loader, *56-58*	125	270	__2
345	Culvert Unloader, *57-59*	185	325	__1
346	Manual Culvert Unloader, *65*	65	150	__1
347	Cannon Firing Range set, *64 u*	170	520	__1
348	Manual Culvert Unloader, *66-69*	80	190	__1
350	Engine Transfer Table, *57-60*	205	360	__2
350-50	Transfer Table Extension, *57-60*	85	190	__1
352	Ice Depot, includes 6352, *55-57*	110	190	__1
353	Trackside Control Signal, *60-61*	17	40	__1
356	Operating Freight Station, *52-57*	55	95	__1
362	Barrel Loader, *52-57*	50	110	__3
362-78	Wooden Barrels, *52-57*	7	18	__1
364	Conveyor Lumber Loader, *48-57*	85	115	__4
364C	On/Off Switch, *48-64*	3	8	__1
365	Dispatching Station, *58-59*	65	115	__1
375	Turntable, *62-64*	160	275	__1
390C	Switch, d.p.d.t., *60-64*	8	13	__1
394	Rotary Beacon, *49-53*	31	40	__2
395	Floodlight Tower, *49-56*	33	55	__1
397	Diesel Operating Coal Loader, *48-57*	90	140	__3
400	B&O RDC Passenger, *56-58*	180	215	__3
404	B&O RDC Baggage-Mail, *57-58*	200	375	__1
410	Billboard Blinker, *56-58*	33	55	__1

		Good	Exc	Cond/$
413	Countdown Control Panel, *62*	44	80	__1
415	Diesel Fueling Station, *55-57*	80	125	__2
419	Heliport Control Tower, *62*	175	410	__1
443	Missile Launch Platform,			
	w/ 943 Ammo Dump, *60-62*	17	41	__1
445	Switch Tower, lighted, *52-57*	39	75	__2
448	Missile Firing Range set, w/ 6448, *61-63*	85	155	__1
450	Signal Bridge, two-track, *52-58*	33	55	__3
450L	Signal Light Head, *52-58*	17	38	__1
452	Signal Bridge, single-track, *61-63*	60	110	__1
455	Operating Oil Derrick, *50-54*	115	170	__2
456	Coal Ramp w/ 3456 Hopper, *50-55*	145	185	__2
460	Piggyback Transportation,			
	includes 3460, *55-57*	65	145	__2
460P	Piggyback Platform, *55-57*	25	65	__1
461	Platform w/ Truck and Trailer, *66*	75	160	__1
462	Derrick Platform set, *61-62*	200	325	__1
464	Lumber Mill, *56-60*	75	145	__2
465	Sound Dispatching Station, *56-57*	49	95	__1
470	Missile Launching Platform w/ 6470, *59-62*	85	115	__2
480-25	Conversion Coupler, *50-60*	1	3	__1
480-32	Conv. Magnetic Coupler, *61-69*	1	2.50	__1
494	Rotary Beacon, *54-66*	24	50	__1
497	Coaling Station, *53-58*	120	205	__1
520	Lionel Lines Box Cab Electric, *56-57*	70	115	__1
600	MKT NW-2 Switcher, *55*			
	(A) Black frame and end rails	80	145	__2
	(B) Gray frame and yellow or black end rails	220	360	__2
601	Seaboard NW-2 Switcher, *56*	95	190	__1
602	Seaboard NW-2 Switcher, *57-58*	90	180	__1
610	Erie NW-2 Switcher, *55*			
	(A) Black frame	85	145	__1
	(B) Yellow frame	285	540	__1
611	Jersey Central NW-2 Switcher, *57-58*	95	145	__1
613	UP NW-2 Switcher, *58*	115	350	__1
614	Alaska NW-2 Switcher, *59-60*			
	(A) Plastic bell, no brake	115	175	__1
	(B) No bell, yellow brake/air	135	205	__1
	(C) (B) w/ "BUILT BY LIONEL"	225	390	__1
616	Santa Fe NW-2 Switcher, *61-62*	130	200	__2
617	Santa Fe NW-2 Switcher, *63*	135	255	__1
621	Jersey Central NW-2 Switcher, *56-57*	75	180	__1
622	Santa Fe NW-2 Switcher, *49-50*			
	(A) Large "GM" decal on cab	190	320	__
	(B) Small "GM" decal on cab	145	290	__
623	Santa Fe NW-2 Switcher, *52-54*	115	215	__

		Good	Exc	Cond/$
624	C&O NW-2 Switcher, *52-54*	120	220	__2
625	LV GE 44-ton Switcher, *57-58*	70	125	__1
626	B&O GE 44-ton Switcher, *59*	115	305	__1
627	LV GE 44-ton Switcher, *56-57*	70	115	__1
628	NP GE 44-ton Switcher, *56-57*	90	130	__1
629	Burlington GE 44-ton Switcher, *56*	130	340	__1
633	Santa Fe NW-2 Switcher, *62*	110	160	__1
634	Santa Fe NW-2 Switcher, *63, 65-66*			
	(A) w/ safety stripes	80	170	__1
	(B) w/o safety stripes	50	110	__1
635	UP NW-2 Switcher, *65 u*	65	125	__1
637	Steam 2-6-4, 2046 W/ 736W Tender, *59-63*			
	(A) 2046W "LIONEL LINES" tender	60	150	__1
	(B) 736W "PENNSYLVANIA" tender	65	155	__1
638-2361	Van Camp's Pork & Beans Boxcar, *62 u*	25	45	__1
645	Union Pacific NW-2 Switcher, *69*	60	115	__1
646	Steam 4-6-4, 2046W Tdr., *54-58*	135	295	__1
665	Steam 4-6-4, 2046W/6026W/736W			
	Tender, *54-59, 66*	100	220	__2
670	Pennsylvania Turbine, 6-8-6, *52*		NM	__
671	Steam 6-8-6, *46-49*			
	(A) 671W Tender	120	215	__2
	(B) 2671W Tender	150	265	__2
671R	Steam 6-8-6, 4424W/4671 Tender, *46-49*	130	280	__1
671RR	Steam 6-8-6, 2046W-50 Tender, *52*	110	200	__1
671S	Smoke Conversion Kit		31	__1
674	Steam 2-6-4, *52*		NM	__
675	Steam 2-6-2, 2466W/2466WX/6466WX			
	Tender, *47-49; 2-6-4, 52*			
	(A) 2-6-2, disc drivers	95	155	__1
	(B) 2-6-4, spoked drivers	95	155	__1
681	Steam Turbine, 6-8-6, 2046W-50/2671W			
	Tender, *50-51, 53*	110	260	__2
682	Steam 6-8-6, 2046W-50 Tender, *54-55*	210	370	__1
685	Steam 4-6-4, 6026W Tender, *53*	95	225	__1
703	Steam 4-6-4, Hudson, *46*		NM	__
703-10	Special Smoke Bulb, *46*		23	__1
725	Steam 2-8-4, Berkshire, *52*		NM	__
726	Steam 2-8-4 Berkshire, *47-49*			
	(A) 2426W Tender, *46*	250	425	__2
	(B) 2426W Tender, *47-49*	270	390	__2
726RR	Steam 2-8-4 Berkshire, 2046W Tender, *52*	215	375	__1
726S	Smoke Conversion kit	NRS	600	__1
736	Steam 2-8-4, 2671WX/2046W/736W			
	Tender, *50-66*	235	390	__5
746	N&W Steam 4-8-4, *57-60*			

		Good	Exc	Cond/$
	(A) Long stripe Tender	550	900	__2
	(B) Short stripe Tender	455	950	__2
760	Curved Track, 16 sec. (O72), *54-57*	17	30	__1
773	Steam 4-6-4 Hudson, 2426W Tender, *50*	870	1700	__2
773	Steam 4-6-4 Hudson, *64-66*			
	(A) w/ 773W Tender	540	1000	__2
	(B) w/ 736W Tender	465	730	__2
902	Elevated Trestle set, *60*		NRS	__
909	Smoke Fluid, *57-66, 68-69*		9	__1
919	Artificial Grass, *46-64*		11	__1
920	Scenic Display set, *57-58*	55	95	__1
920-2	Tunnel Portals, pair, *58-59*	23	38	__1
920-3	Green Grass, *57*		11	__1
920-4	Yellow Grass, *57*		11	__1
920-5	Artificial Rock, *57-58*	3	7	__1
920-8	Dyed Lichen, *57-58*	1	8	__1
925	Lionel Lubricant, lg. tube, *46-69*	1	5	__1
926	Lionel Lubricant, sm. tube, *55*	1	2	__1
926-5	Instruction Booklet, *46-48*	1	5	__1
927	Lubricating Kit, *50-59*	13	29	__1
928	Maint. & Lubricating Kit, *60-63*	28	60	__1
943	Ammo Dump, *59-61*	31	55	__1
950	U.S. Railroad Map, *58-66*	22	50	__1
951	Farm Set w/ Box, *58*	20	55	__1
952	Figure Set w/ Box, *58*	22	50	__1
953	Figure Set w/ Box, *59-62*	27	65	__1
954	Swimming Pool/Playground Set w/ Box, *59*	24	55	__1
955	Highway Set w/ Box, *58*	22	55	__1
956	Stockyard Set w/ Box, *59*	19	42	__1
957	Farm Building and Animal Set w/ Box, *58*	29	65	__1
958	Vehicle Set w/ Box, *58*	15	41	__1
959	Barn Set w/ Box, *58*	18	45	__1
960	Barnyard Set w/ Box, *59-61*	14	39	__1
961	School Set w/ Box, *59*	15	46	__1
962	Turnpike Set w/ Box, *58*	29	75	__1
963	Frontier Set w/ Box, *59-60*	28	80	__1
963-100	Frontier Set for Halloween General Set w/ Box, *60*	105	195	__1
964	Factory Site Set w/ Box, *59*	19	47	__1
965	Farm Set, *59*	20	50	__1
966	Firehouse Set w/ Box, *58*	18	46	__1
967	Post Office Set w/ Box, *58*	18	46	__1
968	TV Transmitter Set w/ Box, *58*	14	40	__1
969	Construction Set w/ Box, *60*	17	48	__2
970	Ticket Booth, *58-60*	50	145	__1
971	Lichen Package w/ Box, *60-64*	9	15	__1

		Good	Exc	Cond/$
972	Landscape Tree Assortment w/ Box, *61-64*	10	17	__1
973	Complete Landscaping Set w/ Box, *60-64*	14	34	__1
974	Scenery Set w/ Box, *58*	7	18	__1
980	Ranch Set w/ Box, *60*	19	55	__1
981	Freight Yard Set w/ Box, *60*	14	48	__1
982	Suburban Split Level Set w/ Box, *60*	14	48	__1
983	Farm Set w/ Box, *60-61*	14	48	__1
984	Railroad Set w/ Box, *61-62*	14	48	__1
985	Freight Area Set w/ Box, *61*	16	46	__1
986	Farm Set w/ Box, *62*	25	45	__1
987	Town Set w/ Box, *62*	25	45	__1
988	Railroad Structure Set w/ Box, *62*	25	44	__1
1001	Steam 2-4-2, 1001T Tender, *48*			
	(A) Plastic	22	41	__1
	(B) Die-cast	275	600	__1
1002	Lionel Gondola, *48-52*			
	(A) Black w/ white lettering	5	9	__1
	(B) Blue w/ white lettering	6	11	__1
	(C) Silver w/ black lettering	105	335	__1
	(D) Yellow w/ black lettering	115	345	__1
	(E) Red w/ white lettering	110	370	__1
	(F) Light blue w/ black lettering		NRS	__
X1004	PRR Baby Ruth Boxcar, *48-52*	5	11	__1
1005	Sunoco 1-D Tank Car, *48-50*	7	11	__1
1007	LL SP-type Caboose, *48-52*	4	10	__1
1008	Camtrol Uncoupling Unit (O27), *57-62*	0.55	1	__1
1008-50	Camtrol w/ track (O27), *48*	0.25	0.90	__1
1010	Transformer, 35 watts, *61-66*	8	19	__1
1011	Transformer, 25 watts, *48-49*	8	18	__1
1012	Transformer, 35 watts, *50-54*	7	14	__1
1013	Curved Track (O27), *45-69*	0.10	0.30	__1
1013-17	Steel Pins (O27), *46-60*		0.05	__1
1013-42	Steel Pins (O27), *61-68*		0.50	__1
1014	Transformer, 40 watts, *55*	13	22	__1
1015	Transformer, 45 watts, *56-60*	8	25	__1
1016	Transformer, 35 watts, *59-60*	7	24	__1
1018	Straight Track (O27), *45-69*	0.15	0.35	__1
1018	1 2 Straight Track (O27), *55-69*	0.15	0.35	__1
1019	R.C. Track set (O27), *46-48*	2	7	__1
1020	90° Crossing (O27), *55-69*	2.50	6	__1
1021	90° Crossing (O27), *45-54*	2	5	__1
1022	Man. Switches, pr. (O27), *53-69*	11	18	__1
1023	45° Crossing (O27), *56-69*	2	5	__1
1024	Man. Switches, pr. (O27), *46-52*	8	14	__1
1025	Illuminated Bumper (O27), *46-47*	9	15	__1
1025	Transformer, 45 watts, *61-69*	13	24	__1

		Good	Exc	
1026	Transformer, 25 watts, *61-64*	5	14	__1
1032	Transformer, 75 watts, *48*	26	46	__1
1033	Transformer, 90 watts, *48-56*	29	46	__2
1034	Transformer, 75 watts, *48-54*	22	38	__1
1035	Transformer, 60 watts, *47*	22	41	__1
1037	Transformer, 40 watts, *46-47*	10	25	__1
1041	Transformer, 60 watts, *45-46*	13	25	__1
1042	Transformer, 75 watts, *47-48*	19	47	__1
1043	Transformer, *53-58*			
	(A) 50 watts, black, *53-57*	13	24	__1
	(B) 60 watts, ivory, *57-58*	55	105	__1
1044	Transformer, 90 watts, *57-69*	37	65	__1
1045	Operating Watchman, *46-50*	19	55	__1
1047	Operating Switchman, *59-61*	55	180	__1
1050	Steam 0-4-0, 1050 Tender, *59 u*	85	265	__1
1053	Transformer, 60 watts, *56-60*	19	40	__1
1055	Texas Special Alco A Unit (adv. cat.), *59-60*	46	80	__1
1060	Steam 2-4-2, 1050T/1060T Tender (adv. cat.), *60-62*	9	30	__1
1061	Steam 0-4-0, 1061T Tender, *64; 2-4-2, 69*			
	(A) Slope-back "LIONEL LINES"	14	33	__1
	(B) 1130T "SOUTHERN PACIFIC"	17	41	__1
1062	Steam 2-4-2, 1062T Tender, *63-64*			
	(A) 0-4-0 wheel arrangement	12	27	__1
	(B) 2-4-2 wheel arrangement	12	27	__1
1063	Transformer, 75 watts, *60-64*	16	45	__1
1065	Union Pacific Alco A Unit (adv. cat.), *61*	31	70	__1
1066	Union Pacific Alco A Unit, *64 u*	45	80	__1
1073	Transformer, 60 watts, *61-66*	19	47	__1
1101	Steam 2-4-2, 1001T Tender, *48*	20	38	__1
1101	Transformer, 25 watts, *48*	8	14	__1
1110	Steam 2-4-2, 1001T Tender, *49, 51-52*	11	27	__1
1120	Steam 2-4-2, 1001T Tender, *50*	19	35	__1
1121	R.C. Switches, pr. (O27), *46-51*	14	27	__1
1122	R.C. Switches, pr. (O27), *52-53*	10	25	__2
1122E	R.C. Switches, pr. (O27), *53-69*	15	27	__1
1122-34	R.C. Switches, pair, *52-53*	14	34	__1
1122-500	Gauge Adapter (O27), *57-66*	0.25	0.90	__1
1130	Steam 2-4-2, 6066T/1130T Tender, *53-54*			
	(A) Plastic body	20	36	__1
	(B) Die-cast body	42	85	__1
1615	Steam 0-4-0, 1615T Tender, *55-57*			
	(A) No grab-irons	95	165	__2
	(B) Grab-irons on chest/tender	165	310	__2
1625	Steam 0-4-0, 1625T Tender, *58*	115	250	__1

		Good	Exc	Cond/$
1640-100	Presidential Kit, *60*	75	220	__1
1654	Steam 2-4-2, 1654W Tender, *46-47*	44	75	__1
1655	Steam 2-4-2, 6654W Tender, *48-49*	35	70	__1
1656	Steam 0-4-0, 6403B Tender, *48-49*	155	365	__2
1665	Steam 0-4-0, 2403B Tender, *46*	180	345	__1
1666	Steam 2-6-2, 2466W/2466WX Tender, *46-47*	37	120	__1
1862	General 4-4-0, 1862T Tender, *59-62*			
	(A) Gray smoke stack	85	205	__1
	(B) Black smoke stack	100	205	__1
1865	Western & Atlantic Coach, *59-62*	25	44	__1
1866	Western & Atlantic Baggage, *59-62*	33	60	__1
1872	General 4-4-0, 1872T Tender, *59-62*	95	285	__1
1875	Western & Atlantic Coach, *59-62*	150	255	__1
1875W	W&A Coach w/ whistle, *59-62*	80	175	__1
1876	Western & Atlantic Baggage, *59-62*	28	70	__1
1877	Flatcar w/ fence and horses, *59-62*	36	70	__1
1882	General 4-4-0, 1882T Tender, *60 u*	205	385	__1
1885	Western & Atlantic Coach, *60 u*	100	265	__1
1887	Flatcar w/ fences and horses, *60 u*	75	150	__1
2001	Track Make-up Kit (O27), *63*		NRS	___
2002	Track Make-up Kit (O27), *63*		NRS	___
2003	Track Make-up Kit (O27), *63*		NRS	___
2016	Steam 2-6-4, 6026W Tender, *55-56*	43	120	__1
2018	Steam 2-6-4, *56-59, 61*			
	(A) 6026T Tender	40	70	__1
	(B) 6026W Tender	60	105	__1
	(C) 1130T Tender	43	75	__1
2020	Steam 6-8-6, 2020W/6020W Tender, *46-49*	100	150	__1
2023	Union Pacific Alco AA Units, *50-51*			
	(A) Yellow body	130	240	__2
	(B) Gray nose and side frames		NRS	___
	(C) Silver body	145	250	__2
2024	C&O Alco A, *69*	30	65	__1
2025	Steam 2-6-2, 2-6-4, with 2466W/6466W Tender, *47-49, 52*	65	150	__2
2026	Steam 2-6-2, 2-6-4, *48-49, 51-53*			
	(A) 6466W or 6466WX	60	115	__2
	(B) 6466T or 6066T	40	80	__2
2028	Pennsylvania GP-7, *55*			
	(A) Gold lettering	165	250	__1
	(B) Yellow lettering	140	260	__1
	(C) Tan frame	275	540	__1
2029	Steam 2-6-4, 234W Tdr., *64-69*			
	(A) 243W "LIONEL LINES" tender	70	115	__1
	(B) 243W "PENNSYLVANIA" tender	255	325	__1
	(C) (A) w/ "HAGERSTOWN, MAR..."	90	135	__1

		Good	Exc	Cond/$
2031	Rock Island Alco AA Units, *52-54*	135	265	_1
2032	Erie Alco AA Units, *52-54*	135	255	_2
2033	Union Pacific Alco AA Units, *52-54*	140	275	_1
2034	Steam 2-4-2, 6066T Tender, *52*	26	47	_1
2035	Steam 2-6-4, 6466W Tender, *50-51*	70	175	_1
2036	Steam 2-6-4, 6466W Tender, *50*	65	125	_1
2037	Steam 2-6-4, black engine, *54-55, 57-63*			
	(A) w/ 6026T, 1130T	45	80	_1
	(B) w/ 6026W, 233W, 234W	70	145	_1
2037-500	Steam 2-6-4, pink engine, w/ 1130T-500 Tender, *57-58*	400	820	_1
2041	Rock Island Alco AA Units, *69*	70	135	_1
2046	Steam 4-6-4, 2046W Tender, *50-51, 53*	155	250	_2
2046	Steam 4-6-4, 2046W Tender, *50-51, 53*	155	250	_2
2055	Steam 4-6-4, 2046W/ 6026W Tender, *53-55*	105	220	_2
2056	Steam 4-6-4, 2046W Tender, *52*	125	200	_2
2065	Steam 4-6-4, 2046W/6026W Tender, *54-56*	115	225	_2
2240	Wabash F-3 AB Units, *56*	425	740	_1
2242	New Haven F-3 AB Units, *58-59*	475	1050	_1
2243	Santa Fe F-3 AB Units, *55-57*	225	310	_2
2243C	Santa Fe F-3 B Unit, *55-57*	90	210	_1
2245	Texas Special F-3 AB Units, *54-55*			
	(A) B unit w/ portholes, *54*	250	455	_2
	(B) B unit w/o portholes, *55*	400	720	_2
2257	Lionel SP-type caboose, *47*	8	13	_1
	(A) Red, no stack	7	11	_1
	(B) Tuscan, w/ stack	55	200	_1
	(C) Red, w/ stack		NRS	_1
2257	Caboose, red w/ plastic stack	85	95	_1
2321	Lackawanna Train Master, *54-56*			
	(A) Gray roof	270	420	_4
	(B) Maroon roof	390	630	_4
2322	Virginian Train Master, *65-66*			
	(A) Unpainted blue stripe	340	610	_2
	(B) Painted blue stripe	400	770	_2
2328	Burlington GP-7, *55-56*	205	355	_3
2329	Virginian Rectifier, *58-59*	300	580	_1
2330	Pennsylvania GG-1, green, *50*	530	1050	_1
2331	Virginian Train Master, *55-58*			
	(A) Black stripe/gold lettering, *55*	550	990	_3
	(B) Blue stripe/yellow lettering, *56-58*	345	640	_
	(C) Blue and yellow, gray mold	680	1200	_
2332	Pennsylvania GG-1, *47-49*			
	(A) Black	880	1750	_
	(B) Green	325	540	_
2333	Santa Fe F-3 AA Units, *48-49*	210	425	_

		Good	Exc	Cond/$
2333	NYC F-3 AA Units, *48-49*			
	(A) Rubber-stamped lettering	410	780	__1
	(B) Heat-stamped lettering	285	610	__1
2337	Wabash GP-7, *58*	125	275	__1
2338	Milwaukee Road GP-7, *55-56*			
	(A) Orange band around shell	900	1700	__3
	(B) Interrupted orange band	145	245	__3
2339	Wabash GP-7, *57*	150	310	__2
2340	Pennsylvania GG-1, *55*			
	(A) Tuscan	630	1050	__2
	(B) Dark green	560	940	__2
2341	Jersey Central Train Master, *56*			
	(A) High gloss orange	1050	2050	__2
	(B) Dull orange	950	1700	__2
2343	Santa Fe F-3 AA Units, *50-52*	175	350	__3
2343C	Santa Fe F-3 B Unit, *50-55*			
	(A) Screen roof vents	100	215	__1
	(B) Louver roof vents	115	220	__1
2344	NYC F-3 AA Units, *50-52*	205	570	__3
2344C	NYC F-3 B Unit, *50-55*	130	275	__2
2345	Western Pacific F-3 AA Units, *52*	620	1250	__2
2346	B&M GP-9, *65-66*	190	315	__1
2347	C&O GP-7, *65 u*	1400	2600	__1
2348	M&St L GP-9, *58-59*	150	315	__2
2349	Northern Pacific GP-9, *59-60*	190	465	__1
2350	New Haven EP-5, *56-58*			
	(A) White "N" painted nose	370	680	__2
	(B) White "N" decal nose	210	380	__2
	(C) Orange "N" painted nose	900	1550	__2
	(D) Orange "N" decal nose	510	910	__2
	(E) White "N" orange paint through doors	395	750	__2
2351	Milwaukee Road EP-5, *57-58*	185	400	__1
2352	Pennsylvania EP-5, *58-59*			
	(A) Tuscan body	225	650	__1
	(B) Chocolate brown body	220	480	__1
2353	Santa Fe F-3 AA units, *53-55*	275	410	__3
2354	NYC F-3 AA units, *53-55*	240	540	__2
2355	Western Pacific F-3 AA units, *53*	740	1350	__1
2356	Southern F-3 AA units, *54-56*	460	750	__1
2356C	Southern F-3 B Unit, *54-56*	175	330	__1
2357	Lionel SP-type Caboose, *47-48*			
	(A) Red w/ red stack	160	350	__1
	(B) Tuscan w/ Tuscan stack	15	31	__1
2358	Great Northern EP-5, *59-60*	345	670	__1
2359	Boston & Maine GP-9, *61-62*	170	315	__1
2360	Penn GG-1, *56-58, 61-63*			

		Good	Exc	
	(A) Tuscan, 5 gold stripes	600	1250	__3
	(B) Dark green, 5 gold stripes	580	1100	__3
	(C) Tuscan, 1 gold stripe, heat-stamped lettering	490	880	__3
	(D) Tuscan, 1 gold stripe, decaled lettering	455	750	__3
2363	Illinois Central F-3 AB Units, *55-56*			
	(A) Black lettering	435	960	__2
	(B) Brown lettering	435	960	__2
2365	C&O GP-7, *62-63*	120	290	__1
2367	Wabash F-3 AB units, *55*	380	820	__1
2368	B&O F-3 AB Units, *56*	550	1300	__1
2373	CP F-3 AA units, *57*	1350	2200	__1
2378	Milwaukee Road F-3 AB Units, *56*			
	(A) w/ yellow roof line stripes	1050	1600	__2
	(B) w/o roof line stripes	870	1300	__2
2379	Rio Grande F-3 AB units, *57-58*	465	760	__2
2383	Santa Fe F-3 AA units, *58-66*	195	430	__2
2400	Maplewood Pullman, green, *48-49*	65	170	__1
2401	Hillside Obs., green, *48-49*	75	150	__1
2402	Chatham Pullman, green, *48-49*	70	160	__1
2404	Santa Fe Vista Dome, *64-65*	31	85	__1
2405	Santa Fe Pullman, *64-65*	30	65	__1
2406	Santa Fe Observation, *64-65*	28	60	__1
2408	Santa Fe Vista Dome, *66*	38	75	__1
2409	Santa Fe Pullman, *66*	38	75	__1
2410	Santa Fe Observation, *66*	34	65	__1
2411	Lionel Lines Flatcar, *46-48*			
	(A) w/ pipes, *46*	50	80	__1
	(B) w/ logs, *47-48*	16	28	__1
2412	Santa Fe Vista Dome, *59-63*	35	110	__1
2414	Santa Fe Pullman, *59-63*	30	105	__1
2416	Santa Fe Observation, *59-63*	30	75	__1
2419	DL&W Work Caboose, *46-47*	25	60	__1
2420	DL&W Work Caboose, w/ light, *46-48*	50	115	__1
2421	"Maplewood" Pullman, *50-53*			
	(A) Gray roof	40	75	__1
	(B) Silver roof	43	70	__1
2422	"Chatham" Pullman, *50-53*			
	(A) Gray roof	39	75	__1
	(B) Silver roof	38	70	__1
2423	"Hillside" Observation, *50-53*			
	(A) Gray roof	40	70	__1
	(B) Silver roof	38	65	__1
2429	"Livingston" Pullman, *52-53*			

		Good	Exc	Cond/$
	(A) Gray roof	44	95	__1
	(B) Aluminum roof, no stripe	55	130	__1
2430	Blue Pullman, *46-47*	27	65	__1
2431	Blue Observation, *46-47*	27	65	__1
2432	"Clifton" Vista Dome, *54-58*	42	95	__1
2434	"Newark" Pullman, *54-58*	34	65	__1
2435	"Elizabeth" Pullman, *54-58*	39	80	__1
2436	"Mooseheart" Observation, *57-58*	26	65	__1
2436	Summit Observation, *54-56*	25	55	__1
2440	Green Pullman, *46-47*	22	55	__1
2441	Green Observation, *46-47*	22	55	__1
2442	"Clifton," Vista Dome, red stripe, *56*	49	105	__1
2442	Brown Pullman, *46-48*			
	(A) Silver lettering	20	75	__1
	(B) White lettering	25	65	__1
2443	Brown Observation, *46-48*			
	(A) Silver lettering	20	75	__1
	(B) White lettering	25	65	__1
2444	"Newark" Pullman, *56*	42	85	__1
2445	"Elizabeth" Pullman, *56*	90	250	__1
2446	"Summit" Observation, *56*	48	115	__1
2452	Pennsylvania Gondola, *45-47*	10	19	__1
2452X	Pennsylvania Gondola, *46-47*	6	18	__1
X2454	Pennsylvania Boxcar, *46*			
	(A) Brown door	75	160	__1
	(B) Orange door	120	210	__1
X2454	Baby Ruth Boxcar, "PRR" logo, *46-47*	11	30	__1
2456	Lehigh Valley Hopper, *48*	10	33	__1
2457	PRR Caboose, metal, N5, *45-47*			
	(A) Red, white lettering	17	34	__1
	(B) Brown, white lettering	18	39	__1
X2458	Pennsylvania Boxcar, *46-48*	18	50	__1
(2458)	Automobile Boxcar (O), postwar trucks, "2758," *41-42*	38	65	__1
2460	Bucyrus Erie Crane, 12-wheel, *46-50*			
	(A) Gray cab	85	180	__1
	(B) Black cab	35	60	__1
2461	Transformer Car, die-cast, *47-48*			
	(A) Red transformer	42	105	__1
	(B) Black transformer	30	75	__1
2465	Sunoco 2-D Tank Car, *46-48*			
	(A) "GAS/SUNOCO/OILs" in diamond	38	85	__1
	(B) "SUNOCO" in diamond	10	21	__1
	(C) "SUNOCO" goes past diamond	10	18	__1
2472	PRR Caboose, metal, N5, *46-47*	11	22	__1
2481	"Plainfield" Pullman, yellow, *50*	125	310	__1

		Good	Exc	Cond/$
2482	"Westfield" Pullman, yellow, *50*	105	260	__1
2483	"Livingston" Observation, yellow, *50*	105	245	__1
2521	"President McKinley" Obs., *62-66*	75	150	__2
2522	"President Harrison" V. D., *62-66*	80	135	__1
2523	"President Garfield" Pullman, *62-66*	80	170	__1
2530	REA Baggage, *54-60*			
	(A) Large doors	310	530	__3
	(B) Small doors	90	165	__3
2531	"Silver Dawn" Observation, *52-60*	65	135	__2
2532	"Silver Range" Vista Dome, *52-60*	55	125	__2
2533	"Silver Cloud" Pullman, *52-59*	60	110	__1
2534	"Silver Bluff" Pullman, *52-59*	70	145	__1
2541	"Alexander Hamilton" Obs., *55-56**	95	200	__1
2542	"Betsy Ross" Vista Dome, *55-56**	85	175	__1
2543	"William Penn" Pullman, *55-56**	70	140	__1
2544	"Molly Pitcher" Pullman, *55-56**	85	175	__1
2550	B&O RDC Baggage/Mail, *57-58*	230	570	__1
2551	"Banff Park" Observation, *57**	145	300	__1
2552	"Skyline 500" Vista Dome, *57**	125	250	__1
2553	"Blair Manor" Pullman, *57**	245	455	__1
2554	"Craig Manor" Pullman, *57**	195	440	__1
2555	Sunoco 1-D Tank Car, *46-48*	21	48	__1
2559	B&O RDC Passenger, *57-58*	150	340	__2
2560	Lionel Lines Crane, 8-wheel, *46-47*			
	(A) Black boom	25	65	__1
	(B) Brown boom	22	55	__1
	(C) Green boom	25	65	__1
2561	"Vista Valley" Observation, *59-61**	115	260	__1
2562	"Regal Pass" Vista Dome, *59-61**	125	295	__1
2563	"Indian Falls" Pullman, *59-61**	125	295	__1
2625	"Madison" Pullman, *46-47**	110	220	__1
2625	"Manhattan" Pullman, *46-47**	100	220	__1
2625	"Irvington" Pullman, *46-50**			
	(A) No silhouettes	80	175	__1
	(B) w/ silhouettes	115	270	__1
2627	"Madison" Pullman, *48-50**			
	(A) No silhouettes	85	215	__1
	(B) w/ silhouettes	80	235	__1
2628	"Manhattan" Pullman, *48-50**			
	(A) No silhouettes	100	205	__1
	(B) w/ silhouettes	115	250	__1
2671	TCA Tender, *68*		65	__1
2855	SUNX 1-D Tank Car, *46-47*			
	(A) Black	70	205	__
	(B) Black, "GAS/OILS" omitted	50	210	__
	(C) Gray	43	185	__

		Good	Exc	Cond/$
2856	B&O Scale Hopper Car, *46-47*		NM	___
2857	NYC Scale Caboose, *46*		NM	___
(3309)	Turbo Missile Launch Car, *63-64*			
	(A) Red body	23	50	_1
	(B) Olive body	100	310	_1
3330	Flatcar w/ Submarine Kit, *60-62*	49	195	_1
3330-100	Oper. Submarine kit, *60-61*	55	105	_1
(3349)	Turbo Missile Launch Car, *62-65*			
	(A) Red body	26	47	_2
	(B) Olive drab body	95	320	_2
3356	Operating Horse Car only, *56-60, 64-66*	55	105	_1
3356	Operating Horse Car and Corral set, *56-60, 64-66*	70	125	_1
3356-100	(9) Black Horses, *56-59*	7	26	_1
3356-150	Horse Car Corral, *57-60*	30	75	_1
3357	Hydraulic Maintenance Car, *62-64*	36	85	_1
3359	Lionel Lines Two-bin Dump, *55-58*	24	60	_1
3360	Operating Burro Crane, *56-57*	140	215	_3
3361	Operating Log Dump Car, *55-58*	26	49	_1
3362	Flatcar w/ helium tanks or logs, *61-63*	13	36	_1
3362/3364	Log Dump Car, *65-69*	15	32	_1
3366	Circus Car Corral set, *59-62*	60	110	_1
3366	Circus Car only, *59-62*	145	235	_1
3366-100	(9) White Horses, *59-60*	31	65	_1
3370	W&A Outlaw Car, *61-64*	28	70	_1
3376	Bronx Zoo Car, *60-66, 69*			
	(A) Blue w/ white lettering	20	55	_2
	(B) Green w/ yellow lettering	35	100	_2
	(C) Blue w/ yellow lettering	115	290	_2
3386	Bronx Zoo Car (adv. cat.), *60*	29	65	_1
3409	Helicopter Car (adv. cat.), *61*	46	100	_1
3410	Helicopter Car, *61-63*	40	85	_1
(3413)	Mercury Capsule Car, *62-64*	85	170	_1
3419	Helicopter Car, *59-65*	48	90	_2
3424	Wabash Operating Boxcar, *56-58*	31	75	_3
3424-100	Low Bridge Signal set, *56-58*	15	55	_1
3428	U.S. Mail Oper. Boxcar, *59-60*	50	115	_1
3429	USMC Helicopter Car, *60*	170	365	_1
3434	Poultry Dispatch car, *59-60, 64-66*	60	120	_1
3435	Traveling Aquarium Car, *59-62*			
	(A) Gold circle	430	970	_1
	(B) Tank 1, Tank 2	280	770	_1
	(C) Gold lettering	155	305	_1
	(D) Yellow rubber stamp	100	230	_1
3444	Erie Operating Gondola, *57-59*	50	90	_2
3451	Operating Log Dump Car, *46-48*	17	34	_1

		Good	Exc	Cond/$
3454	PRR Operating Merchandise Car, *46-47*			
	(A) Red lettering		NRS	__
	(B) Blue lettering	55	115	__1
3456	N&W Operating Hopper Car, *50-55*	17	60	__2
3459	LL Operating Dump Car, *46-48*			
	(A) Aluminum bin	100	295	__1
	(B) Black bin	21	49	__1
	(C) Green bin	27	70	__1
3460	Flatcar w/ trailers, *55-57*	29	70	__1
3461	Lionel Operating Log Car, *49-55*			
	(A) Black car	15	39	__1
	(B) Green car	28	65	__1
3462	Automatic Milk Car, *47-48*	21	55	__1
	(A) Plain	21	55	__1
	(B) Glossy Eggshell White		450	__1
3462P	Milk Car Platform, *47-48*	7	14	__1
X3464	ATSF Operating Boxcar, *49-52*	11	23	__1
X3464	NYC Operating Boxcar, *49-52*	9	23	__1
3469	LL Operating Dump Car, *49-55*	18	49	__1
3470	Target Launcher, *62-64*			
	(A) Dark blue car	30	70	__1
	(B) Light blue car	60	140	__1
3472	Automatic Milk Car, *49-53*	27	60	__2
3474	Western Pacific Boxcar, *52-53*	27	70	__1
3482	Automatic Milk Car, *54-55*			
	(A) "RT3472" number	45	100	__1
	(B) "RT3482" number	35	75	__1
3484	Pennsylvania Operating Boxcar, *53*			
	(A) White lettering	15	45	__1
	(B) Gold lettering	15	45	__1
3484-25	ATSF Operating Boxcar, *54*			
	(A) White lettering	33	90	__1
	(B) Black lettering	38	105	__1
3494-1	NYC Pacemaker Boxcar, *55*	38	90	__1
3494-150	MP Operating Boxcar, *56*	60	120	__1
3494-275	State of Maine Operating Boxcar, *56-58*	60	130	__1
3494-550	Monon Operating Boxcar, *57-58*	130	430	__1
3494-625	Soo Operating Boxcar, *57-58*	150	470	__1
3509	Satellite Car, *61*	24	48	__1
(3510)	Satellite Car (adv. cat.), *62*	40	140	__1
3512	Fireman and Ladder Car, *59-61*			
	(A) Black rooftop ladder	60	110	__2
	(B) Silver rooftop ladder	85	230	__2
3519	Satellite Car, *61-64*	29	65	__1

		Good	Exc	Cond/$
3520	Searchlight Car, *52-53*	22	50	__2
3530	GM Generator Car, *56-58*			
	(A) Orange generator	60	125	__3
	(B) Gray generator	65	135	__3
3530-50	Searchlight w/ pole and base, *56-56*	29	65	__1
3535	A E C Security Car, *60-61*	38	125	__1
3540	Operating Radar Car, *59-60*	50	180	__1
3545	Lionel TV Car, *61-62*	55	185	__1
3559	Operating Coal Dump Car, *46-48*	15	37	__1
3562-1	ATSF Operating Barrel Car, black, *54*			
	(A) Black trough	75	185	__1
	(B) Yellow trough	75	180	__1
3562-25	ATSF Operating Barrel Car, gray, *54*			
	(A) Red lettering	165	390	__1
	(B) Blue lettering	22	55	__1
3562-50	ATSF Oper. Barrel Car, yellow, *55-56*			
	(A) Painted	45	95	__2
	(B) Unpainted	20	50	__2
3562-75	ATSF Operating Barrel Car, orange, *57-58*	30	60	__1
3619	Helicopter Boxcar, *62-64*			
	(A) Light yellow	33	90	__1
	(B) Dark yellow	40	135	__1
3620	Searchlight Car, *54-56*			
	(A) Gray searchlight	27	45	__2
	(B) Orange generator/light	55	130	__2
3650	Extension Searchlight Car, *56-59*			
	(A) Light gray	38	60	__2
	(B) Dark gray	70	140	__2
3656	Armour Operating Cattle Car, *49-55*			
	(A) Black letters, Armour sticker	75	190	__2
	(B) White letters, Armour sticker	34	70	__2
	(C) No "ARMOUR" sticker, black lettering	28	80	__2
	(D) White lettering	28	70	__2
3656	Stockyard w/ cattle	30	90	__2
3662	Automatic Milk Car, *55-60, 64-66*	36	90	__1
3665	Minuteman Operating Car, *61-64*			
	(A) Medium blue roof	75	155	__2
	(B) Dark blue roof	55	110	__2
3666	Minuteman Boxcar w/ missile, *64 u*	205	540	__1
3672	Bosco Operating Boxcar, *59-60*			
	(A) Unpainted	85	220	__1
	(B) Painted	115	315	__1
3820	Flatcar w/ submarine, *60-62*	75	210	__1
3830	Flatcar w/ submarine, *60-63*	42	90	__1
3854	Operating Merchandise Car, *46-47*	160	340	__1
3927	Lionel Lines Track Cleaner, *56-60*	60	85	__5

		Good	Exc	Cond/$
3927-50	Track Cleaning Fluid, *57-69*	3	13	__1
3927-75	Track Cleaning Pads, *57-69*	6	25	__1
4357	PRR SP-type Caboose, elec., *48-49*	55	155	__1
	(A) w/ extra roof plank	65	185	__1
	(B) w/o extra roof plank	55	140	__1
4452	PRR Gondola, electronic, *46-49*	43	75	__1
4454	Baby Ruth PRR Boxcar, elec., *46-49*	60	160	__1
4457	PRR N5 Caboose, electronic, *46-47*	45	150	__1
4681	Steam 6-8-6, electronic, *50*		NM	__
4776-18	(See 2457, 2472)			
5159	Maintenance Kit, *63-65*	2	5	__1
5159-50	Maintenance and Lube Kit, *66-69*	2	5	__1
5160	Viewing Stand, *63*	50	130	__1
5459	LL Dump Car, electronic, *46-49*	49	150	__1
6002	NYC Gondola, *50*	4	10	__1
X6004	Baby Ruth PRR Boxcar, *50*	4	7	__1
6007	Lionel Lines SP-type Caboose, *50*	3	8	__1
6009	R.C. Uncoupling Track, *53-54*	1	5	__1
6012	Lionel Gondola, *51-56*	2	7	__1
6014	Airex Boxcar, *60 u*	25	49	__1
6014	Bosco PRR Boxcar, *58*			
	(A) White body	35	50	__1
	(B) Red body	4	7	__1
	(C) Orange body	4	7	__1
6014	Chun King Boxcar, *57 u*	65	115	__1
6014	Frisco Boxcar, *57, 63-69*			
	(A) White body	4	8	__1
	(B) Red body	4	7	__1
	(C) White w/ coin slot	25	45	__1
	(D) Orange body	22	38	__1
X6014	Baby Ruth PRR Boxcar, *51-56*			
	(A) White	5	9	__1
	(B) Red	10	26	__1
6014-150	Wix Boxcar, *59 u*	85	150	__1
6015	Sunoco 1-D Tank Car, *54-55*			
	(A) Painted tank	45	120	__1
	(B) Unpainted tank	4	9	__1
6017	Lionel Lines SP-type Caboose, *51-62*	3	9	__1
6017	Lionel SP-type Caboose, *56*	14	34	__1
6017-50	USMC SP-type Caboose, *58*	22	50	__1
6017-85	LL SP-type Caboose, gray, *58*	19	43	__1
6017-100	B&M SP-type Caboose, *59, 62, 65-66*			
	(A) Purplish blue	255	475	__1
	(B) Medium or light blue	11	41	__1
6017-185	ATSF SP-type Caboose, *59-60*	11	39	__1
6017-200	U.S. Navy SP-type Caboose, *60*	39	85	__1

		Good	Exc	Cond/$
6017-225	ATSF SP-type Caboose, c. *63 u, 61-62*	15	42	__1
6017-235	ATSF SP-type Caboose, *62*	25	43	__1
6019	RCS Track set (O27), *48-66*	2.50	10	__1
6024	Nabisco Shredded Wheat Boxcar, *57*	13	30	__1
6024	RCA Whirlpool Boxcar, *57 u*	30	65	__1
6025	Gulf 1-D Tank Car, *56-58*			
	(A) Gray, blue lettering	5	14	__1
	(B) Orange, blue lettering	5	14	__1
	(C) Black, red "GULf" emblem	5	14	__1
6027	Alaska SP-type Caboose, *59*	27	75	__1
6029	Remote Control Uncoupling Track, *55-63*	1	5	__1
6032	Lionel Gondola, black (O27), *52-54*	2.50	6	__1
X6034	Baby Ruth PRR Boxcar, *53-54*			
	(A) Orange, blue lettering	5	11	__1
	(B) Red, white lettering	5	11	__1
	(C) Orange, black lettering	5	11	__1
6035	Sunoco 1-D Tank Car, *52-53*	3	8	__1
6037	Lionel Lines SP-type Caboose, *52-54*	3	7	__1
6042	Lionel Gondola, *59-61, 62-64 u*	2	6	__1
6044	Airex Boxcar, orange lettering, *59-60 u*			
	(A) Medium blue	6	16	__1
	(B) Teal blue	40	75	__1
	(C) Dark blue/purple	80	250	__1
6044-1X	Nestles/McCall's Boxcar			
	(no lettering), *62-63 u*	450	810	__1
6045	LL 2-D Tank Car (adv. cat.), *59-64*			
	(A) Gray	15	21	__1
	(B) Orange	15	37	__1
6045	Cities Service 2-D Tank, *60 u*	13	35	__1
6047	Lionel Lines SP-type Caboose, *62*			
	(A) Painted	2	5	__1
	(B) Brown-painted	100	150	__1
6050	Lionel Savings Bank Boxcar, *61*	12	26	__1
	(A) BLT, *61*	13	32	__1
	(B) BUILT, *N/A*		225	__1
6050	Swift Refrigerator Car, *62-63*	11	21	__1
6050	Libby's Boxcar, *63 u*			
	(A) Green stems on tomatoes	18	41	__1
	(B) Green stems missing	21	49	__1
6057	LL SP-type Caboose, *59-62*			
	(A) Unpainted	3	9	__1
	(B) Painted	25	100	__1
6057-50	LL SP-type Caboose, orange, *62*	12	23	__1
6058	C&O SP-type Caboose, *61*			
	(A) Blue lettering	18	45	__1
	(B) Black lettering	18	50	__1

		Good	Exc	Cond/$
6059	M&St L SP-type Caboose, *61-69*			
	(A) Painted, red	13	22	__1
	(B) Unpainted, red	4	8	__1
	(C) Unpainted, maroon	7	12	__1
6062	NYC Gondola, w/ cable reels, *59-62*	12	19	__1
6062-50	NYC Gondola, w/ 2 canisters, *69*	5	18	__1
(6067)	Caboose (no lett.), SP-type, *62*	3	5	__1
6076	ATSF Hopper, *63 u*	10	20	__1
6076	LV Hopper, red, black or gray body, *63*			
	(A) Gray body	7	14	__1
	(B) Black body	7	13	__1
	(C) Red body	7	13	__1
	(D) Yellow body	7	13	__1
(6076)	Hopper, no lettering, gray or yellow body, *63*			
	(A) Yellow Body	50	90	__1
	(B) Gray body	10	18	__1
6110	Steam 2-4-2, 6001T Tender, *50-51*	15	34	__1
(6111)	Flatcar w/ logs, *55-57*	7	15	__1
6112	Lionel Gondola, *56-58*			
	(A) Black body	3	7	__1
	(B) Blue body	4	10	__1
	(C) White body	11	25	__1
6119	DL&W Work Caboose, red, *55-56*	10	26	__1
6119-25	DL&W Work Caboose, orange, *56-59*	11	40	__1
6119-50	DL&W Caboose, brown, *56*	17	55	__1
6119-75	DL&W Caboose, gray, *57*	14	37	__1
6119-100	DL&W Work Caboose, red/gray, *57-66, 69*	13	38	__1
(6119-125)	Rescue Unit Work Caboose (no number), olive drab, *63-64 u.*	65	140	__1
(6120)	Work Caboose (no lettering), yellow (adv. cat.), *61-62*	7	23	__1
(6121)	Flatcar (various colors) w/ pipes, *56-57*	5	15	__1
6130	ATSF Work Caboose, *61, 65-69*	12	35	__1
6139	R.C. Uncoupling Track (O27), *63*	1	4	__1
6142	Lionel Gondola; green, blue or black, *63-66, 69*	2.50	6	__1
6149	Remote Control Uncoupling Track (O27), *64-69*	1	5	__1
(6151)	Flatcar (various colors) w/ patrol truck, *58*			
	(A) Yellow car	40	110	__1
	(B) Orange car	40	110	__1
	(C) Cream car	40	110	__1
6162	NYC Gondola, *59-68*			
	(A) Blue body	5	11	__1
	(B) Red body	60	165	__1
6162-60	Alaska Gondola, *59*	34	85	__1
6167	LL SP-type Caboose, red, *63*			

		Good	Exc	Cond/$
	(A) Unpainted	3	9	__1
	(B) Painted	100	225	__1
(6167)	Unstamped SP-type Caboose w/o end rails			
	(A) Red body	3	9	__1
	(B) Yellow body	10	23	__1
	(C) Brown body	15	36	__1
	(D) Olive body	NRS	395	__1
6167-85	UP SP-type Caboose, *69*	10	27	__1
6175	Flatcar w/ rocket, red or black body, *58-61*			
	(A) Black car	25	65	__1
	(B) Red car	25	65	__1
6176	LV Hopper, yellow, gray or black body, *64-66, 69*			
	(A) Yellow	3	9	__1
	(B) Gray	3	8	__1
	(C) Black	3	8	__1
(6176)	Hopper (no lettering), *64*			
	(A) Yellow	6	16	__1
	(B) Gray	5	14	__1
	(C) Olive	32	75	__1
6219	C&O Work Caboose, *60*	31	75	__1
6220	Santa Fe NW-2 Switcher, *49-50*			
	(A) Large "GM" decal on cab	125	275	__2
	(B) Small "GM" decal on cab	125	265	__2
6250	Seaboard NW-2 Switcher, *54-55*			
	(A) Decals	125	270	__3
	(B) Rubber-stamped	110	255	__3
6257	Lionel SP-type Caboose, *48-56, 63-64*	3	11	__1
6257-100	Lionel Lines SP-type Caboose	7	17	__1
6257-25	Lionel SP-type Caboose	3	7	__1
6257-50	Lionel SP-type Caboose	3	7	__1
6257X	Lionel SP-type Caboose, *48*	15	34	__1
6262	Flatcar w/ wheels, *56-57*			
	(A) Black, *56-57*	30	55	__1
	(B) Red, *56*	170	445	__1
6264	Flatcar w/ lumber for Fork Lift set, *57-60*			
	(A) No box	20	75	__1
	(B) Separate-sale box	100	390	__1
6311	Flatcar w/ three pipes, *55*	19	43	__1
6315	Gulf 1-D Chemical Tank Car, *56-59, 68-69*			
	(A) Early, painted	38	65	__2
	(B) Late, unpainted	30	55	__2
	(C) Late, unpainted w/ built date	43	75	__2
6315	Lionel Lines 1-D Tank Car, *63-66*			
	(A) Unpainted orange body	15	30	__1
	(B) Painted orange body	100	250	__1

		Good	Exc	Cond/$
6342	NYC Gondola, *56-58, 64-66*	15	40	__1
6343	Barrel Ramp Car, *61-62*	15	38	__1
6346	Alcoa Quad Hopper, *56*	27	65	__1
6352	PFE Reefer from 352 Ice Depot, *55-57*			
	(A) No box	65	195	__1
	(B) Separate-sale box	650	1700	__1
6356	NYC Stock Car, 2 level, *54-55*	15	36	__1
6357	Lionel SP-type Caboose, *48-61*	8	26	__1
6357-50	ATSF SP-type Caboose, *60*	325	820	__1
6361	Flatcar w/ timber, *60-61, 64-69*	27	70	__2
6362	Truck Car w/ 3 trucks, *55-56*			
	(A) Shiny orange	22	50	__1
	(B) Dull orange	80	130	__1
6376	LL Circus Stock Car, *56-57*	39	80	__2
(6401)	Flatcar, no load, gray, *60*	2	7	__1
(6402)	Flatcar w/ reels or boat, *62, 64-66, 69*			
	(A) w/ reels	6	14	__1
	(B) w/ boat	25	60	__1
6404	Black Flatcar w/ brown auto, *60*			
	(A) w/ red auto		180	__1
	(B) w/ yellow auto	0.05	445	__1
	(C) w/ brown auto	0.05	800	__1
	(D) w/ green auto	0.05	800	__1
6405	Maroon Flatcar w/ trailer, *61*	15	41	__1
(6406)	Flatcar w/ yellow auto, *61*			
	(A) Maroon w/ red auto	35	75	__1
	(B) Maroon w/ yellow auto	70	255	__1
	(C) Gray w/ dark brown car	100	360	__1
(6407)	Flatcar w/ rocket, *63*	140	440	__1
(6408)	Flatcar w/ pipes, *63*	14	26	__1
(6409)	Flatcar w/ pipes, *63*	14	27	__1
6411	Flatcar w/ logs, *48-50*	17	26	__1
6413	Mercury Project Car, *62-63*			
	(A) Powder blue car	75	130	__1
	(B) Aquamarine car	95	150	__1
6414	Evans Auto Loader w/ 4 cars, *55-66*			
	(A) Early premium cars w/ windows, chrome bumpers and rubber tires; red, yellow, blue and white	49	120	__4
	(B) 4 cheap cars, w/o trim, 2 red, 2 yellow	300	540	__4
	(C) 4 red cars w/ gray bumpers	50	160	__4
	(D) 4 yellow cars w/ gray bumpers	150	365	__4
	(E) Dark yellow, gray bumpers		NRS	__
	(F) Dark brown, chrome bumpers		NRS	__

		Good	Exc	Cond/$
	(G) 4 brown cars w/ gray bumpers	315	780	__4
	(H) Medium green, chrome bumpers		NRS	___
	(I) 4 green cars w/ gray bumpers	360	900	__4
6415	Sunoco 3-D Tank Car, *53-55, 64-66, 69*	13	37	__1
6416	Boat Loader Car, *61-63*	95	215	__1
6417	PRR Porthole Caboose, *53-57*			
	(A) w/ "NEW YORK ZONE"	11	38	__2
	(B) w/o "NEW YORK ZONE"	105	230	__2
6417-3	(See 6417-25)		30	__1
6417-25	Lionel Lines N5C Caboose, *54*	15	36	__1
6417-50	LV porthole Caboose, *54*			
	(A) Tuscan	375	960	__1
	(B) Gray	50	125	__1
6417-51	(See 6417-50)		120	__1
6417-53	(See 6417-25)			
6418	(See 214)			
6418	Flatcar w/ steel girders, *55-57*	45	90	__2
6419	DL&W Work Caboose, early frame, *48-50, 52-57*	17	45	__2
6419-25	DL&W Work Caboose, *54-55*	16	37	__1
6419-50	DL&W Work Caboose, late frame, *56-57*	17	50	__1
6419-57	(See 6419-100)			
6419-75	DL&W Work Caboose, late frame, *56-57*	15	45	__1
6419-100	N&W Work Caboose, *57-58*	38	100	__1
6420	DL&W Work Caboose, w/ light, *48-50*	30	85	__1
6424	Flatcar w/ two autos, *56-59*	22	48	__2
6425	Gulf 3-D Tank Car, *56-58*	16	41	__1
6427	Lionel Lines Porthole Caboose, *54-60*	15	38	__1
6427-60	Virginian Porthole Caboose, *58*	155	420	__1
6427-500	PRR Porthole Caboose, Girls', *57-58**	145	310	__1
6428	U.S. Mail Boxcar, *60-61, 65-66*	21	37	__1
6429	DL&W Work Caboose, AAR trucks, *63*	145	350	__1
6430	Flat. w/ Cooper-Jarrett vans, *56-58*			
	(A) Gray vans	22	60	__1
	(B) White vans	20	55	__1
6431	Flatcar w/ vans, *66*	90	245	__1
6434	Poultry Dispatch, *58-59*	37	70	__1
6436-1	LV Quad Hopper, black, *55*	17	38	__1
6436-25	LV Quad Hopper, maroon, *55-57*	16	29	__1
6436-57	(See 6436-500)			
6436-110	LV Quad Hopper, red, *63-68*			
	(A) w/o cover, no built date	20	35	__1
	(B) w/ cover and "NEW 3-55"	100	275	__1
	(C) w/o cover and "NEW 3-55"	40	80	__1
6436-500	LV Girls' Hopper, lilac, "643657," *57-58**	95	270	__1
6436-1969	TCA Quad Hopper, *69*	55	85	__1

		Good	Exc	
6437	PRR Porthole Caboose, *61-68*	17	34	__1
6440	Flatcar with vans, *61-63*	26	85	__1
6440	Green Pullman, *48-49*	22	46	__1
6441	Green Observation, *48-49*	22	46	__1
6442	Brown Pullman, *49*	38	70	__1
6443	Brown Observation, *49*	33	60	__1
6445	Fort Knox Gold Reserve, *61-63*	55	105	__1
(6446)	N&W Quad Hopper "546446,"			
	black or gray, *54-55*	21	50	__1
6446-25	N&W Quad Hopper "644625," black or gray, *55-57*			
	(A) Black, white lettering	17	65	__1
	(B) Gray, black lettering	17	70	__1
6446-60	See 6436-110(B)			
6447	PRR Porthole Caboose, *63*	155	440	__1
6448	Target Car, *61-64*			
	(A) Red, white lettering	17	35	__1
	(B) White, red lettering	17	35	__1
6452	Pennsylvania Gondola, black, *48-49*	6	19	__1
X6454	Baby Ruth PRR Boxcar, *48*	75	245	__1
X6454	NYC Boxcar, *48*			
	(A) Brown body	20	50	__1
	(B) Orange body	45	125	__1
	(C) Tan body	15	35	__1
X6454	Santa Fe Boxcar, *48*	15	38	__1
X6454	SP Boxcar, *49-52*	15	40	__1
X6454	Erie Boxcar, *49-52*	25	55	__1
X6454	PRR Boxcar, *49-52*	25	65	__1
6456	Lehigh Valley Short Hopper, *48-55*			
	(A) Black	9	16	__2
	(B) Maroon	6	15	__2
	(C) Gray	16	36	__2
	(D) Enamel red, yellow lettering	60	140	__2
	(E) Enamel red, white lettering	225	510	__2
	(F) Enamel gray, maroon letter		NRS	__
6457	Lionel SP-type Caboose, *49-52*	19	36	__2
6460	Bucyrus Erie black cab Crane, 8-wheel, *52-54*			
	(A) Black cab	18	50	__2
	(B) Red cab	29	80	__2
6460-25	Bucyrus Erie red cab Crane,			
	8-wheel, w/ box, *54*	48	105	__1
6461	Transformer Car, *49-50*	25	70	__1
6462	Pennsylvania Gondola, black, *49*	10	25	__
6462	NYC Gondola, *49-57*			
	(A) Black	9	13	__2
	(B) Green	8	22	__2
	(C) Red	5	15	__2

	Good	Exc	Cond/$
6462-500 NYC Girls' Gondola, pink, *57-58**	65	160	__1
6463 Rocket Fuel 2-D Tank, *62-63*	12	48	__1
6464-1 WP Boxcar, *53-54*			
(A) Blue lettering	31	65	__3
(B) Red lettering	450	1150	__3
(C) Orange, silver lettering		NRS	___
6464-25 GN Boxcar, *53-54*	34	75	__3
6464-50 M&St L Boxcar, *53-56*	37	60	__2
6464-75 RI Boxcar, *53-54, 69*	42	85	__3
6464-100 WP Boxcar, *54-55*			
(A) Silver body, yellow feather	60	120	__1
(B) Orange body, blue feather	380	810	__1
(C) Orange, blue feather, "1954"		NRS	___
(D) (C) w/ "6464-100"		NRS	___
6464-125 NYC Boxcar, *54-56*	43	125	__1
6464-150 MP Boxcar, *54-55, 57*	30	100	__2
6464-175 Rock Island Boxcar, *54-55*			
(A) Blue lettering	50	90	__1
(B) Black lettering	450	950	__1
6464-200 Pennsylvania Boxcar, *54-55, 69*	85	145	__1
6464-225 SP Boxcar, *54-56*	65	135	__2
6464-250 WP Boxcar, *66*	115	205	__2
6464-275 State of Maine Boxcar, *55, 57-59*			
(A) Striped doors	48	85	__2
(B) Solid doors	55	135	__2
6464-300 Rutland Boxcar, *55-56*			
(A) Rubber-stamped	40	75	__2
(B) Split door	310	650	__2
(C) Solid shield	850	2250	__2
(D) Heat-stamped	50	135	__2
6464-325 B&O Sentinel Boxcar, *56*	290	540	__1
6464-350 MKT Katy Boxcar, *56*	145	255	__1
6464-375 Central of Georgia Boxcar, *56-57, 66*			
(A) Unpainted, maroon body	50	110	__2
(B) Painted, red body	800	1550	__2
6464-400 B&O Time-saver Boxcar, *56-57, 69*			
(A) Lettered "BLT 5-54"	44	110	__2
(B) Lettered "BLT 2-56"	95	230	__2
6464-425 New Haven Boxcar, *56-58*	27	60	__2
6464-450 Great Northern Boxcar, *56-57, 66*	60	120	__2
6464-475 B&M Boxcar, *57-60, 65-66, 68*	41	90	__2
6464-500 Timken Boxcar, yellow and white, charcoal lettering (Also see 6464-500 in MPC) 57-58, *69*	75	150	__1
6464-510 NYC Pacemaker Boxcar, *57-58*	345	640	__1
6464-515 MKT Boxcar, *57-58*	300	610	__1

		Good	Exc	Cond/$
6464-525	M&StL Boxcar, *57-58, 64-66*			
	(A) Red, white lettering	30	60	__2
	(B) Maroon, white lettering		530	__2
6464-650	D&RGW Boxcar, *57-58, 66*			
	(A) Unpainted yellow body	50	115	__2
	(B) (A) w/o black stripe	150	195	__2
	(C) Painted yellow body and roof	500	900	__2
6464-700	Santa Fe Boxcar, *61, 66*	49	105	__1
6464-725	New Haven Boxcar, *62-66, 68*			
	(A) Orange body	30	55	__1
	(B) Black body	70	225	__1
6464-825	Alaska Boxcar, *59-60*	170	400	__2
6464-900	NYC Boxcar, *60-66*	55	115	__2
6464-1965	TCA Pittsburgh Boxcar, *65*		205	__1
6464-1970	(See MPC)			
6464-1971	(See MPC)			
6465	Sunoco 2-D Tank Car, *48-56*	6	16	__1
6465	Cities Service 2-D Tank, *60-62*	13	30	__1
6465	Gulf 2-D Tank Car, *58*			
	(A) Black tank	25	60	__1
	(B) Gray tank	10	23	__1
6465	LL 2-D Tank Car, *59, 63-64*			
	(A) Black tank	10	26	__1
	(B) Orange tank	5	16	__1
6467	Bulkhead Flatcar, *56*	22	55	__1
6468	B&O Auto Boxcar, *53-55*			
	(A) Tuscan	140	290	__1
	(B) Blue	20	45	__1
6468-25	NH Auto Boxcar, *56-58*			
	(A) Black "N" over white "H"	41	135	__1
	(B) White "N" over black "H"	215	470	__1
(6469)	Lionel Liquefied Gases Car, *63*	60	140	__1
6470	Explosives Boxcar, *59-60*	14	37	__1
6472	Refrigerator Car, *50-53*	20	40	__1
6473	Horse Transport Car, *62-69*	9	24	__1
6475	Heinz 57 Vat Car, post-factory alteration, *65-66*	55	105	__1
6475	Libby's Crushed Pineapple Vat Car, *63 u*	25	75	__1
6475	Pickles Vat Car, *60-62*	22	45	__1
6476	LV Hopper, red, black, and gray body, *57-69*			
	(A) Red body	4	9	__1
	(B) Gray body	4	9	__1
	(C) Black body	4	10	__1
6476-1	LV Hopper, gray, TTOS, *69*	25	70	__1
6476-135	LV Hopper, yellow, *64-66, 68*	6	11	__1
6476-160	LV Hopper, black, *69*	7	16	__1

		Good	Exc	Cond/$
6476-185	LV Hopper, yellow, *69*	6	14	__1
6477	Bulkhead Car w/ pipes, *57-58*	22	60	__1
6480	Explosives Boxcar, red (adv. cat.), *61*	28	48	__1
6482	Refrigerator Car, *57*	30	46	__1
(6500)	Flatcar w/ Bonanza plane, *62, 65*			
	(A) Plane w/ red top and wings	380	730	__2
	(B) Plane w/ white top and wings	320	590	__2
(6501)	Flatcar w/ jet boat, *62-63*	70	130	__1
(6502)	Flatcar w/ bridge girder, *62*	17	38	__1
6511	Flatcar w/ pipes, *53-56*	19	37	__2
(6512)	Cherry Picker Car, *62-63*	35	90	__1
6517	LL Bay Window Caboose, *55-59*			
	(A) Underscored	30	70	__2
	(B) Not underscored	22	65	__2
6517-75	Erie B/W Caboose, *66*	185	445	__1
6517-1966	TCA B/W Caboose, *66*	90	210	__1
6518	Transformer Car, *56-58*	45	105	__1
6519	Allis-Chalmers Flatcar, *58-61*			
	(A) Dark/medium orange base	35	70	__1
	(B) Dull light orange base	40	100	__1
6520	Searchlight Car, *49-51*			
	(A) Tan diesel generator	200	450	__2
	(B) Green diesel generator	175	325	__2
	(C) Maroon or orange diesel gen.	25	60	__2
	(D) Orange generator, gray light	23	55	__2
6530	Fire Fighting Car, red, *60-61*			
	(A) Red, white lettering	40	70	__1
	(B) Black, white lettering		415	__1
6536	M&St L Quad Hopper, *58-59, 63*	20	45	__1
6544	Missile Firing Car, *60-64*			
	(A) White-lettered console	45	100	__1
	(B) Black-lettered console	180	390	__1
6555	Sunoco 1-D Tank Car, *49-50*	17	43	__1
6556	MKT Stock Car, *58*	95	320	__1
6557	Lionel SP-type Caboose, smoke, *58-59*	100	275	__2
6560	Bucyrus Erie Crane w/ stack, 8-wheel, *55-58, 68-69*			
	(A) Reddish-orange or black cab, early construction	65	160	__2
	(B) Gray cab	40	75	__2
	(C) Red cab	24	45	__2
	(D) Dark blue (Hagerstown)	40	85	__2
6560-25	Bucyrus Erie Crane, 8-whl., *56*	39	85	__1
6561	Reel Car, *53-56*			
	(A) Orange reels	22	55	__1
	(B) Gray reels	25	55	__1
6562	NYC Gondola w/ canisters, black, red, or gray, *56-58*			

		Good	Exc	Cond/$
	(A) Gray body, 1956	17	44	__1
	(B) Red body, 1956, 1958	15	38	__1
	(C) Black body, 1957	15	38	__1
6572	REA Refrig. Car, *58-59, 63*	50	105	__1
6630	IRBM Rocket Launcher (adv. cat.), *61*	30	95	__1
6636	Alaska Quad Hopper, *59-60*	17	47	__1
6640	USMC Rocket Launcher, *60*	85	200	__1
6646	Lionel Lines Stock Car, *57*	18	45	__1
6650	IRBM Rocket Launcher, *59-63*	23	50	__1
6650-80	Missile, *60*	3	9	__1
6651	USMC Cannon Car, *64 u*	75	195	__1
6656	Lionel Lines Stock Car, *49-55*			
	(A) With brown "ARMOUR" decal	55	100	__2
	(B) Without decal	10	25	__2
6657	Rio Grande SP-type Caboose, *57-58*	55	140	__1
6660	Flatcar w/ crane, *58*	30	70	__1
6670	Flatcar w/ crane, *59-60*	18	60	__1
6672	Santa Fe Refrigerator Car, *54-56*			
	(A) Blue lettering, 2 lines	25	60	__1
	(B) Black lettering, 2 lines	22	65	__1
	(C) Blue lettering, 3 lines	85	250	__1
6736	Detroit & Mack. Quad Hopper, *60-62*	15	40	__1
6800	Flatcar w/ airplane, *57-60*			
	(A) Yellow plane w/ black top	80	175	__2
	(B) Black plane w/ yellow top	75	160	__2
6801	Flatcar w/ boat, *57-60*			
	(A) Boat with blue hull	45	100	__1
	(B) Brownish-yellow boat hull	45	100	__1
	(C) Boat with white hull	38	85	__1
6802	Flatcar w/ bridge, *58-59*	17	31	__1
6803	Flatcar w/ tank and truck, *58-59*	75	185	__1
6804	Flatcar w/ USMC trucks, *58-59*	80	200	__1
6805	Atomic Disposal Flatcar, *58-59*	55	150	__1
6806	Flatcar w/ USMC trucks, *58-59*	75	175	__1
6807	Lionel Flatcar w/ boat, *58-59*	55	125	__1
6808	Flatcar w/ USMC trucks, *58-59*	100	215	__1
6809	Flatcar w/ USMC trucks, *58-59*	75	170	__1
6810	Flatcar w/ trailer, *58*	25	50	__1
6812	Track Maintenance Car, *59*			
	(A) Dark yellow-gold superstructure	18	80	__1
	(B) Black base and gray top	18	80	__1
	(C) Gray base, black top	18	80	__1
	(D) Cream base and top	19	85	__1
	(E) Light yellow base and top	18	80	__1
6814	Lionel Rescue Caboose, *59-61*	29	100	__1
6816	Flatcar w/ Allis-Chalmers tractor dozer, *59-60*			

		Good	Exc	Cond/$
	(A) Red car	240	425	__1
	(B) Black car	285	640	__1
6816-100	Allis-Chalmers Tractor Dozer, *59-60*			
	(A) No box	75	250	__1
	(B) Separate-sale box	250	1000	__1
6817	Flatcar w/ Allis-Chalmers motor scraper, *59-60*			
	(A) Red car	230	430	__1
	(B) Black car	370	690	__1
6817-100	Allis-Chalmers Motor Scraper, *59-60*			
	(A) No box	105	250	__1
	(B) Separate-sale box		NRS	___
6818	Transformer Car, *58*	21	46	__1
6819	Flatcar w/ helicopter, *59-60*	21	60	__1
6820	Flatcar w/ missile transport helicopter, *60-61*			
	(A) Light blue-painted flatcar	80	205	__1
	(B) Darker blue flatcar	50	135	__1
6821	Flatcar w/ crates, *59-60*	21	33	__1
6822	Searchlight Car, *61-69*			
	(A) Black base, gray light	20	42	__2
	(B) Gray base, black light	21	44	__2
6823	Flatcar w/ IRBM missiles, *59-60*	27	65	__1
6824	USMC Work Caboose, *60*	70	210	__1
6825	Flatcar w/ bridge, *59-62*	16	35	__1
6826	Flatcar w/ trees, *59-60*	45	95	__1
6827	Flatcar w/ steam shovel, *60-63*	60	145	__1
6827-100	Harnischfeger Tractor Shovel, *60*			
	(A) No box	55	110	__1
	(B) Separate-sale box	105	185	__1
6828	Flatcar w/ crane, *60-63, 66*	100	200	__1
6828-100	Harnischfeger Construction Crane, *60*			
	(A) No box	55	135	__1
	(B) Separate-sale box	115	225	__1
6830	Flatcar w/ submarine, *60-61*	45	90	__1
6844	Flatcar w/ missiles, *59-60*			
	(A) Black plastic flatcar	23	85	__1
	(B) Red plastic flatcar	300	590	__1
53132	(See 3464)			
54173	(See 6427 LL)			
65400	(See 2454 or 6454)			
81000	(See 6417 PRR)			
96743	(See 6454)			
159000	(See 3464)			
436155	(See 3361)			
477618	(See 2457 or 2472)			
536417	(See 6417 PRR)			

		Good	Exc	Cond/$
546446	(See 6446)		75	__1
576419	(See 6419-100)			
576427	(See 6427-500)			
641751	(See 6417-50)			
A	Transformer, 90 watts, *47-48*	25	70	__1
CTC	Lockon (O and O27), *47-69*		0.65	__1
ECU-1	Electronic Control Unit, *46*	22	65	__1
KW	Transformer, 190 watts, *50-65*	90	125	__4
LTC	Lockon (O and O27), *50-69*		3	__1
LW	Transformer, 125 watts, *55-56*	80	90	__3
OC	Curved Track (O), *45-61*		1.50	__1
OC1/2	Half Sec. Curve Track (O), *45-66*		1.50	__1
OCS	Curved Insulated Track (O), *46-50*		NRS	___
OS	Straight Track (O), *45-61*		1.50	__1
OSS	Straight Insulated Track, *46-50*		NRS	___
OTC	Lockon Track (O and O27)		3	__1
Q	Transformer, 75 watts, *46*	20	60	__1
R	Transformer, 110 watts, *46-47*	39	65	__1
RW	Transformer, 110 watts, *48-54*	38	65	__1
RCS	Remote Control Track (O), *45-48*	6	11	__1
SP	Smoke Pellets, bottle, *48-69*	7	21	__1
SW	Transformer, 130 watts, *61-66*	49	90	__1
TW	Transformer, 175 watts, *53-60*	65	105	__1
TOC	Curved Track (O), *62-66, 68-69*		1.50	__1
TOC1/2	Half Sec. Str. Trk. (O), *62-66*		1.50	__1
TOS	Straight Track (O), *62-69*		1.50	__1
UCS	Remote Control Track (O), *45-69*	9	18	__1
UTC	Lockon (O, O27, Standard), *45*		1.50	__1
V	Transformer, 150 watts, *46-47*	85	150	__1
VW	Transformer, 150 watts, *48-49*	70	135	__1
Z	Transformer, 250 watts, *45-47*	80	155	__1
ZW	Transformer, 250 watts, *48-49*	105	215	__1
ZW	Transformer, 275 watts, *50-66*	140	230	__5

No Number SP-type Caboose, (see 6067, 6167)
No Number Work Caboose, (see 6119-125, 6120)
No Number Flatcar (see 6401, 6402, 6406)
No Number Gondola (see 6142)
No Number Hopper (see 6176)
No Number Turbo Missile Car (see 3309, 3349)
No Number Rolling Stock (see 3413, 3510, 6111, 6121, 6151, 6407, 6408, 6409, 6469, 6500, 6501, 6502, 6512)

Section 3
MODERN ERA 1970–2005
MPC/LTI/LLC

		Exc	New	Cond/$
3	(See 8104, 8630, 8701)			
[4]	Midwest TCA C&NW F-3 A Unit, shell only, *77 u*		80	—1
4	(See 18008, 18013)			
T-4	(See 12923)			
[00005]	Midwest TCA Covered Quad Hopper, *78 u*	—	50	—1
6	(See 18023)			
[10]	METCA Jersey Central F-3 A Unit, shell only, *71 u*		75	—1
12	(See 16137, 52029)			
14	(See 52032)			
27	(See 18841)			
29	(See 52039)			
36	(See 19042)			
40	(See 11737)			
52	(See 18555)			
65-00637	(See 18927)			
74	(See 19718)			
79C95204C	Sears Santa Fe Diesel set, *71 u*	150	165	—1
79C9715C	Sears 4-unit set, *75 u*	50	65	—1
79C9717C	Sears 7-unit set, *75 u*	150	165	—1
79N95223C	Sears 6-unit set, *74 u*	150	165	—1
79N9552C	Sears 6-unit set, *72 u*	150	165	—1
79N9553C	Sears 6-unit Diesel set, *72 u*	150	165	—1
79N96178C	Sears 4-unit set, *74 u*	50	65	—1
79N97082C	Sears set, *70 u*		NRS	
79N97101C	Sears 5-unit set, *75 u*	150	165	—1
79N98765C	Sears Logging Empire set, *78 u*	100	115	—1
91	(See 18558)			
102	(See 19538)			
109	(See 11809)			
0121	(See 19717)			
125	(See 19724)			
150	(See 18553)			
154	(See 18223)			
155	(See 18224)			
190	(See 17899)			
197	(See 18843)			
200	(See 18117/18118)			
200A	(See 18121)			

		Exc	New	Cond/$
200B	(See 18122)			
D200	(See 18512)			
D202	(See 18506)			
D203	(See 18506)			
211	(See 19136)			
C217	(See 19715)			
D250	(See 18512)			
254	(See 18920)			
260	(See 19133)			
300	(See 17307, 18934/18935)			
C300	(See 19719)			
301	(See 16807, 17308)			
302	(See 17309)			
[303]	LOTS Stauffer Chemical 1-D Tank Car, *85 u*	85	195	—¹
303	(See 17310)			
304	(See 18934/18935)			
342	(See 11903)			
342B	(See 11903)			
343	(See 11903)			
351C	(See 11724)			
366A	(See 11724)			
370B	(See 11724)			
371	(See 18907)			
371B	(See 18108)			
400	(See 18505)			
401	(See 18505)			
425	(See 19135)			
469	(See 19132)			
483	(See 18306)			
484	(See 8587)			
484	(See 18310)			
485	(See 18310)			
490	(See 18043)			
491	(See 7203)			
494	(See 19140)			
495	(See 19141)			
501	(See 17213)			
504	(See 18504)			
507	(See 19128)			
(0511)	TCA St. Louis Baggage Car "1981," *81 u*	50	60	—¹
0512	Toy Fair Reefer, *81 u*	65	80	—¹
537	(See 19143)			
538	(See 19142)			
539	(See 16539)			
550	(See 8378)			
(550C)	Curved Track 31" (O), *70*	0.85	1.50	—¹

		Exc	New	Cond/$
(550S)	Straight Track (O), *70*	0.85	1.50	—[1]
576	(See 19108)			
577	(See 9562)			
577	(See 19139)			
578	(See 9563)			
579	(See 9564)			
580	(See 9565)			
581	(See 9566)			
582	(See 9567)			
582	(See 19144)			
600	(See 18824)			
601	(See 19111)			
611	(See 8100)			
612	(See 18040)			
618	(See 18042)			
619	(See 18041)			
634	Santa Fe NW-2, *70 u*	47	85	—[1]
638	(See 18638)			
639	(See 18639)			
659	(See 8101)			
665E	Johnny Cash "Blue Train" 4-6-4, *71 u*		NRS	—[1]
672	(See 8610)			
680	(See 51229)			
681	(See 51240)			
684	(See 51233)			
685	(See 51245)			
700	(See 18046)			
721	(See 18554)			
725A	(See 11734)			
725B	(See 11734)			
736A	(See 11734)			
779	(See 8215)			
0780	LRRC Boxcar, *82 u*	60	70	—[1]
0781	LRRC Flatcar w/ trailers, *83 u*	65	75	—[1]
0782	LRRC 1-D Tank Car, *85 u*	43	55	—[1]
783	(See 8406)			
0784	LRRC Covered Quad Hopper, *84 u*	55	65	—[1]
784	(See 8606)			
785	(See 18002)			
788	(See 19818)			
789	(See 19134)			
858	(See 18116)			
859	(See 18116)			
863	(See 18309)			
868	(See 18842)			
901	(See 19532)			

		Exc	New	Cond/$
907	(See 16566, 18024)			
914	(See 17893)			
1017	(See 18921)			
[1018-1979]	TCA Mortgage Burning Hi-cube			
	Boxcar, *79 u*	32	37	—1
1041	(See 16538)			
(1050)	New Englander set, *80-81*	155	185	—1
(1051)	T&P Diesel set, *80*		NM	—1
(1052)	Chesapeake Flyer set, *80*	140	150	—1
(1053)	The James Gang set, *80-82*	175	220	—1
(1070)	The Royal Limited set, *80*	310	375	—1
(1071)	Mid Atlantic Limited set, *80*	285	295	—1
(1072)	Cross Country Express set, *80-81*	270	350	—1
(1076)	Lionel Clock, *76-77 u*	510	630	—1
(1081)	Wabash Cannonball set, *70-72*	105	120	—1
(1082)	Yard Boss set, *70*	120	165	—1
(1083)	Pacemaker set, *70*	105	120	—1
(1084)	Grand Trunk & Western set, *70*	120	140	—1
(1085)	Santa Fe Express Diesel Freight set, *70*	175	190	—1
(1086)	The Mountaineer set, *70*		NM	—1
(1087)	Midnight Express set, *70*		NM	—1
(1091)	Sears Special set, *70 u*	150	165	—1
(1092)	79N97081C Sears set, *70 u*	150	165	—1
(1092)	79C97105C Sears 6-unit set, *71 u*	150	165	—1
(1100)	Happy Huff n' Puff, *74-75 u*	50	60	—1
1115	(See 19040)			
1116	(See 19041)			
(1150)	L.A.S.E.R. Train set, *81-82*	165	185	—1
(1151)	Union Pacific Thunder Freight set, *81-82*	150	175	—1
(1153)	JCPenney Thunderball Freight set, *81 u*	165	180	—1
(1154)	Reading Yard King set, *81-82*	180	200	—1
(1155)	Cannonball Freight set, *82*	75	85	—1
(1157)	Lionel Leisure Wabash Cannonball set, *81 u*		250	—1
(1158)	Maple Leaf Limited set, *81*	350	410	—1
(1159)	Toys "R" Us Midnight Flyer set, *81 u*	130	140	—1
(1160)	Great Lakes Limited set, *81*	305	360	—1
(T-1171)	Canadian National Steam Loco set, *71 u*	240	275	—1
(T-1172)	Yardmaster set, *71 u*		200	—1
(T-1173)	Grand Trunk & Western set, *71-73 u*	175	195	—1
(T-1174)	Canadian National set, *71-73 u*	265	300	—1
(1182)	The Yardmaster set, *71-72*	85	105	—
(1183)	The Silver Star set, *71-72*	65	80	—
(1184)	The Allegheny set, *71*	120	150	—
(1186)	Cross Country Express set, *71-72*	210	260	—
(1187)	Illinois Central set (SSS), *71*	400	485	—
(1190)	Sears Special #1 set, *71 u*	85	100	—

		Exc	New	Cond/$
1192	(See 19120)			
(1195)	JCPenney Special set, *71 u*	150	165	—1
(1198)	Unnamed set, *71 u*		175	—1
(1199)	Ford-Autolite Allegheny set, *71 u*	175	195	—1
(1200)	Gravel Gus, *75 u*	75	100	—1
1200	(See 19116)			
1201	(See 18022)			
[1203]	NETCA B&M NW-2, shell only, *72 u*	—	65	—1
1212	(See 19118)			
[1223]	LOTS Seattle & North Coast Hi-cube Boxcar, *86 u*	150	200	—1
1240	(See 19117)			
(1250)	New York Central set (SSS), *72*	350	420	—1
(1252)	Heavy Iron set, *82-83*	95	135	—1
(1253)	Quicksilver Express set, *82-83*	230	285	—1
(1254)	Black Cave Flyer set, *82*	75	105	—1
(1260)	Continental Limited set, *82*	285	375	—1
(1261)	49N95211 Sears Black Cave Flyer set, *82 u*	165	195	—1
(1262)	Toys "R" Us Heavy Iron set, *82 u*	150	165	—1
(1263)	XU671-0701A JCPenney Overland Freight set, *82 u*	150	165	—1
(1264)	Nibco Express set, *82 u*	200	225	—1
(1265)	Tappan Special set, *82 u*	130	155	—1
(T-1272)	Yardmaster set, *72-73 u*	150	165	—1
(T-1273)	Silver Star set, *72-73 u*	90	115	—1
(1280)	Kickapoo Valley & Northern set, *72*	60	75	—1
(1284)	Allegheny set, *72*	140	165	—1
(1285)	Santa Fe Twin Diesel set, *72*	95	140	—1
(1287)	Pioneer Dockside Switcher set, *72*	95	100	—1
[1287]	Midwest TCA C&NW Reefer, *84 u*		NRS	—1
1289	(See 17875)			
(1290)	Sears set, *72 u*	150	165	—1
(1291)	Sears set, *72 u*	150	165	—1
(1300)	Gravel Gus Junior, *75 u*	70	90	—1
1322	(See 19119)			
(1350)	Canadian Pacific set (SSS), *73*	510	690	—1
(1351)	Baltimore & Ohio set, *83-84*	205	245	—1
(1352)	Rocky Mountain Freight set, *83-84*	75	95	—1
(1353)	Southern Streak set, *83-85*	75	95	—1
(1354)	Northern Freight Flyer set, *83-85*	250	305	—1
(1355)	Commando Assault Train set, *83-84*	175	280	—1
(1359)	Train Display Case for set 1355, *83 u*	75	95	—1
(1361)	Gold Coast Limited set, *83*	580	600	—1
1362)	Lionel Leisure BN Express set, *83 u*	200	300	—1
1380)	U.S. Steel Industrial Switcher set, *73-75*	60	75	—1
1381)	Cannonball set, *73-75*	70	75	—1

		Exc	New	Cond/$
(1382)	Yardmaster set, *73-74*	100	120	—¹
(1383)	Santa Fe Freight set, *73-75*	100	125	—¹
(1384)	Southern Express set, *73-76*	75	120	—¹
(1385)	Blue Streak Freight set, *73-74*	100	120	—¹
(1386)	Rock Island Express set, *73-74*	120	140	—¹
(1387)	Milwaukee Road Special set, *73*	185	280	—¹
(1388)	Golden State Arrow set, *73-75*	215	240	—¹
(1390)	Sears 7-unit set, *73 u*	150	165	—¹
1390	(See 18044)			
(1392)	79C95224C Sears 8-unit set, *73 u*	150	165	—¹
(1393)	79C95223C Sears 6-unit set, *73 u*	150	165	—¹
(1395)	JCPenney set, *73 u*	150	165	—¹
(1400)	Happy Huff n' Puff Junior, *75 u*	130	140	—¹
(1402)	Chessie System set, *84-85*	135	160	—¹
(1403)	Redwood Valley Express set, *84-85*	170	205	—¹
1403	(See 19145)			
(1450)	D&RGW set (SSS), *74*	380	470	—¹
(1451)	Erie-Lackawanna Limited set, *84*	540	600	—¹
1458	(See 52031)			
(1460)	Grand National set, *74*	265	305	—¹
(1461)	Black Diamond set, *74 u, 75*	100	120	—¹
(1463)	Coca-Cola Special set, *74 u, 75*	195	245	—¹
(1487)	Broadway Limited set, *74-75*	225	285	—¹
(1489)	Santa Fe Double Diesel set, *74-76*	140	165	—¹
(1492)	79N96185C Sears 7-unit set, *74 u*	150	165	—¹
(1493)	79N96185C Sears 7-unit set, *74 u*	150	165	—¹
(1499)	JCPenney Great Express set, *74 u*	150	165	—¹
(1501)	Midland Freight set, *85-86*	75	95	—¹
1501	(See 18003)			
(1502)	Yard Chief set, *85-86*	200	225	—¹
(1506)	Sears Chessie System set, *85 u*	165	195	—¹
(1512)	JCPenney Midland Freight set, *85 u*	90	115	—¹
1538	(See 18838)			
(1549)	Toys "R" Us Heavy Iron set, *85-89 u*	200	240	—¹
(1552)	Burlington Northern Limited set, *85*	610	690	—¹
1552	(See 52007)			
(1560)	North American Express set, *75*	225	280	—¹
(1562)	Fast Freight Flyer set, *85 u*	120	140	—¹
(1577)	Liberty Special set, *75 u*	165	195	—¹
(1579)	Milwaukee Road set (SSS), *75*	370	470	—¹
(1581)	Thunderball Freight set, *75-76*	85	95	—¹
(1582)	Yard Chief set, *75-76*	115	155	—¹
(1584)	Norfolk & Western "Spirit of America" set, *75*	200	215	—¹
(1585)	75th Anniversary Special set, *75-77*	210	245	—¹
(1586)	Chesapeake Flyer set, *75-77*	160	190	—¹

		Exc	New	Cond/$
(1587)	Capitol Limited set, *75*	255	280	—1
(1593)	Sears set, *75 u*		100	—1
(1595)	79C9716C Sears 6-unit set, *75 u*	150	165	—1
(1602)	Nickel Plate Special set, *86-91*	120	125	—1
(1606)	Sears Nickel Plate Special set, *86 u*	165	195	—1
(1608)	American Express General set, *86 u*	185	280	—1
(1615)	Cannonball Express set, *86-90*	65	75	—1
1623	(See 19146)			
(1632)	Santa Fe Work Train set (SSS), *86*	195	225	—1
(1652)	B&O Freight set, *86*	165	220	—1
(1658)	Town House TV and Appliances set, *86 u*	80	95	—1
(1660)	Yard Boss set, *76*	95	110	—1
(1661)	Rock Island Line set, *76-77*	95	120	—1
(1662)	Black River Freight set, *76-78*	75	95	—1
(1663)	Amtrak Lake Shore Limited set, *76-77*	215	270	—1
(1664)	Illinois Central Freight set, *76-77*	265	355	—1
(1665)	NYC Empire State Express set, *76*	315	450	—1
(1672)	Northern Pacific set (SSS), *76*	240	310	—1
(1685)	True Value Freight Flyer set, *86-87 u*	60	75	—1
(1686)	Kay Bee Toys Freight Flyer set, *86 u*	150	165	—1
(1687)	Freight Flyer set, *87-90*	39	47	—1
(1693)	Toys "R" Us Rock Island Line set, *76 u*	110	130	—1
(1694)	Toys "R" Us Black River Freight set, *76 u*	110	130	—1
(1696)	Sears set, *76 u*	110	130	—1
(1698)	True Value Rock Island Line set, *76 u*	110	130	—1
1750	(See 52035)			
1754	(See 52037)			
(1760)	Trains n' Truckin' Steel Hauler set, *77-78*	90	95	—1
(1761)	Trains n' Truckin' Cargo King set, *77-78*	85	150	—1
(1762)	Wabash Cannonball set, *77*	135	190	—1
(1764)	Heartland Express set, *77*	185	215	—1
(1765)	Rocky Mountain Special set, *77*	205	265	—1
(1766)	B&O Budd Car set (SSS), *77*	285	315	—1
1776	(See 8559, 8665, 9170)			
1776	Seaboard U36B, *74-76*	120	170	—1
(1790)	Lionel Leisure Steel Hauler set, *77 u*	150	200	—1
(1791)	Toys "R" Us Steel Hauler set, *77 u*	130	175	—1
(1792)	True Value Rock IslandLine set, *77 u*	100	135	—1
(1793)	Toys "R" Us Black River Freight set, *77 u*	120	155	—1
(1796)	JCPenney Cargo Master set, *77 u*		200	—1
1803	(See 19147)			
1815	(See 18815)			
1818	(See 18931)			
1821	(See 18840)			
(1860)	Workin' on the Railroad Timberline set, *78*	60	75	—1
(1862)	Workin' on the RR Logging Empire set, *78*	75	95	—1

		Exc	New	Cond/$
(1864)	Santa Fe Double Diesel set, *78-79*	155	190	—¹
(1865)	Chesapeake Flyer set, *78-79*	140	165	—¹
(1866)	Great Plains Express set, *78-79*	195	270	—¹
(1867)	Milwaukee Road Limited set, *78*	245	295	—¹
(1868)	M&St L set (SSS), *78*	220	255	—¹
(1892)	JCPenney Logging Empire set, *78 u*	95	125	—¹
(1893)	Toys "R" Us Logging Empire set, *78 u*	175	225	—¹
1900	(See 18502)			
1905-95	(See 16953)			
1921	(See 52047)			
1947	(See 18830)			
1952	(See 19960)			
(1960)	Midnight Flyer set, *79-81*	55	75	—¹
1960	(See 18943)			
(1962)	Wabash Cannonball set, *79*	90	105	—¹
(1963)	Black River Freight set, *79-81*	75	85	—¹
(1964)	Radio Control Express set, *79 u*		NM	—¹
(1965)	Smokey Mountain Line set, *79*	65	85	—¹
(1970)	Southern Pacific Limited set, *79 u*	375	415	—¹
1970	(See 8615)			
(1971)	Quaker City Limited Set, *1979*	380	415	—¹
[1971-1976]	Rocky Mountain TCA Reefer, *76 u*		50	—¹
1973	(See 9123)			
1973	TCA Bicentennial Observation Car (027), *76 u*	34	50	—¹
1974	TCA Bicentennial Passenger Car (027), *76 u*	34	50	—¹
1975	TCA Bicentennial Passenger Car (027), *76 u*	34	50	—¹
1976	TCA Seaboard U36B, *76 u*	140	185	—¹
[1976]	Southern TCA Florida East Coast F-3 ABA, shells only, *76 u*		250	—¹
[1979]	IETCA Boxcar, *79 u*	—	15	—¹
1980	(See 8068, 9544)			
[1980]	IETCA SP-type Caboose, *80 u*	—	14	—¹
[1980]	Atlantic TCA Flatcar w/ trailers, *80 u*	28	34	—¹
1981	(See 0511)			
[1981]	IETCA Quad Hopper, *81 u*	—	14	—¹
[1981]	LCOL Boxcar, *81 u*	—	23	—¹
1982	(See 7205)			
[1982]	IETCA 3-D Tank Car, *82 u*	—	14	—¹
1983	(See 7206)			
[1983]	IETCA Reefer, *83 u*	—	14	—¹
[1983]	TTOS Phoenix 3-D Tank Car, *83 u*	—	100	—¹
[1983]	Great Lakes TCA Churchill Downs Boxcar, *83 u*		200	—¹
[1983]	Great Lakes TCA Churchill Downs Reefer, *83 u*		250	—¹
1984	(See 7212)			

		Exc	New	Cond/$
[1984]	TTOS Sacramento Northern Boxcar, *84 u*	65	85	—1
[1984-30X]	Ft. Pitt TCA Heinz Ketchup Boxcar, *84 u*		500	—1
[1985]	TTOS Snowbird Covered Quad Hopper, *85 u*	42	55	—1
[1986]	IETCA Bunk Car, *86 u*	—	14	—1
[1986]	Southern TCA Bunk Car, *86 u*	—	30	—1
[1986]	LCOL Work Caboose, shell only, *86 u*	—	14	—1
1987	(See 16205, 16310, 16311, 16507, 18605)			
[1988]	Midwest TCA IC Boxcar, *88 u*		NRS	—1
1989	(See 16110, 17879, 18614)	—	20	—1
(1990)	Mystery Glow Midnight Flyer set, *79 u*	75	90	—1
1990	(See 17883, 18090, 19708)			
(1991)	JCPenney Wabash Cannonball Deluxe Express set, *79 u*	150	165	—1
1992	(See 18818)			
(1993)	Toys "R" Us Midnight Flyer set, *79 u*	110	130	—1
1993	(See 16655, 18713, 19927)			
1993X	(See 52008)			
1994	(See 52043, 52050)	—	300	—1
1995	(See 19934, 19935, 52062)			
1996	(See (52079, 52085), *99 u*	—	300	—1
(1999)	LCCA Ft. Worth & Weston Boxcar, *99 u*	—	50	—1
2000	(See 18710, 18711, 18712, 19131)			
2100	(See 18006)			
2101	(See 18011, 18557)			
2110	Graduated Trestle set (22), *70-88*	9	13	—1
2111	Elevated Trestle set (10), *70-88*	8	11	—1
(2113)	Tunnel Portals (2), *84-87*	11	17	—1
(2115)	Dwarf Signal, *84-87*	12	13	—1
(2117)	Block Target Signal, *84-87*	20	25	—1
(2122)	Extension Bridge w/ rock piers, *76-87*	24	34	—1
2125	Whistling Freight Shed, *71*	36	43	—1
2126	Whistling Freight Shed, *76-87*	25	26	—1
2127	Diesel Horn Shed, *76-87*	25	30	—1
(2128)	Operating Switchman, *83-86*	25	28	—1
2129	Illuminated Freight Station, *83-86*	26	29	—1
(2133)	Lighted Freight Station, *72-78, 80-84*	33	42	—1
2140	Automatic Banjo Signal, *70-84*	17	21	—1
(2145)	Automatic Gateman, *72-84*	36	55	—1
(2151)	Operating Semaphore, *78-82*	15	19	—1
(2152)	Automatic Crossing Gate, *70-84*	21	25	—1
2154	Automatic Highway Flasher, *70-87*	19	24	—1
2156	Illuminated Station Platform, *70-71*	26	34	—1
(2162)	Automatic Crossing Gate and Signal "262," *70-87, 94, 96-98*	20	34	—1
(2163)	Block Target Signal, *70-78*	13	17	—1
(2170)	Street Lamps (3), *70-87*	14	19	—1

		Exc	New	Cond/$
(2171)	Gooseneck Street Lamps (2), *80-81, 83-84*	15	18	—1
(2175)	Sandy Andy Gravel Loader kit, *76-79*	31	50	—1
(2180)	Road Signs (16) "307," *77-98*	—	6	—1
(2181)	Telephone Pole set "150," *77-98*	—	5	—1
2184	(See 17218)			
(2195)	Floodlight Tower, *70-71*	38	50	—1
(2199)	Microwave Tower, *72-75*	30	39	—1
(2214)	Girder Bridge, *70-71, 72 u, 73-87*	5	9	—1
2256	Station Platform, *73-81*	15	19	—1
[2256]	TCA Station Platform, *75 u*	22	30	—1
(2260)	Illuminated Bumper, *70-71, 72 u, 73*	23	35	—1
(2280)	Non-Illuminated Bumpers (3), *73-84*	2.50	4	—1
2282	Die-cast Bumpers (2), *83 u*	17	18	—1
2283	(See 52039)			
(2283)	Die-cast illuminated bumpers "260," *84-99*	19	20	—1
(2290)	Illuminated Bumpers (2), *75 u, 76-86*	9	10	—1
(2292)	Station Platform, *85-87*	5	9	—1
(2300)	Operating Oil Drum Loader, *83-87*	100	120	—1
(2301)	Operating Sawmill, *80-84*	70	75	—2
2302	Union Pacific Manual Gantry Crane, *80-82*	24	31	—1
2303	Santa Fe Manual Gantry Crane, *80-81, 83 u*	17	21	—1
2305	Getty Operating Oil Derrick, *81-84*	105	115	—2
(2306)	Operating Ice Station w/ 6700 PFE Ice Car, *82-83*	120	155	—2
(2307)	Lighted Billboard, *82-86*	17	21	—1
2308	Animated Newsstand, *82-83*	115	140	—1
(2309)	Mechanical Crossing Gate, *82-92*	4	7	—1
(2310)	Mechanical Crossing Gate, *73-77*	2.50	4	—1
(2311)	Mechanical Semaphore, *82-92*	4	7	—1
(2312)	Mechanical Semaphore, *73-77*	2.50	4	—1
(2313)	Floodlight Tower, *75-86*	22	27	—1
(2314)	Searchlight Tower, *75-84*	22	27	—1
(2315)	Operating Coaling Station, *83-84*	95	125	—1
2316	N&W Operating Gantry Crane, *83-84*	95	135	—1
2317	Operating Drawbridge, *75 u, 76-81*	110	145	—1
(2318)	Operating Control Tower, *83-86*	65	75	—1
2319	Illuminated Watchtower, *75-78, 80*	27	30	—1
2320	Flagpole kit, *83-87*	10	14	—1
2321	Operating Sawmill, *84, 86-87*	115	145	—1
2323	Operating Freight Station, *84-87*	65	75	—1
2324	Operating Switch Tower, *84-87*	65	70	—1
(2346)	LCAC TH&B Gondola, *99 u*	—	45	—1
(2354)	LCAC TH&B Gondola, *99 u*	—	45	—1
(2390)	Lionel Mirror, *82 u*	55	95	—1
2400	(See 18305)			
2401	(See 18304)			

		Exc	New	Cond/$
2402	(See 18304)			
2403	(See 18305)			
2487	(See 18833)			
2494	Rotary Beacon, *72-74*	37	44	—[1]
2504	(See 19150)			
2601	(See 52023)			
2626	(See 18016)			
(2709)	Rico Station kit, *81-98*	—	32	—[1]
2710	Billboards (5), *70-84*	4	7	—[1]
(2714)	Tunnel, *75 u, 76-77*	36	43	—[1]
(2716)	Short Extension Bridge, *88-98*	3	8	—[1]
(2717)	Short Extension Bridge, *77-87*	2.50	4	—[1]
(2718)	Barrel Platform kit, *77-84*	3	5	—[1]
(2719)	Watchman's Shanty kit, *77-87*	2.50	4	—[1]
(2720)	Lumber Shed kit, *77-84, 87*	3	5	—[1]
(2721)	Operating Log Mill kit, *78*	2.50	4	—[1]
(2722)	Barrel Loader kit, *78*	2.50	4	—[1]
(2729)	Water Tower kit, *85*		NM	—[1]
(2783)	Freight Station kit, *84*	6	10	—[1]
(2784)	Freight Platform kit, *81-90*	5	8	—[1]
(2785)	Engine House kit, *73-77*	27	34	—[1]
(2786)	Freight Platform kit, *73-77*	4	6	—[1]
(2787)	Freight Station kit, *73-77, 83*	6	9	—[1]
(2788)	Coal Station kit, *75 u, 76-77*	18	30	—[1]
(2789)	Water Tower kit, *75-77, 80*	17	21	—[1]
(2791)	Cross Country set, *70-71*	22	30	—[1]
(2792)	Whistle Stop set, *70-71*	24	34	—[1]
(2792)	Layout Starter Pak, *80-84*	9	21	—[1]
(2793)	Alamo Junction set, *70-71*	22	30	—[1]
(2796)	Grain Elevator kit, *76 u, 77*	50	55	—[1]
(2797)	Rico Station kit, *76-77*	23	34	—[1]
2848	(See 12848)			
(2900)	Lockon, *70-98*	—	1.50	—[1]
(2901)	Track Clips (12) (O27), *71-98*	—	6	—[1]
2902	(See 12902)			
2903	(See 18630)			
(2905)	Lockon and Wire, *74-00*	—	3	—[1]
(2909)	Smoke Fluid, *70-98*	—	4	—[1]
2910	OTC Contactor, *84-86, 88*	4	7	—[1]
(2911)	Smoke Pellets, *70-73*	10	12	—[1]
2925	Lubricant, *70-71, 72 u, 73-75*	—	1.50	—[1]
(2927)	Maintenance kit, *70, 78-98*	—	11	—[1]
2928	Oil, *71*	—	1.50	—[1]
2930	(See 12930)			
2951	Track Layout Book, *70-86*	0.85	1.50	—[1]
2952	Train and Accessory Manual, *70-74*	0.85	1.50	—[1]

		Exc	New	Cond/$
2953	Train and Accessory Manual, *75-86*	0.85	1.50	—1
2956	(See 19721)			
(2960)	Lionel 75th Anniversary Book, *75 u, 76*	9	19	—1
(2980)	Magnetic Conversion Coupler, *70-71*	0.85	1.50	—1
(2985)	The Lionel Train Book, *86-98*	—	11	—1
3000	(See 18009, 33000)			
3004	(See 33004)			
3005	(See 33005)			
3010	(See 23010)			
3011	(See 23011)			
3100	Great Northern 4-8-4 (FARR #3), *81*	375	415	—2
3158	(See 18034)			
3285	(See 16805)			
3400	(See 19109)			
3500	(See 19110)			
[3764]	LOTS Kahn Boxcar, *81 u*	65	75	—1
3768	(See 18028)			
4000	(See 18812, 18825)			
4002	(See 18211)			
4004	(See 18218)			
4023	(See 52030)			
04039	(See 16908)			
04040	(See 16939)			
4044	Transformer, 45-watt, *70-71*	2.50	4	—1
4045	Safety Transformer, *70-71*	2.50	3	—1
4050	Safety Transformer, *72-79*	2.50	3	—1
4060	(See 18831)			
4060	Power Master Transformer, *80-93*	—	13	—1
4065	DC Hobby Transformer, *81-83*	2.50	3	—1
4090	Power Master Transformer, *70-84*	47	65	—1
4100	(See 18030)			
4124	(See 18514)			
4125	Transformer, 25-watt, *72*	2.50	3	—1
4136	(See 18819)			
4150	Trainmaster Transformer, *72-73, 75-77*	4	10	—1
4250	Trainmaster Transformer, *74*	5	10	—1
4410	(See 18007)			
4449	(See 8307)			
4501	(See 8309)			
4501	(See 18018)			
4574	(See 18306)			
4600	(See 18816)			
4651	Trainmaster Transformer, *78-79*	1.50	2.50	—1
4690	MW Transformer, *86-89*	65	80	—1
4851	DC Transformer, *85-91, 94-96*	5	10	—1
4866	(See 18308)			

		Exc	New	Cond/$
4870	DC Hobby Transformer and Throttle Controller, *77-78*	2.50	3	—[1]
4907	(See 18313)			
4935	(See 8150)			
(5012)	Curved Track 27" card of 4 (O27), *70-96*	—	17	—[1]
(5013)	Curved Track 27" (O27), *70-78*	—	0.45	—[1]
(5014)	Half-Curved Track 27" (O27), *70-98*	—	0.70	—[1]
(5016)	36" Straight Track (O27), *87-88*	1.50	2.50	—[1]
(5017)	Straight Track, card of 4 (O27), *70-96*	—	4	—[1]
5017	(See 51230)			
(5018)	Straight Track (O27), *70-78*	0.45	0.65	—[1]
(5019)	Half-Straight Track (O27), *70-98*	—	0.70	—[1]
5020	(See 51234)			
(5020)	90° Crossover (O27), *70-98*	—	7	—[1]
(5021)	Left Manual Switch 27" (O27), *70-98*	—	15	—[1]
(5022)	Right Manual Switch 27" (O27), *70-98*	—	15	—[1]
(5023)	45° Crossover (O27), *70-98*	—	6	—[1]
(5024)	35" Straight Track (O27), *88-98*	—	2.50	—[1]
(5025)	Manumatic Uncoupler, *71-72*	0.85	1.50	—[1]
(5027)	Pair Manual Switches 27" (O27), *74-84*	13	21	—[1]
(5030)	Track Expander set (O27), *71-84*	18	26	—[1]
(5031)	Ford-Autolite Layout Expander set, *71 u*	50	65	—[1]
(5033)	Curved Track 27" (O27), *79-98*	—	0.85	—[1]
(5038)	Straight Track (O27), *79-98*	—	0.85	—[1]
(5041)	Insulator Pins (12) (O27), *70-98*	—	1.50	—[1]
(5042)	Steel Pins (12) (O27), *70-98*	—	1.50	—[1]
(5044)	Curved Track Ballast 42" (O27), *88*		NM	—[1]
(5045)	Curved Track Ballast 54" (O27), *87-88*	0.85	1.50	—[1]
(5046)	Curved Track Ballast 27" (O27), *87-88*	0.85	1.50	—[1]
(5047)	Straight Track Ballast (O27), *87-88*	0.85	1.50	—[1]
(5049)	Curved Track 42" (O27), *88-98*	0.85	1.50	—[1]
(5090)	Three Pair Manual Switches 27" (O27), *78-84*	55	70	—[1]
5100	(See 18001)			
(5113)	Curved Track 54" (O27), *79-98*	0.85	1.50	—[1]
(5121)	Left Remote Switch 27" (O27), *70-98*	20	22	—[1]
(5122)	Right Remote Switch 27" (O27), *70-98*	20	22	—[1]
(5125)	Pair Remote Switches 27" (O27), *71-83*	20	30	—[1]
5132	Right Remote Switch 31" (O), *80-94*	22	30	—[1]
5133	Left Remote Switch 31" (O), *80-94*	22	30	—[1]
(5149)	Remote Uncoupling Section (O27), *70-98*	—	7	—[1]
(5165)	Right Remote Switch 72" (O), *87-98*	20	65	—[1]
(5166)	Left Remote Switch 72" (O), *87-98*	20	75	—[1]
(5167)	Right Remote Switch 42" (O27), *88-98*	25	37	—[1]
(5168)	Left Remote Switch 42" (O27), *88-98*	25	37	—[1]
(5193)	Three Pair Remote Switches 27" (O27), *78-83*	80	95	—[1]
5300	(See 18636)			

		Exc	New	Cond/$
5340	(See 18005, 18012)			
5366	(See 52078)			
5450	(See 18026, 18027, 18029)			
5484	(See 8476)			
5500	(See 18216)			
(5500)	Straight Track 10" (O), *71-98*	—	1.50	—1
(5501)	Curved Track 31" (O), *71-98*	—	1.50	—1
(5502)	Remote Uncoupling Section (O), *71-72*	7	9	—1
(5504)	Half-Curved Track 31" (O), *83-98*	—	0.85	—1
(5505)	Half-Straight Track (O), *83-98*	—	0.85	—1
5512	(See 18221)			
5517	(See 18222)			
5520	90° Crossover (O), *71-72*	6	9	—1
(5522)	36" Straight, *87-88*	—	3	—1
(5523)	40" Straight Track (O), *88-98*	—	4	—1
(5530)	Remote Uncoupling Section (O), *81-98*	—	19	—1
(5540)	90° Crossover (O), *81-98*	—	10	—1
(5543)	Insulator Pins (12) (O), *70-98*	—	1.50	—1
(5545)	45° Crossover (O), *83-98*	—	9	—1
(5551)	Steel Pins (12) (O), *70-98*	—	1.50	—1
(5554)	Curved Track 54" (O), *90-98*	—	2.50	—1
(5560)	Curved Track Ballast 72" (O), *87-88*	0.85	1.50	—1
(5561)	Curved Track Ballast 31" (O), *87-88*	0.85	1.50	—1
(5562)	Straight Track Ballast (O), *87-88*	0.85	1.50	—1
(5572)	Curved Track 72" (O), *79-98*	—	3	—1
5600	Curved Track (TT), *73-74*	0.85	1.50	—1
5601	Curved Track, card of 4 (TT), *73-74*	6	10	—1
5602	Curved Track Ballast, card of 4 (TT), *73-74*	5	9	—1
5605	Straight Track (TT), *73-74*	0.85	1.50	—1
5606	Straight Track, card of 4 (TT), *73-74*	5	9	—1
5607	Straight Track Ballast, card of 4 (TT), *73-74*	5	9	—1
5620	Left Manual Switch (TT), *73-74*	4	13	—1
5625	Left Remote Switch (TT), *73-74*	9	17	—1
5630	Right Manual Switch (TT), *73-74*	4	13	—1
5635	Right Remote Switch (TT), *73-74*	9	17	—1
5640	Left Switch Ballast, card of 2 (TT), *73-74*	5	9	—1
5650	Right Switch Ballast, card of 2 (TT), *73-74*	5	9	—1
5655	Lockon (TT), *73-74*	0.85	1.50	—1
5658	(See 16559)			
5660	Terminal Track w/ lockon (TT), *74*	1.50	3	—1
5700	Oppenheimer Reefer, *81*	35	45	—1
[5700]	Ozark TCA Oppenheimer Reefer, *81 u*	49	95	—1
5701	Dairymen's League Reefer, *81*	27	30	—1
5702	National Dairy Despatch Reefer, *81*	24	34	—1
5703	North American Despatch Reefer, *81*	26	32	—1
5704	Budweiser Reefer, *81-82*	55	80	—1

		Exc	New	Cond/$
5705	Ball Glass Jars Reefer, *81-82*	30	36	__1
5706	Lindsay Brothers Reefer, *81-82*	29	33	__1
5707	American Refrigerator Reefer, *81-82*	24	25	__1
5708	Armour Reefer, *82-83*	17	22	__1
5709	REA Reefer, *82-83*	25	29	__2
5710	Canadian Pacific Reefer, *82-83*	17	19	__1
[5710]	NETCA CP Reefer, *82 u*	33	39	__1
[5710]	LCAC CP Reefer, *83 u*		250	__1
5711	Commercial Express Reefer, *82-83*	17	20	__1
5712	Lionel Lines Reefer, *82 u*	170	200	__2
5713	Cotton Belt Reefer, *83-84*	21	25	__1
5714	Michigan Central Reefer, *83-84*	17	25	__1
[5714]	LCAC Michigan Central Reefer, *85 u*	120	150	__1
5715	Santa Fe Reefer, *83-84*	23	33	__1
5716	Central Vermont Reefer, *83-84*	23	27	__1
[5716]	NETCA Central Vermont Reefer, *83 u*	25	30	__1
5717	Santa Fe Bunk Car, *83*	26	34	__2
5718	(See 9849)			
5719	Canadian National Reefer, *84*	15	16	__1
5720	Great Northern Reefer, *84*	80	90	__1
5721	Soo Line Reefer, *84*	23	26	__1
5722	NKP Reefer, *84*	16	18	__1
5724	PRR Bunk Car, *84*	26	29	__1
[5724]	LCOL PRR Bunk Car, *84 u*	30	39	__1
5726	Southern Bunk Car, *84 u*	27	33	__1
5727	U.S. Marines Bunk Car, *84-85*	28	33	__1
5728	Canadian Pacific Bunk Car, *86*	23	29	__1
5730	Strasburg RR Reefer, *85-86*	23	33	__1
5731	L&N Reefer, *85-86*	17	21	__1
[5731]	TCA Museum L&N Reefer, *90 u*	—	95	__1
5732	Jersey Central Reefer, *85-86*	—	23	__1
5733	Lionel Lines Bunk Car, *86 u*	27	39	__1
5734	TCA REA Reefer, *85 u*	65	90	__2
5735	NYC Bunk Car, *85-86*	36	39	__1
5739	B&O Tool Car, *86*	36	41	__1
5745	Santa Fe Bunk Car (SSS), *86*	40	47	__1
5760	Santa Fe Tool Car (SSS), *86*	35	41	__1
5800	(See 18836)			
5808	(See 18826)			
5900	AC/DC Converter, *79-83*	3	5	__1
6001	(See 18107)			
6002	(See 18107)			
6003	(See 17611)			
6005	(See 18821)			
6006	(See 18210)			
6007	(See 18217)			

		Exc	New	Cond/$
[6014-900]	LCCA Frisco Boxcar (O27), *75-76 u*	19	30	—[1]
6061	(See 16061)			
6062	(See 16062)			
6063	(See 16063)			
6064	(See 16064)			
6065	(See 16065)			
6066	(See 16066)			
6067	(See 16067)			
6068	(See 16068)			
6069	(See 16069)			
6070	(See 16070)			
6071	(See 16071)			
6072	(See 16072)			
6073	(See 16073)			
6074	(See 16074)			
6076	LV Hopper (O27), *70 u*	17	21	—[1]
6076	TTOS Santa Fe Hopper (O27), *70 u*		85	—[1]
6080	(See 16080)			
6081	(See 16081)			
6082	(See 16082)			
6083	(See 16083)			
6084	(See 16084)			
6086	(See 16086)			
6087	(See 16087)			
6088	(See 16088)			
6089	(See 16089)			
6090	(See 16090)			
6100	Ontario Northland Cvrd Quad Hopper, *81-82*	36	40	—[1]
[6100]	LCAC Ontario Northland Covered Quad Hopper, *82 u*		250	—[1]
6101	Burlington Northern Covered Quad Hopper, *81-82*	23	34	—[1]
[6101]	Atlantic TCA Burlington Northern Covered Quad Hopper, *82 u*	21	34	—[1]
6102	GN Covered Quad Hopper (FARR #3), *81*	33	37	—[1]
6103	Canadian National Covered Quad Hopper, *81*	32	34	—[1]
6104	Southern Quad Hopper w/ coal load (FARR #4), *83*	70	85	—[1]
6105	Reading Operating Hopper, *82*	39	45	—[1]
6106	N&W Covered Quad Hopper, *82*	27	35	—[1]
6107	Shell Covered Quad Hopper, *82*	22	26	—[1]
6108	(See 16108)			
6109	C&O Operating Hopper, *83*	31	45	—[1]
6110	Missouri Pacific Covered Quad Hopper, *83-84*	16	25	—[1]
6111	L&N Covered Quad Hopper, *83-84*	13	20	—[1]
[6111]	Southern TCA L&N Covered Quad			

		Exc	New	Cond/$
	Hopper, *83 u*	20	22	—1
[6111]	LOTS L&N Covered Quad Hopper, *83 u*	37	42	—1
6112	LCCA Commonwealth Edison Quad Hopper w/ coal load, *83 u*	45	60	—1
6113	Illinois Central Hopper (O27), *83-85*	11	17	—1
6114	C&NW Covered Quad Hopper, *83*	85	95	—1
6115	Southern Hopper (O27), *83-86*	15	19	—1
6116	Soo Line Ore Car, *84*	31	41	—1
6117	Erie Operating Hopper, *84*	36	38	—1
6118	Erie Covered Quad Hopper, *84*	37	40	—1
6122	Penn Central Ore Car, *84*	28	32	—1
6123	PRR Covered Quad Hopper (FARR #5), *84-85*	50	75	—1
6124	D&H Covered Quad Hopper, *84*	22	32	—1
[6124]	NETCA D&H Covered Quad Hopper, *84 u*	25	30	—1
6126	Canadian National Ore Car, *86*	26	30	—1
6127	(See 5735)			
6127	Northern Pacific Ore Car, *86*	21	26	—1
6131	Illinois Terminal Covered Quad Hopper, *85-86*	20	24	—1
6134	Burlington Northern 2-bay ACF Hopper (Std. O), *86 u*	110	130	—2
6135	C&NW 2-bay ACF Hopper (Std. O), *86 u*	95	120	—2
6137	NKP Hopper (O27), *86-91*	13	17	—1
6138	B&O Quad Hopper w/ coal load, *86*	24	28	—1
6150	Santa Fe Hopper (O27), *85-86, 92 u*	10	15	—1
6177	Reading Hopper (O27), *86-90*	13	17	—1
6200	FEC Gondola w/ canisters, *81-82*	14	24	—1
6200	(See 8404)			
6200	(See 18010)			
6201	Union Pacific Animated Gondola, *82-83*	21	29	—1
6202	WM Gondola w/ coal load, *82*	34	36	—1
(6203)	Black Cave Gondola (O27), *82*	2.50	4	—1
6205	CP Gondola w/ canisters, *83*	23	28	—1
6206	C&IM Gondola w/ canisters, *83-85*	18	26	—1
6207	Southern Gondola w/ canisters (O27), *83-85*	6	8	—1
6208	Chessie System Gondola w/ canisters, *83 u*	23	26	—1
6209	NYC Gondola w/ coal load (Std. O), *84-85*	40	44	—1
6210	Erie-Lackawanna Gondola w/ canisters, *84*	23	30	—1
6211	C&O Gondola w/ canisters, *84-85*	—	10	—1
[6211]	LOTS C&O Gondola w/ canisters, *86 u*	55	80	—1
6214	Lionel Lines Gondola w/ canisters, *84 u*	37	44	—1
6226	(See 16226)			
6230	Erie-Lackawanna Reefer (Std. O), *86 u*	105	140	—1
6231	Railgon Gondola w/ coal load (Std. O), *86 u*	85	95	—1
6232	Illinois Central Boxcar (Std. O), *86 u*	80	105	—1
6233	Canadian Pacific Flatcar w/ stakes (Std. O), *86 u*	65	80	—1

		Exc	New	Cond/$
6234	Burlington Northern Boxcar (Std. O), *85*	41	55	—1
6235	Burlington Northern Boxcar (Std. O), *85*	37	50	—1
6236	Burlington Northern Boxcar (Std. O), *85*	37	50	—1
6237	Burlington Northern Boxcar (Std. O), *85*	38	55	—1
6238	Burlington Northern Boxcar (Std. O), *85*	37	50	—1
6239	Burlington Northern Boxcar (Std. O), *86 u*	43	65	—1
6251	NYC Coal Dump Car, *85*	18	28	—1
6254	NKP Gondola w/ canisters, *86-91*	9	10	—1
6258	Santa Fe Gondola w/ canisters (O27), *85-86, 92 u*	—	3	—1
X6260	NYC Gondola w/ canisters, *85-86*	13	15	—1
6272	Santa Fe Gondola w/ cable reels (SSS), *86*	20	25	—1
6300	Corn Products 3-D Tank Car, *81-82*	20	26	—1
6301	Gulf 1-D Tank Car, *81*	22	29	—1
6302	Quaker State 3-D Tank Car, *81*	43	48	—1
6304	GN 1-D Tank Car (FARR #3), *81*	44	55	—1
6305	British Columbia 1-D Tank Car, *81*	44	65	—1
6306	Southern 1-D Tank Car (FARR #4), *83*	49	55	—1
6307	PRR 1-D Tank Car (FARR #5), *84-85*	70	85	—1
6308	Alaska 1-D Tank Car (O27), *82-83*	27	35	—1
6310	Shell 2-D Tank Car (O27), *83-84*	19	24	—1
6312	C&O 2-D Tank Car (O27), *84-85*	18	26	—1
6313	Lionel Lines 1-D Tank Car, *84 u*	43	50	—1
6314	B&O 3-D Tank Car, *86*	39	47	—1
6315	TCA Pittsburgh 1-D Tank Car, *72 u*	65	70	—1
6317	Gulf 2-D Tank Car (O27), *84-85*	19	23	—1
6323	LCCA Virginia Chemicals 1-D Tank Car, *86 u*	47	75	—1
6325	(See 6579)			
6336	(See 16336)			
6357	Frisco 1-D Tank Car, *83*	49	60	—1
6401	Virginian B/W Caboose, *81*	32	40	—1
[6401]	Sacramento-Sierra TCA Virginian B/W Caboose, *84 u*	—	35	—1
6403	Amtrak Vista Dome Car (O27), *76-77*	30	31	—1
6404	Amtrak Passenger Car (O27), *76-77*	24	31	—1
6405	Amtrak Passenger Car (O27), *76-77*	24	31	—1
6406	Amtrak Observation Car (O27), *76-77*	22	29	—1
6408	(See 16408)			
6410	Amtrak Passenger Car (O27), *77*	21	34	—1
6411	Amtrak Passenger Car (O27), *77*	22	32	—1
6412	Amtrak Vista Dome Car (O27), *77*	20	29	—1
6420	Reading Transfer Caboose, *81-82*	14	19	—1
6421	Joshua L. Cowen B/W Caboose, *82*	36	42	—1
6422	DM&IR B/W Caboose, *81*	32	42	—1
6425	Erie-Lackawanna B/W Caboose, *83-84*	35	48	—1
6426	Reading Transfer Caboose, *82-83*	13	21	—1

		Exc	New	Cond/$
6427	Burlington Northern Transfer Caboose, *83-84*	12	21	—¹
6428	C&NW Transfer Caboose, *83-85*	22	25	—¹
6430	Santa Fe SP-type Caboose, *83-89*	4	7	—¹
6431	Southern B/W Caboose (FARR #4), *83*	42	55	—¹
6432	Union Pacific SP-type Caboose, *81-82*	9	10	—¹
6433	Canadian Pacific B/W Caboose, *81*	65	75	—¹
6435	U.S. Transfer Caboose, *83-84*	9	17	—¹
6438	GN B/W Caboose (FARR #3), *81*	38	47	—¹
6439	Reading B/W Caboose, *84-85*	22	30	—¹
6441	Alaska B/W Caboose, *82-83*	42	47	—¹
6446-25	N&W Covered Quad Hopper, *70 u*	135	175	—¹
6449	Wendy's N5c Caboose, *81-82*	49	60	—¹
6464	(See 19248, 19249, 19250, 19258, 19269, 19275)			
6464-095	(See 52051)			
6464-100	(See 19259, 19260)			
6464-125	(See 19267, 52063)			
6464-150	(See 19268, 52064)			
6464-225	(See 19274)			
6464-275	(See 19273)			
6464-500	Timken Boxcar, *70 u*	150	195	—¹
6464-555	(See 52081)			
6464-1895	(See 52058)			
6464-1970	TCA Chicago Boxcar, *70 u*	105	135	—¹
6464-1971	TCA Disneyland Boxcar, *71 u*	245	275	—¹
6464-1972	(See 52086)			
6464-1993	(See 52009)			
6464-1995	(See 52057)			
6464-1996	(See 52087)			
6464-2003	Maddox Retirement Boxcar, *02*	—	100	—¹
(6476-135)	Lehigh Valley Hopper "25000" (O27), *70-71 u*	6	11	—¹
(6478)	Black Cave SP-type Caboose, *82*	5	9	—¹
6482	Nibco Express SP-type Caboose, *82 u*	26	34	—¹
6483	LCCA Jersey Central SP-type Caboose, *82 u*	26	34	—¹
6485	Chessie System SP-type Caboose, *84-85*	6	10	—¹
6486	Southern SP-type Caboose, *83-85*	5	7	—¹
6490	NKP N5c Caboose, *84 u*		NRS	—¹
6491	Erie-Lackawanna Transfer Caboose, *85-86*	9	17	—¹
6493	L&C B/W Caboose, *86-87*	16	25	—¹
6494	Santa Fe Bobber Caboose, *85-86*	7	9	—¹
6496	Santa Fe Work Caboose (SSS), *86*	24	34	—¹
(6504)	L.A.S.E.R. Flatcar w/ helicopter (O27), *81-82*	18	26	—¹
(6505)	L.A.S.E.R. Radar Car, *81-82*	17	25	—¹
(6506)	L.A.S.E.R. Security Car, *81-82*	18	26	—¹
(6507)	L.A.S.E.R. Flatcar w/ cruise missile, *81-82*	21	30	—¹
6508	Canadian Pacific Crane Car, *81*	65	85	—¹
6508	(See 16508)			

		Exc	New	Cond/$
[6508]	LCOL Canadian Pacific Crane Car, *83 u*	—	40	__1
(6509)	Depressed Flatcar w/ girders, *81*	60	70	__1
6510	Union Pacific Crane Car, *82*	65	70	__1
6515	Union Pacific Flatcar (O27), *83-84, 86*	5	9	__1
6521	NYC Flatcar w/ stakes (Std. O), *84-85*	38	46	__1
6522	C&NW Searchlight Car, *83-85*	27	30	__1
6524	Erie Crane Car, *84*	60	65	__1
6526	U.S. Marines Searchlight Car, *84-85*	27	30	__1
6528	(See 16528)			
6529	NYC Searchlight Car, *85-86*	21	27	__1
6531	Express Mail Flatcar w/ trailers, *85-86*	28	38	__1
6560	Bucyrus Erie Crane Car, *71*	115	130	__1
(6561)	Flatcar w/ cruise missile (O27), *83-84*	13	26	__1
(6562)	Flatcar w/ fences (O27), *83-84*	13	21	__1
(6564)	Flatcar w/ two U.S.M.C. tanks (O27), *83-84*	13	21	__1
(6567)	LCCA ICG Crane Car "100408," *85 u*	55	65	__2
(6573)	Redwood Valley Express Flatcar w/ dump bin (O27), *84-85*	7	13	__1
(6574)	Redwood Valley Express Flatcar w/ crane (O27), *84-85*	7	13	__1
(6575)	Redwood Valley Express Flatcar w/ fences (O27), *84-85*	7	13	__1
6576	Santa Fe Flatcar w/ crane (O27), *85-86, 92 u*	7	10	__1
6579	NYC Crane Car, *85-86*	40	49	__1
6582	TTOS Portland Flatcar w/ wood load, *86 u*	65	95	__1
6585	PRR Flatcar w/ fences (O27), *86-90*	5	9	__1
6587	W&ARR Flatcar w/ horses, *86 u*	18	26	__1
6593	Santa Fe Crane Car (SSS), *86*	41	48	__1
6602	(See 16053)			
6603	(See 16054)			
6609	(See 16079)			
6616	(See 16052, 16077)			
6620	(See 16050, 16075)			
6630	(See 16051, 16076)			
6670	(See 9378)			
6700	PFE Ice Car (See 2306), *82-83*		65	__1
6900	N&W E/V Caboose, *82*	65	75	__1
6901	Ontario Northland E/V Caboose, *82 u*	38	49	__2
6903	Santa Fe E/V Caboose, *83*	105	125	__2
6904	Union Pacific E/V Caboose, *83*	105	125	__1
6905	NKP E/V Caboose, *83 u*	45	55	__1
6906	Erie-Lackawanna E/V Caboose, *84*	75	90	__1
6907	NYC Woodside Caboose (Std. O), *86 u*	80	90	__2
6908	PRR N5c Caboose (FARR #5), *84-85*	60	65	__1
6910	NYC E/V Caboose, *84 u*	50	55	__2
(6912)	Redwood Valley Exp SP-type Caboose, *84-85*	9	16	__1

		Exc	New	Cond/$
6913	Burlington Northern E/V Caboose, *85*	70	90	—1
6916	NYC Work Caboose, *85-86*	16	22	—1
6917	Jersey Central E/V Caboose, *86*	50	60	—1
6918	B&O SP-type Caboose, *86*	10	15	—1
6919	Nickel Plate Road SP-type Caboose, *86-91*	5	9	—1
6920	B&A Woodside Caboose (Std. O), *86 u*	70	80	—2
6921	PRR SP-type Caboose, *86-90*	5	9	—1
6926	TCA New Orleans E/V Caboose, *86 u*	33	50	—1
7000	(See 51301)			
7200	Quicksilver Passenger Car (O27), *82-83*	26	34	—1
7200	(See 19415)			
7201	Quicksilver Passenger Car (O27), *82-83*	26	34	—1
7202	Quicksilver Observation Car (O27), *82-83*	26	34	—1
(7203)	N&W Dining Car "491," *82 u*	180	285	—1
(7204)	Southern Pacific Dining Car, *82 u*	255	335	—1
(7205)	TCA Denver Combination Car "1982," *82 u*	37	50	—1
(7206)	TCA Louisville Passenger Car "1983," *83 u*	40	55	—1
7207	NYC Dining Car, *83 u*	110	160	—1
(7208)	PRR Dining Car, *83 u*	105	120	—2
7210	Union Pacific Dining Car, *84*	85	110	—1
(7211)	Southern Pacific Vista Dome Car, *83 u*	210	250	—1
(7212)	TCA Pittsburgh Passenger Car "1984," *84 u*	41	50	—1
7215	B&O Passenger Car, *83-84*	43	50	—1
7216	B&O Passenger Car, *83-84*	43	50	—1
7217	B&O Baggage Car, *83-84*	43	50	—1
7220	Illinois Central Baggage Car, *85, 87*	105	135	—1
7221	Illinois Central Combination Car, *85, 87*	85	105	—1
7222	Illinois Central Passenger Car, *85, 87*	85	105	—1
7223	Illinois Central Passenger Car, *85, 87*	85	105	—1
7224	Illinois Central Dining Car, *85, 87*	75	90	—1
7225	Illinois Central Observation Car, *85, 87*	95	115	—1
7227	Wabash Dining Car (FF #1), *86-87*	90	100	—1
7228	Wabash Baggage Car (FF #1), *86-87*	90	100	—1
7229	Wabash Combination Car (FF #1), *86-87*	90	100	—1
7230	Wabash Passenger Car (FF #1), *86-87*	90	100	—1
7231	Wabash Passenger Car (FF #1), *86-87*	90	100	—1
7232	Wabash Observation Car (FF #1), *86-87*	75	85	—1
7241	W&ARR Passenger Car, *86 u*	43	50	—1
7242	W&ARR Baggage Car, *86 u*	43	50	—1
7301	Norfolk & Western Stock Car, *82*	37	38	—1
7302	Texas & Pacific Stock Car (O27), *83-84*	12	15	—1
7303	Erie Stock Car, *84*	45	55	—1
7304	Southern Stock Car (FARR #4), *83 u*	46	50	—1
7309	Southern Stock Car (O27), *85-86*	12	16	—1
7312	W&ARR Stock Car (O27), *86 u*	25	30	—1
7401	Chessie System Stock Car (O27), *84-85*	13	17	—1

		Exc	New	Cond/$
7403	LCCA LNAC Boxcar, *84 u*	23	33	—1
7404	Jersey Central Boxcar, *86*	35	45	—1
7420	(See 18513)			
(7500)	Lionel 75th Anniversary U36B, *75-77*	115	135	—1
7500	(See 18214)			
7501	Lionel 75th Anniversary Boxcar, *75-77*	21	28	—1
7502	Lionel 75th Anniversary Reefer, *75-77*	23	32	—1
7503	Lionel 75th Anniversary Reefer, *75-77*	26	37	—1
7504	Lionel 75th Anniversary Covered Quad Hopper, *75-77*	23	33	—1
7505	Lionel 75th Anniversary Boxcar, *75-77*	26	37	—1
7506	Lionel 75th Anniversary Boxcar, *75-77*	20	27	—1
7507	Lionel 75th Anniversary Reefer, *75-77*	26	37	—1
7508	Lionel 75th Anniversary N5c Caboose, *75-77*	22	27	—1
7509	Kentucky Fried Chicken Reefer, *81-82*	34	38	—1
7510	Red Lobster Reefer, *81-82*	31	38	—1
7511	Pizza Hut Reefer, *81-82*	34	39	—1
7512	Arthur Treacher's Reefer, *82*	27	32	—1
7513	Bonanza Reefer, *82*	27	32	—1
7514	Taco Bell Reefer, *82*	41	60	—1
7515	Denver Mint Car, *81*	60	65	—1
7517	Philadelphia Mint Car, *82*	45	49	—1
7518	Carson City Mint Car, *83*	38	45	—1
[7518]	IETCA Carson City Mint Car, *84 u*	—	43	—1
7519	Toy Fair Reefer, *82 u*	49	60	—1
7520	Nibco Express Boxcar, *82 u*	265	440	—1
7521	Toy Fair Reefer, *83 u*	50	65	—1
7522	New Orleans Mint Car, *84 u*	36	43	—2
[7522]	Lone Star TCA New Orleans Mint Car w/ coin, *86 u*		365	—1
7523	Toy Fair Reefer, *84 u*	55	60	—1
7524	Toy Fair Reefer, *85 u*	75	85	—1
7525	Toy Fair Boxcar, *86 u*	70	85	—1
7530	Dahlonega Mint Car, *86 u*	46	60	—1
7600	Frisco "Spirit of '76" N5c Caboose, *74-76*	30	39	—1
[7600]	Midwest TCA Frisco "Spirit of '76" N5c Caboose "00003," *76 u*	—	35	—1
7601	Delaware Boxcar, *74-76*	19	22	—1
7602	Pennsylvania Boxcar, *74-76*	23	31	—1
7603	New Jersey Boxcar, *74-76*	25	29	—1
7604	Georgia Boxcar, *74 u, 75-76*	25	30	—1
7605	Connecticut Boxcar, *74 u, 75-76*	25	34	—1
7606	Massachusetts Boxcar, *74 u, 75-76*	26	33	—1
7607	Maryland Boxcar, *74 u, 75-76*	26	40	—1
7608	South Carolina Boxcar, *75 u, 76*	30	46	—1
7609	New Hampshire Boxcar, *75 u, 76*	49	60	—1

		Exc	New	Cond/$
7610	Virginia Boxcar, *75 u, 76*	155	200	—[1]
7611	New York Boxcar, *75 u, 76*	60	85	—[1]
7612	North Carolina Boxcar, *75 u, 76*	35	55	—[1]
7613	Rhode Island Boxcar, *75 u, 76*	35	55	—[1]
7613	(See 17613)			
7643	(See 18215)			
[7679]	VTC Boxcar, *79 u*	—	17	—[1]
[7681]	VTC N5c Caboose, *81 u*	—	23	—[1]
[7682]	VTC Covered Quad Hopper, *82 u*	—	26	—[1]
[7683]	VTC Virginia Fruit Express Reefer, *83 u*	—	26	—[1]
[7684]	VTC Vitraco Oil 3-D Tank Car, *84 u*	—	26	—[1]
[7685]	VTC Boxcar, *85 u*	—	27	—[1]
[7686]	VTC GP-7, *86 u*	—	100	—[1]
[7692-1]	VTC Baggage Car (O27), *92 u*	35	45	—[1]
[7692-2]	VTC Combination Car (O27), *92 u*	35	45	—[1]
[7692-3]	VTC Dining Car (O27), *92 u*	35	45	—[1]
[7692-4]	VTC Passenger Car (O27), *92 u*	35	45	—[1]
[7692-5]	VTC Vista Dome Car (O27), *92 u*	35	45	—[1]
[7692-6]	VTC Passenger Car (O27), *92 u*	35	45	—[1]
[7692-7]	VTC Observation Car (O27), *92 u*	35	45	—[1]
7694	(See 52060)			
7700	Uncle Sam Boxcar, *75 u*	43	47	—[2]
7701	Camel Boxcar, *76-77*	36	50	—[1]
7702	Prince Albert Boxcar, *76-77*	36	50	—[1]
7703	Beechnut Boxcar, *76-77*	19	28	—[1]
7704	Toy Fair Boxcar, *76 u*	115	125	—[1]
7705	Canadian Toy Fair Boxcar, *76 u*	130	145	—[1]
7706	Sir Walter Raleigh Boxcar, *77-78*	38	50	—[1]
7707	White Owl Boxcar, *77-78*	38	50	—[1]
7708	Winston Boxcar, *77-78*	41	55	—[1]
7709	Salem Boxcar, *78*	37	50	—[1]
7710	Mail Pouch Boxcar, *78*	46	60	—[1]
7711	El Producto Boxcar, *78*	46	60	—[1]
7712	Santa Fe Boxcar (FARR #1), *79*	25	29	—[1]
[7780]	TCA Museum Boxcar, *80 u*	—	26	—[1]
[7781]	TCA Hafner Boxcar, *81 u*	—	26	—[1]
[7782]	TCA Carlisle & Finch Boxcar, *82 u*	—	26	—[1]
[7783]	TCA Ives Boxcar, *83 u*	—	26	—[1]
[7784]	TCA Voltamp Boxcar, *84 u*	—	23	—[1]
[7785]	TCA Hoge Boxcar, *85 u*	—	23	—[1]
7800	Pepsi Boxcar, *76 u, 77*	50	55	—[1]
7801	A&W Boxcar, *76 u, 77*	36	50	—[1]
7802	Canada Dry Boxcar, *76 u, 77*	36	50	—[1]
7803	Trains n' Truckin' Boxcar, *77 u*	22	29	—[1]
7805	(See 16078)			
7806	Season's Greetings Boxcar, *76 u*	70	95	—[1]

		Exc	New	Cond/$
7807	Toy Fair Boxcar, *77 u*	70	95	—1
7808	Northern Pacific Stock Car, *77*	43	50	—1
7809	Vernors Boxcar, *77 u, 78*	40	55	—1
7810	Orange Crush Boxcar, *77 u, 78*	40	55	—1
7811	Dr Pepper Boxcar, *77 u, 78*	40	55	—1
7812	TCA Houston Stock Car, *77 u*	15	24	—1
7813	Season's Greetings Boxcar, *77 u*	65	90	—1
7814	Season's Greetings Boxcar, *78 u*	70	95	—1
7815	Toy Fair Boxcar, *78 u*	65	85	—1
7816	Toy Fair Boxcar, *79 u*	70	95	—1
7817	Toy Fair Boxcar, *80 u*	105	120	—1
7890	(See 17303)			
7900	D&RGW Operating Cowboy Car (O27), *82-83*	22	26	—1
7901	Lionel Lines Cop and Hobo Car (O27), *82-83*	27	31	—1
7902	Santa Fe Boxcar (O27), *82-85*	5	9	—1
7903	Rock Island Boxcar (O27), *83*	7	11	—1
7904	San Diego Zoo Giraffe Car (O27), *83-84*	44	55	—1
(7905)	Black Cave Boxcar (O27), *82*	6	9	—1
7908	Tappan Boxcar (O27), *82 u*	39	55	—1
7909	L&N Boxcar (O27), *83-84*	40	49	—1
7910	Chessie System Boxcar (O27), *84-85*	20	25	—1
7912	Toys "R" Us Giraffe Car (O27), *82-84 u*	70	80	—1
7913	Turtleback Zoo Giraffe Car (O27), *85-86*	39	45	—1
7914	Toys "R" Us Giraffe Car (O27), *85-89 u*	70	90	—1
7920	Sears Centennial Boxcar (O27), *85-86 u*	39	44	—1
7925	Erie-Lackawanna Boxcar (O27), *86-90*	10	18	—1
7926	NKP Boxcar (O27), *86-91*	8	10	—1
7930	True Value Boxcar (O27), *86-87 u*	34	50	—1
7931	Town House TV and Appliances Boxcar (O27), *86 u*	31	39	—1
7932	Kay Bee Toys Boxcar (O27), *86-87 u*	40	49	—1
8001	NKP 2-6-4, *80 u*	55	65	—1
8002	Union Pacific 2-8-4 (FARR #2), *80*	360	450	—3
8003	Chessie System 2-8-4, *80*	340	440	—3
8004	Rock Island 4-4-0, *80-82*	165	190	—2
8004	(See 18004)			
8005	Santa Fe 4-4-0, *80-82*	65	75	—1
8006	ACL 4-6-4, *80 u*	375	450	—1
8007	NYNH&H 2-6-4, *80-81*	65	75	—1
8008	Chessie System 4-4-2, *80*	65	75	—1
8010	Santa Fe NW-2, *70, 71 u*	—	65	—1
8014	(See 18014)			
8020	Santa Fe Alco A Unit, *70-72, 74-76*	65	85	—1
8020	Santa Fe Alco A Unit Dummy, *70*	45	60	—1
8021	Santa Fe Alco B Unit, *71-72, 74-76*	45	65	—1
8022	Santa Fe Alco A Unit, *71 u*	80	105	—1

		Exc	New	Cond/$
8025	CN Alco A Unit, *71-73 u*	85	105	—1
8025	CN Alco A Unit Dummy, *71-73 u*	45	65	—1
8030	Illinois Central GP-9, *70-72*	90	95	—2
8031	Canadian National GP-7, *71-73 u*	85	155	—1
8031	Illinois Central GP-9 Dummy, *70*		NM	—1
8040	NKP 2-4-2, *70-72*	26	34	—1
8040	Canadian National 2-4-2, *71 u*	43	85	—1
8041	NYC 2-4-2, *70*	55	65	—1
8041	PRR 2-4-2, *71 u*	55	65	—1
8042	GTW 2-4-2, *70, 71-73 u*	26	34	—1
8043	NKP 2-4-2, *70 u*	45	65	—1
8050	D&H U36C, *80*	105	220	—1
8051	D&H U36C Dummy, *80*	95	115	—1
[8051]	NETCA Hood's Milk Boxcar, *86 u*	44	65	—1
8054/8055	Burlington F-3 AA set, *80*	360	385	—1
8056	C&NW FM Trainmaster, *80*	220	275	—3
8057	Burlington NW-2, *80*	115	140	—1
8059	Pennsylvania F-3 B Unit, *80 u*	260	375	—1
8060	Pennsylvania F-3 B Unit, *80 u*	335	420	—1
8061	Chessie System U36C, *80*	130	165	—1
8062	Great Northern 4-6-4, *70*		NM	—1
8062	Burlington F-3 B Unit, *80 u*	205	270	—1
8063	Seaboard SD-9, *80*	95	120	—1
8064	Florida East Coast GP-9, *80*	145	195	—1
8065	Florida East Coast GP-9 Dummy, *80*	95	120	—1
8066	TP&W GP-20, *80-81, 83 u*	70	90	—1
8067	Texas & Pacific Alco A Unit, *80*		NM	—1
(8068)	LCCA Rock Island GP-20 "1980," *80 u*	80	105	—1
8071	Virginian SD-18, *80 u*	150	180	—1
8072	Virginian SD-18 Dummy, *80 u*	75	110	—1
(8100)	Norfolk & Western 4-8-4 "611," *81*	400	450	—3
8100	(See 11711)			
(8101)	Chicago & Alton 4-6-4 "659," *81*	320	390	—2
8101	(See 11711)			
(8102)	Union Pacific 4-4-2, *81-82*	49	65	—1
8102	(See 11711)			
[8103]	LCAC Toronto, Hamilton & Buffalo Boxcar, *81 u*	NRS	150	—1
8103	(See 18103)			
(8104)	Union Pacific 4-4-0 "3," *81 u*	190	250	—1
8111	DT&I NW-2, *71-74*	50	65	—1
8119	(See 18119/18120)			
8120	(See 18119/18120)			
8124	(See 51300)			
8140	Southern 2-4-0, *71 u*	22	30	—1
8141	PRR 2-4-2, *71-72*	36	43	—1

		Exc	New	Cond/$
8142	C&O 4-4-2, *71-72*	—	55	—1
(8150)	PRR GG-1 "4935," *81*	355	420	—1
8151	Burlington SD-28, *81*	125	150	—1
8152	Canadian Pacific SD-24, *81*	155	165	—1
8153	Reading NW-2, *81-82*	120	140	—1
8154	Alaska NW-2, *81-82*	110	150	—1
8155	Monon U36B, *81-82*	110	135	—1
8156	Monon U36B Dummy, *81-82*	—	65	—1
8157	Santa Fe FM Trainmaster, *81*	270	290	—3
8158	DM&IR GP-35, *81-82*	80	135	—1
8159	DM&IR GP-35 Dummy, *81-82*	65	85	—1
8160	Burger King GP-20, *81-82*	105	135	—1
8161	L.A.S.E.R. Diesel Switcher, *81-82*	23	55	—1
8162	Ontario Northland SD-18, *81 u*	135	175	—1
8163	Ontario Northland SD-18 Dummy, *81 u*	90	120	—1
8164	Pennsylvania F-3 B Unit, *81 u*	360	510	—1
8182	Nibco Express NW-2, *82 u*	90	130	—1
(8190)	Diesel Horn kit, *81 u*	—	31	—1
8200	"Kickapoo" Dockside 0-4-0T, *72*	30	39	—1
8200	(See 18200)			
8201	(See 18201)			
8203	PRR 2-4-2, *72, 74 u, 75*	26	34	—1
8203	(See 18203)			
8204	C&O 4-4-2, *72*	55	60	—1
[8204]	LCAC Algoma Central Boxcar, *82 u*	—	150	—1
8204	(See 18204)			
8206	NYC 4-6-4, *72-75*	140	155	—1
8206	(See 18206)			
8209	"Pioneer" Dockside 0-4-0T w/ tender, *72*	45	65	—1
8209	"Pioneer" Dockside 0-4-0T w/o tender, *73-76*	42	55	—1
8209	(See 18209)			
8210	Joshua L. Cowen 4-6-4, *82*	340	380	—2
8212	Black Cave 0-4-0, *82*	30	49	—1
8212	(See 18212)			
8213	D&RGW 2-4-2, *82-83, 84-91 u*	55	60	—1
8214	Pennsylvania 2-4-2, *82-83*	55	65	—1
(8215)	Nickel Plate Road 2-8-4 "779," *82 u*	315	370	—2
8223	(See 18835)			
8250	Santa Fe GP-9, *72, 74-75*	95	110	—
(8251-50)	Horn/Whistle Controller, *72-74*	1.50	2.50	—
8252	D&H Alco A Unit, *72*	75	110	—
8253	D&H Alco B Unit, *72*	50	70	—
8254	Illinois Central GP-9 Dummy, *72*	65	75	—
8255	Santa Fe GP-9 Dummy, *72*	65	75	—
8258	Canadian National GP-7 Dummy, *72-73 u*	65	85	—
8260/8262	Southern Pacific F-3 AA set, *82*	490	520	—

		Exc	New	Cond/$
8261	Southern Pacific F-3 B Unit, *82 u*	570	680	—1
8263	Santa Fe GP-7, *82*	65	80	—1
8264	CP Vulcan Switcher w/ snowplow, *82*	115	135	—2
8265	Santa Fe SD-40, *82*	225	245	—2
8266	Norfolk & Western SD-24, *82*	150	225	—1
8268	Quicksilver Alco A Unit, *82-83*	95	120	—1
8269	Quicksilver Alco A Unit Dummy, *82-83*	55	65	—1
8272	Pennsylvania EP-5, *82 u*	225	290	—1
8300	Santa Fe 2-4-0, *73-74*	19	21	—1
8300	(See 18300)			
8301	(See 18301)			
\8302	Southern 2-4-0, *73-76*	29	30	—1
8302	(See 18302)			
8303	Jersey Central 2-4-2, *73-74*	47	49	—1
8303	(See 18303)			
8304	Rock Island 4-4-2, *73-75*	85	105	—1
8304	Pennsylvania 4-4-2, *74-75*	75	105	—1
8304	B&O 4-4-2, *75*	75	105	—1
8304	C&O 4-4-2, *75-77*	75	105	—1
8305	Milwaukee Road 4-4-2, *73*	95	120	—1
(8307)	Southern Pacific 4-8-4 "4449," *83*	700	830	—3
8308	Jersey Central 2-4-2, *73-74 u*	36	43	—1
(8309)	Southern 2-8-2 "4501" (FARR #4), *83*	415	530	—1
8310	Nickel Plate Road 2-4-0, *73 u*	26	50	—1
8310	Santa Fe 2-4-0, *74-75 u*	26	34	—1
8310	Jersey Central 2-4-0, *74-75 u*	26	50	—1
8311	Southern 0-4-0, *73 u*	26	34	—1
8311	(See 18311)			
8313	Santa Fe 0-4-0, *83-84*	13	17	—1
8314	Southern 2-4-0, *83-85*	17	21	—1
8315	B&O 4-4-0, *83-84*	85	120	—1
8341	ACL SP-type Caboose, *86 u, 87-90*	6	8	—1
8350	U.S. Steel Diesel Switcher, *73-75*	18	26	—1
8351	Santa Fe Alco A Unit, *73-75*	55	60	—1
8352	Santa Fe GP-20, *73-75*	60	95	—1
8353	Grand Trunk GP-7, *73-75*	70	105	—1
8354	Erie NW-2, *73, 75*	90	105	—1
8355	Santa Fe GP-20 Dummy, *73-74*	75	105	—1
8356	Grand Trunk GP-7 Dummy, *73-75*	65	75	—1
8357	PRR GP-9, *73-75*	110	125	—1
8358	PRR GP-9 Dummy, *73-75*	55	100	—1
(8359)	Chessie System GP-7 "GM50," *73*	—	105	—2
8360	Long Island GP-20, *73-74*	70	105	—1
8361	Western Pacific Alco A Unit, *73-75*	55	75	—1
8362	Western Pacific Alco B Unit, *73-75*	45	65	—1
8363	B&O F-3 A Unit, *73-75*	285	290	—1

		Exc	New	Cond/$
8364	B&O F-3 A Unit Dummy, *73-75*	125	160	___1
8365/8366	CP F-3 AA set (SSS), *73*	385	435	___1
8367	Long Island GP-20 Dummy, *73-75*	80	100	___1
8368	Alaska Vulcan Switcher, *83*	95	125	___2
8369	Erie-Lackawanna GP-20, *83-85*	125	140	___1
8370/8372	NYC F-3 AA set, *83*	330	435	___1
8371	NYC F-3 B Unit, *83*	105	150	___1
8374	Burlington Northern NW-2, *83-85*	105	110	___1
8375	C&NW GP-7, *83-85*	135	165	___1
8376	Union Pacific SD-40, *83*	180	205	___1
8377	U.S. Diesel Switcher, *83-84*	55	65	___1
(8378)	Wabash FM Trainmaster "550," *83 u*	810	940	___1
8379	PRR Fire Car, *83 u*	105	120	___2
8380	Lionel Lines SD-28, *83 u*	165	210	___2
[8389]	NLOE Long Island Boxcar, *89 u*	70	100	___1
[8390]	NLOE Long Island Covered Quad Hopper, *90 u*	70	100	___1
[8391A]	NLOE Long Island Bunk Car, *91 u*	70	90	___1
[8391B]	NLOE Long Island Tool Car, *91 u*	70	90	___1
8392	NLOE Long Island 1-D Tank Car, *92 u*	70	90	___1
8393	(See 52019, 52020)			
8394	(See 52026)			
8395	(See 52061)			
8396	(See 52076)			
8400	(See 18400)			
8402	Reading 4-4-2, *84-85*	47	55	___1
8403	Chessie System 4-4-2, *84-85*	55	65	___1
(8404)	PRR 6-8-6 "6200" (FARR #5), *84-85*	320	405	___3
8404	(See 18404)			
(8406)	NYC 4-6-4 "783," *84*	520	600	___3
8410	Redwood Valley Express 4-4-0, *84-85*	34	50	___1
8419	(See 18419)	—	125	___1
8446	(See 18832)			
8452	Erie Alco A Unit, *74-75*	75	95	___1
8453	Erie Alco B Unit, *74-75*	55	75	___
8454	D&RGW GP-7, *74-75*	80	110	___
8455	D&RGW GP-7 Dummy, *74-75*	50	85	___
8458	Erie-Lackawanna SD-40, *84*	270	290	___2
8459	D&RGW Vulcan Rotary Snowplow, *84*	155	180	___3
8459	(See 18202)			
8460	MKT NW-2, *74-75*	45	65	___
8463	Chessie System GP-20, *74 u*	110	125	___
8464/8465	D&RGW F-3 AA set (SSS), *74*	235	320	___
8466	Amtrak F-3 A Unit, *74-76*	200	245	___
8467	Amtrak F-3 A Unit Dummy, *74-76*	95	105	___
8468	B&O F-3 B Unit, *74-75*	110	120	___
8469	CP F-3 B Unit (SSS), *74*	105	140	___

		Exc	New	Cond/$
8470	Chessie System U36B, *74*	95	130	—1
8471	Pennsylvania NW-2, *74-76*	165	180	—1
8473	Coca-Cola NW-2, *74 u, 75*	95	120	—1
8474	D&RGW F-3 B Unit (SSS), *74*	100	130	—1
8475	Amtrak F-3 B Unit, *74*	95	120	—1
(8476)	TCA 4-6-4 "5484," *85 u*	320	325	—1
8477	NYC GP-9, *84 u*	190	245	—3
8480/8482	Union Pacific F-3 AA set, *84*	280	365	—1
8481	Union Pacific F-3 B Unit, *84*	180	185	—1
8485	U.S. Marines NW-2, *84-85*	120	155	—1
8490	(See 8690)			
8500	Pennsylvania 2-4-0, *75-76*	17	21	—1
8500	(See 18500, 18550)			
8501	(See 18219, 18501)			
8502	Santa Fe 2-4-0, *75*	17	21	—1
8502	(See 18220)			
8503	(See 18503)			
8506	PRR 0-4-0, *75-77*	105	115	—1
8507	Santa Fe 2-4-0, *75 u*	22	26	—1
[8507]/[8508]	LCAC CN F-3 AA set, shells only, *85 u*		400	—1
8512	Santa Fe 0-4-0T, *85-86*	22	30	—1
8516	NYC 0-4-0, *85-86*	105	115	—1
8550	Jersey Central GP-9, *75-76*	105	135	—1
8551	Pennsylvania EP-5, *75-76*	150	155	—2
8552/8553/8554	Southern Pacific Alco ABA set, *75-76*	200	245	—1
8555/8557	Milwaukee Road F-3 AA set (SSS), *75*	250	335	—1
8556	Chessie System NW-2, *75-76*	155	190	—2
8558	Milwaukee Road EP-5, *76-77*	160	195	—1
(8559)	N&W GP-9 "1776," *75*	115	145	—1
8560	Chessie System U36B Dummy, *75*	65	100	—1
8561	Jersey Central GP-9 Dummy, *75-76*	70	95	—1
8562	Missouri Pacific GP-20, *75-76*	—	130	—1
8563	Rock Island Alco A Unit, *75-76 u*	70	95	—1
8564	Union Pacific U36B, *75*	105	145	—1
8565	Missouri Pacific GP-20 Dummy, *75-76*	55	70	—1
8566	Southern F-3 A Unit, *75-77*	250	340	—1
8567	Southern F-3 A Unit Dummy, *75-77*	115	155	—1
8568	Preamble Express F-3 A Unit, *75 u*	80	105	—1
8569	Soo Line NW-2, *75-77*	60	65	—1
8570	Liberty Special Alco A Unit, *75 u*	75	90	—1
8571	Frisco U36B, *75-76*	75	95	—1
8572	Frisco U36B Dummy, *75-76*	—	55	—1
8573	Union Pacific U36B Dummy, *75 u*	140	165	—1
8575	Milwaukee Road F-3 B Unit (SSS), *75*	95	150	—1
8576	Penn Central GP-7, *75 u, 76-77*	90	105	—1
8578	NYC Ballast Tamper, *85, 87*	115	125	—1

		Exc	New	Cond/$
8580/8582	Illinois Central F-3 AA set, *85, 87*	380	425	—1
8581	Illinois Central F-3 B Unit, *85, 87*	135	160	—1
8585	Burlington Northern SD-40, *85*	340	365	—1
8586	(See 18208)			
(8587)	Wabash GP-9 "484," *85 u*	240	270	—1
8600	NYC 4-6-4, *76*	175	195	—1
8600	(See 18600)			
8601	Rock Island 0-4-0, *76-77*	17	21	—1
8601	(See 18601)			
8602	D&RGW 2-4-0, *76-78*	22	26	—1
8602	(See 18602)			
8603	C&O 4-6-4, *76-77*	135	190	—1
8604	Jersey Central 2-4-2, *76 u*	39	44	—1
8604	(See 18604)			
(8606)	B&A 4-6-4 "784," *86 u*	800	900	—5
8606	(See 18606)			
8607	(See 18607)			
8608	(See 18608)			
8609	(See 18609)			
8610	(See 18610)			
(8610)	Wabash 4-6-2 "672" (FF #1), *86-87*	485	620	—1
8611	(See 18611)			
8612	(See 18612)			
8613	(See 18613)			
(8615)	L&N 2-8-4 "1970," *86 u*	630	740	—1
8615	(See 18615)			
8616	Santa Fe 4-4-2, *86*	60	65	—1
8616	(See 18616)			
8617	Nickel Plate Road 4-4-2, *86-91*	60	65	—1
8618	(See 18618)			
8620	(See 18620)			
8621	(See 18621)			
8622	(See 18622)			
8623	(See 18623)			
8625	(See 18625, 18635)			
8625	Pennsylvania 2-4-0, *86-90*	21	34	—1
8626	(See 18626)			
8627	(See 18627)			
8628	(See 18628)			
(8630)	W&ARR 4-4-0 "3," *86 u*	110	130	—1
8632	(See 18632)			
8633	(See 18627, 18633, 18637)			
8635	Santa Fe 0-4-0 (SSS), *86*	85	100	—1
8640	(See 18640)			
8641	(See 18641)			
8642	(See 18642)			

		Exc	New	Cond/$
8650	Burlington Northern U36B, *76-77*	110	150	—1
8651	Burlington Northern U36B Dummy, *76-77*	75	95	—1
8652	Santa Fe F-3 A Unit, *76-77*	295	380	—1
8653	Santa Fe F-3 A Unit Dummy, *76-77*	150	170	—1
8654	Boston & Maine GP-9, *76-77*	125	160	—1
8655	Boston & Maine GP-9 Dummy, *76-77*	90	110	—1
8656	Canadian National Alco A Unit, *76*	150	195	—1
8657	Canadian National Alco B Unit, *76*	60	75	—1
8658	Canadian National Alco A Unit Dummy, *76*	85	170	—1
8659	Virginian Rectifier, *76-77*	135	165	—2
8660	CP Rail NW-2, *76-77*	100	135	—1
8661	Southern F-3 B Unit, *76*	130	135	—1
8662	B&O GP-7, *86*	120	130	—1
8664	Amtrak Alco A Unit, *76-77*	85	120	—1
8665	BAR "Jeremiah O'Brien" GP-9 "1776," *76 u*	70	115	—1
8666	Northern Pacific GP-9 (SSS), *76*	125	175	—1
8667	Amtrak Alco B Unit, *76-77*	60	80	—1
8668	Northern Pacific GP-9 Dummy (SSS), *76*	100	130	—1
8669	Illinois Central Gulf U36B, *76-77*	90	110	—1
8670	Chessie System Diesel Switcher, *76*	30	55	—1
8679	Northern Pacific GP-20, *86*	100	120	—1
8687	Jersey Central FM Trainmaster, *86*	280	340	—2
8688	(See 18213)			
8689	(See 18207)			
8690	Lionel Lines Trolley, *86*	105	115	—1
8699	(See 18307)			
8700	(See 18700)			
(8701)	W&ARR 4-4-0 "3," *77-79*	220	235	—1
8702	Southern 4-6-4, *77-78*	—	315	—2
8702	(See 18702)			
8703	Wabash 2-4-2, *77*	22	30	—1
8704	(See 18704)			
8705	(See 18705)			
8706	(See 18706)			
8707	(See 18707)			
8716	(See 18716)			
8750	Rock Island GP-7, *77-78*	110	125	—1
8751	Rock Island GP-7 Dummy, *77-78*	45	70	—1
8753	Pennsylvania GG-1, *77 u*	380	415	—2
8754	New Haven Rectifier, *77-78*	135	160	—1
8755	Santa Fe U36B, *77-78*	130	150	—1
8756	Santa Fe U36B Dummy, *77-78*	75	95	—1
8757	Conrail GP-9, *76 u, 77-78*	95	140	—1
8758	Southern GP-7 Dummy, *77 u, 78*	75	95	—1
8759	Erie-Lackawanna GP-9, *77-79*	110	155	—1
8760	Erie-Lackawanna GP-9 Dummy, *77-79*	95	115	—1

		Exc	New	Cond/$
8761	GTW NW-2, *77-78*	95	130	__1
8762	Great Northern EP-5, *77-78*	180	190	__1
8763	Norfolk & Western GP-9, *76 u, 77-78*	95	120	__1
8764	B&O Budd RDC Passenger (SSS), *77*	115	140	__1
8765	B&O Budd RDC Baggage Dummy (SSS), *77*	60	80	__1
8766	B&O Budd RDC Baggage (SSS), *77*	—	265	__1
8767	B&O Budd RDC Passenger Dummy (SSS), *77*	85	105	__1
8768	B&O Budd RDC Passenger Dummy (SSS), *77*	85	105	__1
8769	Republic Steel Diesel Switcher, *77-78*	22	39	__1
8770	EMD NW-2, *77-78*	—	65	__1
8771	Great Northern U36B, *77*	100	125	__1
8772	GM&O GP-20, *77*	85	95	__1
8773	Mickey Mouse U36B, *77-78*	385	530	__2
8774	Southern GP-7, *77 u, 78*	110	135	__1
8775	Lehigh Valley GP-9, *77 u, 78*	85	105	__1
8776	C&NW GP-20, *77 u, 78*	105	135	__1
8777	Santa Fe F-3 B Unit (SSS), *77*	135	145	__1
8778	Lehigh Valley GP-9 Dummy, *77 u, 78*	80	95	__1
8779	C&NW GP-20 Dummy, *77 u, 78*	110	135	__1
8800	Lionel Lines 4-4-2, *78-81*	75	105	__1
8800	(See 18800)			
8801	Blue Comet 4-6-4, *78-80*	385	510	__2
8801	(See 18801)			
8802	(See 18802)			
8803	Santa Fe 0-4-0, *78*	14	24	__1
8803	(See 18803)			
8804	(See 18804)			
8805	(See 18805, 18890)			
8806	(See 18806)			
8807	(See 18807)			
8808	(See 18808)			
8809	(See 18551)			
8810	(See 18810)			
8811	(See 18811)			
8813	(See 18552)			
8814	(See 18814)			
8820	(See 18820)			
8827	(See 18827)			
8834	(See 18834)			
8837	(See 18837)			
8850	Penn Central GG-1, *78 u, 79*	330	400	__2
8851/8852	New Haven F-3 AA set, *78 u, 79*	280	375	__1
8854	CP Rail GP-9, *78-79*	100	120	__1
8855	Milwaukee Road SD-18, *78*	—	120	__1
8857	Northern Pacific U36B, *78-80*	105	135	__1
8858	Northern Pacific U36B Dummy, *78-80*	55	85	__1

		Exc	New	Cond/$
8859	Conrail Rectifier, *78-82*	120	175	—[1]
8860	Rock Island NW-2, *78-79*	85	105	—[1]
8861	Santa Fe Alco A Unit, *78-79*	65	85	—[1]
8862	Santa Fe Alco B Unit, *78-79*	36	43	—[1]
8864	New Haven F-3 B Unit, *78*	85	105	—[1]
8866	M&St L GP-9 (SSS), *78*	90	125	—[1]
8867	M&St L GP-9 Dummy (SSS), *78*	65	95	—[1]
8868	Amtrak Budd RDC Baggage, *78, 80*	135	175	—[1]
8869	Amtrak Budd RDC Passenger Dummy, *78, 80*	75	95	—[1]
8870	Amtrak Budd RDC Passenger Dummy, *78, 80*	75	100	—[1]
8871	Amtrak Budd RDC Baggage Dummy, *78, 80*	75	95	—[1]
8872	Santa Fe SD-18, *78 u, 79*	110	155	—[1]
8873	Santa Fe SD-18 Dummy, *78 u, 79*	65	95	—[1]
8900	Santa Fe 4-6-4 (FARR #1), *79*	310	335	—[2]
8900	(See 18900)			
8901	(See 18901/18902)			
8902	(See 18901/18902)			
8902	ACL 2-4-0, *79-82, 86 u, 87-90*	13	17	—[1]
8903	D&RGW 2-4-2, *79-81*	17	21	—[1]
8903	(See 18903/18904)			
8904	Wabash 2-4-2, *79, 81 u*	30	34	—[1]
8904	(See 18903/18904)			
8905	"Smokey Mountain" Dockside 0-4-0T, *79*	9	17	—[1]
8906	(See 18906)			
8908	(See 18908/18909)			
8909	(See 18908/18909)			
8910	(See 18910)			
8911	(See 18911)			
8912	(See 18912)			
[8912]	LCAC Canada Southern Operating Hopper, *89 u*	—	95	—[1]
8913	(See 18913)			
8915	(See 18915)			
8916	(See 18916)			
8918	(See 18918)			
8919	(See 18919)			
8922	(See 18922)			
8923	(See 18923)			
8924	(See 18924)			
8925	(See 18925)			
8926	(See 18926)			
8932	(See 18932)			
8933	(See 18933)			
8936	(See 18936)			
8937	(See 18937)			
8950	Virginian FM Trainmaster, *79*	265	300	—[3]
8951	Southern Pacific FM Trainmaster, *79*	320	370	—[3]

		Exc	New	Cond/$
8952/8953	PRR F-3 AA set, *79*	—	520	—[1]
8955	Southern U36B, *79*	120	195	—[1]
8956	Southern U36B Dummy, *79*	75	120	—[1]
8957	Burlington Northern GP-20, *79*	120	150	—[1]
[8957]	Detroit-Toledo TCA Burlington Northern GP-20, *80 u*		200	—[1]
8958	Burlington Northern GP-20 Dummy, *79*	95	105	—[1]
[8958]	Detroit-Toledo TCA Burlington Northern GP-20 Dummy, *80 u*		150	—[1]
8960	Southern Pacific U36C, *79 u*	95	125	—[1]
8961	Southern Pacific U36C Dummy, *79 u*	65	75	—[1]
8962	Reading U36B, *79*	110	120	—[1]
8970/8971	PRR F-3 AA set, *79 u, 80*	405	495	—[1]
8977	(See 18000)			
8999	Lone Star Aquarium Car, *99*		NRS	—[1]
9001	Conrail Boxcar (O27), *86-87 u, 88-90*	5	10	—[1]
9010	GN Hopper (O27), *70-71*	6	8	—[1]
9011	GN Hopper (O27), *70 u, 75-76, 78-83*	6	9	—[1]
9011	(See 19011)			
9012	TA&G Hopper (O27), *71-72*	7	8	—[1]
9013	Canadian National Hopper (O27), *72-76*	4	8	—[1]
9014	Trailer Train Flatcar (O27), *78-79*		NM	—[1]
9015	Reading Hopper (O27), *73-75*	17	21	—[1]
9015	(See 19015)			
9016	Chessie System Hopper (O27), *75-79, 87-88, 89 u*	4	6	—[1]
[9016]	LCCA Chessie System Hopper (O27), *79-80 u*	16	20	—[1]
9016	(See 19016)			
9017	Wabash Gondola w/ canisters (O27), *78-82*	3	5	—[1]
9017	(See 19017)			
9018	DT&I Hopper (O27), *78-79, 81-82*	4	7	—[1]
9018	(See 19018)			
(9019)	Unlettered Flatcar (O27), *78*	2.50	3	—[1]
9019	(See 19019)			
9020	Union Pacific Flatcar (O27), *70-78*	3	5	—[1]
9021	Santa Fe Work Caboose, *70-71, 73-75*	9	13	—[1]
9022	Santa Fe Bulkhead Flatcar (O27), *70-72, 75-79*	7	13	—[1]
9023	MKT Bulkhead Flatcar (O27), *73-74*	7	10	—[1]
9023	(See 19023)			
9024	C&O Flatcar (O27), *73-75*	3	6	—[1]
9024	(See 19024)			
9025	DT&I Work Caboose, *71-74, 77-78*	7	9	—[1]
9025	(See 19025)			
9026	Republic Steel Flatcar (O27), *75-82*	5	7	—[1]
9026	(See 19026)			
9027	Soo Line Work Caboose, *75-76*	7	9	—[1]

		Exc	New	Cond/$
9027	(See 19027)			
(9030)	"Kickapoo" Gondola (O27), *72, 79*	5	9	—[1]
9031	(See 19031)			
9031	NKP Gondola w/ canisters (O27), *73-75, 82-83, 84-91 u*	4	7	—[1]
9032	Southern Pacific Gondola w/ canisters (O27), *75-78*	—	3	—[1]
9032	(See 19032)			
9033	(See 19033)			
9033	PC Gondola w/ canisters (O27), *76-78, 82, 86 u, 87-90, 92 u*	—	3	—[1]
9034	Lionel Leisure Hopper (O27), *77 u*	27	34	—[1]
9035	Conrail Boxcar (O27), *78-82*	5	9	—[1]
9036	Mobilgas 1-D Tank Car (O27), *78-82*	7	13	—[1]
[9036]	LCCA Mobilgas 1-D Tank Car (O27), *78-79 u*	20	22	—[1]
9037	Conrail Boxcar (O27), *78 u, 80*	6	9	—[1]
9038	Chessie System Hopper (O27), *78 u, 80*	15	19	—[1]
9039	Mobilgas 1-D Tank Car (O27), *78 u, 80*	10	15	—[1]
9040	General Mills Wheaties Boxcar (O27), *70-72*	9	13	—[1]
9041	Hershey's Boxcar (O27), *70-71, 73-76*	15	25	—[1]
9042	Ford-Autolite Boxcar (O27), *71 u, 72, 74-76*	11	18	—[1]
9043	Erie-Lackawanna Boxcar (O27), *73-75*	13	20	—[1]
9044	D&RGW Boxcar (O27), *75-76*	5	8	—[1]
9045	Toys "R" Us Boxcar (O27), *75 u*	36	43	—[1]
9046	True Value Boxcar (O27), *76 u*	26	34	—[1]
9047	Toys "R" Us Boxcar (O27), *76 u*	40	43	—[1]
9047	(See 19047)			
9048	Toys "R" Us Boxcar (O27), *76 u*	33	41	—[1]
9048	(See 19048)			
(9049)	Toys "R" Us Boxcar (O27), *78 u*		NRS	—[1]
9049	(See 19049)			
9050	Sunoco 1-D Tank Car (O27), *70-71*	17	23	—[1]
9050	(See 19050)			
9051	Firestone 1-D Tank Car (O27), *74-75, 78*	15	19	—[1]
9052	Toys "R" Us Boxcar (O27), *77 u*	26	34	—[1]
9053	True Value Boxcar (O27), *77 u*	28	40	—[1]
9054	JCPenney Boxcar (O27), *77 u*	14	19	—[1]
9055	Republic Steel Gondola w/ canisters, *78 u*	9	10	—[1]
9057	CP Rail SP-type Caboose, *78-79*	10	15	—[1]
9058	Lionel Lines SP-type Caboose, *78-79, 83*	5	7	—[1]
9059	Lionel Lines SP-type Caboose, *79 u, 81 u*	7	9	—[1]
9060	Nickel Plate Road SP-type Caboose, *70-72*	5	7	—[1]
9061	Santa Fe SP-type Caboose, *70-76*	5	8	—[1]
9062	Penn Central SP-type Caboose, *70-72, 74-76*	6	9	—[1]
9063	GTW SP-type Caboose, *70, 71-73 u*	14	19	—[1]
9064	C&O SP-type Caboose, *71-72, 75-77*	7	10	—[1]

		Exc	New	Cond/$
9065	Canadian National SP-type Caboose, *71-73 u*	19	24	—[1]
9066	Southern SP-type Caboose, *73-76*	7	9	—[1]
(9067)	Kickapoo Valley Bobber Caboose, *72*	6	9	—[1]
9068	Reading Bobber Caboose, *73-76*	5	7	—[1]
[9068]	Gateway TCA Reading Bobber Caboose, *76 u*	—	20	—[1]
9069	Jersey Central SP-type Caboose, *73-74, 75-76 u*	5	8	—[1]
9070	Rock Island SP-type Caboose, *73-74*	11	17	—[1]
9071	Santa Fe Bobber Caboose, *74 u, 77-78*	7	9	—[1]
9073	Coca-Cola SP-type Caboose, *74 u, 75*	15	19	—[1]
9075	Rock Island SP-type Caboose, *75-76 u*	13	17	—[1]
9076	"We The People" SP-type Caboose, *75 u*	19	28	—[1]
9077	D&RGW SP-type Caboose, *76-83, 84-91 u*	6	8	—[1]
9078	Rock Island Bobber Caboose, *76-77*	5	7	—[1]
9079	GTW Hopper (O27), *77*	21	30	—[1]
9080	Wabash SP-type Caboose, *77*	9	10	—[1]
9085	Santa Fe Work Caboose, *79-82*	4	5	—[1]
9090	General Mills Mini-Max Car, *71*	24	28	—[1]
9100	(See 18205, 19100)			
9101	(See 19101)			
9102	(See 19102)			
9103	(See 19103)			
9104	(See 19104)			
9105	(See 19105)			
9106	Miller Vat Car, *84-85*	31	46	—[1]
9106	(See 19106)			
9107	Dr Pepper Vat Car, *86-87*	24	33	—[1]
9110	B&O Quad Hopper, *71*	25	30	—[1]
9111	N&W Quad Hopper, *72-75*	17	22	—[1]
9112	D&RGW Covered Quad Hopper, *73-75*	20	24	—[1]
9113	Norfolk & Western Quad Hopper (SSS), *73*	27	32	—[1]
[9113]	Three Rivers TCA N&W Quad Hopper, *76 u*	27	30	—[1]
9114	Morton Salt Covered Quad Hopper, *74-76*	18	26	—[1]
9115	Planter's Covered Quad Hopper, *74-76*	21	27	—[1]
9116	Domino Sugar Covered Quad Hopper, *74-76*	19	25	—[1]
9117	Alaska Covered Quad Hopper (SSS), *74-76*	24	29	—[1]
9118	LCCA Corning Covered Quad Hopper, *74 u*	65	85	—[1]
9119	Detroit & Mackinac Covered Quad Hopper (SSS), *75*	25	30	—[1]
[9119]	Detroit-Toledo TCA Detroit & Mackinac Covered Quad Hopper, *77 u*	20	27	—[1]
[9119]	North Texas TCA Detroit & Mackinac Covered Quad Hopper, *78 u*	22	30	—[1]
9120	Northern Pacific Flatcar w/ trailers, *70-71*	28	33	—[1]
9121	L&N Flatcar w/ bulldozer and scraper, *71-79*	50	65	—[1]
9121	(See 19121)			
9122	Northern Pacific Flatcar w/ trailers, *72-75*	26	33	—[1]

		Exc	New	Cond/$
9123	C&O Auto Carrier (3-tier), *72 u, 73-74*	20	30	—¹
(9123)	TCA Dearborn Auto Carrier "1973" (3-tier), *73 u*	25	33	—¹
9124	P&LE Flatcar w/ log load, *73-74*	18	25	—¹
9125	Norfolk & Western Auto Carrier (2-tier), *73-77*	23	28	—¹
9126	C&O Auto Carrier (3-tier), *73-75*	23	34	—¹
9128	Heinz Vat Car, *74-76*	21	31	—¹
9129	N&W Auto Carrier (3-tier), *75-76*	22	26	—¹
9129	(See 19129)			
9130	B&O Quad Hopper, *70*	19	20	—¹
9131	D&RGW Gondola w/ canisters, *73-77*	5	8	—¹
9132	Libby's Vat Car (SSS), *75-77*	16	23	—¹
9133	Burlington Northern Flatcar w/ trailers, *76-77, 80*	21	29	—¹
9134	Virginian Covered Quad Hopper, *76-77*	—	28	—¹
9135	N&W Covered Quad Hopper, *70 u, 71, 75*	17	22	—¹
9136	Republic Steel Gondola w/ canisters, *72-76, 79*	9	11	—¹
9138	Sunoco 3-D Tank Car (SSS), *78*	35	40	—¹
9139	PC Auto Carrier (3-tier), *76-77*	23	32	—¹
9140	Burlington Gondola w/ canisters, *70, 73-82, 87-89*	7	9	—¹
9141	Burlington Northern Gondola w/ canisters, *70-72*	8	10	—¹
9142	Republic Steel Gondola w/ canisters, *71*	7	9	—¹
[9142]	LCCA Republic Steel Gondola w/ canisters, *77-78 u*	14	19	—¹
9143	Canadian National Gondola w/ canisters, *71-73 u*	30	34	—¹
9144	D&RGW Gondola w/ canisters (SSS), *74-76*	9	13	—¹
9145	ICG Auto Carrier (3-tier), *77-80*	18	25	—¹
9146	Mogen David Vat Car, *77-81*	21	26	—¹
9146	(See 19821)			
9147	Texaco 1-D Tank Car, *77-78*	35	47	—¹
9148	Du Pont 3-D Tank Car, *77-81*	20	24	—¹
9149	CP Rail Flatcar w/ trailers, *77-78*	23	37	—¹
9150	Gulf 1-D Tank Car, *70 u, 71*	19	24	—¹
9151	Shell 1-D Tank Car, *72*	30	34	—¹
9152	Shell 1-D Tank Car, *73-76*	29	35	—¹
9153	Chevron 1-D Tank Car, *74-76*	29	33	—¹
9154	Borden 1-D Tank Car, *75-76*	33	47	—¹
9155	LCCA Monsanto 1-D Tank Car, *75 u*	45	55	—¹
9156	Mobilgas 1-D Tank Car, *76-77*	26	37	—¹
9157	C&O Flatcar w/ crane, *76-78, 81-82*	34	40	—¹
9158	PC Flatcar w/ shovel, *76-77, 80*	32	39	—¹

		Exc	New	Cond/$
9159	Sunoco 1-D Tank Car, *76*	35	50	—1
9160	Illinois Central N5c Caboose, *70-72*	17	27	—1
9161	CN N5c Caboose, *72-74*	18	29	—1
9162	PRR N5c Caboose, *72-76*	28	30	—1
9163	Santa Fe N5c Caboose, *73-76*	17	24	—1
9165	Canadian Pacific N5c Caboose (SSS), *73*	21	30	—1
9166	D&RGW SP-type Caboose (SSS), *74-75*	19	24	—1
9167	Chessie System N5c Caboose, *74-76*	24	31	—1
9168	Union Pacific N5c Caboose, *75-77*	22	25	—1
9169	Milwaukee Road SP-type Caboose (SSS), *75*	23	29	—1
(9170)	N&W N5c Caboose "1776," *75*	27	30	—1
9171	Missouri Pacific SP-type Caboose, *75 u, 76-77*	21	24	—1
9172	Penn Central SP-type Caboose, *75 u, 76-77*	22	30	—1
9173	Jersey Central SP-type Caboose, *75 u, 76-77*	23	35	—1
9174	NYC P&E B/W Caboose, *76*	65	75	—1
9175	Virginian N5c Caboose, *76-77*	26	28	—1
9176	BAR N5c Caboose, *76 u*	18	30	—1
9177	Northern Pacific B/W Caboose (SSS), *76*	30	43	—1
9178	ICG SP-type Caboose, *76-77*	21	27	—1
9179	Chessie System Bobber Caboose, *76*	5	9	—1
9180	Rock Island N5c Caboose, *77-78*	15	30	—1
9181	B&M N5c Caboose, *76 u, 77*	29	38	—1
[9181]	NETCA B&M N5c Caboose, *77 u*	22	34	—1
9182	N&W N5c Caboose, *76 u, 77-80*	24	32	—1
9183	Mickey Mouse N5c Caboose, *77-78*	35	55	—1
9184	Erie B/W Caboose, *77-78*	24	31	—2
[9184]	North Texas TCA Erie B/W Caboose, *77 u*	19	24	—1
[9184]	LCOL Erie B/W Caboose, *82 u*	17	21	—1
9185	GTW N5c Caboose, *77*	21	29	—1
9186	Conrail N5c Caboose, *76 u, 77-78*	27	35	—1
[9186]	Atlantic TCA Conrail N5c Caboose, *79 u*	22	30	—1
9187	GM&O SP-type Caboose, *77*	15	26	—1
9188	GN N5c Caboose, *77*	26	32	—1
9189	Gulf 1-D Tank Car, *77*	43	50	—1
9193	Budweiser Vat Car, *83-84*	90	145	—1
[9193]	Atlantic TCA Budweiser Vat Car, *84 u*	80	110	—1
9200	Illinois Central Boxcar, *70-71*	18	24	—1
9201	Penn Central Boxcar, *70*	16	24	—1
9202	Santa Fe Boxcar, *70*	—	37	—1
9203	Union Pacific Boxcar, *70*	—	27	—1
9204	Northern Pacific Boxcar, *70*	—	26	—1
9205	Norfolk & Western Boxcar, *70*	23	28	—1
9206	Great Northern Boxcar, *70-71*	—	20	—1
9207	Soo Line Boxcar, *71*	17	25	—1

		Exc	New	Cond/$
9208	CP Rail Boxcar, *71*	20	22	—1
9209	Burlington Northern Boxcar, *71-72*	16	21	—1
9210	B&O DD Boxcar, *71*	19	23	—1
9211	Penn Central Boxcar, *71*	19	31	—1
9212	LCCA SCL Flatcar w/ trailers, *76 u*	21	25	—1
9213	M&St L Covered Quad Hopper (SSS), *78*	19	27	—1
9214	Northern Pacific Boxcar, *71-72*	18	24	—1
9215	Norfolk & Western Boxcar, *71*	20	27	—1
9215	(See 52004)			
9216	Great Northern Auto Carrier (3-tier), *78*	26	40	—1
9217	Soo Line Operating Boxcar, *82-84*	24	29	—1
9218	Monon Operating Boxcar, *81*	28	33	—1
9219	Missouri Pacific Operating Boxcar, *83*	23	28	—1
9220	Borden Milk Car, *83-86*	115	150	—1
9221	Poultry Dispatch Operating Chicken Car, *83-85*	43	47	—1
9222	L&N Flatcar w/ trailers, *83-84*	29	44	—1
9223	Reading Operating Boxcar, *84*	28	34	—1
9224	Churchill Downs Operating Horse Car, *84-86*	105	125	—1
9225	Conrail Operating Barrel Car, *84*	55	75	—1
9226	Delaware & Hudson Flatcar w/ trailers, *84-85*	32	44	—1
9228	Canadian Pacific Operating Boxcar, *86*	22	34	—1
9229	Express Mail Operating Boxcar, *85-86*	27	37	—2
9230	Monon Boxcar (SSS), *71, 72 u*	15	21	—1
9231	Reading B/W Caboose, *79*	27	36	—1
9232	Allis-Chalmers Condenser Car, *80-81, 83 u*	46	55	—1
9233	Depressed Flatcar w/ transformer, *80*	65	70	—1
9234	Lionel Radioactive Waste Car, *80*	55	85	—1
9235	Union Pacific Derrick Car, *83-84*	16	22	—1
9236	C&NW Derrick Car, *83-85*	22	30	—1
9237	UPS Operating Boxcar, *84*		NM	—1
9238	Northern Pacific Log Dump Car, *84*	15	22	—1
9239	Lionel Lines N5c Caboose, *83 u*	47	55	—1
9240	NYC Operating Hopper, *86*	32	40	—1
9240	NYC Hopper (O27), *87 u*	17	24	—1
9241	PRR Log Dump Car, *85-86*	17	22	—1
9245	Illinois Central Derrick Car, *85*		NM	—1
9247	(See 6529)			
9250	WaterPoxy 3-D Tank Car, *70-71*	23	28	—1
X9259	LCCA Southern B/W Caboose, *77 u*	36	41	—1
9260	Reynolds Aluminum Covered Quad Hopper, *75-76*	19	23	—1
9261	Sun-maid Raisins Covered Quad Hopper, *75 u, 76*	17	25	—1
9262	Ralston Purina Covered Quad Hopper,			

		Exc	New	Cond/$
	75 u, 76	47	60	—2
9263	PRR Covered Quad Hopper, *75 u, 76-77*	30	41	—1
9264	Illinois Central Covered Quad Hopper, *75 u, 76-77*	34	38	—1
[9264]	Midwest TCA Museum Express Illinois Central Covered Quad Hopper, *78 u*	22	26	—1
9265	Chessie System Covered Quad Hopper, *75 u, 76-77*	24	27	—1
9266	Southern "Big John" Covered Quad Hopper, *76*	49	65	—1
9267	Alcoa Covered Quad Hopper (SSS), *76*	24	32	—1
9268	Northern Pacific B/W Caboose, *77 u*	32	42	—1
9269	Milwaukee Road B/W Caboose, *78*	35	48	—1
9270	Northern Pacific N5c Caboose, *78*	11	21	—1
9271	M&St L B/W Caboose (SSS), *78-79*	19	38	—1
9272	New Haven B/W Caboose, *78-80*	20	34	—1
[9272]	METCA New Haven B/W Caboose, *79 u*	21	25	—1
[9272]	Detroit-Toledo TCA New Haven B/W Caboose, *79 u*	19	22	—1
9273	Southern B/W Caboose, *78 u*	39	50	—1
9274	Santa Fe B/W Caboose, *78 u*	50	55	—1
9276	Peabody Quad Hopper, *78*	24	33	—1
9277	Cities Service 1-D Tank Car, *78*	47	55	—1
9278	Life Savers 1-D Tank Car, *78-79*	100	165	—2
9279	Magnolia 3-D Tank Car, *78, 79 u*	20	26	—1
9280	Santa Fe Operating Stock Car (027), *77-81*	20	24	—1
9281	Santa Fe Auto Carrier (3-tier), *78-80*	23	29	—1
9282	Great Northern Flatcar w/ trailers, *78-79, 81-82*	29	37	—1
9283	Union Pacific Gondola w/ canisters, *77*	15	21	—1
9284	Santa Fe Gondola w/ canisters, *77*	19	27	—1
9285	ICG Flatcar w/ trailers, *77*	43	50	—1
9286	B&LE Covered Quad Hopper, *77*	18	30	—1
9287	Southern N5c Caboose, *77 u, 78*	16	26	—1
[9287]	Southern TCA Southern N5c Caboose, *77 u*	15	21	—1
9288	Lehigh Valley N5c Caboose, *77 u, 78, 80*	35	45	—1
9288	(See 18844)			
9289	C&NW N5c Caboose, *77 u, 78, 80*	27	39	—1
[9289]	Midwest TCA Museum Express C&NW N5c Caboose, *80 u*	36	43	—1
9290	Union Pacific Operating Barrel Car, *83*	75	85	—1
9300	PC Log Dump Car, *70-75, 77*	14	18	—1
9301	U.S. Mail Operating Boxcar, *73-84*	27	35	—1
[9301]	Sacramento-Sierra TCA U.S. Mail Operating Boxcar, *76 u*	26	38	—1
9302	L&N Searchlight Car, *72 u, 73-78*	21	24	—1

		Exc	New	Cond/$
9303	Union Pacific Log Dump Car, *74-78, 80*	13	22	—1
9304	C&O Coal Dump Car, *74-78*	11	22	—1
9305	Santa Fe Operating Cowboy Car (O27), *80-82*	16	23	—1
9306	Santa Fe Flatcar w/ horses, *80-82*	18	26	—1
9307	Erie Animated Gondola, *80-84*	50	65	—1
9308	Aquarium Car, *81-84*	175	185	—2
9309	TP&W B/W Caboose, *80-81, 83 u*	21	29	—1
9310	Santa Fe Log Dump Car, *78 u, 79-83*	13	24	—1
9311	Union Pacific Coal Dump Car, *78 u, 79-82*	13	24	—1
9312	Conrail Searchlight Car, *78 u, 79-83*	15	22	—1
9312	(See 18905)			
9313	Gulf 3-D Tank Car, *79 u*	47	55	—1
9315	Southern Pacific Gondola w/ canisters, *79 u*	22	32	—1
9316	Southern Pacific B/W Caboose, *79 u*	60	70	—2
9317	Santa Fe B/W Caboose, *79*	30	44	—1
9319	TCA Silver Jubilee Mint Car, *79 u*	145	170	—2
9320	Fort Knox Mint Car, *79 u*	175	225	—1
9321	Santa Fe 1-D Tank Car (FARR #1), *79*	28	36	—1
9322	Santa Fe Covered Quad Hopper (FARR #1), *79*	50	60	—1
9323	Santa Fe B/W Caboose (FARR #1), *79*	39	48	—1
9324	Tootsie Roll 1-D Tank Car, *79-81*	55	80	—1
9325	(See 9363, 9364)			
9325	Norfolk & Western Flatcar w/ fences, *79-81 u*	6	10	—1
9326	Burlington Northern B/W Caboose, *79-80*	31	40	—1
[9326]	TTOS Burlington Northern B/W Caboose, *82 u*	—	22	—1
9327	Bakelite 3-D Tank Car, *80*	22	30	—1
9328	Chessie System B/W Caboose, *80*	37	47	—1
9329	Chessie System Crane Car, *80*	55	65	—1
(9330)	"Kickapoo" Dump Car, *72, 79*	3	7	—1
9331	Union 76 1-D Tank Car, *79*	50	60	—1
9332	Reading Crane Car, *79*	48	70	—1
9333	Southern Pacific Flatcar w/ trailers, *79-80*	31	41	—1
9334	Humble 1-D Tank Car, *79*	21	26	—1
9335	B&O Log Dump Car, *86*	16	22	—1
9336	CP Rail Gondola w/ canisters, *79*	24	34	—1
9338	Penn Power Quad Hopper, *79*	70	95	—1
9339	Great Northern Boxcar (O27), *79-83, 85 u, 86*	7	10	—1
9340	Illinois Central Gondola w/ canisters (O27), *79-81, 82 u, 83*	5	9	—1
9341	ACL SP-type Caboose, *79-82, 86 u, 87-90*	6	8	—1
9344	Citgo 3-D Tank Car, *80*	—	42	—1
9345	Reading Searchlight Car, *84-85*	19	25	—1
9346	Wabash SP-type Caboose, *79*	6	10	—1
9347	TTOS Niagara Falls 3-D Tank Car, *79 u*	38	46	—1
9348	Santa Fe Crane Car (FARR #1), *79 u*	60	70	—1

		Exc	New	Cond/$
9349	San Francisco Mint Car, *80*	75	100	—2
9351	PRR Auto Carrier (3-tier), *80*	20	36	—1
9352	Trailer Train Flatcar w/ C&NW trailers, *80*	35	65	—1
9353	Crystal Line 3-D Tank Car, *80*	18	26	—1
9354	Pennzoil 1-D Tank Car, *80, 81 u*	50	65	—1
9355	Delaware & Hudson B/W Caboose, *80*	34	41	—1
[9355]	TTOS D&H B/W Caboose, *82 u*		NRS	—1
9356	Life Savers Stik-O-Pep 1-D Tank Car, *80 u*		NM	—1
9357	Smokey Mountain Bobber Caboose, *79*	8	10	—1
9358	LCCA Sands of Iowa Covered Quad Hopper, *80 u*	22	28	—1
9359	National Basketball Association Boxcar (O27), *79-80 u*	19	24	—1
9360	National Hockey League Boxcar (O27), *79-80 u*	21	26	—1
9361	C&NW B/W Caboose, *80*	55	65	—1
[9361]	TTOS C&NW B/W Caboose, *82 u*	—	50	—1
9362	Major League Baseball Boxcar (O27), *79-80 u*	17	21	—1
(9363)	N&W Flatcar w/ dump bin "9325" (O27), *79*	4	7	—1
(9364)	N&W Flatcar w/ crane "9325" (O27), *79*	7	9	—1
9365	Toys "R" Us Boxcar (O27), *79 u*	30	37	—1
9366	Union Pacific Covered Quad Hopper (FARR #2), *80*	24	27	—1
9367	Union Pacific 1-D Tank Car (FARR #2), *80*	28	40	—1
9368	Union Pacific B/W Caboose (FARR #2), *80*	33	42	—1
9369	Sinclair 1-D Tank Car, *80*	55	75	—1
9370	Seaboard Gondola w/ canisters, *80*	20	25	—1
9371	Atlantic Sugar Covered Quad Hopper, *80*	25	34	—1
9372	Seaboard B/W Caboose, *80*	30	40	—1
9373	Getty 1-D Tank Car, *80-81, 83 u*	36	44	—1
9374	Reading Covered Quad Hopper, *80-81, 83 u*	40	45	—1
9375	Union Pacific Flatcar w/ fences (O27), *80*		NM	—1
9376	Texas & Pacific SP-type Caboose, *80*		NM	—1
9376	Soo Line Boxcar (O27), *81 u*	40	50	—1
9377	Missouri Pacific Boxcar (O27), *80*		NM	—1
9378	Lionel Derrick Car, *80-82*	20	24	—1
9379	Santa Fe Gondola w/ canisters, *80-81, 83 u*	22	30	—1
9380	NYNH&H SP-type Caboose, *80-81*	9	10	—1
9381	Chessie System SP-type Caboose, *80*	7	9	—1
9382	Florida East Coast B/W Caboose, *80*	39	55	—1
[9382]	TTOS Florida East Coast B/W Caboose, *82 u*	—	80	—1
9383	Union Pacific Flatcar w/ trailers (FARR #2), *80 u*	35	42	—1
9384	Great Northern Operating Hopper, *81*	55	65	—1
9385	Alaska Gondola w/ canisters, *81*	33	41	—1
9386	Pure Oil 1-D Tank Car, *81*	55	60	—1

		Exc	New	Cond/$
9387	Burlington B/W Caboose, *81*	42	55	__¹
9388	Toys "R" Us Boxcar (O27), *81 u*	38	45	__¹
9389	Lionel Radioactive Waste Car, *81-82*	60	75	__¹
9398	PRR Coal Dump Car, *83-84*	22	27	__¹
9399	C&NW Coal Dump Car, *83-85*	17	22	__¹
9400	Conrail Boxcar, *78*	16	22	__¹
[9400]	NETCA Conrail Boxcar, *78 u*	23	27	__¹
9401	Great Northern Boxcar, *78*	16	20	__¹
[9401]	Detroit-Toledo TCA GN Boxcar, *78 u*	—	23	__¹
9402	Susquehanna Boxcar, *78*	29	31	__¹
9403	Seaboard Coast Line Boxcar, *78*	16	22	__¹
[9403]	Southern TCA SCL Boxcar, *78 u*	—	18	__¹
9404	NKP Boxcar, *78*	19	22	__¹
9405	Chattahoochee Boxcar, *78*	16	21	__¹
[9405]	Southern TCA Chattahoochee Boxcar, *79 u*	—	21	__¹
9405	(See 19716)			
9406	D&RGW Boxcar, *78-79*	17	21	__¹
9407	Union Pacific Stock Car, *78*	33	36	__¹
9408	Lionel Lines Circus Stock Car (SSS), *78*	28	36	__¹
9411	Lackawanna "Phoebe Snow" Boxcar, *78*	45	55	__¹
9412	RF&P Boxcar, *79*	21	30	__¹
[9412]	WB&A TCA RF&P Boxcar, *79 u*	—	26	__¹
9413	Napierville Junction Boxcar, *79*	14	19	__¹
[9413]	LCAC Napierville Junction Boxcar, *80 u*		NRS	__¹
9414	Cotton Belt Boxcar, *79*	17	21	__¹
[9414]	Sacramento-Sierra TCA Cotton Belt Boxcar, *80 u*	—	35	__¹
[9414]	LOTS Cotton Belt Boxcar, *80 u*	39	55	__¹
9415	Providence & Worcester Boxcar, *79*	15	22	__¹
[9415]	NETCA Providence & Worcester Boxcar, *79 u*	28	34	__¹
9416	MD&W Boxcar, *79, 81*	11	15	__¹
9417	CP Rail Boxcar, *79*	38	50	__¹
9418	FARR Boxcar, *79 u*	42	50	__¹
9419	Union Pacific Boxcar (FARR #2), *80*	23	32	__¹
9420	B&O "Sentinel" Boxcar, *80*	33	39	__¹
9421	Maine Central Boxcar, *80*	12	20	__¹
9422	EJ&E Boxcar, *80*	13	21	__¹
9423	NYNH&H Boxcar, *80*	15	24	__¹
[9423]	NETCA NYNH&H Boxcar, *80 u*	25	30	__¹
9424	TP&W Boxcar, *80*	17	21	__¹
9425	British Columbia DD Boxcar, *80*	23	27	__¹
9426	Chesapeake & Ohio Boxcar, *80*	20	32	__¹
9427	Bay Line Boxcar, *80-81*	14	18	__¹
[9427]	Sacramento-Sierra TCA Bay Line Boxcar, *81 u*	—	30	__¹
9428	TP&W Boxcar, *80-81, 83 u*	—	23	__¹
9429	"The Early Years" Boxcar, *80*	29	40	__¹

		Exc	New	Cond/$
9430	"The Standard Gauge Years" Boxcar, *80*	21	24	__1
9431	"The Prewar Years" Boxcar, *80*	20	25	__1
9432	"The Postwar Years" Boxcar, *80*	65	75	__1
9433	"The Golden Years" Boxcar, *80*	60	75	__1
9434	Joshua Lionel Cowen "The Man" Boxcar, *80 u*	33	42	__1
9435	LCCA Central of Georgia Boxcar, *81 u*	24	30	__1
9436	Burlington Boxcar, *81*	35	43	__1
9437	Northern Pacific Stock Car, *81*	25	40	__1
9438	Ontario Northland Boxcar, *81*	27	38	__1
9439	Ashley Drew & Northern Boxcar, *81*	11	20	__1
9440	Reading Boxcar, *81*	50	65	__1
9441	Pennsylvania Boxcar, *81*	44	60	__1
9442	Canadian Pacific Boxcar, *81*	14	22	__1
9443	Florida East Coast Boxcar, *81*	17	19	__1
[9443]	Southern TCA Florida East Coast Boxcar, *81 u*	—	23	__1
9444	Louisiana Midland Boxcar, *81*	16	21	__1
[9444]	Sacramento-Sierra TCA Louisiana Midland Boxcar, *82 u*	—	35	__1
9445	Vermont Northern Boxcar, *81*	15	19	__1
[9445]	NETCA Vermont Northern Boxcar, *81 u*	29	34	__1
9446	Sabine River & Northern Boxcar, *81*	15	21	__1
9447	Pullman Standard Boxcar, *81*	17	22	__1
9448	Santa Fe Stock Car, *81-82*	34	40	__1
9449	Great Northern Boxcar (FARR #3), *81*	33	39	__1
9450	Great Northern Stock Car (FARR #3), *81 u*	65	70	__1
9451	Southern Boxcar (FARR #4), *83*	33	37	__1
9452	Western Pacific Boxcar, *82-83*	13	18	__1
[9452]	Sacramento-Sierra TCA WP Boxcar, *83 u*	—	35	__1
9453	MPA Boxcar, *82-83*	13	18	__1
9454	New Hope & Ivyland Boxcar, *82-83*	18	25	__1
9455	Milwaukee Road Boxcar, *82-83*	13	17	__1
9456	PRR DD Boxcar (FARR #5), *84-85*	28	35	__1
9460	LCCA D&TS DD Boxcar, *82 u*	26	32	__1
9461	Norfolk & Southern Boxcar, *82*	29	49	__1
9462	Southern Pacific Boxcar, *83-84*	18	23	__1
9463	Texas & Pacific Boxcar, *83-84*	15	19	__1
9464	NC&St L Boxcar, *83-84*	14	19	__1
9465	Santa Fe Boxcar, *83-84*	14	21	__1
9466	Wanamaker Boxcar, *82 u*	60	70	__1
[9466]	Atlantic TCA Wanamaker Boxcar, *83 u*	105	135	__1
9467	Tennessee World's Fair Boxcar, *82 u*	30	37	__1
9468	Union Pacific DD Boxcar, *83*	35	38	__1
9469	NYC "Pacemaker" Boxcar (Std. O), *84-85*	55	65	__2
9470	Chicago Beltline Boxcar, *84*	15	20	__1
9471	Atlantic Coast Line Boxcar, *84*	14	19	__1

		Exc	New	Cond/$
[9471]	Southern TCA Atlantic Coast Line Boxcar, *84 u*	—	23	—1
9472	Detroit & Mackinac Boxcar, *84*	23	27	—1
9473	Lehigh Valley Boxcar, *84*	22	26	—1
9474	Erie-Lackawanna Boxcar, *84*	29	35	—1
9475	D&H "I Love NY" Boxcar, *84 u*	24	35	—1
[9475]	LCOL D&H "I Love New York" Boxcar, *85 u*	—	30	—1
9476	PRR Boxcar (FARR #5), *84-85*	38	41	—1
9480	MN&S Boxcar, *85-86*	17	21	—1
9481	Seaboard System Boxcar, *85-86*	15	18	—1
9482	Norfolk & Southern Boxcar, *85-86*	16	22	—1
[9482]	Southern TCA Norfolk & Southern Boxcar, *85 u*	—	23	—1
9483	Manufacturers Railway Boxcar, *85-86*	17	23	—1
9484	Lionel 85th Anniversary Boxcar, *85*	20	24	—2
9486	GTW "I Love Michigan" Boxcar, *86*	22	33	—1
9486	Artrain GTW "I Love Michigan" Boxcar, *87 u*	—	305	—1
9490	Christmas Boxcar for Lionel Employees, *85 u*	—	1750	—1
9491	Christmas Boxcar, *86 u*	33	47	—1
9492	Lionel Lines Boxcar, *86*	26	32	—1
9500	Milwaukee Road Passenger Car, *73*	34	65	—1
9501	Milwaukee Road Passenger Car, *73 u, 74-76*	30	39	—1
9502	Milwaukee Road Observation Car, *73*	30	48	—1
9503	Milwaukee Road Passenger Car, *73*	30	48	—1
9504	Milwaukee Road Passenger Car, *73 u, 74-76*	30	38	—1
9505	Milwaukee Road Passenger Car, *73 u, 74-76*	30	38	—1
9506	Milwaukee Road Combination Car, *74 u, 75-76*	29	39	—1
9507	PRR Passenger Car, *74-75*	37	55	—1
9508	PRR Passenger Car, *74-75*	34	50	—1
9509	PRR Observation Car, *74-75*	42	60	—1
9510	PRR Combination Car, *74 u, 75-76*	31	42	—1
9511	Milwaukee Road Passenger Car, *74 u*	27	50	—1
9512	TTOS Summerdale Junct Passenger Car, *74 u*	44	55	—1
9513	PRR Passenger Car, *75-76*	27	44	—1
9514	PRR Passenger Car, *75-76*	23	36	—1
9515	PRR Passenger Car, *75-76*	21	34	—1
9516	B&O Passenger Car, *76*	27	42	—1
9517	B&O Passenger Car, *75*	45	65	—1
9517	(See 52005)			
9518	B&O Observation Car, *75*	45	65	—1
9519	B&O Combination Car, *75*	55	85	—1
9520	TTOS Phoenix Combination Car, *75 u*	26	29	—1
9521	PRR Baggage Car, *75 u, 76*	70	85	—1
9522	Milwaukee Road Baggage Car, *75 u, 76*	65	80	—1
9523	B&O Baggage Car, *75 u, 76*	65	70	—1

		Exc	New	Cond/$
9524	B&O Passenger Car, *76*	27	37	—[1]
9525	B&O Passenger Car, *76*	30	43	—[1]
9526	TTOS Snowbird Observation Car, *76 u*	36	42	—[1]
(9527)	Milwaukee Road Campaign Observation Car, *76 u*	45	65	—[1]
(9528)	PRR Campaign Observation Car, *76 u*	55	75	—[1]
(9529)	B&O Campaign Observation Car, *76 u*	49	80	—[1]
9530	Southern Baggage Car, *77-78*	45	65	—[1]
9531	Southern Combination Car, *77-78*	36	50	—[1]
9532	Southern Passenger Car, *77-78*	39	55	—[1]
9533	Southern Passenger Car, *77-78*	34	48	—[1]
9534	Southern Observation Car, *77-78*	36	55	—[1]
9535	TTOS Columbus Baggage Car, *77 u*	33	43	—[1]
9536	Blue Comet Baggage Car, *78-80*	34	47	—[1]
9537	Blue Comet Combination Car, *78-80*	35	50	—[1]
9538	Blue Comet Passenger Car, *78-80*	35	47	—[1]
9539	Blue Comet Passenger Car, *78-80*	36	50	—[1]
9540	Blue Comet Observation Car, *78-80*	32	47	—[1]
9541	Santa Fe Baggage Car, *80-82*	21	30	—[1]
(9544)	TCA Chicago Observation Car "1980," *80 u*	—	50	—[1]
9545	Union Pacific Baggage Car, *84*	95	135	—[1]
9546	Union Pacific Combination Car, *84*	85	105	—[1]
9547	Union Pacific Observation Car, *84*	85	105	—[1]
(9548)	Union Pacific "Placid Bay" Passenger Car, *84*	85	105	—[1]
(9549)	Union Pacific "Ocean Sunset" Pass. Car, *84*	85	105	—[1]
9551	W&ARR Baggage Car, *77 u, 78-80*	46	60	—[1]
9552	W&ARR Passenger Car, *77 u, 78-80*	46	60	—[1]
9553	W&ARR Flatcar w/ horses, *77 u, 78-80*	34	42	—[1]
(9554)	Chicago & Alton Baggage Car, *81*	50	75	—[1]
(9555)	Chicago & Alton Combination Car, *81*	50	75	—[1]
(9556)	Chicago & Alton "Wilson" Passenger Car, *81*	50	75	—[1]
(9557)	Chicago & Alton "Webster Groves" Passenger Car, *81*	50	75	—[1]
(9558)	Chicago & Alton Observation Car, *81*	50	75	—[1]
9559	Rock Island Baggage Car, *81-82*	37	55	—[1]
9560	Rock Island Passenger Car, *81-82*	39	60	—[1]
9561	Rock Island Passenger Car, *81-82*	37	55	—[1]
(9562)	Norfolk & Western Baggage Car "577," *81*	80	110	—[1]
(9563)	Norfolk & Western Combination Car "578," *81*	80	105	—[1]
(9564)	Norfolk & Western Passenger Car "579," *81*	90	100	—[1]
(9565)	Norfolk & Western Passenger Car "580," *81*	85	100	—[1]
(9566)	Norfolk & Western Observation Car "581," *81*	100	110	—[1]
(9567)	Norfolk & Western Vista Dome Car			

		Exc	New	Cond/$
	"582," *81 u*	205	320	—[1]
9569	PRR Combination Car, *81 u*	115	160	—[1]
9570	PRR Baggage Car, *79*	85	115	—[1]
9571	PRR Passenger Car, *79*	125	145	—[1]
9572	PRR Passenger Car, *79*	110	125	—[1]
9573	PRR Vista Dome Car, *79*	95	120	—[1]
9574	PRR Observation Car, *79*	85	100	—[1]
9575	PRR Passenger Car, *79-80 u*	100	135	—[1]
9576	Burlington Baggage Car, *80*	105	120	—[1]
9577	Burlington Passenger Car, *80*	95	105	—[1]
9578	Burlington Passenger Car, *80*	105	110	—[1]
9579	Burlington Vista Dome Car, *80*	95	110	—[1]
9580	Burlington Observation Car, *80*	95	110	—[1]
9581	Chessie System Baggage Car, *80*	47	55	—[1]
9582	Chessie System Combination Car, *80*	47	55	—[1]
9583	Chessie System Passenger Car, *80*	40	47	—[1]
9584	Chessie System Passenger Car, *80*	34	40	—[1]
9585	Chessie System Observation Car, *80*	55	65	—[1]
9586	Chessie System Dining Car, *86 u*	85	90	—[1]
9588	Burlington Vista Dome Car, *80 u*	110	120	—[1]
(9589)	Southern Pacific Baggage Car, *82-83*	100	120	—[1]
(9590)	Southern Pacific Combination Car, *82-83*	100	120	—[1]
(9591)	Southern Pacific "Pullman" Passenger Car, *82-83*	95	115	—[1]
(9592)	Southern Pacific "Chair" Passenger Car, *82-83*	95	115	—[1]
(9593)	Southern Pacific Observation Car, *82-83*	100	130	—[1]
9594	NYC Baggage Car, *83-84*	110	135	—[1]
9595	NYC Combination Car, *83-84*	90	105	—[1]
(9596)	NYC "Wayne County" Passenger Car, *83-84*	80	95	—[1]
(9597)	NYC "Hudson River" Passenger Car, *83-84*	70	85	—[1]
(9598)	NYC Observation Car, *83-84*	85	100	—[1]
(9599)	Chicago & Alton Dining Car, *86 u*	75	85	—[1]
9600	Chessie System Hi-cube Boxcar, *75 u, 76-77*	21	30	—[1]
9601	ICG Hi-cube Boxcar, *75 u, 76-77*	22	24	—[1]
[9601]	Gateway TCA ICG Hi-cube Boxcar, *77 u*	—	21	—[1]
9602	Santa Fe Hi-cube Boxcar, *75 u, 76-77*	19	20	—[1]
9603	Penn Central Hi-cube Boxcar, *76-77*	21	23	—[1]
9604	Norfolk & Western Hi-cube Boxcar, *76-77*	21	23	—[1]
9605	NH Hi-cube Boxcar, *76-77*	19	25	—[1]
9606	Union Pacific Hi-cube Boxcar, *76 u, 77*	21	23	—[1]
9607	Southern Pacific Hi-cube Boxcar, *76 u, 77*	21	23	—[1]
9608	Burlington Northern Hi-cube Boxcar, *76 u, 77*	21	23	—[1]
9610	Frisco Hi-cube Boxcar, *77*	28	39	—[1]
9611	TCA Boston Hi-cube Boxcar, *78 u*	26	31	—[1]
9620	NHL Wales Boxcar, *80*	24	31	—[1]

		Exc	New	Cond/$
9621	NHL Campbell Boxcar, *80*	21	26	—¹
9622	NBA Western Boxcar, *80*	24	31	—¹
9623	NBA Eastern Boxcar, *80*	24	31	—¹
9624	National League Baseball Boxcar, *80*	21	26	—¹
9625	American League Baseball Boxcar, *80*	21	27	—¹
9626	Santa Fe Hi-cube Boxcar, *82-84*	13	18	—¹
9627	Union Pacific Hi-cube Boxcar, *82-83*	18	25	—¹
9628	Burlington Northern Hi-cube Boxcar, *82-84*	14	19	—¹
9629	Chessie System Hi-cube Boxcar, *83-84*	23	34	—¹
9660	Mickey Mouse Hi-cube Boxcar, *77-78*	36	50	—¹
9661	Goofy Hi-cube Boxcar, *77-78*	48	55	—¹
9662	Donald Duck Hi-cube Boxcar, *77-78*	41	50	—¹
9663	Dumbo Hi-cube Boxcar, *77 u, 78*	35	60	—¹
9664	Cinderella Hi-cube Boxcar, *77 u, 78*	50	75	—¹
9665	Peter Pan Hi-cube Boxcar, *77 u, 78*	48	75	—¹
9666	Pinocchio Hi-cube Boxcar, *78*	120	175	—²
9667	Snow White Hi-cube Boxcar, *78*	325	440	—¹
9668	Pluto Hi-cube Boxcar, *78*	125	160	—¹
9669	Bambi Hi-cube Boxcar, *78 u*	60	100	—¹
9670	Alice In Wonderland Hi-cube Boxcar, *78 u*	55	90	—¹
9671	Fantasia Hi-cube Boxcar, *78 u*	50	90	—¹
9672	Mickey Mouse 50th Anniversary Hi-cube Boxcar, *78 u*	370	460	—¹
9678	TTOS Hollywood Hi-cube Boxcar, *78 u*	21	24	—¹
9695	(See 52077)			
9700	Southern Boxcar, *72-73*	24	31	—¹
9700-1976	(See 9779)			
9701	B&O DD Boxcar, *72*	16	22	—¹
9701	TCA B&O DD Boxcar, *72 u*	50	65	—¹
[9701]	LCCA B&O DD Boxcar, *72 u*	—	170	—¹
9702	Soo Line Boxcar, *72-73*	16	22	—¹
9703	CP Rail Boxcar, *72*	34	44	—¹
9704	Norfolk & Western Boxcar, *72*	12	20	—¹
9705	D&RGW Boxcar, *72*	15	23	—¹
[9705]	Sacramento-Sierra TCA D&RGW Boxcar, *75 u*	—	38	—¹
9706	C&O Boxcar, *72*	19	22	—¹
9706	(See 19706)			
9707	MKT Stock Car, *72-75*	17	24	—¹
9708	U.S. Mail Boxcar, *72-75*	19	24	—¹
9708	U.S. Mail Toy Fair Boxcar, *73 u*	75	85	—¹
9709	BAR "State of Maine" Boxcar (SSS), *72-74*	34	38	—¹
9710	Rutland Boxcar (SSS), *72-74*	22	26	—¹
9711	Southern Boxcar, *74-75*	17	25	—¹
9712	B&O DD Boxcar, *73-74*	27	30	—¹
9713	CP Rail Boxcar, *73-74*	21	26	—¹
9713	CP Rail Season's Greetings Boxcar, *74 u*	95	120	—¹

		Exc	New	Cond/$
9714	D&RGW Boxcar, *73-74*	20	24	—¹
9715	C&O Boxcar, *73-74*	17	22	—¹
9716	Penn Central Boxcar, *73-74*	20	27	—¹
9717	Union Pacific Boxcar, *73-74*	24	29	—¹
9718	Canadian National Boxcar, *73-74*	21	27	—¹
[9718]	LCAC Canadian National Boxcar, *79 u*		NRS	—¹
9719	New Haven DD Boxcar, *73 u*	25	35	—¹
9723	Western Pacific Boxcar (SSS), *73-74*	26	28	—¹
9723	Western Pacific Toy Fair Boxcar, *74 u*	75	85	—¹
[9723]	Sacramento-Sierra TCA WP Boxcar, *73 u*	—	29	—¹
9724	Missouri Pacific Boxcar (SSS), *73-74*	24	28	—¹
9725	MKT Stock Car (SSS), *73-75*	17	21	—¹
[9725]	Midwest TCA Stock Car "00002," *75 u*		NRS	—¹
9726	Erie-Lackawanna Boxcar (SSS), *78*	25	30	—¹
[9726]	Sacramento-Sierra TCA Erie-Lack. Boxcar, *79 u*—		31	—¹
9727	LCCA TA&G Boxcar, *73 u*	115	125	—¹
9728	LCCA Union Pacific Stock Car, *78 u*	24	27	—²
9729	CP Rail Boxcar, *78*	—	32	—¹
9730	CP Rail Boxcar, *74-75*	22	26	—¹
[9730]	Detroit-Toledo TCA CP Rail Boxcar, *76 u*	—	27	—¹
[9730]	Sacramento-Sierra TCA CP Rail Boxcar, *77 u*	—	30	—¹
[9730]	Western Michigan TCA CP Rail Boxcar, *74 u*	—	25	—¹
9731	Milwaukee Road Boxcar, *74-75*	14	19	—¹
9732	Southern Pacific Boxcar, *79 u*	30	40	—¹
9733	LCCA Airco Boxcar w/ tank, *79 u*	42	55	—¹
9734	Bangor & Aroostook Boxcar, *79*	31	41	—¹
9735	Grand Trunk Boxcar, *74-75*	16	22	—¹
9737	Central Vermont Boxcar, *74-76*	18	23	—¹
9738	Illinois Terminal Boxcar, *82*	47	60	—¹
9739	D&RGW Boxcar (SSS), *74-76*	17	25	—¹
[9739]	North Texas TCA D&RGW Boxcar, *76 u*	—	20	—¹
[9739]	LCCA D&RGW Boxcar, *78 u*	—	150	—¹
9740	Chessie System Boxcar, *74-75*	15	19	—¹
[9740]	Great Lakes TCA Chessie System Boxcar, *76 u* —		23	—¹
[9740]	WB&A TCA Chessie System Boxcar, *76 u*	—	23	—¹
9742	M&St L Boxcar, *73 u*	22	26	—¹
9742	M&StL Season's Greetings Boxcar, *73 u*	85	105	—¹
9743	Sprite Boxcar, *74 u, 75*	15	21	—¹
9744	Tab Boxcar, *74 u, 75*	15	21	—¹
9745	Fanta Boxcar, *74 u, 75*	15	24	—¹
9747	Chessie System DD Boxcar, *75-76*	27	28	—¹
9748	CP Rail Boxcar, *75-76*	15	20	—¹
9749	Penn Central Boxcar, *75-76*	16	21	—¹
9750	DT&I Boxcar, *75-76*	16	25	—¹
9751	Frisco Boxcar, *75-76*	15	19	—¹
9752	L&N Boxcar, *75-76*	17	22	—¹

		Exc	New	Cond/$
9753	Maine Central Boxcar, *75-76*	16	22	__1
[9753]	NETCA Maine Central Boxcar, *75 u*	24	34	__1
9754	NYC "Pacemaker" Boxcar (SSS), *75-77*	22	34	__2
[9754]	METCA NYC "Pacemaker" Boxcar, *76 u*	—	27	__1
9755	Union Pacific Boxcar, *75-76*	22	28	__1
9757	Central of Georgia Boxcar, *74 u*	21	25	__1
9758	Alaska Boxcar (SSS), *75-77*	30	38	__1
9759	Paul Revere Boxcar, *75 u*	36	43	__1
9760	Liberty Bell Boxcar, *75 u*	40	49	__1
9761	George Washington Boxcar, *75 u*	36	43	__1
(9762)	Toy Fair Boxcar, *75 u*	115	150	__1
9763	D&RGW Stock Car, *76-77*	18	23	__1
9764	GTW DD Boxcar, *76-77*	28	35	__1
9767	Railbox Boxcar, *76-77*	20	23	__1
[9767]	Gateway TCA Railbox Boxcar, *78 u*	—	20	__1
9768	B&M Boxcar, *76-77*	22	35	__1
[9768]	NETCA B&M Boxcar, *76 u*	28	34	__1
9769	B&LE Boxcar, *76-77*	19	24	__1
9770	Northern Pacific Boxcar, *76-77*	17	22	__1
9771	Norfolk & Western Boxcar, *76-77*	16	24	__1
[9771]	TCA Museum N&W Boxcar, *77 u*	24	31	__1
[9771]	WB&A TCA N&W Boxcar, *78 u*	—	30	__1
[9771]	LCCA N&W Boxcar, *77 u*		NRS	__1
9772	Great Northern Boxcar, *76*	55	75	__1
9773	NYC Stock Car, *76*	31	38	__1
9774	TCA Orlando Southern Belle Boxcar, *75 u*	30	39	__1
9775	M&St L Boxcar (SSS), *76*	21	24	__1
9776	Southern Pacific "Overnight" Boxcar (SSS), *76*	40	46	__1
9777	Virginian Boxcar, *76-77*	22	25	__1
9778	Season's Greetings Boxcar, *75 u*	165	185	__1
(9779)	TCA Philadelphia Boxcar "9700-1976," *76 u*	27	33	__1
9780	Johnny Cash Boxcar, *76 u*	33	48	__1
9781	Delaware & Hudson Boxcar, *77-78*	19	23	__1
9782	Rock Island Boxcar, *77-78*	17	21	__1
9783	B&O "Time-Saver" Boxcar, *77-78*	27	30	__1
[9783]	WB&A TCA B&O "Time-Saver" Boxcar, *77 u*	—	30	__1
9784	Santa Fe Boxcar, *77-78*	19	25	__1
9785	Conrail Boxcar, *78*		NRS	__1
9785	Conrail Boxcar, *77-78*	19	24	__1
[9785]	Midwest TCA Museum Express Conrail Boxcar, *77 u*		NRS	__*
[9785]	NETCA Conrail Boxcar, *78 u*	22	26	__*
[9785]	Sacramento-Sierra TCA Conrail Boxcar, *78 u*	—	27	__*
9786	C&NW Boxcar, *77-79*	18	26	__*
[9786]	Midwest TCA Museum Express C&NW			

		Exc	New	Cond/$
	Boxcar, *79 u*		NRS	—1
9787	Jersey Central Boxcar, *77-79*	17	25	—1
9788	Lehigh Valley Boxcar, *77-79*	18	25	—1
[9788]	Atlantic TCA Lehigh Valley Boxcar, *78 u*	19	24	—1
9789	Pickens Boxcar, *77*	25	33	—1
9790	(See 19243)			
9791	(See 19244)			
9801	B&O "Sentinel" Boxcar (Std. O), *73-75*	27	41	—3
9802	Miller High Life Reefer (Std. O), *73-75*	34	39	—1
9803	Johnson Wax Boxcar (Std. O), *73-75*	28	41	—3
9805	Grand Trunk Reefer (Std. O), *73-75*	30	34	—2
9806	Rock Island Boxcar (Std. O), *74-75*	38	44	—2
9807	Stroh's Beer Reefer (Std. O), *74-76*	60	85	—1
9808	Union Pacific Boxcar (Std. O), *75-76*	50	70	—2
9809	Clark Reefer (Std. O), *75-76*	34	41	—1
9811	Pacific Fruit Express Reefer (FARR #2), *80*	25	32	—1
9812	Arm & Hammer Reefer, *80*	18	26	—1
9813	Ruffles Reefer, *80*	24	34	—1
9814	Perrier Reefer, *80*	25	36	—1
9815	NYC "Early Bird" Reefer (Std. O), *84-85*	50	55	—2
9816	Brach's Candy Reefer, *80*	21	26	—1
9817	Bazooka Gum Reefer, *80*	24	31	—1
9818	Western Maryland Reefer, *80*	22	29	—1
9819	Western Fruit Express Reefer (FARR #3), *81*	30	40	—1
9820	Wabash Gondola w/ coal load (Std. O), *73-74*	32	40	—1
9821	Southern Pacific Gondola w/ coal load (Std. O), *73-75*	39	42	—1
9822	Grand Trunk Gondola w/ coal load (Std. O), *74-75*	30	32	—1
9823	Santa Fe Flatcar w/ crates (Std. O), *75-76*	60	70	—1
9824	NYC Gondola w/ coal load (Std. O), *75-76*	39	55	—1
9825	Schaefer Reefer (Std. O), *76-77*	50	70	—2
9826	P&LE Boxcar (Std. O), *76-77*	55	60	—2
9827	Cutty Sark Reefer, *84*	21	25	—1
9828	J&B Reefer, *84*	23	27	—1
9829	Dewar's White Label Reefer, *84*	21	23	—1
9830	Johnnie Walker Red Label Reefer, *84*	21	25	—1
9831	Pepsi Cola Reefer, *82*	45	60	—1
9832	Cheerios Reefer, *82*	110	140	—1
9833	Vlasic Pickles Reefer, *82*	23	29	—1
9834	Southern Comfort Reefer, *83-84*	25	34	—1
9835	Jim Beam Reefer, *83-84*	25	31	—1
9836	Old Grand-Dad Reefer, *83-84*	25	31	—1
9837	Wild Turkey Reefer, *83-84*	34	55	—1
9840	Fleischmann's Gin Reefer, *85*	24	28	—1

		Exc	New	Cond/$
9841	Calvert Gin Reefer, *85*	24	29	—[1]
9842	Seagram's Gin Reefer, *85*	26	29	—[1]
9843	Tanqueray Gin Reefer, *85*	27	29	—[1]
9844	Sambuca Reefer, *86*	27	34	—[1]
9845	Baileys Irish Cream Reefer, *86*	33	55	—[1]
9846	Seagram's Vodka Reefer, *86*	24	30	—[1]
9847	Wolfschmidt Vodka Reefer, *86*	25	30	—[1]
9849	Lionel Lines Reefer, *83 u*	42	49	—[1]
9850	Budweiser Reefer, *72 u, 73-75*	41	50	—[1]
9851	Schlitz Reefer, *72 u, 73-75*	23	31	—[1]
9852	Miller Reefer, *72 u, 73-77*	23	29	—[1]
9853	Cracker Jack Reefer, caramel, *72 u, 73-75*			
	(A) Caramel color body.	27	30	—[1]
	(B) White body, black logo border.	21	26	—[1]
9854	Baby Ruth Reefer, *72 u, 73-76*	19	25	—[1]
9855	Swift Reefer, *72 u, 73-77*	24	29	—[1]
9856	Old Milwaukee Reefer, *75-76*	25	33	—[1]
9858	Butterfinger Reefer, *73 u, 74-76*	22	31	—[1]
9859	Pabst Reefer, *73 u, 74-75*	23	31	—[1]
9860	Gold Medal Reefer, *73 u, 74-76*	19	24	—[1]
9861	Tropicana Reefer, *75-77*	23	35	—[1]
9862	Hamm's Reefer, *75-76*	22	31	—[1]
9863	REA Reefer (SSS), *74-76*	26	30	—[1]
9864	TCA Seattle Reefer, *74 u*	31	34	—[1]
9866	Coors Reefer, *76-77*	40	55	—[1]
9867	Hershey's Reefer, *76-77*	50	65	—[1]
9868	TTOS Oklahoma City Reefer, *80 u*	36	44	—[1]
9869	Santa Fe Reefer (SSS), *76*	27	32	—[1]
9870	Old Dutch Cleanser Reefer, *77-78, 80*	18	25	—[1]
9871	Carling Black Label Reefer, *77-78, 80*	27	33	—[1]
9872	Pacific Fruit Express Reefer, *77-79*	22	26	—[1]
[9872]	Midwest TCA PFE Reefer, *79 u*		NRS	—[1]
9873	Ralston Purina Reefer, *78*	26	33	—[1]
9874	Miller Lite Beer Reefer, *78-79*	35	50	—[2]
9875	A&P Reefer, *78-79*	20	28	—[1]
9876	Central Vermont Reefer, *78*	27	31	—[1]
9877	Gerber Reefer, *79-80*	65	75	—[1]
9878	Good and Plenty Reefer, *79*	24	31	—[1]
9879	Hills Bros. Reefer, *79-80*	21	27	—[1]
9879	Kraft Reefer, *79 u*		NM	—[1]
9880	Santa Fe Reefer (FARR #1), *79*	32	37	—[1]
9881	Rath Packing Reefer, *79 u*	32	38	—[2]
9882	NYC "Early Bird" Reefer, *79*	26	31	—
9883	Nabisco Oreo Reefer, *79*	70	85	—
[9883]	TTOS Phoenix Reefer, *83 u*	—	50	—
9884	Fritos Reefer, *81-82*	23	30	—

		Exc	New	Cond/$
9885	Lipton Tea Reefer, *81-82*	27	35	—1
9886	Mounds Reefer, *81-82*	20	25	—1
9887	Fruit Growers Express Reefer (FARR #4), *83*	29	38	—1
9888	Green Bay & Western Reefer, *83*	47	55	—1
10001	(See 19251)			
10009	(See 17008)			
10131	(See 16541)			
(11006)	Lionel Lion Set, *03 u*	—	200	—1
(11700)	Conrail Limited set, *87*	400	465	—1
(11701)	Rail Blazer set, *87-88*	—	55	—1
(11702)	Black Diamond set, *87*	195	265	—1
(11703)	Iron Horse Freight set, *88-91*	100	105	—1
(11704)	Southern Freight Runner set (SSS), *87*	230	305	—1
(11705)	Chessie System Unit Train set, *88*	405	415	—1
(11706)	Dry Gulch Line set (SSS), *88*	180	245	—1
(11707)	Silver Spike set, *88-89*	190	220	—1
(11708)	Midnight Shift set, *88 u, 89*	60	75	—1
(11710)	CP Rail Freight set, *89*	345	435	—1
(11711)	Santa Fe F3 ABA set "8100," "8101," "8102," *91*	450	550	—5
(11712)	Great Lakes Express set (SSS), *90*	275	295	—1
(11713)	Santa Fe Dash 8-40B set, *90*	370	445	—1
(11714)	Badlands Express set, *90-91*	49	60	—1
(11715)	Lionel 90th Anniversary set, *90*	240	290	—1
(11716)	Lionelville Circus Special set, *90-91*	195	245	—2
(11717)	CSX Freight set, *90*	190	250	—1
(11718)	Norfolk Southern Dash 8-40C Unit Train set, *92*	530	620	—1
(11719)	Coastal Freight set (SSS), *91*	200	260	—1
(11720)	Santa Fe Special set, *91*	49	60	—1
(11721)	Mickey's World Tour Train set, *91, 92 u*	105	135	—1
(11722)	Girl's Train set, *91*	610	900	—1
(11723)	Amtrak Maintenance Train set, *91, 92 u*	215	250	—1
(11724)	Great Northern F3 ABA set "366A," "370B," "351C," *92*	750	850	—3
(11726)	Erie-Lackawanna Freight set, *91 u*	235	285	—1
(11727)	Coastal Limited set, *92*	80	100	—1
(11728)	High Plains Runner set, *92*	120	130	—1
(11729)	L&N Express set, *92*		NM	—1
11730	Evergreen Intermodal Container (See 12805)			
11731	Maersk Intermodal Container (See 12805)			
11732	American President Lines Intermodal Container (See 12805)			
(11733)	Feather River set (SSS), *92*	270	310	—1
(11734)	Erie Alco ABA set "725A," "725B," "736a" (FF #7), *93*	295	360	—1

		Exc	New	Cond/$
(11735)	NYC Flyer Freight set "1735WS," *93-99*	125	140	__1
(11736)	Union Pacific Express set, *93-95*	110	130	__1
(11737)	TCA F3 ABA set "40," *93 u*	600	790	__1
(11738)	Soo Line set (SSS), *93*	240	270	__1
(11739)	Super Chief set, *93-94*	120	135	__1
(11740)	Conrail Consolidated set, *93*	235	255	__1
(11741)	Northwest Express set, *93*	130	155	__1
(11742)	Coastal Limited set, *93 u*	80	100	__1
(11743)	Chesapeake & Ohio Freight set, *94*	230	265	__1
(11744)	NYC Passenger/Freight set (SSS), *94*	300	340	__1
(11745)	U.S. Navy set, *94-95*	190	230	__1
(11746)	Seaboard Freight set, *94, 95 u*	80	100	__1
(11747)	Lionel Lines Steam set, *95*	260	280	__1
(11748)	Amtrak Alco Passenger set, *95-96*	115	160	__1
(11749)	Western Maryland set (SSS), *95*	240	255	__1
(11750)	McDonald's Nickel Plate Special set, *87 u*	135	145	__1
(11751)	49C95171C Sears Pennsylvania Passenger set, *87 u*	120	155	__1
(11752)	JCPenney Timber Master set, *87 u*	75	115	__1
(11753)	Kay Bee Toys Rail Blazer set, *87 u*	80	100	__1
(11754)	Key America set, *87 u*	150	165	__1
(11755)	Timber Master set, *87 u*	150	165	__1
(11756)	Hawthorne Freight Flyer set, *87-88 u*	65	85	__1
(11757)	Chrysler Mopar Express set, *88 u*	235	255	__1
(11758)	The Desert King set (SSS), *89*	175	220	__1
(11759)	JCPenney Silver Spike set, *88 u*	175	250	__1
(11761)	JCPenney Iron Horse Freight set, *88 u*	120	125	__1
(11762)	True Value Cannonball Express set, *89 u*	85	130	__1
(11763)	United Model Freight Hauler set, *88 u*	135	145	__1
(11764)	49N95178 Sears Iron Horse Freight set, *88 u*	155	190	__1
(11765)	Spiegel Silver Spike set, *88 u*	175	250	__1
(11767)	Shoprite Freight Flyer set, *88 u*	85	130	__1
(11769)	JCPenney Midnight Shift set, *89 u*	100	175	__1
(11770)	49GY95280 Sears Circus set, *89 u*	185	220	__1
(11771)	K-Mart Microracers set, *89 u*	70	95	__1
(11772)	Macy's Freight Flyer set, *89 u*	150	190	__1
(11773)	49GY95281 Sears NYC Passenger set, *89 u*	175	200	__1
(11774)	Ace Hardware Cannonball Express set, *89 u*	145	175	__1
(11775)	Anheuser-Busch set, *89-92 u*	175	215	__1
(11776)	Pace Iron Horse Freight set, *89 u*	115	135	__1
(11777)	49N95265 Sears Lionelville Circus Special set, *90 u*	175	190	__1
(11778)	49N95264 Sears Badlands Express set, *90 u*	49	60	__1
(11779)	49N95267 Sears CSX Freight set, *90 u*	190	230	__1
(11780)	49N95266 Sears Northern Pacific			

		Exc	New	Cond/$
	Passenger set, *90 u*	155	190	—1
(11781)	True Value Cannonball Express set, *90 u*	75	115	—1
(11783)	Toys "R" Us Heavy Iron set, *90-91 u*	155	190	—1
(11784)	Pace Iron Horse Freight set, *90 u*	115	135	—1
(11785)	Costco Union Pacific Express set, *90 u*	175	200	—1
(11789)	Sears Illinois Central Passenger set, *91 u*	155	175	—1
(11793)	Santa Fe set w/ mailer, *91 u*	49	60	—1
(11794)	Mickey's World Tour set w/ mailer, *91 u*	80	100	—1
(11796)	Union Pacific Express set, *91 u*	145	155	—1
(11797)	Sears Coastal Limited set w/ mailer, *92 u*	80	100	—1
(11800)	Toys "R" Us Heavy Iron Thunder			
	Limited set, *92-93 u*	185	215	—1
(11803)	Mall Promotion Nickel Plate Special			
	set, *92 u*	135	145	—1
(11804)	K-Mart Coastal Limited set, *92 u*	80	100	—1
(11809)	Lionel Village Trolley Company set			
	"1809" (O), *95-97*	55	80	—1
(11810)	Budweiser Modern Era set, *93-94 u*	170	205	—1
(11811)	United Auto Workers set, *93 u*	170	590	—1
(11812)	Mall Promotion Coastal Limited set, *93 u*	95	115	—1
(11813)	Crayola Activity Train set, *94 u, 95*	65	90	—1
(11814)	Ford Limited Edition set, *94 u*	175	205	—1
(11818)	Chrysler Mopar set, *94 u*	175	195	—1
(11819)	Georgia Power set, *95 u*	450	630	—1
(11820)	Red Wing Shoes NYC Flyer set, *95 u*	200	255	—1
(11821)	Sears Zenith set, *95 u*	—	760	—1
(11822)	Chevrolet set, *96 u*	235	305	—1
(11825)	Bloomingdale's set, *96 u*	—	305	—1
(11826)	Sears Freight set, *95-96 u*	—	700	—1
(11826)	Sears Freight set, *95-96 u*	—	700	—1
(11827)	Zenith employees set, *96 u*	—	675	—1
(11827)	Zenith employees set, *96 u*	—	675	—1
(11828)	NJ Transit Passenger set, *96 u*	—	235	—1
(11833)	NJ Transit GP38 Passenger Set, *97*	230	245	—1
(11837)	Union Pacific GP9 Unit Train set, *97*	—	600	—2
(11838)	AT&SF Warhorse Hudson Freight set, *97*	—	780	—2
(11839)	SP&S 4-6-2 Steam Freight set, *97*	—	280	—1
(11841)	Bloomingdale's set, *97 u*	—	250	—1
(11843)	Boston & Maine GP9 A-B-A Diesel			
	Locomotive Set, *98*	—	570	—1
(11844)	Union Pacific Die-Cast Ore Cars 4-pack, *98*	—	225	—1
(11846)	Kal Kan Pet Care Train Set, *01u*	—	920	—1
(11849)	1998 Lionel Centennial Series Reefer			
	4-pack, *98*	—	130	—1
(11850)	Rice A Roni Trolley Set, *02u*	—	325	—1
(11851)	PFE Reefer 6-pack (Std. O), *02*	250	285	—1

		Exc	New	Cond/$
(11863)	Southern Pacific GP9 "2383," *98*	—	220	—¹
(11864)	New York Central GP9 "2383," *98*	—	270	—¹
(11865)	Alaska GP7 "1802," *98-99*	—	95	—¹
(11900)	SF Special Freight set "1900Ws" (O), *96-01*	—	130	—¹
(11903)	Atlantic Coast Line F3 ABA set "342," "342B," "343," *96*	—	670	—³
(11905)	U.S. Coast Guard set, *96*	175	200	—¹
(11906)	Factory Selection Special set, *95 u*	—	85	—¹
(11909)	N&W J 4-8-4 Warhorse set, *96*	500	630	—²
(11910)	Lionel Lines set (O27), *96*	125	140	—¹
(11912)	"57" Switcher Service Exclusive, *96*	—	450	—³
(11913)	SP GP9 Freight set, *97*	—	425	—¹
(11914)	NYC GP9 Freight set, *97*	—	375	—¹
(11918)	Conrail SD20 Service Exclusive "X1144" (SSS), *97*	—	340	—²
(11919)	Lionel Docksider set "1919" (O), *97*	—	70	—¹
(11920)	Port of Lionel City Dive Team set "1920," *97*	—	185	—¹
(11921)	Lionel Lines Freight set "1113WS," *97*	—	140	—¹
(11929)	AT&SF Warbonnet Passenger set "1929W," *97-99*	—	165	—¹
(11930)	AT&SF Warbonnet Passenger 2-pack "2404-05," *97-99*	—	95	—¹
(11931)	Chessie Flyer Freight set "1931s" (O), *97-99*	—	165	—¹
(11933)	Dodge Motorsports Freight Set, *96 u*	—	245	—¹
(11934)	Virginian Rectifier Freight set, *97-99*	—	310	—²
(11935)	Lionel NYC Flyer Freight set, *97*	—	155	—¹
(11936)	Little League Baseball Steam Set, *97*	185	225	—¹
(11939)	SP&S 4-6-2 Steam Freight Set, *97*	—	220	—¹
(11940)	Southern Pacific SD40 Warhorse Coal Set, *98*	—	570	—¹
(11944)	Lionel Lines 4-4-2 Steam Freight Set, *98*	—	175	—¹
(11956)	UP GP9 "2380," "2381" (Powered & Dummy), *97*	325	375	—¹
(11957)	Mobil Oil Steam Special Set, *97*	—	560	—¹
(11971)	D&H 4-4-2 Steam Freight Set, *98*	125	155	—¹
(11972)	Alaska GP7 Train set, *98-99*	155	175	—¹
(11974)	Station Accessory Set, *98*	—	22	—¹
(11975)	Freight Accessory Pack, *98*	—	25	—¹
(11977)	NP 4-pack Freight Cars, *98*	—	185	—¹
(11979)	N&W 4-4-2 Steam Freight Set, *98*	—	75	—¹
(11981)	1998 Holiday Trolley Set, *98*	—	75	—¹
11982	New Jersey Transit Ore Car Set, *98*	—	250	—¹
(11983)	Farmrail Agricultural Set, *99*	—	375	—¹
(11984)	Corvette GP7 Set, *99*	—	450	—¹
(11988)	NYC Firecar "18444" & Instruction Car "19853" Set, *99*	—	155	—¹
12000	(See 52000)			

		Exc	New	Cond/$
(12014)	Straight Track 10" (FasTrack), *03-04*		CP	__1
(12015)	Curved Track 0-36 (FasTrack), *03-04*		CP	__1
(12016)	Terminal Track 10" (FasTrack), *03-04*		CP	__1
(12017)	Left Manual Switch 0-36 (FasTrack), *03-04*		CP	__1
(12018)	Right Manual Switch 0-36 (FasTrack), *03-04*		CP	__1
(12019)	90° Crossover (FasTrack), *03-04*		CP	__1
(12020)	Uncoupling Track 5" (FasTrack), *03-04*		CP	__1
(12022)	Half Curved Track 0-36 (FasTrack), *03-04*		CP	__1
(12023)	Quarter Curved Track 0-36 (FasTrack), *03-04*		CP	__1
(12024)	Half Straight Track (FasTrack), *03-04*		CP	__1
(12025)	Straight Track 4½" (FasTrack), *03-04*		CP	__1
(12026)	Straight Track 1¾" (FasTrack), *03-04*		CP	__1
(12027)	Insulated Track 5" (FasTrack), *03-04*		CP	__1
(12028)	Inner Passing Loop Track Pack (FasTrack), *03-04*		CP	__1
(12029)	Accessory Activator Pack (FasTrack), *03-04*		CP	__1
(12030)	Figure 8 Track Pack (FasTrack), *03-04*		CP	__1
(12031)	Outer Passing Loop Track Pack (FasTrack), *03-04*		CP	__1
(12032)	Straight Track 10" 4-Pack (FasTrack), *03-04*		CP	__1
(12033)	Curved Track 0-36 4-Pack (FasTrack), *03-04*		CP	__1
12035	FasTrack Lighted Bumper 2-pack, *04*		CP	__1
12036	Grade Crossing (FasTrack), *04*		CP	__1
12039	Railer (FasTrack), *04*		CP	__1
12040	O Gauge Transition Piece (FasTrack), *04*		CP	__1
12041	Curved Track O-72 (FasTrack), *04*		CP	__1
12042	Straight Track 30" (FasTrack), *04*		CP	__1
12043	Curved Track O-48 (FasTrack), *04*		CP	__1
12044	FasTrack Siding Track Add-on Track Plan, *04*		CP	__1
12045	Left Remote Switch O-36 (FasTrack), *04*		CP	__1
12046	Right Remote Switch O-36 (FasTrack), *04*		CP	__1
12047	Wye Remote Switch O-72 (FasTrack), *04*		CP	__1
12048	Left Remote Switch O-72 (FasTrack), *04*		CP	__1
12049	Right Remote Switch O-72 (FasTrack), *04*		CP	__1
12050	22.5° Crossover (FasTrack), *04*		CP	__1
12051	45° Crossover (FasTrack), *04*		CP	__1
12053	Accessory Power Wire (FasTrack), *04*		CP	__1
12055	Half Curved Track O-72 (FasTrack), *04*		CP	__1
12059	Earthen Bumper (FasTrack), *04*		CP	__1
12700	Erie Magnetic Gantry Crane, *87*	140	165	__1
(12701)	Operating Fueling Station, *87*	65	80	__1
(12702)	Control Tower, *87*	70	85	__1
(12703)	Icing Station, *88-89*	70	75	__2
(12704)	Dwarf Signal, *88-93*	9	11	__1
(12705)	Lumber Shed kit "832K," *88-99*	—	10	__1
(12706)	Barrel Loader Building kit, *87-99*	—	10	__1

		Exc	New	Cond/$
(12707)	Billboards (3), *87-99*	—	4	—¹
(12708)	Street Lamps (3), *88-93*	6	9	—¹
(12709)	Banjo Signal "140," *87-91, 95-00*	—	33	—¹
(12710)	Engine House kit, *87-91*	21	25	—¹
(12711)	Water Tower kit, *87-99*	—	13	—¹
(12712)	Automatic Ore Loader, *87-88*	17	21	—¹
(12713)	Automatic Gateman "145," *87-88, 94-00*	—	40	—¹
(12714)	Crossing Gate "252," *87-91, 93-04*	—	26	—¹
(12715)	Illuminated Bumpers "261," *87-04*	—	3	—¹
(12716)	Searchlight Tower, *87-89, 91-92*	19	22	—¹
(12717)	Non-Illuminated Bumpers (3), *87-04*		CP	—¹
(12718)	Barrel Shed kit, *87-99*	—	10	—¹
(12719)	Animated Refreshment Stand, *88-89*	70	80	—¹
12720	Rotary Beacon, *88-89*	40	45	—¹
(12721)	Illuminated Extension Bridge w/ rock piers, *89*	26	38	—¹
(12722)	Roadside Diner w/ smoke, *88-89*	21	29	—¹
(12723)	Microwave Tower, *88-91, 94-95*	19	25	—¹
(12724)	Double Signal Bridge, *88-90*	46	60	—¹
12725	Lionel Tractor and Trailer, *88-89*	18	21	—¹
(12726)	Grain Elevator kit, *88-91, 94-99*	—	40	—¹
(12727)	Operating Semaphore "151," *89-99*	—	24	—¹
(12728)	Illuminated Freight Station, *89*	29	38	—¹
(12729)	Mail Pick-up set, *88-91, 95*	13	18	—¹
(12730)	Girder Bridge "314," *88-03*	—	11	—¹
(12731)	Station Platform "158," *88-00*	—	9	—¹
(12732)	Coal Bag "206," *88-04*		CP	—¹
(12733)	Watchman Shanty kit, *88-99*	—	5	—¹
(12734)	Passenger/Freight Station, *89-99*	—	18	—¹
(12735)	Diesel Horn Shed, *88-91*	19	24	—¹
(12736)	Coaling Station kit, *88-91*	21	31	—¹
(12737)	Whistling Freight Shed "118," *88-99*	—	31	—¹
(12739)	Lionel Gas Company Tractor and Tanker, *89*	20	25	—¹
(12740)	Genuine Wood Logs (3), *88-92, 94-95, 97-99*	—	5	—¹
12741	Union Pacific Intermodal Crane, *89*	170	190	—¹
(12742)	Gooseneck Lamps "58," *89-00*	—	30	—¹
(12743)	Track Clips (12) (O), *89-04*		CP	—¹
(12744)	Rock Piers (2) "920-5," *89-92, 94-03*	—	10	—¹
(12745)	Barrel Pack (6), *89-04*		CP	—¹
(12746)	Operating/Uncoupling Track (O27), *89-04*	—	7	—¹
(12748)	Illuminated Passenger Platform "157," *89-99*	—	18	—¹
(12749)	Rotary Radar Antenna, *89-92, 95*	32	36	—¹
(12750)	Crane kit, *89-91*	8	10	—¹
(12751)	Shovel kit, *89-91*	8	10	—¹
(12752)	History of Lionel Trains video (VHS), *89-92, 94*	19	21	—¹

		Exc	New	Cond/$
(12753)	Ore Load (2), *89-91, 95*	1.50	2.50	—¹
(12754)	Graduated Trestle set (22) "110," *89-03*	—	15	—¹
(12755)	Elevated Trestle set (10) "111," *89-03*	—	15	—¹
(12756)	The Making of the Scale Hudson video (VHS), *91-94*	20	22	—¹
(12759)	Floodlight Tower "195," *90-00*	—	25	—¹
(12760)	Automatic Highway Flasher, *90-91*	26	30	—¹
(12761)	Animated Billboard, *90-91, 93, 95*	19	22	—¹
(12762)	Freight Station w/ train control and sounds, *90-91*		NM	—¹
(12763)	Single Signal Bridge, *90-91, 93*	25	28	—¹
(12765)	Die-cast Auto Assortment (6), *90*		NM	—¹
(12767)	Steam Clean and Wheel Grind Shop, *92-93, 95*	265	300	—¹
(12768)	Burning Switch Tower, *90, 93*	95	110	—¹
(12770)	Arch-Under Bridge "332," *90-03*	—	25	—¹
(12771)	Mom's Roadside Diner w/ smoke, *90-91*	34	50	—¹
(12772)	Truss Bridge w/ Flasher and Piers "318," *90-04*		CP	—¹
(12773)	Freight Platform kit, *90-98*	—	32	—¹
(12774)	Lumber Loader kit, *90-99*	—	17	—¹
12777	Chevron Tractor and Tanker, *90-91*	10	17	—¹
12778	Conrail Tractor and Trailer, *90*	10	17	—¹
12779	Lionelville Grain Company Tractor and Trailer, *90*	11	19	—¹
(12780)	RS-1 50 Watt Transformer, *90-93*	95	130	—¹
12781	N&W Intermodal Crane, *90-91*	180	210	—¹
12782	Lift Bridge, *91-92*	620	780	—¹
12783	Monon Tractor and Trailer, *91*	11	19	—¹
(12784)	Intermodal Containers (3), *91*	11	15	—¹
12785	Lionel Gravel Company Tractor and Trailer, *91*	10	17	—¹
12786	Lionel Steel Company Tractor and Trailer, *91*	10	16	—¹
12787	Family Lines Intermodal Container (See 12784)			
12788	UP Intermodal Container (See 12784)			
12789	B&M Intermodal Container (See 12784)			
(12790)	ZW-II Transformer, *91*		NM	—¹
(12791)	Animated Passenger Station, *91*	75	80	—¹
(12794)	Lionel Tractor, *91*	8	14	—¹
(12795)	Lionel Cable Reels (2) "40-15," *91-98*	3	5	—¹
(12797)	Crossing Gate and Signal, *91*		NM	—¹
(12798)	Forklift Loader Station, *92-95*	46	55	—²
(12800)	Scale Hudson Replacement Pilot Truck, *91 u*	13	17	—¹
(12802)	"Chat & Chew" Roadside Diner w/ smoke and lights, *92-95*	37	44	—¹
(12804)	Highway Lights "72," *92-99, 02-04*	10	14	—¹
(12805)	Intermodal Containers (3), *92*	9	12	—¹

		Exc	New	Cond/$
12806	Lionel Lumber Company Tractor and Trailer, *92*	8	13	—[1]
(12807)	Little Caesars Tractor and Trailer, *92*	9	15	—[1]
12808	Mobil Tractor and Tanker, *92*	8	13	—[1]
(12809)	Animated Billboard, *92-93*	22	26	—[1]
(12810)	American Flyer Tractor and Trailer "DX26925," *94*	12	18	—[1]
12811	Alka Seltzer Tractor and Trailer, *92*	12	22	—[1]
(12812)	Illuminated Freight Station "133," *93-00*	—	31	—[1]
(12818)	Animated Freight Station, *92, 94-95*	55	65	—[1]
12819	Inland Steel Tractor and Trailer, *92*	10	17	—[1]
(12821)	Lionel Catalog video (VHS), *92*	13	17	—[1]
(12826)	Intermodal Containers (3), *93*	10	15	—[1]
(12827)	CSX Intermodal Container "610584" (See 12826)			
(12828)	NYC Intermodal Container (See 12826)			
(12829)	Great Northern Container (See 12826)			
12831	Rotary Beacon, *93-95*	25	32	—[1]
(12832)	Block Target Signal "253," *93-98*	—	25	—[1]
(12833)	RoadRailer Tractor and Trailer, *93*	10	16	—[1]
12834	Pennsylvania Magnetic Gantry Crane, *93*	150	200	—[1]
(12835)	Operating Fueling Station, *93*	65	75	—[1]
12836	Santa Fe Quantum Tractor and Trailer, *93*	8	14	—[1]
(12837)	Humble Oil Tractor and Tanker, *93*	10	17	—[1]
(12838)	Crate Load (2), *93-97*	—	3	—[1]
(12839)	Grade Crossing (2), *93-04*	—	5	—[1]
(12897)	Engine House kit, *96-98*	—	29	—[1]
(12840)	Insulated Straight Track (O), *93-04*		CP	—[1]
(12841)	Insulated Straight Track (O27), *93-04*		CP	—[1]
(12842)	Dunkin' Donuts Tractor and Trailer, *92 u*	32	35	—[1]
(12843)	Die-cast Metal Sprung Trucks (2), *93-99*		NRS	—[1]
(12844)	Coil Covers (2) (O), *93-98*	—	3	—[1]
(12847)	Animated Ice Depot "352," *94-99*	—	75	—[1]
(12848)	Lionel Oil Company Oil Derrick "2848," *94*	65	80	—[2]
(12849)	Lionel Controller w/ wall pack, *94, 95 u*		NRS	—[1]
(12852)	Die-cast Intermodal Trailer Frame, *94-01*	—	4	—[1]
(12853)	Coil Covers (2) (Std. O), *94-98*	—	7	—[1]
(12854)	U.S. Navy Tractor and Tanker, *94-95*	—	39	—[1]
(12855)	Intermodal Containers (3), *94-95*	9	13	—[1]
12856	CP Rail Intermodal Container (See 12855)			
12857	Frisco Intermodal Container (See 12855)			
2858	Vermont Railways Intermodal Container (See 12855)			
(12860)	Lionel Visitor's Center Tractor and Trailer, *94 u*	12	18	—[1]
(12861)	Lionel Leasing Company Tractor, *94*	5	9	—[1]
(12862)	Oil Drum Loader, *94-95*	80	95	—[1]

		Exc	New	Cond/$
(12864)	Little Caesars Tractor and Trailer, *94*	8	14	—1
(12865)	Wisk Tractor and Trailer, *94*	12	55	—1
(12866)	TMCC 135-Watt PowerHouse Power Supply, *94 u, 95-03*	—	46	—1
(12867)	TMCC 135 PowerMaster Power Distribution Center, *94 u, 95-04*	—	46	—1
(12868)	TMCC CAB-1 Remote Controller, *94 u, 95-04*		CP	—1
(12869)	Marathon Oil Tractor and Tanker, *94*	16	25	—1
(12873)	Operating Sawmill "464," *95-97*	—	70	—1
(12874)	Classic Street Lamps "71," *94-00*	—	13	—1
(12875)	Lionel Railroader Club Tractor and Trailer, *94 u*	15	22	—1
(12877)	Operating Fueling Station, *95*	70	75	—1
(12878)	Control Tower, *95*	55	65	—1
(12880)	Power Station Transformer, *96*		NM	—1
(12881)	Chrysler Mopar Tractor and Trailer, *94 u*	32	42	—1
(12882)	Lighted Billboard, *95*	9	13	—1
(12883)	Dwarf Signal "148," *95-03*	—	25	—1
(12884)	Truck Loading Dock kit, *95-98*	—	16	—1
(12885)	40-Watt Control System, *94 u, 95-03*	—	26	—1
(12886)	Floodlight Tower "395," *95-98*	—	37	—1
(12887)	Lionel Conductor Display, *95*		NM	—1
(12888)	Railroad Crossing Flasher "154," *95-04*	—	38	—1
(12889)	Operating Windmill "453," *95-98*	—	45	—1
(12890)	Big Red Control Button, *94 u, 95-00*	—	45	—1
(12891)	Lionel Lines Refrigerator Tractor and Trailer, *95*	13	17	—1
(12892)	Automatic Flagman "1045," *92-98*	—	26	—1
(12893)	TMCC PowerMaster Power Adapter Cable, *94 u, 95-04*		CP	—1
(12894)	Signal Bridge "452," *95-01*	—	35	—1
(12895)	Double-track Signal Bridge "450," *95-00*	—	44	—1
(12896)	Tunnel Portals (2) "920-2," *95-04*	—	5	—1
(12898)	Flagpole "89," *95-97*	—	8	—1
(12899)	Searchlight Tower "496," *95-98*	—	25	—1
(12900)	Crane kit "6828-100," *95-98*	—	7	—1
(12901)	Shovel kit "6827-100," *95-98*	—	7	—1
(12902)	Marathon Oil Derrick "2902," *94 u, 95*	170	260	—1
(12903)	Diesel Horn Shed "114," *95-98*	—	29	—1
(12904)	Coaling Station kit, *95-98*	—	19	—1
(12905)	Factory kit, *95-98*	—	20	—1
(12906)	Maintenance Shed kit, *95-98*	—	20	—1
(12907)	Intermodal Containers (3), *95*	8	12	—1
(12908)	Western Pacific Intermodal Container (See 12907)			
(12909)	Northern Pacific Intermodal Container "33621"			

		Exc	New	Cond/$
	(See 12907)			
(12910)	CP Rail Intermodal Container "680441"			
	(See 12907)			
(12911)	TMCC Command Base, *95-04*	—	45	—1
(12912)	Oil Pumping Station "457," *95-98*	—	65	—1
(12914)	SC-1 Switch and Accessory Controller, *95-98*	—	35	—1
(12915)	Log Loader "164," *96*	—	160	—2
(12916)	Water Tower "138," *96-97*	—	65	—1
(12917)	Animated Switch Tower "445," *96-98*	—	25	—1
(12921)	LRRC Illuminated Station Platform, *95 u*	24	29	—1
12922	NYC Operating Gantry Crane			
	w/ coil covers, *96*	90	105	—1
(12923)	Red Wing Shoes Tractor and Trailer			
	"T-4," *95 u*	32	39	—1
(12925)	Curved Track Section 42" (O), *96-04*		CP	—1
(12926)	Globe Street Lamps "64," *96-03*	—	10	—1
(12927)	Yard Light "65," *96-04*		CP	—1
(12929)	Rail-truck Loading Dock, *96*	—	37	—1
(12930)	Lionelville Oil Company Oil Derrick			
	"2930," *95 u, 96*	75	95	—1
(12931)	Electrical Substation, *96*	—	22	—1
(12932)	Laimbeer Packaging Tractor & Trailer set, *96*	—	14	—1
(12936)	SP Intermodal Crane "292," *97*	—	200	—1
(12937)	NS Intermodal Crane "292," *97*	—	200	—1
(12938)	PS PowerStation—PowerHouse set, *97-00*	—	150	—1
(12939)	PG PowerGrid—PowerHouse set, *97*	—	NM	—1
(12943)	Illuminated Station Platform, *97-00*	—	24	—1
(12944)	Sunoco Oil Derrick "455," *97*	—	95	—1
(12945)	Sunoco Pumping Oil Station "457," *97*	—	80	—1
(12948)	Bascule Bridge "313," *97*	—	325	—2
(12949)	Billboard set "310," *97-00*	—	7	—1
(12951)	Airplane Hangar kit "837K," *97-98*	—	21	—1
(12952)	Big L Diner kit "838K," *97*	—	22	—1
(12953)	Linex Gas Tall Oil Tank "840K," *97*	—	9	—1
(12954)	Linex Gas Wide Oil Tank "839K," *97*	—	10	—1
(12955)	Road Runner & Wile E. Coyote Ambush			
	Shack "145," *97*	—	85	—1
(12958)	Industrial Water Tower "193," *97-98*	—	50	—1
(12960)	Rotary Radar Antenna "197," *97*	—	26	—1
(12961)	Lionel News Stand w/ diesel horn "114," *97*	—	30	—1
(12962)	LL Passenger Service Train Whistle			
	"118," *97-99*	—	28	—1
(12964)	Donald Duck Radar Antenna "197," *97*	—	60	—1
(12965)	Goofy Rotary Beacon "494," *97*	—	55	—1
(12966)	Lionel Rotary Aicraft Beacon "494," *97-00*	—	37	—1
(12968)	Girder Bridge Building kit "841K," *97*	—	22	—1

		Exc	New	Cond/$
(12969)	TMCC Command Set, *97-04*		80	—[1]
(12974)	Blinking Light Billboard "410," *97-00*	—	15	—[1]
(12975)	"Steiner" Victorian Building kit "842K," *97-98*	—	31	—[1]
(12976)	"Dobson" Victorian Building kit "843K," *97-98*	—	35	—[1]
(12977)	"Kindler" Victorian Building kit "844K," *97-98*	—	35	—[1]
(12982)	Culvert Loader (Conventional), *98-00*	—	190	—[1]
(12982)	Culvert Loader (Conventional), *98-00*	—	190	—[1]
(12983)	Culvert Unloader (Conventional), *99*	—	215	—[1]
(12987)	Intermodal 3-pack, *98*	—	15	—[1]
(12989)	Lionel Logo Tractor-Trailer, *98*	—	16	—[1]
(12991)	Linex Gas Tractor-Tanker, *98*	—	17	—[1]
(14000)	Operating Forklift Platform "264," *00*	—	185	—[1]
(14001)	Operating Belt Lumber Loader "364," *00*	—	105	—[1]
(14002)	ZW Amp/Volt Meter (for new ZW's), *00-04*	—	80	—[1]
(14003)	80-Watt Transformer/Controller, *00-03*	—	70	—[1]
(14004)	Operating Coal Loader "397," *00*	—	185	—[1]
(14004)	Operating Coal Loader "397," *00*	—	185	—[1]
(14005)	Operating Coal Ramp "456," *00*	—	165	—[1]
(14018)	ElectroCoupler Kit for Command Upgradeable GP9s, *00*	—	20	—[1]
(14062)	O31 Remote Switch (LH), *01-04*		CP	—[1]
(14063)	O31 Remote Switch (RH), *01-04*		CP	—[1]
(14065)	463 Nuclear Reactor, *00*	—	195	—[1]
(14071)	#70 Yard Light, *00-04*	—	24	—[1]
(14072)	Haunted House, *01*	—	170	—[1]
(14073)	Video: History of Lionel, The First 90 Years, *00*	—	15	—[1]
(14075)	Video: A Century of Lionel, 1900-1969, *00*	—	15	—[1]
(14076)	Video: A Century of Lionel, 1970-2000, *00*	—	15	—[1]
(14077)	ZW Amp/Volt Meter (for older ZW's), *00-03*		CP	—[1]
(14078)	Die-Cast Sprung Trucks, *00-04*		CP	—[1]
(14079)	Operating North Pole Pylon, *01*	—	90	—[1]
(14080)	Hobo Hotel, *01*	—	55	—[1]
(14081)	Shell Oil Derrick, *01*	—	145	—[1]
(14082)	Pedestrian Walkover w/Speed Sensor, *01-03*	—	50	—[1]
(14083)	Pedestrian Walkover, *01-03*	—	30	—[1]
(14084)	Lionel Heliport, *01*	—	60	—[1]
(14085)	Newsstand, *01*	—	85	—[1]
(14086)	Water Tower "38," *00*	—	100	—[1]
(14087)	Lionel Lighthouse, *01*	—	125	—[1]
(14090)	Banjo Signal, *01-04*		CP	—[1]
(14091)	Automatic Gateman, *01-03*		CP	—[1]
(14092)	Floodlight Tower, *01-04*		CP	—[1]

		Exc	New	Cond/$
(14093)	Single Signal Bridge, *01-04*		CP	__1
(14094)	Double Signal Bridge, *01-04*		CP	__1
(14095)	Illuminated Station Platform, *01-04*		CP	__1
(14096)	Station Platform, *01-04*		CP	__1
(14097)	Rotary Aircraft Beacon, *01-04*		CP	__1
(14098)	Auto Crossing Gate, *01-04*		CP	__1
(14099)	Block Target Signal, *01-04*		CP	__1
(14100)	Blinking Light Billboard, *01-03*		CP	__1
(14101)	Red Baron Pylon, *01*	—	100	__1
(14102)	Rocket Launcher "175," *01*	—	250	__1
(14104)	Burning Switch Tower, *00*	—	80	__1
(14105)	Lionel "505" Aquarium, *01*	—	205	__1
(14106)	Operating Freight Station "356," *00*	—	70	__1
(14107)	Lionel Postwar Coaling Station, "497," *01-03*	—	95	__1
(14109)	Carousel, *01*	—	315	__1
(14110)	Operating Ferris Wheel, *01-02, 04*	—	150	__1
(14111)	1531R Controller, *00-04*		CP	__1
(14112)	Lighted Lock-on, *01-03*		CP	__1
(14113)	Engine Transfer Table, *01*	—	175	__1
(14114)	Engine Transfer Table Extension, *01*	—	60	__1
(14116)	PRR Die-Cast Girder Bridge, *01*	—	20	__1
(14117)	NYC Die-Cast Girder Bridge, *01*	—	20	__1
(14119)	Gooseneck Lamps, Green, *01-04*	—	22	__1
(14121)	Classic Billboard Set (3), *01-03*		CP	__1
14124	ZW Controller w/ two 135 W Packs, *01*	—	300	__1
(14125)	Christmas Tree w/400E Train Set, *00*	—	50	__1
(14133)	Madison Hobby Shop, *01*	—	315	__1
(14134)	Triple Action Magnetic Crane, *01*	—	230	__1
(14135)	NS Black Die-Cast Girder Bridge, *02*	—	15	__1
(14137)	Generic Die-Cast Girder Bridge, *01-04*	—	18	__1
(14142)	Industrial Smokestack, *02-04*		CP	__1
(14143)	Industrial Tank, *02-04*		CP	__1
(14145)	Operating Lumberjacks, *02-03*	—	70	__1
(14147)	Die-cast Old Style Clock Tower, *02-04*	—	43	__1
(14148)	Operating Billboard Signmen, *02-03*	—	70	__1
(14149)	Scale-sized Banjo Signal, *02-03*		CP	__1
(14151)	Die-cast Dwarf Signal, *02-04*	—	28	__1
(14152)	Passenger Station "133," *02-04*	—	37	__1
(14153)	Lion Oil Derrick, *02-03*	—	50	__1
(14154)	Water Tower "193," *01-02*	—	50	__1
(14155)	Floodlight Tower "395," *02-03*	—	50	__1
(14156)	Lion Oil Diesel Fueling Station "415," *02-03*	—	70	__1
(14157)	Coal Loader "397," *01-03*	—	120	__1
(14158)	Icing Station "352," *01-02*	—	75	__1
(14159)	Animated Billboard, *02-04*		CP	__1
(14160)	Frank's Hotdog Stand, *03-04*		CP	__1

		Exc	New	Cond/$
(14161)	Smoking Hobo Shack, *02*	—	60	—[1]
(14162)	Missile Launching Platform "470," *02-03*	—	50	—[1]
(14163)	Industrial Power Station "840," *02-03*	—	550	—[1]
(14164)	Lionelville Bandstand, *02*	—	140	—[1]
14166	Train Orders Building, *04*		CP	—[1]
(14167)	Operating Lift Bridge "213," *02*	—	310	—[1]
(14168)	Operating Harry's Barber Shop, *02-04*	—	110	—[1]
(14170)	Amusement Park Swing Ride, *03-04*	—	150	—[1]
(14171)	Pirate Ship Ride, *02-04*	—	125	—[1]
(14172)	NYC Railroad Tugboat, *02*	—	180	—[1]
(14173)	Drawbridge, *02-04*		CP	—[1]
(14175)	Santa Fe Die-Cast Girder Bridge, *01-03*	—	15	—[1]
(14176)	Norfolk Southern Die-Cast Girder Bridge, *02-03*	—	18	—[1]
(14178)	TMCC Direct Lock-on, *02-03*		CP	—[1]
(14179)	TMCC Track Power Controller "400," *02-04*	—	130	—[1]
(14180)	B&O Railroad Tugboat, *02-03*	—	155	—[1]
(14181)	TMCC Action Recorder Controller, *02-04*	—	60	—[1]
(14182)	TMCC Accessory Switch Controller, *02-04*	—	55	—[1]
(14183)	TMCC Accessory Motor Controller, *02-04*	—	60	—[1]
(14184)	TMCC Block Power Controller, *02-04*	—	55	—[1]
(14185)	TMCC Operating Track Controller, *02-04*	—	49	—[1]
(14186)	TMCC Accessory Voltage Controller, *02-04*	—	90	—[1]
(14187)	TMCC How-To Video, *02-04*	—	11	—[1]
(14189)	TMCC Track Power Controller "300," *02-04*	—	90	—[1]
14190	"The Lionel Train Book," *04*		CP	—[1]
(14191)	TMCC Command Base Cable (6 feet), *02-04*	—	6	—[1]
(14192)	TMCC 3-Wire Command Base Cable, *02-04*	—	8	—[1]
(14193)	TMCC Controller to Controller Cable (1 foot), *02-04*		CP	—[1]
(14194)	TMCC TPC Cable Set, *02-04*	—	9	—[1]
(14195)	TMCC Command Base Cable (20 feet), *02-04*	—	8	—[1]
(14196)	TMCC Controller to Controller Cable (6 feet), *02-04*	—	4	—[1]
(14197)	TMCC Controller to Controller Cable (20 feet), *02-04*	—	6	—[1]
(14198)	CW-80 80-Watt Transformer, *03-04*		CP	—[1]
(14199)	Playground Swings, *03-04*	—	50	—[1]
(14500)	KCS F3 AA "2388" Passenger Set, *01*	350	610	—[1]
(14512)	EMD F3 ABA "291," CC, *01*	400	475	—[1]
(14517)	Santa Fe Powered F3 B Unit "2343C," *01*	—	305	—[1]
(14518)	CP F3 B Unit w/RailSounds "2373C," CC, *01*	—	280	—[1]
(14520)	Texas Special F3 B-unit w/ Railsounds, *01*	—	340	—[1]
(14521)	Rock Island E-6 AA, *01*	—	530	—[1]
(14524)	Atlantic Coast Line E-6 AA, *01*	—	630	—[1]
(14532)	Lionel Century Club PRR Sharknose AA			

		Exc	New	Cond/$
	"9744," CC, *00 u*	—	600	—1
(14539)	Santa Fe F3 B Unit, *03*	—	300	—1
(14540)	D&RGW F3 B Unit w/RailSounds, CC, *01*	—	275	—1
(14541)	C&O F3 B Unit w/RailSounds, CC, *01*	—	275	—1
(14542)	KCS F3 B Unit w/RailSounds "2388C," CC, *01*	—	350	—1
(14543)	SP F3 B Unit w/RailSounds, CC, *01*	—	250	—1
(14544)	Southern EMD E6 AA Diesels, CC, *02*	—	520	—1
(14547)	Burlington EMD E5 AA Diesels, CC, *02*	—	540	—1
(14555)	NYC F3 B Unit, *03*	—	200	—1
(14557)	WP F3 B Unit (Non-powered), *03-04*	—	165	—1
(14558)	B&O F3 B Unit (Non-powered), *03-04*	—	165	—1
(14559)	D&RG F-3 AA, *01*	—	620	—1
(14560)	NP F3 B Unit (Freight) "2390B," *02*	—	175	—1
(14561)	NP F3 B Unit (Passenger) "2390B," *02*	—	190	—1
(14562)	Milwaukee Road F3 B Unit "75C," *02*	—	190	—1
(14563)	Erie Lackawanna F3 B Unit "7094," *02*	—	175	—1
(14564)	CP F3 B Unit "237C," CC, *02*	—	305	—1
(14565)	B&O F3 A-A Set, *03-04*	—	650	—1
(14568)	WP F3 A-A Set, *03-04*	—	650	—1
(14571)	Santa Fe PA A-A Set "51-51," CC, *03*	—	580	—1
(14574)	D&H PA A-A Set "18-19," CC, *03*	—	580	—1
(14584)	Wabash F3 A Unit (Non-Powered), *03*	—	165	—1
(14586)	D&H PB Unit, *03*	—	125	—1
(14587)	Santa Fe PB Unit, *03*	—	125	—1
14588	Santa Fe EMD F3 A-B-A Set "19" CC, *04*		CP	—1
14592	PRR EMD F3 A-B-A Set "9500/9501" CC, *04*		CP	—1
14596	NH Alco PA A-A Set "0767/0768," *04*		CP	—1
14599	NH Alco PB Unit "0767-B," *04*		CP	—1
(14536)	Santa Fe F3 A-A Set w/RailSounds, CC, *03-04*	—	700	—1
(14552)	NYC F3 A-A Set w/RailSounds, CC, *03-04*	—	700	—1
15000	D&RGW Waffle-side Boxcar, *95*	17	19	—1
15001	Seaboard Waffle-side Boxcar, *95*	15	19	—1
(15002)	Chesapeake & Ohio Waffle-sided Boxcar, *96*	20	25	—1
(15003)	Green Bay & Western Waffle-sided Boxcar, *96*	18	22	—1
(15004)	Bloomingdales Boxcar, *97 u*	—	40	—1
(15005)	I Love NY Boxcar, *97 u*	—	65	—1
(15008)	CP Rail Boxcar		NRS	—1
15013	L&N Waffleside Boxcar "102402," *00*	—	29	—1
15014	Seaboard Waffleside Boxcar "125925," *00*	—	25	—1
(15015)	C&NW Waffle-sided Boxcar "161013," *03*	—	18	—1
15016	IC Waffle-sided Boxcar "12981," *04*		CP	—1
(15100)	Amtrak Passenger Car, *95-97*	—	34	—1
15101	Reading Baggage Car (O27), *96*	—	23	—1
15102	Reading Combination Car (O27), *96*	—	23	—1

		Exc	New	Cond/$
15103	Reading Passenger Car (O27), *96*	—	23	—1
15104	Reading Vista Dome Car (O27), *96*	—	26	—1
15105	Reading Full Vista Dome Car (O27), *96*	—	26	—1
15106	Reading Observation Car (O27), *96*	—	23	—1
(15107)	Amtrak Vista Dome Car, *96*	—	33	—1
(15108)	Northern Pacific Vista Dome Car, *96*	—	34	—1
(15109)	AT&SF Combine Car "2407," *97*	—	35	—1
(15110)	AT&SF Vista Dome Car "2404," *97*	—	35	—1
(15111)	AT&SF Observation Car "2406," *97*	—	35	—1
(15112)	AT&SF Coach Albuquerque, "2405," *97*	—	34	—1
(15113)	AT&SF Vista Dome Culebra, "2404," *97*	—	34	—1
(15114)	NJ Transit Coach "5610," *96 u*	—	45	—1
(15115)	NJ Transit Coach "5611," *96 u*	—	45	—1
(15116)	NJ Transit Coach "5612," *96 u*	—	45	—1
(15117)	Annie Passenger Coach, surprised face, *97*	—	26	—1
(15118)	Clarabel Passenger Coach, smiling face, *97*	—	26	—1
(15122)	NJ Transit Passenger Coach "5613," *97u*	—	45	—1
(15123)	NJ Transit Passenger Coach "5614," *97u*	—	45	—1
(15124)	NJ Transit Passenger Coach "5615," *97u*	—	45	—1
(15125)	Amtrak Observation Car, *97u*	—	50	—1
(15126)	Stars & Stripes General Coach "Abraham Lincoln," *99*	—	60	—1
(15127)	Stars & Stripes General Coach "Ulysses S. Grant," *99*	—	60	—1
15128	Pride of Richmond General Coach "Robert E. Lee," *99*	—	60	—1
15129	Pride of Richmond General Coach "Jefferson Davis," *99*	—	60	—1
(15136)	Custom Series Short Observation (blue), *99*	—	40	—1
(15137)	Custom Series Short Observation (red), *99*	—	40	—1
(15138)	Pratt's Hollow Baggage Car, *98*	NRS		—1
(15139)	Pratt's Hollow Vista Dome, *98*	NRS		—1
(15140)	Pratt's Hollow Coach, *98*	NRS		—1
(15141)	Pratt's Hollow Observation, *98*	NRS		—1
(15142)	U.S. Army "Baby" Heavyweight Coach, *00*	—	50	—1
(15143)	U.S. Army "Baby" Heavyweight Coach, *00*	—	50	—1
(15153)	Pullman Baby Madison Set 4-pack, *01*	—	190	—1
(15163)	T&P "Baby" Heavyweight Coach, *01*	—	30	—1
(15169)	C&O Streamliner Passenger Car 4-Pack, *03*	—	140	—1
(15170)	L&N Streamliner Passenger Car 4-Pack, *03*	—	140	—1
15180	NYC Streamliner Passenger Car 4-pack, *04*	CP		—1
15185	UP Streamliner Passenger Car 4-pack, *04*	CP		—1
(15300)	NYC Superliner Aluminum Passenger Car 4-pack, *02*	—	360	—1
(15301)	NYC Superliner Passenger Car "Manhattan," *02*	CP		—1
(15302)	NYC Superliner Passenger Car "Queens," *02*	CP		—1

		Exc	New	Cond/$
(15304)	NYC Superliner Passenger Car "Staten Island," *02*	CP		__1
(15305)	NYC Superliner Passenger Car "Brooklyn," *02*	CP		__1
(15311)	CB&Q California Zephyr Aluminum Passenger Car 4-Pack, *03*	—	350	__1
(15312)	Santa Fe Super Chief Aluminum Passenger Car 4-Pack, *03*	—	275	__1
(15314)	Amtrak Superliner 2-Pack, *03*	CP		__1
(15315)	Santa Fe Superliner 2-Pack, *03*	CP		__1
(15316)	NYC Superliner 2-Pack, *03*	CP		__1
(15317)	Southern The Southemer Aluminum Passenger Car 4-Pack, *03*	—	350	__1
15318	Lionel Lines Aluminum Passenger Car 2 pack, *03*	NRS		__1
(15319)	Santa Fe Superliner Aluminum Passenger Car 2-Pack, *03*	CP		__1
(15326)	NYC 20th Century Limited Aluminum Passenger Car 6-pack, *02*	—	485	__1
(15333)	N&W Powhatan Arrow Aluminum Passenger Car 6-pack, *02*	—	435	__1
(15340)	Pennsylvania South Wind Aluminum Passenger Car 6-pack, *02*	—	435	__1
15379	Lionel Lines Aluminum combo car "Silver Valley," *03*	CP		__1
15380	Lionel Lines Aluminum Dining Car "Silver Spoon," *03*	CP		__1
15381	Santa Fe Aluminum Baggage Car "2571," *03*	CP		__1
15382	Santa Fe Aluminum Vista Dome "Regal Dome," *03*	CP		__1
(15383)	NYC 20th Century Limited Station Sounds Diner, *03*	—	195	__1
(15384)	N&W Powhattan Arrow StationSounds Diner, *03*	—	190	__1
(15385)	Pennsylvania South Wind StationSounds Diner, *03*	—	190	__1
(15394)	Amtrak Streamliner Passenger Car 4-Pack, *03-04*	—	355	__1
(15395)	Alaska Streamliner Passenger Car 4-Pack, *03-04*	—	355	__1
(15396)	Amtrak Superliner Diner w/StationSounds, *03*	CP		__1
(15397)	Santa Fe Superliner Diner w/ StationSounds, *03*	CP		__1
(15398)	NYC Superliner Diner w/ StationSounds, *03*	CP		__1
(15405)	50th Anniversary Heavyweight Diner "Hillside" w/ StationSounds, *02*	—	195	__1

		Exc	New	Cond/$
(15406)	Blue Comet Heavyweight Diner "Giacobini" w/ StationSounds, *02*	—	235	—¹
(15504)	Alton Limited StationSounds Diner, *03*	—	200	—¹
(15507)	Phantom III Passenger Car 4-pack, *02*	—	245	—¹
(15512)	Phantom II Passenger Car 4-pack, *02*	—	250	—¹
(15517)	Southern Crescent Limited Heavyweight Passenger Car 2-Pack, *03-04*	—	200	—¹
(15520)	Southern Crescent Limited Heavyweight Diner w/ StationSounds, *03-04*	—	200	—¹
15521	NYC "Twentieth Century Limited" Heavyweight Passenger Car 4-pack, *04*		CP	—¹
15526	Santa Fe "The Chief" Heavyweight Passenger Car 4-pack, *04*		CP	—¹
15538	NYC "Twentieth Century Limited" Heavyweight Passenger Car 2-pack, *04*		CP	—¹
15541	NYC "Twentieth Century Limited" Heavyweight Diner w/StationSounds, *04*		CP	—¹
15542	Santa Fe "The Chief" Heavyweight Passenger Car 2-pack, *04*		CP	—¹
15545	Santa Fe "The Chief" Heavyweight Diner w/ StationSounds, *04*		CP	—¹
15791	(See 17889)			
15906	RailSounds Trigger Button, *90-95*	—	12	—¹
16000	PRR Vista Dome Car (O27), *87-88*	30	44	—¹
16001	PRR Passenger Car (O27), *87-88*	30	36	—¹
16002	PRR Passenger Car (O27), *87-88*	24	29	—¹
16003	PRR Observation Car (O27), *87-88*	24	29	—¹
16009	PRR Combination Car (O27), *88*	36	38	—¹
16010	Virginia & Truckee Passenger Car (SSS), *88*	36	43	—¹
16011	Virginia & Truckee Passenger Car (SSS), *88*	36	43	—¹
16012	Virginia & Truckee Baggage Car (SSS), *88*	36	43	—¹
16013	Amtrak Combination Car (O27), *88-89*	21	34	—¹
16014	Amtrak Vista Dome Car (O27), *88-89*	21	34	—¹
16015	Amtrak Observation Car (O27), *88-89*	21	34	—¹
16016	NYC Baggage Car (O27), *89*	30	44	—¹
16017	NYC Combination Car (O27), *89*	21	29	—¹
16018	NYC Passenger Car (O27), *89*	21	29	—¹
16019	NYC Vista Dome Car (O27), *89*	21	29	—¹
16020	NYC Passenger Car (O27), *89*	23	33	—¹
16021	(See 17210)	—	40	—¹
16021	NYC Observation Car (O27), *89*	21	29	—¹
16022	(See 17211)			
16022	Pennsylvania Baggage Car (O27), *89*	27	38	—¹
16023	(See 17212)			
16023	Amtrak Passenger Car (O27), *89*	21	30	—¹
16024	NP Dining Car (O27), *92*	39	44	—¹

		Exc	New	Cond/$
16027	LL Combination Car (027) (SSS), *90*	39	48	—¹
16028	LL Passenger Car (027) (SSS), *90*	35	42	—¹
16029	LL Passenger Car (027) (SSS), *90*	35	42	—¹
16030	LL Observation Car (027) (SSS), *90*	35	42	—¹
16031	Pennsylvania Dining Car (027), *90*	35	39	—¹
16033	Amtrak Baggage Car (027), *90*	28	38	—¹
16034	NP Baggage Car (027), *90-91*	21	30	—¹
16035	NP Combination Car (027), *90-91*	18	26	—¹
16036	NP Passenger Car (027), *90-91*	21	30	—¹
16037	NP Vista Dome Car (027), *90-91*	18	26	—¹
16038	NP Passenger Car (027), *90-91*	17	25	—¹
16039	NP Observation Car (027), *90-91*	18	26	—¹
16040	Southern Pacific Baggage Car, *90-91*	22	30	—¹
16041	NYC Dining Car (027), *91*	40	50	—¹
16042	Illinois Central Baggage Car (027), *91*	24	34	—¹
16043	Illinois Central Combination Car (027), *91*	22	30	—¹
16044	Illinois Central Passenger Car (027), *91*	24	34	—¹
16045	Illinois Central Vista Dome Car (027), *91*	22	30	—¹
16046	Illinois Central Passenger Car (027), *91*	24	34	—¹
16047	Illinois Central Observation Car (027), *91*	24	34	—¹
16048	Amtrak Dining Car (027), *91-92*	33	40	—¹
16049	Illinois Central Dining Car (027), *92*	24	33	—¹
(16050)	C&NW Baggage Car "6620," *93*	44	55	—¹
(16051)	C&NW Combination Car "6630," *93*	40	50	—¹
(16052)	C&NW Passenger Car "6616," *93*	34	42	—¹
(16053)	C&NW Passenger Car "6602," *93*	37	46	—¹
(16054)	C&NW Observation Car "6603," *93*	38	47	—¹
16055	Santa Fe Passenger Car (027), *93-94*	27	35	—¹
16056	Santa Fe Vista Dome Car (027), *93-94*	28	37	—¹
16057	Santa Fe Passenger Car (027), *93-94*	30	40	—¹
16058	Santa Fe Combination Car (027), *93-94*	27	35	—¹
16059	Santa Fe Vista Dome Car (027), *93-94*	26	34	—¹
16060	Santa Fe Observation Car (027), *93-94*	25	31	—¹
(16061)	N&W Baggage Car "6061," *94*	43	55	—¹
(16062)	N&W Combination Car "6062," *94*	38	50	—¹
(16063)	N&W Passenger Car "6063," *94*	37	46	—¹
(16064)	N&W Passenger Car "6064," *94*	37	46	—¹
(16065)	N&W Observation Car "6065," *94*	36	48	—¹
(16066)	NYC Combination Car "6066" (SSS), *94*	44	55	—¹
(16067)	NYC Passenger Car "6067" (SSS), *94*	38	47	—¹
(16068)	UP Baggage Car "6068" (027), *94*	36	43	—¹
(16069)	UP Combination Car "6069" (027), *94*	36	43	—¹
(16070)	UP Passenger Car "6070" (027), *94*	36	43	—¹
(16071)	UP Dining Car "6071" (027), *94*	36	46	—¹
(16072)	UP Vista Dome Car "6072" (027), *94*	36	43	—¹
(16073)	UP Passenger Car "6073" (027), *94*	36	42	—¹

		Exc	New	Cond/$
(16074)	UP Observation Car "6074" (O27), *94*	36	43	__1
(16075)	Missouri Pacific Baggage Car "6620," *95*	36	44	__1
(16076)	Missouri Pacific Combination Car "6630," *95*	34	41	__1
(16077)	Missouri Pacific Passenger Car "6616," *95*	34	41	__1
(16078)	Missouri Pacific Passenger Car "7805," *95*	34	39	__1
(16079)	Missouri Pacific Observation Car "6609," *95*	34	41	__1
(16080)	New Haven Baggage Car "6080" (O27), *95*	35	44	__1
(16081)	New Haven Combination Car "6081" (O27), *95*	28	37	__1
(16082)	New Haven Passenger Car "6082" (O27), *95*	28	37	__1
(16083)	New Haven Vista Dome Car "6083" (O27), *95*	30	39	__1
(16084)	New Haven Full Vista Dome Car "6084" (O27), *95*	33	39	__1
(16086)	New Haven Observation Car "6086" (O27), *95*	31	40	__1
(16087)	NYC Baggage Car "6087" (SSS), *95*	38	49	__1
(16088)	NYC Passenger Car "6088" (SSS), *95*	36	43	__1
(16089)	NYC Dining Car "6089" (SSS), *95*	36	43	__1
(16090)	NYC Observation Car "6090" (SSS), *95*	40	48	__1
(16091)	NYC Passenger Cars, set of 4 (SSS), *95*	135	160	__1
16092	Santa Fe Full Vista Dome Car (O27), *95*	30	38	__1
16093	Illinois Central Full Vista Dome Car (O27), *95*	29	38	__1
16094	Pennsylvania Full Vista Dome Car (O27), *95*	30	39	__1
16095	Amtrak Combination Car (O27), *95*	19	23	__1
16096	Amtrak Vista Dome Car (O27), *95*	19	23	__1
16097	Amtrak Observation Car (O27), *95*	19	23	__1
(16098)	Amtrak Passenger Car, *95-97*	18	29	__1
(16099)	Amtrak Vista Dome Car, *95-97*	18	29	__1
16102	Southern 3-D Tank Car (SSS), *87*	23	30	__1
16103	Lehigh Valley 2-D Tank Car (O27), *88*	19	25	__1
16104	Santa Fe 2-D Tank Car (O27), *89*	19	23	__1
16105	D&RGW 3-D Tank Car (SSS), *89*	48	65	__1
(16106)	Mopar Express 3-D Tank Car, *88 u*	70	120	__1
16107	Sunoco 2-D Tank Car (O27), *90*	18	22	__1
(16108)	Racing Fuel 1-D Tank Car "6108" (O27), *89 u, 92 u*	9	13	__1
16109	B&O 1-D Tank Car (SSS), *91*	29	34	__1
(16110)	Circus Animals Operating Stock Car "1989" (O27), *89 u*	24	34	__1
16111	Alaska 1-D Tank Car (O27), *90-91*	19	24	__1
16112	Dow Chemical 3-D Tank Car, *90*	21	28	__1
16113	Diamond Shamrock 2-D Tank Car (O27), *91*	22	27	__1
16114	Hooker Chemicals 1-D Tank Car (O27), *91*	13	17	__1
16115	MKT 3-D Tank Car, *92*	20	25	__1
16116	U.S. Army 1-D Tank Car, *91 u*	44	55	__1

		Exc	New	Cond/$
16119	MKT 2-D Tank Car (O27), *92, 93 u*	14	19	—[1]
16121	C&NW Stock Car (SSS), *92*	65	75	—[1]
16123	Union Pacific 3-D Tank Car, *93-95*	16	22	—[1]
16124	Penn Salt 3-D Tank Car, *93*	19	24	—[1]
16125	Virginian Stock Car, *93*	20	25	—[1]
16126	Jefferson Lake 3-D Tank Car, *93*	24	28	—[1]
16127	Mobil 1-D Tank Car, *93*	25	30	—[1]
16128	Alaska 1-D Tank Car, *94*	21	25	—[1]
16129	Alaska 1-D Tank Car (O27), *93 u, 94*	23	30	—[1]
16130	SP Stock Car (O27), *93 u, 94*	9	11	—[1]
16131	T&P Reefer, *94*	19	24	—[1]
16132	Deep Rock 3-D Tank Car, *94*	25	30	—[1]
16133	Santa Fe Reefer, *94*	23	29	—[1]
16134	Reading Reefer, *94*	17	21	—[1]
16135	C&O Stock Car, *94*	23	27	—[1]
16136	B&O 1-D Tank Car, *94*	28	32	—[1]
16137	Ford 1-D Tank Car "12," *94 u*	34	39	—[1]
16138	Goodyear 1-D Tank Car, *95*	28	34	—[1]
16140	Domino Sug, *95*	25	30	—[1]
16141	Erie Stock Car, *95*	24	28	—[1]
16142	Santa Fe 1-D Tank Car, *95*	29	33	—[1]
16143	Reading Reefer, *95*	18	23	—[1]
16144	San Angelo 3-D Tank Car, *95*	21	24	—[1]
16146	Dairy Despatch Reefer, *95*	17	22	—[1]
(16147)	Clearly Canadian 1-D Tank Car (O27), *94 u*	70	90	—[1]
16149	Zep Chemical 1-D Tank Car (O27), *95 u*	60	85	—[1]
(16150)	Sunoco 1-D Tank Car "6315," *97*	30	33	—[1]
(16152)	Sunoco 3-D Tank Car "6415," *97*	—	26	—[1]
(16153)	AEC Reactor Fluid "6315-1" SD Tank Car, *97*	—	100	—[1]
(16154)	AEC Reactor Fluid "6315-2" SD Tank Car, *97*	—	100	—[1]
(16155)	AEC Reactor Fluid "6315-3" SD Tank Car, *97*	—	100	—[1]
(16157)	Gatorade Little League Baseball 1-Dome TankCar "6315," *97u*	—	45	—[1]
(16160)	Atomic Energy Commission Tank Car w/ Reactor Fluid "6515," *98*	—	49	—[1]
(16162)	Hooker 1-Dome Tank Car "6315-1," *97*	—	50	—[1]
(16163)	Hooker 1-Dome Tank Car "6315-2," *97*	—	50	—[1]
(16164)	Hooker 1-Dome Tank Car "6315-3," *97*	—	50	—[1]
(16165)	Mobilfuel 3-Dome Tank Car "6415," *97u*	—	50	—[1]
(16171)	Alaska 1-Dome Tank Car "6171," *98-99*	—	30	—[1]
(16173)	Harold the Helicopter Flatcar, *98*	—	48	—[1]
(16175)	NJ Transit Ore Car "9125" Port Morris, *98*	—	45	—[1]
(16176)	NJ Transit Ore Car "9126" Raritan Yard, *98u*	—	45	—[1]
(16177)	NJ Transit Ore Car "9127" Gladstone Yard, *98u*	—	45	—[1]
(16178)	NJ Transit Ore Car "9128" Bay Head			

		Exc	New	Cond/$
	Yard, *98u*	—	45	—1
(16179)	NJ Transit Ore Car "9129" Dover Yard, *98u*	—	45	—1
(16180)	Tabasco Single-Dome Tank Car, *98*	50	65	—1
(16181)	Biohazard Tank Car with Lights, *98*	—	60	—1
(16182)	Gatorade 1-Dome Tank Car "6315," *98u*	—	50	—1
(16187)	Linex 3D Tank Car "6425," *99*	—	30	—1
(16188)	Kodak SD Tank Car "6515," *99*	75	105	—1
(16196)	Lava Lite SD Tank Car "9968," *99*		NM	—1
(16199)	UP 1-D Tank Car "6035," *99-00*	—	25	—1
16200	Rock Island Boxcar (O27), *87-88*	7	10	—1
16201	Wabash Boxcar (O27), *88-91*	7	10	—1
16203	Key America Boxcar (O27), *87 u*	45	65	—1
16204	Hawthorne Boxcar (O27), *87 u*	50	85	—1
(16205)	Mopar Express Boxcar "1987" (O27), *87-88 u*	47	55	—1
16206	D&RGW Boxcar (SSS), *89*	38	43	—1
16207	True Value Boxcar (O27), *88 u*	32	47	—1
16208	PRR Auto Carrier w/ autos (3-tier), *89*	30	49	—1
16209	Disney Magic Boxcar (O27), *88 u*	80	100	—1
16211	Hawthorne Boxcar (O27), *88 u*	45	65	—1
16213	Shoprite Boxcar (O27), *88 u*	55	80	—1
16214	D&RGW Auto Carrier, *90*	29	40	—1
16215	Conrail Auto Carrier, *90*	28	40	—1
16217	Burlington Northern Auto Carrier, *92*	29	40	—1
16219	True Value Boxcar (O27), *89 u*	48	65	—1
(16220)	Ace Hardware Boxcar (O27), *89 u*	50	70	—1
(16221)	Macy's Boxcar (O27), *89 u*	50	70	—1
16222	Great Northern Boxcar (O27), *90-91*	8	15	—1
(16223)	Budweiser Reefer, *89-92 u*	47	65	—1
16224	True Value "Lawn Chief" Boxcar (O27), *90 u*	45	60	—1
16225	Budweiser Vat Car, *90-91 u*	120	160	—1
(16226)	Union Pacific Boxcar "6226" (O27), *90-91 u*	15	19	—1
16227	Santa Fe Boxcar (O27), *91*	13	17	—1
16228	Union Pacific Auto Carrier, *92*	28	36	—1
16229	Erie-Lackawanna Auto Carrier, *91 u*	45	55	—1
16232	Chessie System Boxcar, *92, 93 u, 94, 95 u*	25	30	—1
16233	MKT DD Boxcar, *92*	20	29	—1
16234	ACY Boxcar (SSS), *92*	34	41	—1
16235	Railway Express Agency Reefer, *92*	25	31	—1
16236	NYC "Pacemaker" Boxcar, *92 u*	29	32	—1
16237	Railway Express Agency Boxcar, *92 u*	31	34	—1
16238	NYNH&H Boxcar, *93-95*	—	3	—1
16239	Union Pacific Boxcar, *93-95*	15	20	—1
16241	Toys "r" Us Boxcar, *92-93 u*	39	45	—1
16242	Grand Trunk Auto Carrier, *93*	35	40	—1
16243	Conrail Boxcar, *93*	26	34	—1

		Exc	New	Cond/$
16244	Duluth, South Shore & Atlantic Boxcar, *93*	19	23	—¹
16245	(See 52068)			
16245	Contadina Boxcar, *93*	15	19	—¹
16247	(See 52046)			
16247	ACL Boxcar, *94*	17	21	—¹
16248	Budweiser Boxcar, *93-94 u*	32	46	—¹
16249	United Auto Workers Boxcar, *93 u*	—	55	—¹
16250	Santa Fe Boxcar (O27), *93 u, 94*	8	10	—¹
16251	Columbus & Greenville Boxcar, *94*	14	15	—¹
(16252)	U.S. Navy Boxcar "6106888," *94-95*	—	30	—¹
16253	Santa Fe Auto Carrier, *94*	32	38	—¹
16255	Wabash DD Boxcar, *95*	21	27	—¹
16256	Ford DD Boxcar, *94 u*	30	34	—¹
(16257)	Crayola Boxcar, *94 u, 95*	15	20	—¹
16258	Lehigh Valley Boxcar, *95*	18	23	—¹
16259	Chrysler Mopar Boxcar, *97 u*	29	34	—¹
16260	Chrysler Mopar Auto Carrier, *96 u*	47	55	—¹
16261	Union Pacific DD Boxcar, *95*	26	29	—¹
(16263)	AT&SF Boxcar, *96-99*	—	25	—¹
16264	Red Wing Shoes Boxcar, *95*	23	28	—¹
16265	Georgia Power "Atlanta '96" Boxcar, *95 u*	155	200	—¹
16266	Crayola Boxcar, *95*	17	23	—¹
16267	Sears/Zenith Boxcar, *95-96 u*	—	46	—¹
16268	GM/AC Delco Boxcar, *95 u*	—	50	—¹
(16270)	Dept. 56 Boxcar "9746," *96 u*	—	65	—¹
(16272)	1997 Christmas Boxcar "9700," *97*	—	36	—¹
(16274)	Marvin the Martian Boxcar "9700," *97*	—	40	—¹
16275	Eastwood Radio Flyer Boxcar "16275," *96*		NRS	—¹
(16279)	Dodge Motorsports Boxcar, *96 u*	105	145	—¹
(16284)	Galveston Wharves Boxcar "9700," *98*	—	28	—¹
(16285)	Savannah State Docks Boxcar "9700," *98*	—	26	—¹
(16291)	1998 Christmas Boxcar, *98*	—	43	—¹
(16292)	Lionel Christmas Employee Boxcar "9700," *98*	280	350	—¹
(16293)	J.C. Penny Boxcar, *97*	—	100	—¹
(16294)	Pedigree Boxcar, *97*	110	130	—¹
(16295)	Kal Kan Boxcar, *97*	110	130	—
(16296)	Whiskas Boxcar, *97*	110	130	—
(16297)	Sheba Boxcar, *97*	110	130	—¹
(16298)	Mobil Boxcar "9700," *97*	—	45	—¹
16300	Rock Island Flatcar w/ fences (O27), *87-88*	8	10	—
16301	Lionel Barrel Ramp Car, *87*	14	19	—
16303	PRR Flatcar w/ trailers, *87*	25	32	—
16304	Rock Island Gondola w/ cable reels (O27), *87-88*	5	9	—
16305	Lehigh Valley Ore Car, *87*	85	135	—

		Exc	New	Cond/$
16306	Santa Fe Barrel Ramp Car, *88*	13	16	—[1]
16307	NKP Flatcar w/ trailers, *88*	28	35	—[1]
16308	Burlington Northern Flatcar w/ trailer, *88-89*	24	30	—[1]
16309	Wabash Gondola w/ canisters, *88-91*	9	13	—[1]
(16310)	Mopar Express Gondola w/ canisters "1987," *87-88 u*	30	34	—[1]
(16311)	Mopar Express Flatcar w/trailers "1987," *87-88 u*	85	125	—[1]
(15313)	D&H Aluminum Passenger Car 4-Pack, *03*	—	350	—[1]
16313	PRR Gondola w/ cable reels (O27), *88 u, 89*	9	10	—[1]
16314	Wabash Flatcar w/ trailers, *89*	27	31	—[1]
16315	PRR Flatcar w/ fences (O27), *88 u, 89*	7	9	—[1]
16317	PRR Barrel Ramp Car, *89*	17	21	—[1]
(15318)	Lionel Lines Superliner Aluminum Passenger Car 2-Pack, *03*		CP	—[1]
16318	Lionel Lines Depressed Flatcar w/ cable reels, *89*	21	25	—[1]
16320	Great Northern Barrel Ramp Car, *90*	12	16	—[1]
16321/16322	Sealand TTUX Flatcar set w/ trailers, *90*	65	85	—[1]
16323	Lionel Lines Flatcar w/ trailers, *90*	22	26	—[1]
16324	PRR Depressed Flatcar w/ cable reels, *90*	17	21	—[1]
16325	Microracers Exhibition Ramp Car, *89 u*	20	27	—[1]
16326	Santa Fe Depressed Flatcar w/ cable reels, *91*	18	23	—[1]
(16327)	"The Big Top" Circus Gondola w/ canisters, *89 u*	19	24	—[1]
16328	NKP Gondola w/ cable reels, *90-91*	17	23	—[1]
16329	SP Flatcar w/ horses (O27), *90-91*	19	24	—[1]
16330	MKT Flatcar w/ trailers, *91*	25	30	—[1]
16331	Southern Barrel Ramp Car, *91*		NM	—[1]
16332	Lionel Lines Depressed Flatcar w/ transformer, *91*	25	30	—[1]
16333	Frisco Bulkhead Flatcar w/ wood load, *91*	20	27	—[1]
16334)	C&NW TTUX Flatcar set w/ trailers "16337" and "16338," *91*	55	60	—[2]
16335	NYC "Pacemaker" Flatcar w/ trailer (SSS), *91*	50	70	—[1]
16336)	UP Gondola w/ canisters "6336," *90-91 u*	17	21	—[1]
6337/16338	C&NW TTUX Flatcars w/ trailers (See 16334)			
6339	Mickey's World Tour Gondola w/ canisters (O27), *91, 92 u*	17	21	—[1]
6340	Amtrak Flatcar w/ stakes, *91*		NM	—[1]
6341	NYC Depressed Flatcar w/ transformer, *92*	25	29	—[1]
6342	CSX Gondola w/ coil covers, *92*	18	23	—[1]
6343	Burlington Gondola w/ coil covers, *92*	20	23	—[1]
6345/16346	SP TTUX Flatcar set w/ trailers, *92*	55	65	—[1]

		Exc	New	Cond/$
16347	Ontario Northland Bulkhead Flatcar w/ pulp load, *92*	28	31	—¹
16348	Lionel-Erie Liquefied Gas Car, *92*	31	33	—¹
16349	Allis Chalmers Condenser Car, *92*	27	33	—¹
16350	CP Rail Bulkhead Flatcar w/ wood load, *91 u*	20	29	—¹
16351	Lionel Flatcar w/ U.S.N. submarine, *92*	38	49	—²
16352	U.S. Military Flatcar w/ cruise missile, *92*	32	45	—¹
16353	B&M Gondola w/ coil covers, *91 u*	30	34	—¹
16355	Burlington Gondola, *92, 93 u, 94-95*	9	14	—¹
16356	MKT Depressed Flatcar w/ cable reels, *92*	17	21	—¹
16357	L&N Flatcar w/ trailer, *92*	26	33	—²
16358	L&N Gondola w/ coil covers, *92*	19	23	—¹
16359	Pacific Coast Gondola w/ coil covers (SSS), *92*	33	38	—¹
(16360)	N&W Maxi-Stack Flatcar set w/ containers "16361" and "16362," *93*	47	60	—²
16361/16362	N&W Maxi-Stack Flatcars w/ containers (See 16360)			
(16363)	Southern TTUX Flatcar set w/ trailers "16364" and "16365," *93*	47	60	—¹
16364/16365	Southern TTUX Flatcars w/ trailers (See 16363)			
16367	Clinchfield Gondola w/ coil covers, *93*	18	21	—¹
16368	MKT Liquid Oxygen Car, *93*	24	26	—¹
16369	Amtrak Flatcar w/ wheel load, *92 u*	19	28	—¹
16370	Amtrak Flatcar w/ rail load, *92 u*	19	28	—¹
16371	BN I-Beam Flatcar w/ load, *92 u*	27	32	—²
16372	Southern I-Beam Flatcar w/ load, *92 u*	20	25	—²
16373	Erie-Lackawanna Flatcar w/ stakes, *93*	19	23	—¹
16374	D&RGW Flatcar w/ trailer, *93*	24	29	—¹
16375	NYC Bulkhead Flatcar, *93-95*	19	23	—
16376	UP Flatcar w/ trailer, *93-95*	32	38	—
16378	Toys "R" Us Flatcar w/ trailer, *92-93 u*	65	100	—¹
16379	NP Bulkhead Flatcar w/ pulp load, *93*	16	23	—
16380	(See 52084)			
16380	UP I-Beam Flatcar w/ load, *93*	29	32	—
16381	CSX I-Beam Flatcar w/ load, *93*	21	25	—
16382	Kansas City Southern Bulkhead Flatcar, *93*	14	18	—
16383	Conrail Flatcar w/ trailer, *93*	47	55	—
16384	Soo Line Gondola w/ cable reels, *93*	14	19	—
16385	Soo Line Ore Car, *93*	55	65	—
16386	SP Flatcar w/ wood load, *94*	17	21	—
16387	Kansas City Southern Gondola w/ coil covers, *94*	15	19	—
16388	LV Gondola w/ canisters, *94*	18	22	—
16389	PRR Flatcar w/ wheel load, *94*	25	30	—

		Exc	New	Cond/$
16390	Lionel Flatcar w/ water tank, *94*	25	32	—1
16391	Lionel Lines Gondola, *93 u*	—	15	—1
16392	Wabash Gondola w/ canisters (O27), *93 u, 94*	7	9	—1
16393	Wisconsin Central Bulkhead Flatcar, *94*	13	19	—1
16394	Central Vermont Bulkhead Flatcar, *94*	20	30	—1
16395	CP Flatcar w/ rail load, *94*	18	23	—1
16396	Alaska Bulkhead Flatcar, *94*	17	22	—1
16397	Milwaukee Road I-Beam Flatcar w/ load, *94*	38	43	—1
16398	C&O Flatcar w/ trailer, *94*	60	65	—1
16399	Western Pacific I-Beam Flatcar w/ load, *94*	29	33	—1
16400	PRR Hopper (O27), *88 u, 89*	15	18	—1
16402	Southern Quad Hopper w/ coal load (SSS), *87*	30	42	—1
16406	CSX Quad Hopper w/ coal load, *90*	29	34	—1
16407	B&M Covered Quad Hopper (SSS), *91*	30	40	—1
(16408)	Union Pacific Hopper "6408" (O27), *90-91 u*	17	21	—1
16410	MKT Hopper (O27), *92, 93 u*	19	24	—1
16411	L&N Quad Hopper w/ coal load, *92*	28	32	—1
16412	C&NW Covered Quad Hopper, *94*	14	19	—1
16413	(See 52059)			
16413	Clinchfield Quad Hopper w/ coal load, *94*	16	22	—1
16414	CCC&St L Hopper (O27), *94*	14	19	—1
16416	D&RGW Covered Quad Hopper, *95*	18	23	—1
16417	Wabash Quad Hopper w/ coal load, *95*	19	23	—1
16418	C&NW Hopper w/ coal load (O27), *95*	16	22	—1
(16419)	Tennessee Central Hopper, *96*	—	17	—1
16420	Western Maryland Quad Hopper w/ coal load (SSS), *95*	27	30	—1
16421	Western Maryland Quad Hopper w/ coal load (SSS), *95*	30	33	—1
16422	Western Maryland Quad Hopper w/ coal load (SSS), *95*	—	31	—1
16423	Western Maryland Quad Hopper w/ coal load (SSS), *95*	—	31	—1
16424	Western Maryland Covered Quad Hopper (SSS), *95*	30	34	—1
16425	Western Maryland Covered Quad Hopper (SSS), *95*	26	29	—1
16426	Western Maryland Covered Quad Hopper (SSS), *95*	24	27	—1
16427	Western Maryland Covered Quad Hopper (SSS), *95*	27	30	—1
16429)	Western Maryland Quad Hoppers w/ coal loads (2)	—	70	—1

		Exc	New	Cond/$
(16430)	Georgia Power Quad Hopper w/ coal load "82947," *95 u*	—	105	—[1]
(16431)	Lionel Corporation 2-Bay Hopper "6456-1," *96*	—	23	—[1]
(16432)	Lionel Corporation 2-Bay Hopper "6456-2," *96*	—	19	—[1]
(16433)	Lionel Corporation 2-Bay Hopper "6456-3," *96*	—	20	—[1]
(16434)	LV 2-bay Hopper "6456," "TLDX," *97*	—	25	—[1]
(16435)	Virginian 2-Bay Hopper "6456-1," *97*	—	30	—[1]
(16436)	N&W 2-Bay Hopper "6456-2," *97*	—	30	—[1]
(16437)	C&O 2-Bay Hopper "6456-3," *97*	—	30	—[1]
(16438)	Frisco 4-Bay Covered Hopper "87538," *98*	—	30	—[1]
(16439)	Southern 4-Bay Covered Hopper "87538," *98*	—	31	—[1]
(16440)	Alaska 2-Bay Hopper "7100," *98-99*	—	35	—[1]
(16441)	New York Central 4-bay Hopper 6446 "886888," *99*	—	25	—[1]
(16442)	Bethlehem Gondola "6462" (SSS), *99*	—	40	—[1]
(16443)	GN 2-bay Hopper "172364," *99-00*	—	20	—[1]
(16444)	CNJ 2-bay Hopper "643," *00*	—	20	—[1]
(16445)	Frisco 2-Bay Hopper "93108," *00*	—	20	—[1]
(16446)	Burlington 2-Bay Hopper, *00*	—	20	—[1]
(16447)	PRR Tuscan 2-Bay Hopper, *00u*	—	30	—[1]
(16448)	PRR Gray 2-Bay Hopper, *00u*	—	30	—[1]
(16449)	PRR Black 2-Bay Hopper, *00u*	—	30	—[1]
(16450)	PRR Green 2-Bay Hopper, *00u*	—	30	—[1]
(16451)	Lionel Mines 2-Bay Hopper, *00u*	—	50	—[1]
(16453)	SP 2-bay Hopper "460604," *01*	—	15	—[1]
(16454)	Bethlehem Steel Hopper "41025," *01*	—	35	—[1]
(16455)	Pioneer Seed 2-Bay Hopper, *00u*	—	55	—[1]
(16456)	B&O 2-Bay Hopper, *01*	—	20	—[1]
(16459)	LV 2-Bay Hopper "51102," *01*	—	23	—[1]
(16460)	Reading 2-Bay Hopper "79636," *02*	—	22	—[1]
(16463)	Rio Grande Icebreaker Tunnel Car "18936," *02*	—	32	—[1]
(16464)	NYC Icebreaker Tunnel Car "X3200," *02*	—	32	—[1]
(16465)	WP 2-Bay Hopper "100340," *03*	—	20	—[1]
(16466)	Pennsylvania Icebreaker Tunnel Car "16466," *03*	—	32	—[1]
(16467)	Naughty and Nice Hopper 2-pack, *02*	—	60	—[1]
(16469)	B&O Hopper "435351," *02*	—	22	—[1]
(16470)	Naughty & Nice Ore Car 2-Pack, *03*	—	45	—[1]
(16473)	Rock Island Ore Car "99122," *03*	—	18	—[1]
16474	Alaska Ore Car "16474," *04*	CP		—
16475	Santa Fe Hopper "16475," *04*	CP		—
16480	Lionelville Snow Transport Quad Hopper, *04*	CP		—

		Exc	New	Cond/$
16500	Rock Island Bobber Caboose, *87-88*	9	13	__1
16501	Lehigh Valley SP-type Caboose, *87*	19	24	__1
16503	NYC Transfer Caboose, *87*	16	22	__1
16504	Southern N5c Caboose (SSS), *87*	17	30	__1
16505	Wabash SP-type Caboose, *88-91*	10	15	__1
16506	Santa Fe B/W Caboose, *88*	25	33	__1
(16507)	Mopar Express SP-type Caboose "1987," *87-88 u*	40	49	__1
(16508)	Lionel Lines SP-type Caboose "6508," *89 u*	13	17	__1
16509	D&RGW SP-type Caboose (SSS), *89*	19	24	__1
16510	New Haven B/W Caboose, *89*	25	30	__1
16511	PRR Bobber Caboose, *88 u, 89*	9	13	__1
16513	Union Pacific SP-type Caboose, *89*	14	21	__1
16515	Lionel Lines RailScope SP-type Caboose, *89*	22	26	__1
16516	Lehigh Valley SP-type Caboose, *90*	15	26	__1
16517	Atlantic Coast Line B/W Caboose, *90*	21	25	__1
16518	Chessie System B/W Caboose, *90*	39	48	__1
16519	Rock Island Transfer Caboose, *90*	13	17	__1
(16520)	"Welcome To The Show" Circus SP-type Caboose, *89 u*	13	21	__1
16521	PRR SP-type Caboose, *90-91*	8	11	__1
16522	"Chills & Thrills" Circus N5c Caboose, *90-91*	10	15	__1
16523	Alaska SP-type Caboose, *91*	26	34	__1
(16524)	Anheuser-Busch SP-type Caboose, *89-92 u*	30	39	__1
16525	D&H B/W Caboose (SSS), *91*	27	35	__1
16526	Kansas City Southern SP-type Caboose, *91*	17	21	__1
16527	Western Pacific Work Caboose, *92*		NM	__1
(16528)	Union Pacific SP-type Caboose "6528," *90-91 u*	17	21	__1
(16529)	Santa Fe SP-type Caboose "16829," *91*	9	13	__1
(16530)	Mickey's World Tour SP-type Caboose "16830," *91, 92 u*	13	17	__1
16531	Texas &Pacific SP-type Caboose, *92*	18	23	__1
16533	C&NW B/W Caboose, *92*	26	36	__1
16534	Delaware & Hudson SP-type Caboose, *92*	17	22	__1
16535	Erie-Lackawanna B/W Caboose, *91 u*	34	44	__1
16536	Chessie System SP-type Caboose, *92, 93 u, 94, 95 u*	—	23	__1
16537	MKT SP-type Caboose, *92, 93 u*	17	21	__1
(16538)	L&N B/W Caboose "1041," *92 u*	29	33	__1
16538	L&N/Family Lines Steelside Caboose w/ smoke (Std. O), *92*		NM	__1
(16539)	WP Steelside Caboose w/ smoke "539" (Std. O) (SSS), *92*	60	65	__1
(16541)	Montana Rail Link E/V Caboose w/ smoke "10131," *93*	55	65	__1

		Exc	New	Cond/$
(16543)	NYC SP-type Caboose, *93-95*	—	20	—¹
16544	(See 16564)			
16544	Union Pacific SP-type Caboose, *93-95*	22	26	—¹
16546	Clinchfield SP-type Caboose, *93*	22	26	—¹
16547	Happy Holidays SP-type Caboose, *93-95*	38	44	—¹
16548	Conrail SP-type Caboose, *93*	22	30	—¹
16549	Soo Line Work Caboose, *93*	18	26	—¹
16550	U.S. Navy Searchlight Caboose, *94-95*	17	21	—¹
16551	Budweiser SP-type Caboose, *93-94 u*	24	29	—¹
16552	Frisco Searchlight Caboose, *94*	30	34	—¹
16553	United Auto Workers SP-type Caboose, *93 u*	—	40	—¹
(16554)	GT E/V Caboose w/ smoke "79052," *94*	40	47	—¹
16555	C&O SP-type Caboose, *94*	22	26	—¹
16556	(See 16909)			
16557	Ford SP-type Caboose, *94 u*	19	24	—¹
(16558)	Crayola SP-type Caboose, *94 u, 95*	17	21	—¹
(16559)	Seaboard CC Caboose "5658," *95*	26	28	—¹
16560	Chrysler Mopar Caboose, *94 u*	22	24	—¹
(16561)	Union Pacific CC Caboose "25766," *95*	27	31	—¹
16562	Reading CC Caboose, *95*	29	33	—¹
(16563)	Lionel Lines SP-type Caboose, *95*	22	26	—¹
16564	Western Maryland CC Caboose (SSS), *95*	30	34	—¹
16565	Milwaukee Road B/W Caboose, *95*	55	65	—¹
(16566)	U.S. Army SP-type Caboose "907," *95*	—	26	—¹
(16568)	AT&SF SP-type Caboose, *96-99*	—	23	—¹
16570	NdeM E/V Caboose, *96*		NM	—¹
(16571)	Georgia Power SP-type Caboose "52789," *95 u*	—	60	—¹
(16575)	Sears Zenith, SP-type Caboose, *95*	—	38	—¹
(16577)	U.S. Coast Guard Work Caboose, *96*	—	26	—¹
16578	Lionel Lines SP-type Caboose, *95 u*	—	20	—¹
(16579)	GM/AC Delco, SP-type Caboose, *95*	—	35	—¹
(16580)	Lionel SP-type Caboose, *96-99*	—	11	—¹
(16581)	Union Pacific Illuminated Caboose, *96*	—	30	—¹
(16585)	LL Illuminated Caboose "6257," *97*		NM	—¹
(16586)	SP Illuminated Caboose "6357," *97*	—	29	—¹
(16590)	Dodge Motorsports SP-type Caboose, "6950," *96*	—	40	—¹
(16591)	Little League Baseball SP-type Caboose "6397," *97*	—	30	—¹
(16593)	Lionel Belt Line Caboose "6257," *98*	—	33	—¹
(16594)	Lionel Caboose "6357," *98*	—	35	—¹
16600	Illinois Central Coal Dump Car, *88*	13	21	—¹
16601	Canadian National Searchlight Car, *88*	19	24	—¹
16602	Erie-Lackawanna Coal Dump Car, *87*	16	26	—¹
16603	Detroit Zoo Giraffe Car (O27), *87*	40	49	—¹

		Exc	New	Cond/$
16604	NYC Log Dump Car, *87*	14	24	—1
16605	Bronx Zoo Giraffe Car (O27), *88*	39	44	—1
16606	Southern Searchlight Car, *87*	13	21	—1
[16606]	Southern TCA Southern Searchlight Car, *88 u*	17	24	—1
(16607)	Southern Coal Dump Car "16707" (SSS), *87*	18	26	—1
16608	Lehigh Valley Searchlight Car, *87*	22	30	—1
16609	Lehigh Valley Derrick Car, *87*	22	30	—1
16610	Lionel Track Maintenance Car, *87-88*	14	24	—1
16611	Santa Fe Log Dump Car, *88*	15	23	—1
16612	Soo Line Log Dump Car, *89*	14	24	—1
16613	MKT Coal Dump Car, *89*	15	23	—1
16614	Reading Cop and Hobo Car (O27), *89*	27	29	—1
16615	Lionel Lines Extension Searchlight Car, *89*	20	28	—1
16616	D&RGW Searchlight Car (SSS), *89*	22	30	—1
16617	C&NW Boxcar w/ ETD, *89*	21	32	—1
16618	Santa Fe Track Maintenance Car, *89*	13	21	—1
16619	Wabash Coal Dump Car, *90*	14	24	—1
16620	C&O Track Maintenance Car, *90-91*	16	22	—1
16621	Alaska Log Dump Car, *90*	21	27	—1
16622	CSX Boxcar w/ ETD, *90-91*	21	30	—1
16623	MKT DD Boxcar w/ ETD, *91*	16	23	—1
16624	NH Cop and Hobo Car (O27), *90-91*	23	31	—1
16625	NYC Extension Searchlight Car, *90*	18	24	—1
16626	CSX Searchlight Car, *90*	18	26	—1
16627	CSX Log Dump Car, *90*	19	23	—1
16628	"Laughter" Circus Animated Gondola, *90-91*	36	43	—1
16629	"Animal Car" Circus Elephant Car (O27), *90-91*	38	50	—1
16630	SP Operating Cowboy Car (O27), *90-91*	22	26	—1
16631	RI Boxcar w/ Steam RailSounds, *90*	110	130	—1
16632	BN Boxcar w/ Diesel RailSounds, *90*	100	110	—1
16633	Great Northern Cop and Hobo Car (O27), *91*		NM	—1
16634	WM Coal Dump Car, *91*	25	31	—1
16635	CP Rail Track Maintenance Car, *91*		NM	—1
16636	D&RGW Log Dump Car, *91*	17	22	—1
16637	WP Extension Searchlight Car, *91*	27	30	—1
16638	Lionelville Circus Operating Animal Car (O27), *91*	60	65	—1
16639	B&O Boxcar w/ Steam RailSounds, *91*	100	120	—1
16640	Rutland Boxcar w/ Diesel RailSounds, *91*	100	120	—1
16641	Toys "R" Us Giraffe Car (O27), *90-91 u*	45	65	—1
16642	Mickey's World Tour Goofy Car (O27), *91, 92 u*	38	47	—1
16643	Amtrak Coal Dump Car, *91*		NM	—1
16644	Amtrak Crane Car, *91, 92 u*	39	46	—1
16645	Amtrak Searchlight Caboose, *91, 92 u*	27	30	—1

		Exc	New	Cond/$
16646	Railbox Boxcar w/ ETD, *92*		NM	—¹
16649	Railway Express Agency Boxcar			
	w/ Steam RailSounds, *92*	115	145	—¹
16650	NYC "Pacemaker" Boxcar			
	w/ Diesel RailSounds, *92*	110	145	—¹
16651	Circus Operating Clown Car (O27), *92*	33	38	—²
16652	Lionel Radar Car, *92*	25	30	—²
16653	Western Pacific Crane Car (SSS), *92*	48	65	—¹
16654	(See 17214)			
(16655)	Steam Tender w/ RailSounds "1993," *93*	115	140	—¹
16656	Burlington Log Dump Car, *92 u*	17	23	—¹
16657	Lehigh Valley Coal Dump Car, *92 u*	22	29	—¹
16658	Erie-Lackawanna Crane Car, *93*	47	65	—¹
16659	Union Pacific Searchlight Car, *93-95*	17	21	—¹
16660	Lionel Fire Car w/ ladders, *93-94*	30	32	—²
16661	Lionel Flatcar w/ boat, *93*	20	24	—³
16662	Looney Tunes Operating Bugs Bunny			
	and Yosemite Sam Car (O27), *93-94*	30	31	—¹
16663	Missouri Pacific Searchlight Car, *93*	19	22	—¹
16664	L&N Coal Dump Car, *93*	22	25	—¹
16665	Maine Central Log Dump Car, *93*	25	30	—¹
16666	Lionel Toxic Waste Car, *93-94*	32	42	—¹
16667	Conrail Searchlight Car, *93*	27	30	—¹
16668	Ontario Northland Log Dump Car, *93*	21	25	—¹
16669	Soo Line Searchlight Car, *93*	17	21	—¹
16670	Lionel TV Car, *93-94*	21	25	—²
(16673)	Lionel Lines Tender w/ whistle, *94-97*	30	37	—¹
16674	Pinkerton Animated Gondola, *94*	32	37	—¹
16675	Great Northern Log Dump Car, *94*	22	26	—¹
16676	Burlington Coal Dump Car, *94*	23	28	—¹
16677	NATO Flatcar w/ Royal Navy submarine, *94*	30	34	—²
16678	Rock Island Searchlight Car, *94*	25	27	—¹
16679	U.S. Mail Operating Boxcar, *94*	45	50	—¹
16680	Lionel Cherry Picker Car, *94*	23	26	—¹
16681	Aquarium Car, *95*	55	60	—³
16682	Lionelville Farms Operating Stock Car			
	(O27), *94*	23	27	—¹
16683	Los Angeles Zoo Elephant Car (O27), *94*	24	29	—¹
16684	U.S. Navy Crane Car, *94-95*	35	40	—¹
16685	Erie Extension Searchlight Car, *95*	30	34	—¹
16686	Mickey Mouse and Big Bad Pete			
	Animated Boxcar, *95*	35	45	—¹
16687	U.S. Mail Operating Boxcar, *94*	36	46	—¹
16688	Lionel Fire Car w/ ladders, *94*	42	55	—¹
16689	Lionel Toxic Waste Car, *94*	31	35	—¹
16690	Looney Tunes Operating Bugs Bunny and			

		Exc	New	Cond/$
	Yosemite Sam Car (O27), *94*	32	40	—[1]
16701	Southern Tool Car (SSS), *87*	43	55	—[1]
16702	Amtrak Bunk Car, *91, 92 u*	25	27	—[1]
16703	NYC Tool Car, *92*	23	30	—[1]
16704	Lionel TV Car, *94*	28	31	—[1]
16705	Chesapeake &Ohio Cop and Hobo Car, *95*	28	34	—[1]
16706	Animal Transport Service Giraffe Car, *95*	25	28	—[1]
16707	(See 16607)			
16708	C&NW Track Maintenance Car, *95*	25	31	—[1]
16709	New York Central Derrick Car, *95*	25	32	—[1]
16710	U.S. Army Operating Missile Car, *95*	39	41	—[2]
16711	Pennsylvania Searchlight Car, *95*	27	31	—[1]
16712	Pinkerton Animated Gondola, *95*	30	34	—[1]
16713	Great Northern Log Dump Car, *95*		NM	—[1]
16714	Burlington Coal Dump Car, *95*		NM	—[1]
(16715)	AT&SF Log Dump Car, *96-99*	—	25	—[1]
16717	Jersey Central Crane Car, *96*	—	41	—[1]
16718	U.S.M.C. Missile Launching Flatcar, *96*	37	39	—[1]
(16719)	Exploding Boxcar, *96*	—	32	—[1]
(16720)	Lionel Lines Searchlight Car "3650," *96-97*	—	45	—[1]
(16724)	Mickey and Friends Submarine Car, *96*	—	38	—[1]
(16725)	Rhino Transport Car, *97*	—	26	—[1]
(16726)	US Army Fire Ladder Car, *96*	—	43	—[1]
(16734)	U.S.C.G Searchlight Car, *96*	—	30	—[1]
(16735)	U.S.C.G Flatcar w/ Radar, *96*	—	35	—[1]
16736	U.S.C.G. Derrick Car, *96*	—	34	—[1]
(16737)	Warner Bros. Road Runner & Wile E. Coyote ACME Gondola "3444," *96*		40	—[1]
(16738)	Warner Bros. Pepe Le Pew & Penelope Boxcar "3370," *96*	—	44	—[1]
(16739)	Warner Bros. Foghorn Leghorn Poultry Car "6434," *96*	—	48	—[1]
(16740)	Lionel Corporation Mail Car "3428," *96*	—	44	—[1]
(16741)	Union Pacific Illuminated Bunk Car, *97*	—	28	—[1]
(16742)	Trout Ranch Aquarium Car "3435," *96*	—	50	—[2]
(16744)	Port of Lionel City Searchlight Car, *97*	—	30	—[1]
(16745)	Port of Lionel City Flatcar w/ Radar, *97*	—	30	—[1]
(16746)	Port of Lionel City Derrick Car, *97*	—	30	—[1]
(16747)	Breyer Animated Horsecar "6473," *97*	—	33	—[1]
(16748)	US Forest Service Log-Dump Car "3361," *97*	—	34	—[1]
(16749)	Midget Mines Ore-Dump Car "3479," *97*	—	36	—[1]
(16750)	Lionel City Aquarium Car "3436," *97*	—	36	—[1]
(16751)	WLNL Channel 7-AIREX Sports TV Car "3545," *97*	—	32	—[1]
(16752)	Warner Bros. Marvin the Martian Missile-Launching Flatcar "6655," *97*	75	105	—[1]

		Exc	New	Cond/$
(16754)	Warner Bros. Porky Pig & Instant Martians "6805," *97*	95	120	—¹
(16755)	Warner Bros. Daffy Duck Animated Balloon Car "3470," *97*	75	105	—¹
(16757)	Johnny Lightning Auto Carrier "3435," *96u*	—	80	—¹
(16760)	Pluto and Cats Animated Gondola "3444," *97*	—	46	—¹
(16765)	Bureau of Land Management Log Car "3351," *98*	—	33	—¹
(16766)	Bureau of Land Management Ore Car "3479," *98*	—	31	—¹
(16767)	New York Central Ice Docks Ice Car "6352," *98*	—	47	—¹
(16776)	Lionel Holiday Railsounds Boxcar, *98*	—	100	—¹
(16777)	Lionel Cola Animated Car & Platform, *98*	—	100	—¹
(16782)	Bethlehem Ore Dump Car "3479," *99*	—	95	—¹
(16783)	Westside Lumber Log Dump Car "3351," *99*	—	32	—¹
(16784)	Pratt's Hollow Seed Dump Car "3479," *99*	—	45	—¹
(16785)	Happy Holidays Music Reefer "5700," *99*	—	135	—¹
(16789)	Easter Operating Boxcar "9700," *99*	—	39	—¹
(16790)	UP Crowsounds Stock Car "3356," *99*	—	100	—¹
(16791)	NY City Lights Boxcar "9700," *99*	—	42	—¹
(16792)	Constellation Boxcar "9600," *99*	—	44	—¹
(16793)	Animated Glow-in-the-Dark Alien Boxcar "9700," *99*	—	42	—¹
(16794)	Wicked Witch Halloween Boxcar "9700," *99*	—	40	—¹
(16795)	Elf Chasing Rudolph Gondola "6462," *99*	—	60	—¹
(16796)	Snowman Loading Ice Car "6352," *99*	—	55	—¹
16800	Lionel Railroader Club Ore Car, *86 u*	60	65	—¹
16801	Lionel Railroader Club Bunk Car, *88 u*	28	42	—¹
16802	Lionel Railroader Club Tool Car, *89 u*	27	33	—¹
16803	Lionel Railroader Club Searchlight Car, *90 u*	26	30	—²
16804	Lionel Railroader Club B/W Caboose, *91 u*	27	38	—¹
(16805)	Budweiser Malt Nutrine Reefer "3285," *91-92 u*	70	95	—¹
16806	Toys "R" Us Boxcar, *92 u*	27	31	—²
(16807)	H.J. Heinz Reefer "301," *93*	24	28	—¹
16808	Toys "R" Us Boxcar, *93 u*	37	43	—¹
16811	Rutland Boxcar TCA, *96*		NRS	—¹
(16812)	LOTS Grand Trunk 2-bay Hopper, *96 u*	—	60	—¹
(16813)	LOTS Pa. Power and Light Hopper (Std. O), *97 u*	—	90	—¹
(16817)	Ambassador 1-D Tank Car "1999," *00 u*	—	80	—¹
(16818)	Engineer Award Tank Car, *00u*	—	680	—¹
(16819)	JLC Award Tank Car, *00u*	—	750	—¹
(16820)	Ambassador Thank You Boxcar "2000," *00 u*	295	330	—¹
16829	(See 16529)			
16830	(See 16530)			
(16901)	Lionel Catalog video (VHS), *91 u*	17	21	—¹

		Exc	New	Cond/$
16903	CP Bulkhead Flatcar w/ pulp load (SSS), *94*	22	25	__1
(16904)	NYC "Pacemaker" TTUX Flatcar set w/ trailers "16905" and "16906," *94*	60	65	__2
16905/16906	NYC "Pacemaker" TTUX Flatcars w/ trailers (See 16904)			
16907	Lionel Flatcar w/ farm tractors, *94*	29	36	__1
(16908)	U.S. Navy Flatcar "04039" w/ submarine "930," *94-95*	43	50	__1
(16909)	U.S. Navy Gondola w/ canisters "16556," *94-95*	16	22	__1
16910	Missouri Pacific Flatcar w/ trailer, *94*	23	28	__1
16911	NETCA B&M Flatcar w/ trailer "1985," *95*	—	120	__1
16911	B&M Flatcar w/ trailer, *94*	25	30	__1
(16912)	CN Maxi-Stack Flatcar set w/ containers "640000" and "640001," *94*	60	65	__1
(16913)/(16914)	CN Maxi-Stack Flatcars w/ containers "640000" and "640001" (See 16912)			
16915	Lionel Lines Gondola (O27), *93-94 u*	6	9	__1
16916	Ford Flatcar w/ trailer, *94 u*	40	47	__1
(16917)	Crayola Gondola w/ crayons, *94 u, 95*	8	9	__1
(16918)	Budweiser Flatcar w/Trailer, *94*		NM	__1
(16919)	Chrysler Mopar Gondola w/ coil covers, *94-96*	33	36	__1
16920	Lionel Flatcar w/ construction block helicopter, *95*		NM	__1
16922	Chesapeake &Ohio Flatcar w/ trailer, *95*	24	29	__1
16923	Lionel Intermodal Service Flatcar w/ wheelchocks, *95*	21	27	__1
(16924)	Lionel Corporation Flatcar w/ trailer "6424," *96*	—	29	__1
16925	New York Central Flatcar w/ trailer, *95*	65	85	__1
16926	Frisco Flatcar w/ trailers, *95*	22	28	__1
16927	New York Central Flatcar w/ gondola, *95*	18	23	__1
16928	Soo Line Flatcar w/ dump bin (O27), *95*	14	19	__1
16929	BCRail Gondola w/ cable reels, *95*	19	23	__1
16930	Santa Fe Flatcar w/ wheel load, *95*	20	25	__1
16932	Erie Flatcar w/ rail load, *95*	18	23	__1
16933	Lionel Lines Flatcar w/ automobiles, *95*	22	23	__2
16934	Pennsylvania Flatcar w/ Ertl road grader, *95*	31	45	__2
16935	UP Depressed Flatcar w/ Ertl bulldozer, *95*	28	45	__2
(16936)	Sealand Maxi-Stack Flatcar set w/ containers "16937" and "16938," *95*	70	80	__1
16937/16938	Sealand Maxi-Stack Flatcars w/ containers (See 16936)			
(16939)	U.S. Navy Flatcar w/ boat "04040," *95*	22	27	__1
(16940)	AT&SF Flatcar w/ Trailer, *96-99*	—	40	__1
(16941)	AT&SF Flatcar w/ Autos, *96-99*	—	25	__1

		Exc	New	Cond/$
16943	Jersey Central Gondola, *96*	—	18	—[1]
(16944)	Georgia Power Depressed Flatcar w/ transformer "31438," *95 u*	—	50	—[1]
(16945)	Georgia Power Depressed Flatcar w/ cable reels "31950," *95 u*	—	50	—[1]
(16946)	C&O F9 Well Car "3840," *96*	—	32	—[2]
(16951)	Southern I-Beam Flatcar w/ load "9823," *97*	—	33	—[1]
16952	U.S. Navy Flatcar w/ Ertl helicopter, *96*	—	30	—[2]
(16953)	NYC Flatcar w/ Red Wing Shoes trailer "1905-95," *95 u*	33	38	—[1]
(16954)	NYC Flatcar w/ Ertl Scraper "6424," *96*	—	32	—[1]
(16955)	AT&SF Flatcar w/ Ertl Challenger, *96*	—	34	—[1]
(16956)	Zenith Flatcar w/Trailer, *95 u*	—	130	—[1]
(16957)	Lionel Depressed-Center Flatcar w/ Ertl Case 4WD Tractor "6461," *96*	—	29	—[1]
(16958)	Lionel Flatcar w/ Ertl New Holland Loader, *96*	—	29	—[1]
(16960)	U.S.C.G Flatcar w/ boat, *96*	—	40	—[1]
(16961)	GM/AC Delco Flatcar w/Trailer, *95*	—	70	—[1]
(16963)	Lionel Corporation Flatcar "6411," *96-97*	—	33	—[1]
(16964)	Lionel Corporation Gondola "6462," *97*	—	19	—[1]
(16965)	Lionel Scout Flatcar w/ stakes "6424," *96-97*	—	20	—[1]
(16967)	Lionel Depressed-Center Flatcar w/ Transformer "6461," *96*	—	29	—[1]
(16968)	Lionel Aviation Depressed-Center Flatcar w/ General Hospital LifeFlight Ertl Helicopter "6461," *96*	—	29	—[2]
(16969)	Flatcar w/ Beechcraft Bonanza "6411," *96*	—	30	—[2]
(16970)	LA County Flatcar w/ motorized LA County Lifeguard Powerboat "6424," *96*	—	22	—[1]
(16971)	Port of Lionel City Flatcar w/ boat, *97*	—	35	—[1]
(16972)	P&LE Gondola "6462," *97*	—	22	—[1]
(16975)	Lionel Doublestack Set "6480," 2 well cars, *97*	—	75	—[1]
(16978)	MILW Flatcar "6424" w/ P&H shovel kit, *97*	—	43	—[1]
(16980)	Warner Bros. Speedy Gonzales Missile Flatcar "6823," *97*	—	39	—[1]
(16982)	BC Rail Bulkhead Flatcar w/ wood load "9823," *97*	—	33	—[1]
(16983)	PRR F9 Well Car w/ cable reels "6983," *97*	—	37	—[1]
(16985)	Ford Eastwood Flatcar w/ Vans, *97 u*	—	55	—[1]
(16986)	Sears Zenith Flatcar w/ Bulkheads, *96 u*	—	45	—[1]
(16987)	Musco Lighting Flatcar w/ Bulkheads, *97 u*	—	35	—[1]
(16997)	Lionel Lines Recovery Crane Car, *99*	—	50	—[1]
17000	(See 17107)			
17002	Conrail 2-bay ACF Hopper (Std. O), *87*	60	65	—[1]
17003	Du Pont 2-bay ACF Hopper (Std. O), *90*	50	60	—[1]

		Exc	New	Cond/$
17004	MKT 2-bay ACF Hopper (Std. O), *91*	24	27	—1
17005	Cargill 2-bay ACF Hopper (Std. O), *92*	31	41	—1
17006	Soo Line 2-bay ACF Hopper (Std. O)			
	(SSS), *93*	46	55	—1
(17007)	GN 2-bay ACF Hopper "173872" (Std. O), *94*	29	35	—1
(17008)	D&RGW 2-bay ACF Hopper "10009"			
	(Std. O), *95*	—	28	—1
(17009)	New York Central 2-bay ACF Hopper, *96*	—	32	—1
(17010)	Government du Canada ACF 2-bay			
	Covered Hopper "7000," *98*	—	32	—1
(17011)	NP ACF 2-Bay Covered Hoppers "75052," *98*	—	44	—1
(17012)	Government du Canada ACF 2-bay Covered			
	Hopper "7001," *98*	—	41	—1
(17013)	NYC Graffiti 2-Bay Covered Hopper			
	"7000," *99*	—	50	—1
(17014)	Graffiti 2-Bay Covered Hopper "7000"			
	(Std O), *99*	—	39	—1
(17015)	Corning 2-Bay Hopper "90409" (Std. O), *01*	—	40	—1
(17016)	C&NW 2-Bay Hopper "96644" (Std. O), *01*	—	46	—1
(17017)	Chessie System 2-Bay Hopper "605527"			
	(Std. O), *02*	—	32	—1
(17018)	Nickel Plate Road Offset Hopper "33074," *02*	—	43	—1
(17019)	Santa Fe Offset Hopper "78299," *02*	—	43	—1
(17020)	Frisco Offset Hopper "92092," *02*	—	43	—1
(17021)	NYC Offset Hopper "867999," *02*	—	43	—1
(17022)	Burlington 2-Bay ACF Hopper "183925"			
	(Std. O), *03*	—	30	—1
17023	BNSF 2-Bay Hopper "409038" (Std. O), *04*		CP	—1
(17024)	Reading Offset Hopper "81089"			
	(Std. O), *03-04*	—	43	—1
(17025)	C&O Offset Hopper "300027" (Std. O), *03-04*	—	43	—1
(17026)	D&H Offset Hopper "7215" (Std. O), *03-04*	—	43	—1
(17027)	IC Offset Hopper "92142" (Std. O), *03-04*	—	43	—1
(17028)	GE PS-2 2-Bay Covered Hopper "326"			
	(Std. O), *03-04*		CP	—1
(17029)	CNJ PS-2 2-Bay Covered Hopper "803"			
	(Std. O), *03-04*		CP	—1
(17030)	Milwaukee Road PS-2 2-Bay Covered			
	Hopper "99708" (Std. O), *03-04*		CP	—1
(17031)	SP PS-2 2-Bay Covered Hopper "401306"			
	(Std. O), *03-04*		CP	—1
17100	Chessie System 3-bay ACF Hopper			
	(Std. O), *88*	38	65	—1
17101	Chessie System 3-bay ACF Hopper			
	(Std. O), *88*	37	45	—1
17102	Chessie System 3-bay ACF Hopper			

		Exc	New	Cond/$
	(Std. O), *88*	35	41	—[1]
17103	Chessie System 3-bay ACF Hopper (Std. O), *88*	31	34	—[1]
17104	Chessie System 3-bay ACF Hopper (Std. O), *88*	38	46	—[1]
17105	Chessie System 3-bay ACF Hopper (Std. O), *95*	39	46	—[1]
17107	Sclair 3-bay ACF Hopper (Std. O), *89*	70	80	—[1]
17108	Santa Fe 3-bay ACF Hopper (Std. O), *90*	50	55	—[1]
17109	N&W 3-bay ACF Hopper (Std. O), *91*	23	35	—[1]
17110	Union Pacific Hopper w/ coal load (Std. O), *91*	23	29	—[2]
17111	Reading Hopper w/ coal load (Std. O), *91*	26	34	—[1]
17112	Erie-Lack. 3-bay ACF Hopper (Std. O), *92*	23	34	—[1]
17113	LV Hopper w/ coal load (Std. O), *92-93*	27	33	—[1]
17114	Peabody Hopper w/ coal load (Std. O), *92-93*	40	47	—[1]
(17118)	Archer Daniels Midland 3-bay ACF Hopper "60029" (Std. O), *93*	32	40	—[1]
(17120)	CSX Hopper w/ coal load "295110" (Std. O), *94*	33	42	—[1]
(17121)	ICG Hopper w/ coal load "72867" (Std. O), *94*	26	33	—[1]
(17122)	RI 3-bay ACF Hopper "800200" (Std. O), *94*	32	39	—[1]
(17123)	Cargill Covered Grain Hopper "844304" (Std. O), *95*	29	40	—[1]
(17124)	Archer Daniels Midland 3-bay ACF Hopper "50224" (Std. O), *95*	26	33	—[1]
(17125)	Goodyear 3-bay ACF Hopper (Std. O), *95*		NM	—[1]
(17127)	Delaware & Hudson 3-bay Hopper, *96*	—	37	—[1]
(17128)	Chesapeake & Ohio 3-bay hopper, *96*	—	35	—[1]
(17129)	WM 3-bay hopper w/ coal load "9300" (Std O), *97*	—	35	—[1]
(17132)	PRR 3-Bay ACF Hopper "260815," *98*	—	46	—[1]
(17133)	BNSF ACF 3-Bay Covered Hopper "403698," *98*	—	38	—[1]
(17134)	BNSF 3-Bay Covered Hopper "403698" (Std. O), *01*	—	38	—[1]
(17135)	BNSF ACF 3-Bay Covered Hopper With ETD, *98*	—	42	—[1]
(17137)	Cargill 3-Bay Covered Hopper "1219" (Std. O), *99*	—	45	—[1]
(17138)	Farmers Elevator 3-Bay Covered Hopper (Std. O), *99*	—	45	—[1]
(17139)	Grain Train 3-bay Hopper "BLMR 1025," *99-00*	—	44	—[1]
(17140)	Virginian 3-bay Hopper "5260-5265"			

		Exc	New	Cond/$
	(6-pack), *99*	—	190	—[1]
(17143)	Gondola w/ parts load (SSS), 00			
	(6-pack), *99*	—	25	—[1]
(17147)	C&O 3-bay Hopper "156330-156335"			
	(6-pack), *99*	—	190	—[1]
(17154)	Alberta Cylindrical Hopper "628373"			
	(Std. O), *01*	—	35	—[1]
(17155)	Shell Cylindrical Hopper "3527" (Std. O), *01*	—	40	—[1]
(17155)	Shell Cylindrical Hopper "3527" (Std. O), *01*	—	40	—[1]
(17156)	ACF Pressureaide 3-Bay Hopper "59267"			
	(Std. O), *01*	—	30	—[1]
(17157)	Wonder Bread "56670" 3-bay Hopper			
	(Std. O), *01*	—	40	—[1]
(17158)	Conrail Coal Hopper "487739" (Std. O), *01*	—	42	—[1]
(17159)	N&W Coal Hopper "1776" (Std. O), *01*	—	45	—[1]
(17170)	General Mills 3-Bay Covered Hopper			
	(Std. O), *00u*	—	65	—[1]
17171	Lionel Lion Cylindrical Hopper (Std. O), *01*	—	45	—[1]
(17172)	CP Rail Cylindrical Hopper "385206"			
	(Std. O), *02*	—	37	—[1]
17173	Government of Canada Cylindrical Hopper			
	"111031" (Std. O), *02*	—	33	—[1]
(17174)	GN 3-Bay Hopper "171250" (Std. O), *02*	—	33	—[1]
(17175)	IC PS-2CD 4427 Covered Hopper "57031"			
	(Std. O), *02*	—	40	—[1]
(17176)	Cargill PS-2CD 4427 Covered Hopper "2514"			
	(Std. O), *02*	—	40	—[1]
(17177)	Demonstrator PS-2CD 4427 Covered Hopper			
	2500 (Std. O), *02*	—	40	—[1]
(17178)	Santa Fe PS-2CD 4427 Covered Hopper			
	304774 (Std. O), *02*	—	40	—[1]
(17179)	Indianapolis Power & Light Coal Hopper			
	"10074," (Std. O) , *02*	—	40	—[1]
(17180)	Rock Island Coal Hopper "700665,"			
	Std. O, *02*	—	40	—[1]
(17181)	NYC 4-Bay ACF Centerflow Hopper			
	"892138" (Std. O), *03*	—	45	—[1]
(17182)	Sigco, Hybrids 4-Bay ACF Centerflow			
	Hopper "1100" (Std. O), *03*	—	45	—[1]
(17183)	C&O Hopper "156341" (Std. O), *01*	—	30	—[1]
(17184)	Virginian Hopper "5271" (Std. O), *01*	—	30	—[1]
(17185)	LLCX Bathtub Gondola "877900" (Std. O), *01*	—	36	—[1]
(17186)	Cannonaide 4-Bay ACF Centerflow Hopper			
	"96169" (Std. O), *03*	—	45	—[1]
(17187)	Rio Grande 4-Bay ACF Centerflow Hopper			
	"15521" (Std. O), *03*	—	45	—[1]

		Exc	New	Cond/$
(17188)	Govt. of Canada 3-Bay Cylindrical Hopper "106068" (Std. 0), *03*	—	42	—[1]
(17189)	Saskatchewan Grain 3-Bay Cylindrical Hopper "1625338" (Std. 0), *03*	—	42	—[1]
(17190)	Soo/CP 3-Bay ACF Hopper "119303" (Std. 0), *03*	—	32	—[1]
(17191)	BN PS-2CD 4427 Hopper "450669" (Std. 0), *03-04*	—	45	—[1]
(17192)	Lehigh Valley PS-2CD 4427 Hopper "51118" (Std. 0), *03-04*	—	45	—[1]
(17193)	Chessie System/WM PS-2CD 4427 Hopper "4673" (Std. 0), *03-04*	—	45	—[1]
(17194)	MKT PS-2CD 4427 Hopper "1122" (Std. 0), *03-04*	—	45	—[1]
17195	L&N 3-Bay Hopper "240850" (Std. 0), *04*		CP	—[1]
17196	Firestone 4-Bay Hopper "53240" (Std. 0), *04*		CP	—[1]
17197	Diamond Chemicals 4-Bay Hopper "53286" (Std. 0), *04*		CP	—[1]
17198	Hercules 4-Bay Hopper "50503" (Std. 0), *04*		CP	—[1]
17199	Conrail 4-Bay Hopper "888367" (Std. 0), *04*		CP	—[1]
17200	Canadian Pacific Boxcar (Std. 0), *89*	37	38	—[1]
17201	Conrail Boxcar (Std. 0), *87*	39	45	—[1]
17202	Santa Fe Boxcar w/ Diesel RailSounds (Std. 0), *90*	85	90	—[1]
17203	Cotton Belt DD Boxcar (Std. 0), *91*	33	36	—[1]
17204	Missouri Pacific DD Boxcar (Std. 0), *91*	28	30	—[2]
17207	C&IM DD Boxcar (Std. 0), *92*	32	36	—[1]
17208	Union Pacific DD Boxcar (Std. 0), *92*	30	32	—[1]
(17209)	B&O DD Boxcar "296000" (Std. 0), *93*	38	44	—[1]
(17210)	Chicago & Illinois Midland Boxcar "16021" (Std. 0), *92 u*	30	39	—[1]
(17211)	Chicago & Illinois Midland Boxcar "16022" (Std. 0), *92 u*	30	39	—[1]
(17212)	Chicago & Illinois Midland Boxcar "16023" (Std. 0), *92 u*	24	31	—[1]
(17213)	Susquehanna Boxcar "501" (Std. 0), *93*	31	34	—[1]
17214	Railbox Boxcar w/ Diesel RailSounds (Std. 0), *93*	95	105	—[1]
(17216)	PRR DD Boxcar "60155" (Std. 0), *94*	40	44	—[1]
(17217)	New Haven "State of Maine" Boxcar "45003" (Std. 0), *95*	28	40	—[1]
(17218)	BAR "State of Maine" Boxcar "2184" (Std. 0), *95*	23	36	—[1]
17219	Tazmanian Devil 40th Birthday Boxcar (Std. 0), *95*	32	38	—[1]
17220	Pennsylvania Boxcar (Std. 0), *96*	—	38	—[1]

		Exc	New	Cond/$
17221	NYCBoxcar (Std. 0), *96*	—	38	—[1]
17222	Western Pacific Boxcar (Std. 0), *96*	—	38	—[1]
(17223)	Milwaukee Road DD Boxcar Std. 0, *96*	—	36	—[1]
(17224)	Central of Georgia Boxcar "9464-197" (Std 0), *97*	15	34	—[1]
(17225)	Penn Central Boxcar "9464-297" (Std 0), *97*	15	34	—[1]
(17226)	Milwaukee Road Boxcar "9464-397" (Std 0), *97*	—	34	—[1]
(17227)	UP DD Boxcar "9200" (Std 0), *97*	—	36	—[1]
(17231)	Wisconsin Central Double-door Boxcar w/ Auto Frames "9200," *98*	—	40	—[1]
(17232)	Southern Pacific/Union Pacific Merger Double-door Boxcar "9200," *98*	—	45	—[1]
(17233)	Western Pacific Boxcar "9464-198," *98*	—	27	—[1]
17234	LCCA/LOTS Port Huron & Detroit Boxcar "9464-298," *1999*	—	60	—[1]
(17234)	Port Huron & Detroit Boxcar "9464-298," *98*	—	36	—[1]
(17235)	Boston & Maine Boxcar "9464-398," *98*	—	40	—[1]
(17239)	AT&SF Texas Chief Boxcar "9464-1," *97*	—	50	—[1]
(17240)	AT&SF Super Chief Boxcar "9464-2," *97*	—	50	—[1]
(17241)	AT&SF El Capitan Boxcar "9464-3," *97*	—	50	—[1]
(17242)	AT&SF Grand Canyon Boxcar "9464-4," *97*	—	60	—[1]
(17243)	NP Boxcar "8722," *98*	—	48	—[1]
(17244)	Santa Fe Chief Boxcar, *98*	—	39	—[1]
(17245)	C&O Boxcar with Chessie Kitten, *98*	—	43	—[1]
(17246)	NYC Pacemaker Rolling Stock 4-pack, *98*	—	220	—[1]
(17247)	NYC 9464 Boxcar "174940," *98*	—	135	—[1]
(17248)	NYC 9464 Boxcar "174945," *98*	—	115	—[1]
(17249)	NYC 9464 Boxcar "174949," *98*	—	115	—[1]
(17250)	UP Boxcar "507406" (Std. 0), *99*	—	45	—[1]
(17251)	BNSF Modern Boxcar "103277," *99*	—	37	—[1]
(17252)	NS Modern Boxcar "564824" (Std 0), *99*	—	39	—[1]
(17253)	CSX Modern Boxcar "141756" (Std 0), *99*	—	39	—[1]
(17254)	Union Pacific Modern Boxcar "551967" (Std 0), *99*	—	42	—[1]
(17255)	Chevy Modern Double Door Boxcar "9200" (Std 0), *99*	—	43	—[1]
(17257)	Atlantic Coast Line Boxcar 9464 "28809" Std. 0, *99*	—	36	—[1]
(17258)	D&H 9464 Boxcar "29055" (Std. 0) , *99*	—	42	—[1]
(17259)	MKT 9464 Boxcar "1422" (Std. 0), *99*	—	39	—[1]
(17260)	CP Rail 9464 Boxcar "286138" (Std. 0), Silver, *00*	—	45	—[1]
(17261)	CP Rail 9464 Boxcar "85154," Green, *00*	—	45	—[1]
(17262)	CP Rail 9464 Boxcar "56776" (Std. 0), Red, *00*	—	48	—[1]

			Exc	New	Cond/$
(17263)	NYC Modern Boxcar "45725" (Std O), *00*		—	35	—1
(17264)	C&O Modern Boxcar "6054" (Std O), *00*		—	40	—1
(17265)	U.S. Army Modern Boxcar, (Std O), *00*		—	39	—1
(17266)	Monon Modern Boxcar "911" (Std O), *00*		—	43	—1
(17268)	C&O 9464 Boxcar "12700" (Std.O), *01*		—	44	—1
(17269)	Western Maryland 9464 Boxcar "29140" (Std. O), *01*		—	44	—1
(17270)	B&O TimeSaver 9464 Boxcar "467439" (Std. O), *01*		—	42	—1
(17271)	The Rock Modern Boxcar "300324" (Std. O), *01*		—	37	—1
(17272)	Railbox Modern Boxcar "15150" (Std. O), *01*		—	30	—1
(17273)	DT&I DD Boxcar "26852" (Std. O), *01*		—	42	—1
(17274)	Soo Line DD Boxcar "177587" (Std. O), *01*		—	42	—1
(17275)	NYC PS-1 Boxcar "175008" (Std. O), *02*		—	46	—1
(17276)	SSW (Cotton Belt) PS-1 Boxcar "75000" (Std. O), *02*		—	43	—1
(17277)	Rio Grande PS-1 Boxcar "69676" (Std. O), *02*		—	44	—1
(17278)	WP PS-1 Boxcar "1953" (Std. O), *02*		—	43	—1
(17279)	Ontario Northland Modern Boxcar "7428" (Std. O), *02*		—	38	—1
(17280)	Santa Fe 2-Door Boxcar with Automobile Frames 600194 (Std. O), *02*		—	45	—1
17281	PRR Double-Door Boxcar "83158" (Std. O), *04*			CP	—1
17282	UP Double-Door Boxcar "160300" (Std. O), *04*			CP	—1
17283	GM&O Double-Door Boxcar "9077" (Std. O), *04*			CP	—1
17284	Erie Double-Door Boxcar "66000" (Std. O), *04*			CP	—1
(17285)	CSX Big Blue Modern Boxcar "151296" (Std. O), *03*		—	35	—1
(17287)	BAR Modern Boxcar "5976" (Std. O), *03*		—	35	—1
(17288)	NYC PS-1 Boxcar "175012" (Std. O), *03-04*		—	40	—1
(17289)	GN PS-1 Boxcar "18485" (Std. O), *03*		—	40	—1
(17290)	Seaboard PS-1 Boxcar "24452" (Std. O), *03-04*		—	40	—1
(17291)	Rock Island PS-1 Boxcar "21110" (Std. O), *03-04*		—	40	—1
17292	B&M PS-1 Boxcar "76182" (Std. O), *04*			CP	—1
17293	IC PS-1 Boxcar "400666" (Std. O), *04*			CP	—1

		Exc	New	Cond/$
17294	TP&W PS-1 Boxcar "5036" (Std. O), *04*		CP	—1
17295	Santa Fe PS-1 Boxcar "276749" (Std. O), *04*		CP	—1
17300	Canadian Pacific Reefer (Std. O), *89*	31	36	—2
17301	Conrail Reefer (Std. O), *87*	32	37	—1
17302	Santa Fe Reefer w/ ETD (Std. O), *90*	37	43	—1
(17303)	C&O Reefer "7890" (Std. O), *93*	26	34	—1
(17304)	Wabash Reefer "26269" (Std. O), *94*	27	33	—1
(17305)	Pacific Fruit Express Reefer "459400" (Std. O), *94*	30	40	—1
(17306)	Pacific Fruit Express Reefer "459401" (Std. O), *94*	24	32	—1
(17307)	Tropicana Reefer "300" (Std. O), *95*	30	43	—1
(17308)	Tropicana Reefer "301" (Std. O), *95*	24	37	—1
(17309)	Tropicana Reefer "302" (Std. O), *95*	25	35	—1
(17310)	Tropicana Reefer "303" (Std. O), *95*	27	38	—1
17311	Railway Express Agency Reefer (Std. O), *96*	34	38	—1
(17314)	Pacific Fruit Express Reefer "9800-198," *98*	—	37	—1
(17315)	Pacific Fruit Express Reefer "9800-298," *98*	—	37	—1
(17316)	NP Reefer "98583," *98*	—	50	—1
(17317)	PRR Reefer FGE "91904," *96*	—	43	—1
(17318)	UP Refrigerator Car "170650" (Std. O), *99*	—	55	—1
(17319)	PFE Standard O Reefer 6-pack, *01*	—	300	—1
(17331)	Hood's General American Milk Car "802" (Std. O), *02*	—	100	—1
(17332)	Pfaudler General American Milk Car "501" (Std. O), *02*	—	80	—1
(17334)	REA General American Milk Car "1741" (Std. O), *02*	—	100	—1
(17335)	New Haven General American Milk Car "102" (Std. O), *02*	—	90	—1
(17336)	PFE Steel-sided Refrigerator Car "17760" (Std. O), *03*	—	50	—1
(17337)	CN Steel-sided Refrigerator Car "209712" (Std. O), *03*	—	38	—1
(17338)	Merchants Dispatch Transit Steel-sided Refrigerator Car "12322" (Std. O), *03*	—	39	—1
(17339)	Burlington Steel-sided Refrigerator Car "74825" (Std. O), *03*	—	39	—1
(17340)	White Bros. General American Milk Car "891" (Std. O), *03*	—	43	—1
(17341)	Dairymen's League General American Milk Car "779" (Std. O), *03*	—	43	—1
(17342)	Miller Beer Steel-sided Refrigerator Car (Std. O), *03 u*	—	50	—1
(17343)	Miller Beer Steel-sided Refrigerator Car (Std. O), *03 u*	—	50	—1

		Exc	New	Cond/$
(17349)	NYC General American Milk Car "6581" (Std. 0), *03*	—	43	—¹
(17350)	Hood's General American Milk Car "503" (Std. 0), *03*	—	43	—¹
17351	Santa Fe Steel-sided Refrigerator Car "3526" (Std. 0), *04*		CP	—¹
17352	Pacific Fruit Express Steel-sided Refrigerator Car "20043" (Std. 0), *04*		CP	—¹
17353	Needham Packing Co. Steel-sided Refrigerator Car "60507" (Std. 0), *04*		CP	—¹
17354	Swift Steel-sided Refrigerator Car "15392" (Std. 0), *04*		CP	—¹
17355	Hood's Steel-sided Refrigerator Car "550" (Std. 0), *04*		CP	—¹
17356	Nestle Nesquik Steel-sided Refrigerator Car (Std. 0), *04*		CP	—¹
17357	Borden's Steel-sided Refrigerator Car "522" (Std. 0), *04*		CP	—¹
17358	Fairfield Farms Steel-sided Refrigerator Car (Std. 0), *04*		CP	—¹
(17360)	Hood's General American Milk Car "810" (Std. 0), *03*	—	43	—¹
(17361)	Hood's General American Milk Car "811" (Std. 0), *03*	—	43	—¹
(17362)	Pfaudler General American Milk Car "502" (Std. 0), *03*	—	43	—¹
(17363)	Pfaudler General American Milk Car "503" (Std. 0), *03*	—	43	—¹
(17364)	REA General American Milk Car "1742" (Std. 0), *03*	—	43	—¹
(17365)	REA General American Milk Car "1743" (Std. 0), *03*	—	43	—¹
(17366)	NH General American Milk Car "103" (Std. 0), *03*	—	43	—¹
(17367)	NH General American Milk Car "104" (Std. 0), *03*	—	43	—¹
(17368)	White Brothers General American Milk Car "892" (Std. 0), *03*	—	43	—¹
(17369)	White Brothers General American Milk Car "893" (Std. 0), *03*	—	43	—¹
(17370)	Dairymen's League General American Milk Car "780" (Std. 0), *03*	—	43	—¹
(17371)	Dairymen's League General American Milk Car "781" (Std. 0), *03*	—	43	—¹
(17372)	NYC General American Milk Car "6582" (Std. 0), *03*	—	43	—

		Exc	New	Cond/$
(17373)	NYC General American Milk Car "6583" (Std. O), *03*	—	43	—¹
(17374)	Hood's General American Milk Car (2nd version) "504" (Std. O), *03*	—	43	—¹
(17375)	Hood's General American Milk Car (2nd version) "505" (Std. O), *03*	—	43	—¹
17400	CP Rail Gondola w/ coal load (Std. O), *89*	35	40	—¹
17401	Conrail Gondola w/ coal load (Std. O), *87*	34	40	—¹
17402	Santa Fe Gondola w/ coal load (Std. O), *90*	25	31	—¹
(17403)	Chessie System Gondola w/ coil covers "371629" (Std. O), *93*	25	26	—¹
(17404)	Illinois Central Gulf Gondola w/ coil covers "245998" (Std. O), *93*	32	36	—¹
(17405)	Reading Gondola w/ coil covers "24876" (Std. O), *94*	31	35	—¹
(17406)	PRR Gondola w/ coil covers "385405" (Std. O), *95*	40	45	—¹
(17407)	NKP Gondola w/ scrap load, *96*	—	33	—¹
(17408)	Cotton Belt Gondola w/ scrap load "9820" (Std O), *97*	—	33	—¹
(17410)	UP Gondola w/Scrap "903004" (Std. O), *99*	—	30	—¹
(17413)	Service Center Gondola w/ parts load (SSS), *00*	—	25	—¹
(17414)	Nickel Plate PS-5 Gondola "44801" (Std. O), *01-02*	—	40	—¹
(17415)	Frisco PS-5 Gondola "61878" (Std. O), *01-02*	—	40	—¹
(17416)	D&H Gondola w/ Scrap "14011" (Std. O), *01*	—	35	—¹
(17417)	BN Rotary Bathtub Gondola 3-pack, *01*	—	140	—¹
(17421)	CSX Rotary Bathtub Gondola 3-pack, *01*	—	135	—¹
(17425)	Western Maryland PS-5 Gondola "354903" (Std. O), *01-02*	—	40	—¹
(17426)	Maine Central PS-5 Gondola "1116" (Std. O), *01-02*	—	40	—¹
(17427)	CSX Rotary Bathtub Gondola Single Unit Add-on (Std. O), *02*	—	47	—¹
(17428)	BN Rotary Bathtub Gondola Single Unit Add-on (Std. O), *02*	—	42	—¹
(17429)	Conrail Rotary Bathtub Gondola 3-pack (Std. O), *02-03*	—	105	—¹
17433	BNSF Rotary Bathtub Gondola 3-pack (Std. O), *02-03*	—	115	—¹
17439	UP PS-5 Gondola "229606" (Std. O), *03*	—	35	—¹
17440	Algoma Central PS-5 Gondola "801" (Std. O), *03*	—	32	—¹

		Exc	New	Cond/$
(17441)	Conrail Rotary Bathtub Gondola "507673" (Std. 0), *03*	—	40	—[1]
(17442)	BNSF Rotary Bathtub Gondola "668330" (Std. 0), *03*	—	40	—[1]
(17443)	NS Rotary Bathtub Gondola 3-Pack (Std. 0), *03*	—	90	—[1]
(17447)	UP Rotary Bathtub Gondola 3-Pack (Std. 0), *03*	—	100	—[1]
(17455)	(See 52168), *98*		NRS	—[1]
(17457)	GN PS-5 Gondola "72839" (Std. 0), *03*	—	35	—[1]
(17458)	Reading PS-5 Gondola "33267" (Std. 0), *03*	—	35	—[1]
17459	CP Rail PS-5 Gondola "338966" (Std. 0), *04*		CP	—[1]
17460	NYC PS-5 Gondola "749592" (Std. 0), *04*		CP	—[1]
17461	Pennsylvania PS-5 Gondola "374256" (Std. 0), *04*		CP	—[1]
17462	Santa Fe PS-5 Gondola "167340" (Std. 0), *04*		CP	—[1]
17462	Santa Fe PS-5 Gondola "167340" (Std. 0), *04*		CP	—[1]
17463	NS Bathtub Gondola "10303" (Std. 0), *04*		CP	—[1]
17464	UP Bathtub Gondola "28100" (Std. 0), *04*		CP	—[1]
17465	CP Rail Bathtub Gondola 3-pack (Std. 0), *04*		CP	—[1]
17500	CP Flatcar w/ logs (Std. 0), *89*	35	38	—[1]
17501	Conrail Flatcar w/ stakes (Std. 0), *87*	37	45	—[1]
17502	Santa Fe Flatcar w/ trailer (Std. 0), *90*	65	70	—[1]
17503	NS Flatcar w/ trailer (Std. 0), *92*	55	65	—[1]
17504	NS Flatcar w/ trailer (Std. 0), *92*	55	65	—[1]
17505	NS Flatcar w/ trailer (Std. 0), *92*	55	60	—[1]
17506	NS Flatcar w/ trailer (Std. 0), *92*	50	60	—[1]
17507	NS Flatcar w/ trailer (Std. 0), *92*	55	60	—[1]
17508	BN I-Beam Flatcar w/ load (Std. 0), *92*		NM	—[1]
17509	Southern Flatcar w/ load (Std. 0), *92*		NM	—[1]
(17510)	NP Flatcar w/ logs "61200" (Std. 0), *94*	31	36	—[1]
(17511)	WM Flatcars w/ logs, set of 3 (Std. 0), *95*	—	190	—[1]
17512	WM Flatcar w/ logs (Std. 0), *95*	39	46	—[1]
17513	WM Flatcar w/ logs (Std. 0), *95*	43	50	—[1]
17514	WM Flatcar w/ logs (Std. 0), *95*	43	50	—[1]
17515	Norfolk Southern Flatcar w/ tractors (Std. 0), *95*	24	43	—[1]
(17516)	T&P Flatcar w/ 2 Beechcraft Bonanzas "9823" (Std 0), *97*	—	39	—[2]
(17517)	WP Flatcar w/ Ertl Caterpillar Frontloader "9823" (Std 0), *97*		42	—[1]
(17518)	PRR Flatcar w/ 2 Corgi Mack Trucks "9823" (Std 0), *97*	45	46	—[1]
(17522)	Flatcar with Plymouth Prowler, *98*	—	40	—[1]
(17527)	Flatcar with Pair of Dodge Vipers, *98*	—	44	—[1]
(17529)	AT&SF Flatcar w/ Ford Milk Truck			

		Exc	New	Cond/$
	"90010," *99*	—	46	—¹
(17533)	MTTX Ford Flatcar w/ Auto Frames, *99*	—	38	—¹
(17534)	Diamond T Flat w/ Mack Trucks "9823," *99*	—	65	—¹
(17536)	Route 66 Flatcar w/2 Luxury Coupes "9823-3," *99*	—	37	—¹
(17537)	Route 66 Flatcar w/2 Touring Coupes "9823-4," *99*	—	39	—¹
(17538)	NYC Flatcar w/Ford Tow Truck, *99*	—	39	—¹
(17539)	Flatcar with 2 Corvettes "9823" (Std. O), *99*	—	70	—¹
(17540)	Flatcar with 2 Corvettes "9823" (Std. O), *99*	––	70	—¹
(17546)	Lionel Lines Recovery Flatcar w/ rails "6424," *99*	—	50	—¹
(17547)	Lionel Lines Recovery Flatcar w/ machinery "6429," *99*	—	50	—¹
(17548)	Route 66 Flatcar w/2 Luxury Coupes "9823-6," *99*	—	43	—¹
(17549)	Route 66 Flatcar w/Touring Station Wagon & Trailer "9823-5," *99*	—	43	—¹
(17550)	B&N Center Beam Flatcar w/ Lumber Load "6216" (Std O), *99*	—	39	—¹
(17551)	NYC Flatcar with NYC Pickups "499," *99*	—	50	—¹
(17553)	Trailer Train Flatcar with Combine "98102" (Std. O), *99*	—	125	—¹
(17554)	GN Flat w/ Logs "61042," *00*	—	38	—¹
(17555)	Ford Mustang Flatcar with 2 Cars (Std. O), *01*		NRS	—¹
(17556)	Ford Mustang Flatcar with 2 Cars (Std. O), *01*		NRS	—¹
(17557)	Route 66 Flatcar w/Black Sedans "9823-7," *99-00*	—	41	—¹
(17558)	Route 66 Flatcar w/Brown Sedans "9823-8," *99*	—	40	—¹
(17559)	Route 66 Flatcar w/ 2 Wagons "9823-9" (Std. O), *01*	—	40	—¹
(17560)	Route 66 Flatcar with 2 Sedans "9823-10" (Std. O), *01*	—	40	—¹
(17563)	Santa Fe Flatcar with Railroad Pick-up Trucks "90011" (Std. O), *01*	—	49	—¹
(17564)	West Side Lumber Shay Log Car 3-pack #2 (Std. O), *01*	—	105	—¹
(17568)	PRR Flatcar with MOW Pick-up Trucks 470333 (Std. O), *02*	—	50	—¹
(17571)	UP Flatcar with MOW Pick-up Trucks "909231" (Std. O), *03*		50	—¹
(17572)	Pioneer Seed Flatcar with Peddle Cars, *02 u*		210	—¹
(17573)	WM PS-4 Flatcar "2631" (Std. O), *03*		35	—¹

		Exc	New	Cond/$
(17574)	Santa Fe PS-4 Flatcar "90081" (Std. 0), *03*		35	—¹
(17575)	NYC PS-4 Flatcar "506098" (Std. 0), *03*		35	—¹
(17576)	Ontario Northland PS-4 Flatcar "2020" (Std. 0), *03*		35	—¹
17577	B&O PS-4 Flatcar "8651" (Std. O), *04*		CP	—¹
17578	B&M PS-4 Flatcar "34007" (Std. O), *04*		CP	—¹
17579	Milwaukee Road PS-4 Flatcar "64073" (Std. O), *04*		CP	—¹
17580	UP PS-4 Flatcar "54603" (Std. O), *04*		CP	—¹
17581	Great Northern Flatcar w/Pickup Trucks "X4168" (Std. O), *04*		CP	—¹
17600	NYC Wood-sided Caboose (Std. O), *87 u*	40	47	—²
17601	Southern Wood-sided Caboose (Std. O), *88*	42	50	—¹
17602	Conrail Wood-sided Caboose (Std. O), *87*	95	110	—¹
17603	Rock Island Wood-sided Caboose (Std. O), *88*	28	60	—²
17604	Lackawanna Wood-sided Caboose (Std. O), *88*	40	44	—¹
17605	Reading Wood-sided Caboose (Std. O), *89*	30	33	—²
17606	NYC Steel-sided Caboose w/ smoke (Std. O), *90*	70	75	—¹
17607	Reading Steel-sided Caboose w/ smoke (Std. O), *90*	55	65	—¹
17608	C&O Steel-sided Caboose w/ smoke (Std. O), *91*	55	65	—¹
17610	Wabash Steel-sided Caboose w/ smoke (Std. O), *91*	42	60	—¹
(17611)	NYC Wood-sided Caboose "6003" (Std. O), *90 u, 91*	48	65	—²
17612	NKP Steel-sided Caboose w/ smoke (FF #6) (Std. O), *92*	65	70	—¹
(17613)	Southern Steel-sided Caboose w/ smoke "7613" (Std. O), *92*	65	70	—¹
17615	Northern Pacific Wood-sided Caboose w/ smoke (Std. O), *92*	60	65	—¹
17617	D&RGW Steel-sided Caboose (Std. O), *95*	65	75	—²
17618	Frisco Wood-sided Caboose (Std. O), *95*	65	75	—¹
(17620)	NP Wood-sided Caboose "1746," *98*	—	70	—¹
(17623)	Farmrail EV Caboose, *99*	—	65	—¹
(17624)	Conrail E/V Caboose "6900," *99*	—	50	—¹
(17625)	Burlington Northern Steel-sided Caboose "7606," *99*		65	—¹
(17626)	Service Center E/V Caboose (SSS), *00*		30	—¹
(17627)	C&O E/V Caboose, *01*	—	65	—
(17628)	BNSF E/V Caboose, *01*	—	65	—
(17629)	Santa Fe E/V Caboose, *01*	—	65	—

		Exc	New	Cond/$
(17630)	UP E/V Caboose, *01*	—	75	—1
(17631)	Virginian B/W Caboose, *01*	—	70	—1
(17632)	CSX B/W Caboose, *01*	—	65	—1
(17633)	NYC B/W Caboose, *01*	—	75	—1
(17634)	Delaware & Hudson B/W Caboose, *01*	—	75	—1
(17635)	100th Anniversary Die-cast Gold Caboose "2000," *00*	—	300	—1
(17636)	NYC Die-cast Semi-scale Caboose "18096," *00-01*	—	110	—1
(17637)	NYC/P&LE Die-cast Semi-scale Caboose "21," *00*	—	110	—1
(17638)	Rock Island Extended-Vision Caboose "17011," (Std. O) , *02*	—	55	—1
(17639)	Chessie System Extended-Vision Caboose "3322," (Std. O) , *02*	—	55	—1
(17640)	CP Rail Extended-Vision Caboose "434604," (Std. O), *02*	—	55	—1
(17641)	Soo Line Extended-Vision Caboose "2," (Std. O), *02*	—	55	—1
(17642)	Conrail Bay Window Caboose "21023," (Std. O), *02*	—	55	—1
(17643)	Nickel Plate Road Bay Window Caboose "480" (Std. O), *02*	—	55	—1
(17644)	Erie Bay Window Caboose "C307," (Std. O), *02*	—	55	—1
(17645)	N&W Bay Window Caboose "C-6," (Std. O), *02*	—	55	—1
(17646)	UP Bay Window Caboose "24555," (Std. O), *02*	—	55	—1
17647)	B&O Caboose "C-2820" (Std. O), *03-04*	CP		—1
17648)	Chessie System Caboose "C-2800" (Std. O), *03-04*	CP		—1
17649)	Lionel Lines Caboose "7649" (Std. O), *03-04*	CP		—1
17650)	Rio Grande Extended Vision Caboose "01500" (Std. O), *03*	65		—1
17652)	NYC Bay-Window Caboose "20200" (Std. O), *03*	70		—1
17653)	SP Bay-Window Caboose "1337" (Std. O), *03*	60		—1
17654)	Alaska Extended Vision Caboose "989" (Std. O), *03*	60		—1
17655)	WP Bay-Window Caboose "448" (Std. O), *03-04*	65		—1
7658	Burlington E/V Caboose "13611" (Std. O), *04*	CP		—1

		Exc	New	Cond/$
17659	CN E/V Caboose "79646" (Std. O), *04*		CP	—¹
17660	Seaboard E/V Caboose "5700" (Std. O), *04*		CP	—¹
17661	C&NW B/W Caboose "10871" (Std.O), *04*		CP	—¹
(17651)	BN Extended Vision Caboose "10531" (Std. 0), *03*		65	—¹
17662	PC B/W Caboose "21001" (Std. O), *04*		CP	—¹
17663	Southern B/W Caboose "X546" (Std. O), *04*		CP	—¹
(17664)	B&O Caboose "C-2824" (Std. O), *03-04*		CP	—¹
(17665)	Chessie System Caboose "C-2802" (Std. O), *03-04*		CP	—¹
(17700)	UP ACF 40-ton Stock Car "47456" (Std. O), *01-02*	—	75	—¹
(17701)	Rio Grande ACF 40-ton Stock Car "39269" (Std. O), *01-02*	—	60	—¹
(17702)	CP ACF 40-ton Stock Car "277083" (Std. O), *01-02*	—	70	—¹
(17703)	NYC ACF 40-ton Stock Car "23334" (Std. O), *01-02*	—	75	—¹
(17704)	B&O ACF 40-ton Stock Car "110234," Std. 0, *02*	—	40	—¹
(17705)	CB&Q ACF 40-ton Stock Car "52886," Std. 0, *02*	—	40	—¹
(17707)	Pennsylvania ARF 40-ton Stockcar "128994" (Std. O), *03*		CP	—¹
(17708)	CP Rail ACF 40-Ton Stockcar "277313" (Std. O), *03*		CP	—¹
17709	UP Stockcar "48154" (Std. O), *04*		CP	—¹
17710	Great Northern Stockcar "56385" (Std. O), *04*		CP	—¹
(17800)	Ontario Northland Ore Car "6126/6021" *00*	—	30	—¹
(17801)	CN Ore Car "6126/345165," *00*	—	37	—
(17802)	CP Ore Car "377249," *00*	—	28	—
(17803)	DMIR Ore Car "51456," *00*	—	28	—
(17804)	UP Ore Car "8023," *01*	—	29	—
(17805)	CP Rail Ore Car "377238," *01*	—	29	—
(17806)	UP Ore Car "27250," *03*		30	—
(17807)	BN Ore Car "95887," *02*	—	28	—
17870	LCCA East Camden & Highland Boxcar (Std. O), *87 u*	36	50	—
(17871)	TTOS NYC Flatcar w/ Kodak and Xerox trailers "81487," *87 u*	330	400	—
(17872)	TTOS Anaconda Ore Car "81988," *88 u*	70	95	—
17873	LCCA Ashland Oil 3-D Tank Car, *88 u*	49	60	—
(17874)	LOTS MILW Log Dump Car "59629," *88 u*	115	155	—
(17875)	LOTS PHD Boxcar "1289," *89 u*	55	65	—
17876	LCCA Columbia Newberry & Laurens			

		Exc	New	Cond/$
	Boxcar (Std. O), *89 u*	37	40	—2
(17877)	TTOS MKT 1-D Tank Car "3739469," *89 u*	55	70	—1
17878	Gadsden Pacific Magma Ore Car w/ load, *89 u*	80	95	—1
(17879)	TCA Valley Forge Dining Car "1989," *89 u*	—	65	—1
17880	LCCA D&RGW Wood-sided Caboose (Std. O), *90 u*	65	70	—1
17881	Gadsden Pacific Phelps-Dodge Ore Car w/ load, *90 u*	36	42	—1
(17882)	LOTS B&O DD Boxcar w/ ETD "298011," *90 u*	60	70	—1
(17883)	TCA New Georgia RR Passenger Car "1990," *90 u*	50	60	—1
17884	TTOS Columbus & Dayton Terminal Boxcar (Std. O), *90 u*	36	47	—1
17885	Artrain 1-D Tank Car, *90 u*	70	80	—1
17886	Gadsden Pacific Cyprus Ore Car w/ load, *91 u*	35	39	—1
17887	LCCA Conrail Flatcar w/ Armstrong Tile trailer (Std. O), *91 u*	44	85	—1
17888	LCCA Conrail Flatcar w/ Ford New Holland trailer (Std. O), *91 u*	49	80	—1
(17889)	TTOS SP Flatcar w/ trailer "15791" (Std. O), *91 u*	46	60	—1
(17890)	LOTS CSX Auto Carrier "151161," *91 u*	85	90	—1
17891	Artrain Grand Trunk Boxcar, *91 u*	85	110	—1
(17892)	LCCA Conrail Flatcars w/ trailers (Std. O) (See 17887, 17888)			
(17893)	(See 8392)			
[17893]	LCAC BAOC 1-D Tank Car "914," *91 u*	—	85	—1
(17894)	TTOS Southern Pacific Tractor, *91 u*	17	21	—1
(17895)	LCCA Tractor, *91 u*	14	22	—1
(17896)	LCCA Lancaster Lines Tractor, *91 u*	22	30	—1
[17897]	VTC Passenger Cars (See 7692)			
(17898)	TCA Wabash Reefer "21596," *92 u*	45	55	—1
(17899)	LCCA NASA Uni-body Tank Car "190" (Std. O), *92 u*	65	80	—2
17900	Santa Fe Uni-body Tank Car (Std. O), *90*	34	41	—1
17901	Chevron Uni-body Tank Car (Std. O), *90*	29	35	—2
17902	NJ Zinc Uni-body Tank Car (Std. O), *91*	30	37	—1
17903	Conoco Uni-body Tank Car (Std. O), *91*	28	34	—1
17904	Texaco Uni-body Tank Car (Std. O), *92*	35	44	—1
17905	Archer Daniels Midland Uni-body Tank Car (Std. O), *92*	36	46	—1
17906)	SCM Uni-body Tank Car "78286" (Std. O), *93*	43	50	—1

		Exc	New	Cond/$
17908	Marathon Oil Uni-body Tank Car (Std. O), *95*	44	55	__1
17909	Hooker Chemicals Uni-body Tank Car (Std. O), *96*	—	50	__1
(17910)	Sunoco Uni-body Tank Car "7900," *97*	—	45	__1
(17913)	J.M. Huber Tankcar, *98*	—	34	__1
(17914)	Englehard Tank Car, *98*	—	38	__1
(17915)	Gulf Uni-Body Tank Car "8438," *00*	—	43	__1
(17916)	Burlington Uni-body Tank Car "130000," *00*	—	42	__1
(17918)	Southern Unibody Tank Car, *01*	—	32	__1
(17919)	Koppers Unibody Tank Car, *01*	—	39	__1
(17924)	Safety Kleen Unibody Tank Car "77603" (Std. O), *02*	—	40	__1
(17925)	Beefmaster Unibody Tank Car "120021," (Std. O), *02*	—	40	__1
(17926)	Cargill Unibody 1-DomeTank Car "5836" (Std. O), *03*	—	40	__1
(17927)	Union Starch Unibody 1-DomeTank Car "59137" (Std. O), *03*	—	35	__1
(17928)	Merck 1-Dome Tank Car "25421" (Std. O), *03*	—	35	__1
(17929)	Wyandotte Chemicals 1-Dome Tank Car "1325" (Std. O), *03*	—	32	__1
17930	CSX Unibody Tank Car "993369" (Std. O), *04*		CP	__1
17931	UP Unibody Tank Car "6" (Std. O), *04*		CP	__1
17932	CIBRO TankTrain Intermediate Car "26263" (Std. O), *04*		CP	__1
17933	GATX TankTrain Intermediate Car 3-pack (Std. O), *04*		CP	__1
17946	Candy Cane Unibody Tank Car, *04*		CP	__1
(18000)	PRR 0-6-0 "8977" 89, *91*	420	475	__4
(18001)	Rock Island 4-8-4 "5100," *87*	285	355	__3
(18002)	NYC 4-6-4 "785," *87 u*	540	590	__4
(18003)	Delaware Lackawanna & Western 4-8-4 "1501," *88*	285	370	__2
(18004)	Reading 4-6-2 "8004," *89*	215	250	__2
(18005)	NYC 4-6-4 "5340" w/ display case, *90*	890	940	__4
(18006)	Reading 4-8-4 "2100," *89 u*	480	540	__3
(18007)	Southern Pacific 4-8-4 "4410," *91*	590	620	__4
(18008)	Disneyland 35th Anniversary 4-4-0 "4" w/ display case, *90*	225	275	__1
(18009)	NYC 4-8-2 "3000," *90 u, 91*	570	750	__3
(18010)	PRR 6-8-6 Steam Turbine "6200," *91-92*	1050	1350	__1
(18011)	Chessie System 4-8-4 "2101," *91*	600	740	__2
(18012)	NYC 4-6-4 "5340," *90*	710	1000	__1
(18013)	Disneyland 35th Anniversary 4-4-0 "4," *90*	205	260	__1
(18014)	Lionel Lines 2-6-4 "8014," *91*	125	165	__1
(18016)	Northern Pacific 4-8-4 "2626," *92*	345	395	__1

		Exc	New	Cond/$
(18018)	Southern 2-8-2 "4501," *92*	940	980	__2
18021	(See 18030)			
(18022)	Pere Marquette 2-8-4 "1201," *93*	550	650	__1
(18023)	Western Maryland Shay "6," *92*	1200	1550	__3
(18024)	Sears T&P 4-8-2 "907"			
	w/ display case, *92 u*	730	780	__2
(18025)	T&P 4-8-2 "907" (See 18024), *92 u*			
(18026)	Smithsonian NYC Dreyfuss 4-6-4 "5450"			
	(2-rail), *92 u*	—	2300	__1
(18027)	NYC Dreyfuss 4-6-4 "5450" (3-rail), *93 u*	—	1700	__2
(18028)	Smithsonian Pennsylvania 4-6-2 "3768"			
	(2-rail), *93 u*	—	2500	__1
(18029)	NYC Dreyfuss 4-6-4 "5454" (3-rail)			
	w/ operating roller base, *93 u*	1900	2150	__1
(18030)	Frisco 2-8-2 "4100," *93 u*	630	750	__3
(18031)	Bundesbahn BR-50 2-10-0 (2-rail), *93 u*		NRS	__1
(18034)	Santa Fe 2-8-2 "3158," *94*	485	560	__1
(18035)	Reichsbahn BR-50 2-10-0 (2-rail), *93 u*		NRS	__1
(18036)	French BR-50 2-10-0 (2-rail), *93 u*		NRS	__1
(18040)	N&W 4-8-4 "612," *95*	780	870	__3
(18041)	Boston & Albany 4-6-4 "619," *95*		NM	__1
(18042)	Boston & Albany 4-6-4 "618," *95*	—	295	__1
(18043)	Chesapeake & Ohio 4-6-4 "490," *95*	940	1100	__3
(18044)	Southern 4-6-2 "1390," *96*	—	300	__1
(18045)	"777" Commodore Vanderbilt, *96*	—	780	__4
(18046)	Wabash 4-6-4 "700," *96*	225	445	__3
(18049)	N&W Warhorse 4-8-2 "600," *96*	—	470	__1
(18050)	JC Penney 4-6-2 Steam "2055," *96*	320	355	__1
(18052)	Pennsylvania Torpedo "238E," *97*	—	540	__2
(18053)	Berkshire Steam Locomotive 2-8-4 "726," *97*	—	910	__3
(18054)	NYC Switcher 0-4-0 black "1665," *97*	—	140	__1
(18056)	NYC J1-e Hudson Steam Locomotive			
	"763e" and Vanderbilt Tender, *97*	—	820	__2
(18057)	Century Steam Locomotive 6-8-6			
	"671," *97*	375	900	__2
(18058)	Hudson Steam Locomotive 4-6-4 "773," *97*	—	980	__1
(18059)	Western Maryland Baby Pacific 4-6-2			
	Deluxe "209," *98*		NM	__1
18062)	AT&SF 4-6-4 Hudson L/T "3447," *97*	—	790	__1
18063)	NYC Commodore Vanderbilt 4-6-4, *99*	—	1150	__1
18064)	New York Central 4-8-2 Mohawk L-3A			
	Steam Engine w/ Tender "3000," *98*	630	870	__2
18067)	Commodore Vanderbilt Special Edition, *97*	—	1100	__2
18070)	Western Maryland Baby Pacific 4-6-2			
	Locomotive "208," *98*		NM	__1
18071)	Southern Pacific Daylight Locomotive			

		Exc	New	Cond/$
	"4449," *98*	—	710	—2
(18072)	Lionel Lines Torpedo Engine w/ Tender, *98*	—	400	—2
(18079)	NYC Mikado 2-8-2 "1967," *99*	—	710	—1
(18080)	Denver & Rio Grande Mikado 2-8-2 "1210," *99*	—	700	—1
(18082)	NYC Hudson 4-6-4 "5404," *99*	—	220	—1
(18083)	C&O Hudson 4-6-4 "305," *99*	—	205	—1
(18084)	Santa Fe Hudson 4-6-4 "305," *99*	—	215	—1
(18085)	NH Pacific 4-6-2 "1334," *99*	—	275	—1
(18086)	NYC Pacific 4-6-2 "4929," *99*	—	265	—1
(18087)	Santa Fe Pacific 4-6-2 "3448," *99*	—	275	—1
(18088)	SP Pacific 4-6-2 "1407," *99*	—	350	—1
(18089)	CNJ Camelback 4-6-0 "771," *99*	—	405	—1
(18090)	LCCA D&RGW 4-6-2 "1990," *90 u*	255	345	—1
(18091)	PRR Camelback 4-6-0 "821," *99*	—	420	—1
(18092)	SP Camelback 4-6-0 "2283," *99*	—	395	—1
(18093)	C&NW Camelback 4-6-0 "3006," *99*	—	375	—1
(18094)	B&O E6 4-4-2 Atlantic Steam Loco, Command Control, *99-00*	—	385	—1
(18095)	Pennsylvania E6 4-4-2 Atlantic Steam Loco, Command Control, *99-00*	275	455	—1
(18096)	AT&SF E6 4-4-2 Atlantic Steam Loco, Command Control, *99-00*	—	435	—1
(18097)	CNJ Camelback 4-6-0 "770," *99*	—	330	—1
(18098)	PRR Camelback 4-6-0 "820," *99*	—	355	—1
(18099)	SP Camelback 4-6-0 "2282," *99*	—	370	—1
(18100)	Santa Fe F-3 A Unit "8100" (See 11711)			
(18101)	Santa Fe F-3 B Unit "8101" (See 11711)			
(18102)	Santa Fe F-3 A Unit Dummy "8102" (See 11711)			
(18103)	Santa Fe F-3 B Unit Dummy "8103," *91 u*	220	235	—2
(18104)	Great Northern F-3 A Unit Dummy "366a" (See 11724)			
(18105)	Great Northern F-3 B Unit Dummy "370b" (See 11724)			
(18106)	Great Northern F-3 A Unit Dummy "351c" (See 11724)			
(18107)	D&RGW Alco PA-1 ABA set "6001" and "6002," *92*	720	860	—3
(18108)	Great Northern F-3 B Unit "371B," *93*	95	115	—1
(18109)	Erie Alco A Unit "725a" (See 11734)			
(18110)	Erie Alco B Unit "725b" (See 11734)	—	160	—
(18111)	Erie Alco A Unit Dummy "736a" (See 11734)			
(18112)	TCA F-3 A Unit "40" (See 11737)			
(18113)	TCA F-3 B Unit (See 11737)			
(18114)	TCA F-3 A Unit Dummy "40" (See 11737)			

		Exc	New	Cond/$
(18115)	Santa Fe F-3 B Unit, *93*	105	135	—[1]
(18116)	Erie-Lackawanna Alco PA-1 AA set "858"			
	and "859," *93*	465	670	—[3]
(18117)/(18118)	Santa Fe F-3 AA set "200," *93*	300	360	—[1]
(18119)/(18120)	UP Alco AA set "8119" and			
	"8120," *94*	215	255	—[1]
(18121)	Santa Fe F-3 B Unit "200A," *94*	70	95	—[1]
(18122)	Santa Fe F-3 B Unit "200B," *95*	195	220	—[1]
(18123)	ACL F-3 A Unit "342" (See 11903)			
(18124)	ACL F-3 B Unit "342b" (See 11903)			
(18125)	Atlantic Coast Line F-3 A Unit Dummy			
	"343" (See 11903)			
(18128)	Santa Fe F-3 A Unit "2343," *96*	—	435	—[1]
(18129)	Santa Fe F-3 B Unit w/ RS II, *96*	—	325	—[1]
(18130)	Santa Fe F-3 Diesel Locomotive AB set, *96*	—	700	—[2]
(18131)	NP F-3 AB set, "2390A," "2390C," *97*	390	475	—[2]
(18132)	Santa Fe F-3 A Powered (See 18130)			
(18133)	Santa Fe F-3 A Dummy (See 18130)			
(18134)	Santa Fe F-3 A Unit Dummy "2343," *97*	—	220	—[1]
(18135)	NYC F-3 AA Diesel "2333," *97*	—	800	—[2]
(18136)	AT&SF F-3 B Unit w/ Railsounds			
	"2343C," *97*	190	250	—[1]
(18138)	Milwaukee Road F3 A, "75A,"			
	(See 18140), *98*		NRS	—[1]
(18139)	Milwaukee Road F3 B, "2378B," *98*		NRS	—[1]
(18140)	Milwaukee Road F3 A-B Diesel Locomotive			
	"75A," *98*	400	610	—[2]
(18145)	NP F-3 A Unit "2390A," *97*	270	315	—[1]
(18146)	NP F-3 B Unit "2390C," *97*	—	170	—[1]
(18147)	NP F-3 AB Units "2390A, 2390C," *97*	450	580	—[2]
(18149)	Union Pacific Veranda Gas Turbine			
	"61," *98*	900	1000	—[1]
(18154)	Deluxe Santa Fe FT AA "168," *98-00*	—	375	—[1]
(18155)	Deluxe Santa Fe FT A Powered (See 18154)			
(18156)	Deluxe Santa Fe FT A Dummy			
	(See 18154), *N/A*			
(18157)	Santa Fe FT AA "158," *98-00*	—	240	—[1]
(18158)	Santa Fe FT A Powered (See 18157), *N/A*			
(18159)	Santa Fe FT A Dummy (See 18157), *N/A*			
(18160)	New York Central Deluxe FT AA "1603,"			
	"2403," *98-00*	—	435	—[1]
(18161)	(See 18160)			
(18162)	(See 18160)			
(18163)	New York Central FT AA Unit, "1600,"			
	"2400," *98-00*	—	300	—[1]
(18164)	(See 18163)			

		Exc	New	Cond/$
(18165)	(See 18163)			
(18166)	B&O FT AA, Command Control, *99-00*	—	340	—[1]
(18169)	B&O FT AA, Traditional, *99-00*	—	280	—[1]
(18178)	NYC F-3 B-unit Century Club, *98 u*	—	200	—[1]
(18189)	Army of Potomoc Operating Stockcar, *99*	—	45	—[1]
(18190)	McNeil's Rangers Operating Stockcar "2," *99*	—	45	—[1]
(18191)	WP F-3 A-A, *98*	—	780	—[2]
(18192)	WP F3 A Powered (See 18191), *98*		NRS	—[1]
(18193)	WP F-3 A Dummy (See 18191)			
(18197)	WP F3 B-Unit "2355C," *99*	—	230	—[1]
(18198)	WP F3 B-Unit "2355c" Command Control, *99*	—	325	—[1]
(18200)	Conrail SD-40 "8200," *87*	210	235	—[1]
(18201)	Chessie System SD-40 "8201," *88*	280	330	—[1]
(18202)	Erie-Lackawanna SD-40 Dummy "8459," *89 u*	120	190	—[1]
(18203)	CP Rail SD-40 "8203," *89*	230	295	—[2]
(18204)	Chessie System SD-40 Dummy "8204," *90 u*	140	195	—[1]
(18205)	Union Pacific Dash 8-40C "9100," *89*	190	230	—[4]
(18206)	Santa Fe Dash 8-40B "8206," *90*	205	250	—[2]
(18207)	Norfolk Southern Dash 8-40C "8689," *92*	220	255	—[1]
(18208)	BN SD-40 Dummy "8586," *91 u*	155	225	—[1]
(18209)	CP Rail SD-40 Dummy "8209," *92 u*	185	250	—[1]
(18210)	Illinois Central SD-40 "6006," *93*	200	220	—[1]
(18211)	Susquehanna Dash 8-40B "4002," *93*	190	220	—[1]
(18212)	Santa Fe Dash 8-40B Dummy "8212," *93*	160	185	—[1]
(18213)	Norfolk Southern Dash 8-40C "8688," *94*	220	235	—[2]
(18214)	CSX Dash 8-40C "7500," *94*	270	290	—[1]
(18215)	CSX Dash 8-40C "7643," *94*	265	290	—[2]
(18216)	Conrail SD-60M "5500," *94*	330	355	—[2]
(18217)	Illinois Central SD-40 "6007," *94*	235	250	—[1]
(18218)	Susquehanna Dash 8-40B "4004," *94*	200	220	—[1]
(18219)	C&NW Dash 8-40C "8501," *95*	335	340	—[1]
(18220)	C&NW Dash 8-40C "8502," *95*	255	280	—[2]
(18221)	D&RGW SD-50 "5512," *95*	435	495	—[1]
(18222)	D&RGW SD-50 "5517," *95*	305	355	—[2]
(18223)	Milwaukee Road SD-40 "154," *95*	375	380	—[1]
(18224)	Milwaukee Road SD-40 "155," *95*	260	290	—[1]
(18226)	GE Dash 9 Diesel Locomotive, *97*	—	315	—[2]
(18228)	SP Dash 9 "8228," gray, red nose, *97*	—	345	—[2]
(18229)	SP SD40 Diesel Warhorse "7333," *98*	300	425	—[1]
(18231)	BNSF Dash 9 Diesel Locomotive Deluxe "739," *98*	—	435	—[2]
(18232)	SOO Line SD-60 Diesel "5500," *97*	—	390	—[1]

		Exc	New	Cond/$
(18233)	BNSF Dash 9 Diesel Locomotive "745," *98*	—	330	—1
(18234)	BNSF Dash 9 "740" Command Control, *98-99*	—	405	—1
(18235)	BNSF Dash 9 Diesel Locomotive 2-pack "739," "740," *98*	—	710	—1
(18238)	Conrail SD70 "4145," *99-00*	—	300	—1
(18239)	(See 18229), *98*	—	400	—1
(18240)	Conrail Dash 8-40B "5065" Command Control, *98*	—	285	—1
(18241)	BN SD70 "9413," *99-00*	—	385	—1
(18245)	PRR Alco PA-1 AA "5750," *99*	—	540	—1
(18248)	PRR Alco PB-1 "5750B," *99*	—	250	—1
(18249)	Erie Alco PB-1 "850B," *00*	—	250	—1
(18250)	BNSF SD70 "9870," *99-00*	—	365	—1
(18251)	CSX SD60 "8701," *99-00*	—	350	—1
(18252)	Amtrak Dash 9, Command Control, *99*	—	285	—1
(18253)	BNSF Dash 9, Command Control, *99*	—	305	—1
(18254)	AT&SF Dash 9, Command Control, *99*	—	340	—1
(18255)	NS Dash 9, Commmand Control, *99*	—	315	—1
(18256)	Amtrak Dash 9, Traditional, *99*	—	190	—1
(18257)	BNSF Dash 9, Traditional, *99*	—	190	—1
(18258)	AT&SF Dash 9, Traditional, *99*	—	205	—1
(18259)	NS Dash 9, Traditional, *99*	—	215	—1
(18260)	Conrail SD70 "4144," *99-00*	—	265	—1
(18261)	BN SD60 "9412," *99-00*	—	255	—1
(18262)	BNSF SD70 "9869," *99-00*	—	250	—1
(18263)	CSX SD60 "8700," *99-00*	—	235	—1
(18264)	Southern Pacific SD70M "8238," *99-00*	—	245	—1
(18265)	Southern Pacific SD70M "9803," *99-00*	—	340	—1
(18266)	Norfolk Southern SD60 "6552," CC, *01-02*	—	400	—1
(18268)	Lionel Centennial SD90MAC "2000," Command Control, *00*	—	320	—1
(18269)	UP SD90MAC "8006," Command Control, *00*	—	375	—1
(18270)	UP SD90MAC "8007," Traditional, *00*		NM	—1
(18271)	CP SD90MAC "9129," Command Control, *00*	—	350	—1
(18272)	CP SD90MAC "9130," Traditional, *00*		NM	—1
(18273)	UP SD40MAC "8071," *99-00*	—	300	—1
(18274)	Burlington U30C "891"(CC), *01*	—	325	—1
(18276)	Seaboard U30C "7274," CC, *01*	—	295	—1
(18278)	UP U30C "2938," CC, *01*	—	330	—1
(18280)	Maersk SD70, CC, *00*	—	300	—1
(18281)	BNSF Dash 9-44CW "788," Command Control, *00*	—	340	—1
(18282)	BNSF Dash 9-44CW "789," Traditional, *00*	—	225	—1
(18283)	CSX Dash 9-44CW "9019," Command Control, *00*	—	340	—1

		Exc	New	Cond/$
(18284)	CSX Dash 9-44CW "9020," Traditional, 00	—	300	—[1]
(18285)	UP Dash 9-44C "9659," CC, 01	—	325	—[1]
(18286)	Amtrak Dash 8-32BWh "509," CC, 01	CP	325	—[1]
(18287)	CN Dash 9-44C "2529," CC, 01	CP	370	—[1]
(18288)	Odyssey System SD70, CC, 00u	—	400	—[1]
(18290)	UP Dash 9-44CW "9717," CC, 01	—	355	—[1]
(18291)	BNSF Dash 8-32BWH "580," CC, 02	—	340	—[1]
(18292)	Chessie GE U30C Diesel "3312," CC, 02	—	340	—[1]
(18293)	Santa Fe U30C, CC, 03	CP	395	—[1]
(18294)	Alaska SD70MAC "4005," CC, 01-02	—	385	—[1]
(18295)	Conrail SD80MAC "7200," CC, 02-03	—	365	—[1]
(18296)	CSX SD80MAC "801," CC, 02-03	—	380	—[1]
(18297)	NYC SD80MAC "9914," CC, 02-03	—	380	—[1]
(18298)	UP Desert Victory SD40-2 "3593," CC, 02-03	—	360	—[1]
(18299)	CP Rail SD40-2 "5420," CC, 02-03	—	355	—[1]
(18300)	PRR GG-1 "8300," 87	430	510	—[2]
(18301)	Southern FM Train Master "8301," 88	220	250	—[3]
(18302)	GN EP-5 "8302" (FF#3), 88	225	300	—[2]
(18303)	Amtrak GG-1 "8303," 89	360	440	—[5]
(18304)	Lackawanna MU Car set Powered and Dummy "2401" and "2402," 91	455	520	—[2]
(18305)	Lackawanna MU Car set, Dummies "2400" and "2403," 92	250	275	—[1]
(18306)	PRR MU Car set, Powered and Dummy "4574" and "483," 92	285	345	—[2]
(18307)	PRR FM Train Master "8699," 94	265	295	—[2]
(18308)	PRR GG-1 "4866," 92	275	315	—[2]
(18309)	Reading FM Train Master "863," 93	260	290	—[2]
(18310)	PRR MU Car set, Dummies "484" and "485," 93	265	345	—[1]
(18311)	Disney EP-5 "8311," 94	260	360	—[3]
(18313)	Pennsylvania GG-1 "4907," 96	—	335	—[2]
(18314)	Pennsylvania GG-1 "2332," 5 gold stripes, 97	600	710	—[2]
(18315)	Virginian E33 Recifier Electric "2329," 97	—	255	—[1]
(18319)	New Haven EP-5 (Rectifier), 99	300	355	—[1]
(18321)	CNJ Train Master "2341," 99	—	415	—[2]
(18322)	Lackawanna Train Master "2321," 99	—	475	—[2]
(18326)	PRR GG-1 Congressional, 00	—	600	—
(18327)	Virginian "2331" FM Train Master, 99-00	—	435	—[5]
(18328)	NH MU Commuter Set "4082/4083," CC, 00	—	450	—
(18331)	Reading MU Commuter Set "9109/10," CC, 00	—	475	—
(18334)	NH MU Dummy Set "4084/5," CC, 01	—	180	—
(18337)	Reading MU Dummy Set "9111/2," CC, 01	—	220	—
(18340)	Lionel Century Club II Demo FM Train			

		Exc	New	Cond/$
	Master, "TM-1," "TM-2," *00 u*	—	900	—1
(18343)	PRR GG-1 "2332" Black, CC, *01*	—	530	—1
(18344)	LI MU Powered Set"1163/4," CC, *01*	—	470	—1
(18347)	IC MU Powered Set "1204/5," CC, *01*	—	470	—1
(18350)	Archive Lionel EP-5 "2350," CC, *01*		NM	—1
(18353)	Pennsylvania E-33 Rectifier "4403," CC, *02*	—	290	—1
18354	PRR GG1 "4918" (Tuscan) CC, *04*		CP	—1
18355	PRR GG1 "4876" (Brunswick Green) CC, *04*		CP	—1
18356	Penn Central GG1 "4901" CC, *04*		CP	—1
(18400)	Santa Fe Vulcan Rotary Snowplow "8400," *87*	165	215	—2
(18401)	Workmen Handcar, *87-88*	36	46	—2
18402	Lionel Lines Burro Crane, *88*	75	90	—2
18403	Santa Claus Handcar, *88*	29	39	—1
18404	San Francisco Trolley "8404," *88*	75	125	—2
18405	Santa Fe Burro Crane, *89*	85	105	—2
18406	Lionel Track Maintenance Car, *89, 91*	46	65	—1
(18407)	Snoopy and Woodstock Handcar, *90-91*	55	85	—1
(18408)	Santa Claus Handcar, *89*	34	46	—1
18410	PRR Burro Crane, *90*	110	130	—1
18411	Canadian Pacific Fire Car, *90*	90	115	—1
18412	Union Pacific Fire Car, *91*		NM	—1
(18413)	Charlie Brown and Lucy Handcar, *91*	31	60	—1
(18416)	Bugs Bunny and Daffy Duck Handcar, *92-93*	105	150	—1
18417	Lionel Gang Car, *93*	60	75	—1
(18419)	Lionelville Electric Trolley "8419," *94*	95	115	—2
(18421)	Sylvester and Tweety Handcar, *94*	48	65	—1
(18422)	Santa and Snowman Handcar, *94*	39	46	—1
(18423)	On-Track Step Van, *95*	28	35	—2
(18424)	On-Track Pick-up Truck, *95*	27	35	—2
(18425)	Goofy and Pluto Handcar, *95*	32	49	—1
(18426)	Santa and Snowman Handcar, *95*	32	38	—1
(18427)	Tie-Jector "55," *97*	—	65	—2
(18429)	Workmen Handcar, *96*	40	44	—1
(18430)	Crew Car, *96*	—	37	—2
(18431)	Trolley Car, *96-97*	—	60	—1
(18433)	Mickey and Minnie Handcar, *96-97*	40	55	—1
(18434)	Porky and Petunia Handcar, *96*	—	38	—1
(18436)	Dodge Ram Track Inspection Vehicle, *97*	—	50	—2
(18438)	Pennsylvania High-rail Vehicle "49," *98*	—	45	—1
(18439)	Union Pacific High Rail Maintenance Vehicle, *98*	—	38	—1
(18440)	NJ Transit High Rail Inspection Vehicle, *98*	—	50	—1
(18444)	Lionelville Fire Car (SSS), *98*	—	150	—1
(18445)	NYC Fire Car, *98*	—	90	—1
(18446)	Postwar GN Rotary Snowplow "58," *99*	—	210	—2

		Exc	New	Cond/$
(18447)	Executive Inspection Vehicle, *99*	—	150	—²
(18452)	Boston Trolley "3321," *99-00*	—	55	—¹
(18454)	Blue Executive Inspection Car (#68), *00*	—	95	—²
(18455)	NYC Tie-Jector "X-2," *00-01*	—	70	—¹
(18456)	Postwar Minuteman Motorized Unit "59," *01-02*	—	230	—¹
(18457)	Postwar Handcar "65," *00-01*	—	45	—¹
(18458)	Postwar D&RGW Snowplow "53," *00*	—	185	—¹
(18459)	Christmas Handcar, *01*	—	40	—¹
(18461)	Lionel Track Cleaner, *02-03*	—	100	—¹
(18463)	Hot Rod Inspection Vehicle, *01-02*	—	100	—¹
(18464)	Postwar Track Ballast Tamper "54," *02-03*	—	170	—¹
(18465)	Postwar Gang Car "50," *03*	—	85	—¹
(18466)	UP Rotary Snow Plow, *01-02*	—	160	—¹
(18468)	CN Railroad Speeder, *03-04*	—	49	—¹
(18469)	Chessie System Railroad Speeder, *03-04*	—	49	—¹
(18470)	Lionel Postwar Fire Car "52," *02*	—	125	—¹
(18471)	UP GP20 "1977," *03*	—	105	—¹
(18473)	Lehigh Valley GP20 "310," *03*	—	160	—¹
(18476)	Mickey and Minnie Mouse Handcar, *03-04*	—	55	—¹
(18474)	Postwar U.S. Army Switcher "41," *03-04*	—	165	—¹
(18475)	Toy Story Handcar, *03*	—	55	—¹
(18481)	Christmas Yuletide Trolley, *03*	—	50	—¹
18482	New Haven Rail Bonder "16," *04*		CP	—¹
18483	C&O Ballast Tamper "48," *04*		CP	—¹
18484	NS Dodge Inspection Vehicle, *04*		CP	—¹
18485	NYC Gang Car, *04*		CP	—¹
18486	Donald and Daisy Duck Handcar, *04*		CP	—¹
18487	Postwar M&StL Mine Transport "56," *04*		CP	—¹
18489	Great Northern Rail Bonder "HR-73," *04*		CP	—¹
18490	UP Ballast Tamper, *04*		CP	—¹
18491	MOW Ballast Tamper "325," *04*		CP	—¹
18492	MOW Rail Bonder "58," *04*		CP	—¹
(18500)	Milwaukee Road GP-9 "8500" (FF#2), *87*	200	225	—²
(18501)	WM NW-2 "8501" (FF#4), *89*	220	245	—²
(18502)	Lionel Lines 90th Anniversary GP-9 "1900," *90*	135	155	—¹
(18503)	Southern Pacific NW-2 "8503," *90*	230	250	—³
(18504)	Frisco GP-7 "504" (FF#5), *91*	140	160	—²
(18505)	NKP GP-7 Powered and Dummy set "400" and "401" (FF#6), *92*	270	330	—¹
(18506)	CN Budd RDC Powered and Dummy set "D202" and "D203," *92*	210	240	—³
(18507)	CN Budd RDC Baggage Powered "D202," *92*	50	75	—¹
(18508)	CN Budd RDC Passenger Dummy			

		Exc	New	Cond/$
	"D203," *92*	125	150	—¹
(18510)	CN Budd RDC Passenger Dummy "D200"	50	75	—¹
(18511)	CN Budd RDC Passenger Dummy "D250"	50	75	—¹
(18512)	CN Budd RDC Dummies set "D200" and "D250," *93*	125	195	—¹
(18513)	NYC GP-7 "7420," *94*	125	145	—²
(18514)	Missouri Pacific GP-7 "4124," *95*	200	245	—¹
(18515)	Lionel Steel Vulcan Diesel "57" (SSS), *96*	—	190	—¹
(18516)	Phantom III Locomotive, CC, *02*	—	300	—¹
(18550)	JCPenney MILW GP-9 "8500" w/ display case, *87 u*	180	245	—¹
(18551)	JCPenney Susquehanna RS-3 "8809" w/ display case, *89 u*	175	190	—¹
(18552)	JCPenney DM&IR SD-18 "8813" w/ display case, *90 u*	165	190	—¹
(18553)	Sears UP GP-9 "150" w/ display case, *91 u*	180	215	—¹
(18554)	JCPenney GM&O RS-3 "721" w/ display case, *92-93 u*	200	230	—¹
(18555)	Sears C&IM SD-9 "52," *92 u*	165	190	—¹
(18556)	Sears Chicago & Illinois Midland Caboose and Freight Car set, *92 u*	145	155	—¹
(18557)	Chessie System 4-8-4 "2101" w/ display case for export, *92 u*		NRS	—¹
(18558)	JCPenney MKT GP-9 "91" w/ display case, *94 u*	165	190	—¹
(18562)	SP GP-9 "2380," *96*	—	215	—¹
(18563)	NYC GP-9 "2380," *96*	—	215	—¹
(18564)	CP GP-9 "2380," *97*	—	235	—¹
(18565)	Milwaukee GP-9 "2338," *97*	—	220	—¹
(18566)	CR SD-20 "8495" (SSS), *97*	—	155	—¹
(18567)	PRR GP-9 "2028," *97*	—	225	—¹
(18569)	Chicago Burlington & Quincy GP9 Diesel "2380," *98*	—	245	—²
(18573)	Santa Fe GP9 Diesel Freight "2380," *98*	—	155	—¹
(18574)	Milwaukee Road GP20 "975," *98*	—	250	—¹
(18575)	Custom Series I GP9 "2398," *98*	—	340	—¹
(18576)	Southern Pacific GP9 non-powered B Unit "2385," *98*	—	135	—¹
(18577)	New York Central GP9 non-powered B Unit "2385," *98*	—	145	—¹
(18579)	Milwaukee GP9 Non-Powered "2384," *99*	—	135	—¹
(18580)	Pennsylvania GP-9 B-Unit "2027," *98*	—	145	—¹
(18582)	Seaboard NW-2 Switcher, *98*	450	455	—¹
(18583)	AEC-57 Switcher, *98*	—	245	—¹
(18585)	Centennial SD40 "1999," *99*	—	540	—¹
(18587)	Nickel Plate C-420 "577," CC, *99-01*	250	265	—¹

Exc New Cond/$

		Exc	New	Cond/$
(18588)	D&H C-420 "412," CC, *99-01*	250	275	—¹
(18589)	LV C-420 "409," CC, *99-01*	250	295	—¹
(18590)	Nickel Plate C-420"578," Traditional, *99-01*	—	170	—¹
(18591)	D&H C-420 "411," Traditional, *99-01*	—	185	—¹
(18592)	LV C-420 "410," Traditional, *99-01*	—	180	—¹
(18595)	D&H RS-11 (Traditional) "5002," *99-00*		NM	—¹
(18596)	D&H RS-11 "5001," CC, *99-01*	—	370	—¹
(18597)	NYC RS-11 (Traditional) "8011," *99-00*		NM	—¹
(18598)	NYC RS-11 "8010," CC, *99-01*	—	365	—¹
(18599)	C&O GP-38 "3855," *99-00*	—	145	—¹
(18600)	ACL 4-4-2 "8600," *87 u*	65	75	—¹
(18601)	Great Northern 4-4-2 "8601," *88*	80	95	—¹
(18602)	PRR 4-4-2 "8602," *87*	75	85	—¹
(18604)	Wabash 4-4-2 "8604," *88-91*	65	75	—¹
(18605)	Mopar Express 4-4-2 "1987," *87-88 u*	75	120	—¹
(18606)	NYC 2-6-4 "8606," *89*	150	165	—¹
(18607)	Union Pacific 2-6-4 "8607," *89*	130	155	—¹
(18608)	D&RGW 2-6-4 "8608" (SSS), *89*	105	125	—¹
(18609)	Northern Pacific 2-6-4 "8609," *90*	150	170	—¹
(18610)	Rock Island 0-4-0 "8610," *90*	105	115	—¹
(18611)	Lionel Lines 2-6-4 "8611" (SSS), *90*	120	135	—¹
(18612)	C&NW 4-4-2 "8612," *89*	75	90	—¹
(18613)	NYC 4-4-2 "8613," *89 u*	75	95	—¹
(18614)	Circus Train 4-4-2 "1989," *89 u*	85	110	—¹
(18615)	GTW 4-4-2 "8615," *90*	70	85	—¹
(18616)	Northern Pacific 4-4-2 "8616," *90 u*	85	110	—¹
(18617)	Adolphus III 4-4-2, *89-92 u*	100	125	—¹
(18618)	B&O 4-4-2 "8618," *91*		NM	—¹
(18620)	Illinois Central 2-6-2 "8620," *91*	170	195	—¹
(18621)	Western Pacific 0-4-0 "8621," *92*		NM	—¹
(18622)	Union Pacific 4-4-2 "8622," *90-91 u*	65	80	—¹
(18623)	Texas & Pacific 4-4-2 "8623," *92*	80	110	—¹
(18625)	Illinois Central 4-4-2 "8625," *91 u*	70	95	—¹
(18626)	Delaware & Hudson 2-6-2 "8626," *92*	125	135	—¹
(18627)	C&O 4-4-2 "8627" or "8633," *92, 93 u, 94, 95 u*	75	95	—¹
(18628)	MKT 4-4-2 "8628," *92, 93 u*	70	85	—¹
(18630)	C&NW 4-6-2 "2903," *93*	295	325	—¹
(18632)	NYC 4-4-2 "8632," *93-95*	75	95	—¹
(18632)	C&O 4-4-2 Columbia Steam Locomotive "8632," *97-99*	75	95	—¹
(18633)	C&O 4-4-2 "8633," *94-95*	65	85	—¹
(18633)	Union Pacific 4-4-2 "8633," *93-95*	65	85	—¹
(18635)	Santa Fe 2-6-4 "8625," *93*	135	155	—¹
(18636)	B&O 4-6-2 "5300," *94*	330	350	—¹
(18637)	United Auto Workers 4-4-2 "8633," *93 u*	—	90	—¹

		Exc	New	Cond/$
(18638)	Norfolk & Western 2-6-4 "638," *94*	170	220	—¹
(18639)	Reading 4-6-2 "639," *95*	130	155	—¹
(18640)	Union Pacific 4-6-2 "8640," *95*	110	130	—¹
(18641)	Ford 4-4-2 "8641," *94 u*	65	85	—¹
(18642)	Lionel Lines 4-6-2 "8642," *95*	110	130	—¹
(18644)	AT&SF 4-4-2 Columbia Steam Locomotive "8644," *96-99*	75	90	—¹
(18648)	Sears Zenith 4-4-2 "8632," *96 u*	—	100	—¹
(18649)	Chevrolet 4-4-2 "USA-1," *96 u*	—	100	—¹
(18650)	Lionel Lines 4-4-2 Columbia Steam Locomotive "X-1110," *96-99*	95	120	—¹
(18653)	B&A 4-6-2 Pacific "2044," *97*	—	150	—¹
(18654)	SP 4-6-2 Pacific "2044," *97*	—	140	—¹
(18656)	Bloomingdales 4-4-2 Columbia Steam Locomotive "8632," *96*	—	100	—¹
(18657)	Sears Zenith 4-4-2 Columbia Steam Locomotive "8632," *96*	—	100	—¹
(18658)	LL Little League 4-4-2 Columbia Steam Locomotive "X-1110," *97*	—	90	—¹
(18660)	Canadian National 4-2 Steam Loco w/ Tender "2044," *98*	—	175	—¹
(18661)	Norfolk & Western 4-2 Steam Locomotive w/ Tender "2044," *98*	—	160	—¹
(18662)	Pennsylvania 0-4-0 Switcher, *98*	150	210	—¹
(18666)	SP&S 4-6-2 Pacific "2044," *97*	—	200	—¹
(18668)	Bloomingdales 4-4-2 Columbia Steam Locomotive "8632," *97*	—	120	—¹
(18669)	IC/J.C. Penny 4-6-2 Pacific "2099," *98*	—	235	—¹
(18670)	D&H 4-4-2 Columbia Steam Locomotive "1400," *98*	—	80	—¹
(18671)	N&W 4-4-2 Columbia Steam Locomotive "1201," *98*	—	70	—¹
(18678)	Quaker Oats 4-4-2 Columbia Steam Locomotive "8632," *98*	—	150	—¹
(18679)	JC Penney T&P 4-6-2, 99 "2000," Traditional, *00 u*	—	250	—¹
(18680)	Lionel RR Club Countdown 4-6-4 Hudson "2000" Steam Locomotive, Traditional, *00u*	—	300	—¹
(18681)	PRR 4-4-2 Steam Engine "460," *99*	—	75	—¹
(18682)	Santa Fe 4-4-2 Columbia "524" Steam Locomotive, Traditional, *00-01*	—	70	—¹
(18684)	LRRC Pacific 4-6-2 "1999," *99 u*	—	235	—¹
(18689)	(See 18207)	140	265	—¹
(18696)	ACL 4-6-4 "1800," *01*	—	120	—¹
(18697)	Santa Fe 4-6-4 "3465," *01*	—	80	—¹
(18699)	Alaska 4-4-2 "64," *01*	—	105	—¹

		Exc	New	Cond/$
(18700)	Rock Island 0-4-0T "8700," *87-88*	36	43	—1
(18702)	V&TRR 4-4-0 "8702" (SSS), *88*	140	170	—1
(18704)	Lionel Lines 2-4-0 "8704," *89 u*	36	43	—1
(18705)	"Neptune" 0-4-0T "8705," *90-91*	35	42	—1
(18706)	Santa Fe 2-4-0 "8706," *91*	36	43	—1
(18707)	Mickey's World Tour 2-4-0 "8707," *91, 92 u*	55	65	—1
(18709)	Lionel Employee Learning Center "Blue Engine" 0-4-0T, *92 u*	—	120	—1
(18710)	SoSouthern 2-4-0 "2000," *93*	30	38	—1
(18711)	Southern 2-4-0 "2000," *93*	30	38	—1
(18712)	Jersey Central 2-4-0 "2000," *93*	30	38	—1
(18713)	Chessie System 2-4-0 "1993," *94-95*	30	38	—1
(18716)	Lionelville Circus 4-4-0 "8716," *90-91*	90	110	—1
(18718)	Lionel Lines 0-4-0 Dockside Switcher "8200," *97-98*	—	40	—1
(18719)	Thomas the Tank Engine 0-6-0 "1," *97*	—	155	—1
(18720)	Union Cavalry 4-4-0 General "1865," *99*	—	175	—1
(18721)	Confederate States 4-4-0 General "1861," *99*	—	175	—1
(18722)	Percy the Tank Engine "6," *99*	—	155	—1
18799	Bethlehem Steel Diesel Switcher "44," *99*	—	100	—1
(18800)	Lehigh Valley GP-9 "8800," *87*	100	115	—1
(18801)	Santa Fe U36B "8801," *87*	90	105	—1
(18802)	Southern GP-9 "8802" (SSS), *87*	100	115	—1
(18803)	Santa Fe RS-3 "8803," *88*	90	105	—2
(18804)	Soo Line RS-3 "8804," *88*	85	100	—1
(18805)	Union Pacific RS-3 "8805," *89*	90	110	—1
(18806)	New Haven SD-18 "8806," *89*	90	105	—1
(18807)	Lehigh Valley RS-3 "8807," *90*	80	105	—1
(18808)	ACL SD-18 "8808," *90*	95	120	—1
(18809)	Susquehanna RS-3 "8809" (See 18551), *89 u*	—	150	—1
(18810)	CSX SD-18 "8810," *90*	95	130	—1
(18811)	Alaska SD-9 "8811," *91*	135	190	—1
(18812)	Kansas City Southern GP-38 "4000," *91*	115	140	—1
(18813)	DM&IR SD-18 "8813" (See 18552), *90 u*	—	110	—1
(18814)	D&H RS-3 "8814" (SSS), *91*	110	145	—1
(18815)	Amtrak RS-3 "1815," *91, 92 u*	90	115	—1
(18816)	C&NW GP-38-2 "4600," *92*	100	125	—1
(18817)	UP GP-9 "150" (See 18553), *91 u*	—	160	—1
(18818)	Lionel Railroader Club GP-38-2 "1992," *92 u*	135	185	—1
(18819)	L&N GP-38-2 "4136," *92*	140	185	—1
(18820)	WP GP-9 "8820" (SSS), *92*	105	120	—1
(18821)	Clinchfield GP-38-2 "6005," *93*	125	150	—1
(18822)	Gulf, Mobile & Ohio RS-3 "721" (See 18554), *92-93 u*			

		Exc	New	Cond/$
(18823)	Chicago & Illinois Midland SD-9 "52" (See 18555), *92 u*	—	140	—[1]
(18824)	Montana Rail Link SD-9 "600," *93*	150	180	—[1]
(18825)	Soo Line GP-38-2 "4000" (SSS), *93*	120	140	—[1]
(18826)	Conrail GP-7 "5808," *93*	110	135	—[1]
(18827)	"Happy Holidays" RS-3 "8827," *93*	150	225	—[1]
(18830)	Budweiser GP-9 "1947," *93-94 u*	110	150	—[1]
(18831)	SP GP-20 "4060," *94*	115	130	—[1]
(18832)	PRR RSD-4 "8446," *95*	105	125	—[1]
(18833)	Milwaukee Road RS-3 "2487," *94*	100	110	—[1]
(18834)	C&O SD-28 "8834," *94*	100	130	—[1]
(18835)	NYC RS-3 "8223" (SSS), *94*	115	165	—[1]
(18836)	CN/Grand Trunk GP-38-2 "5800," *94*	155	180	—[1]
(18837)	"Happy Holidays" RS-3 "8837," *94-95*	150	190	—[1]
(18838)	Seaboard RSC-3 "1538," *95*	120	155	—[1]
(18840)	U.S.Army GP-7 "1821," *95*	100	140	—[1]
(18841)	Western Maryland GP-20 "27" (SSS), *95*	110	140	—[1]
(18842)	JC Penney/B&LE SD-38 "868," *95 u*	—	245	—[1]
(18843)	Great Northern RS-3 "197," *96*	—	130	—[1]
(18844)	NdeM GP-38 "9288," *96*		NM	—[1]
(18845)	D&RGW RS-3 "5204," *97*	—	115	—[1]
(18846)	1997 Lionel Centennial Series GP-9 Diesel Locomotive, *98*	—	250	—[1]
(18847)	Santa Fe H-12-44 Switcher "9087," *99*	—	430	—[1]
(18848)	PRR H-12-44 Switcher "502," *99*	—	420	—[1]
(18853)	Santa Fe JC Penney GP-9 "2370," *97u*	—	150	—[1]
(18854)	Union Pacific GP-9 set "2380"-"2387" dummy, *97*	—	450	—[1]
(18855)	Union Pacific GP-9 Dummy (See 18854)			
(18856)	NJ Transit GP-38-2 "4303," *99*	—	315	—[1]
(18857)	Union Pacific GP-9 "2397," *97*	—	240	—[1]
(18858)	1998 Lionel Centennial GP20 Diesel Engine "1998," *98*	—	280	—[2]
(18859)	The Phantom II, *99*	—	340	—[1]
(18860)	The Pratt's Hollow Collection I: The Phantom, *98*	—	400	—[1]
(18864)	Southern Pacific GP-9 B-Unit, *98*	—	110	—[1]
(18865)	New York Central GP-9 B-Unit, *98*	—	170	—[1]
(18868)	NJ Transit GP-38-2 "4300," *98u*	—	140	—[1]
(18870)	Pennsylvania GP-9 Diesel "2029," *98*	—	235	—[1]
(18872)	Wabash GP7 3-Unit Set "453, 454, 455," *99*	—	510	—[1]
(18876)	C&NW H-12-44 Switcher "1053," *99*	—	415	—[1]
(18877)	Union Pacific GP9 Non-Powered "2399," *99*	—	170	—[1]
(18878)	Alaska GP7 "1803," *99*	—	115	—[1]
(18879)	B&O GP9 "5616," *99*	—	260	—[1]
(18881)	Custom GP9 "5616," *99*	—	290	—[1]

		Exc	New	Cond/$
(18890)	LOTS UP RS-3 "8805," *89 u*	125	150	—[1]
(18892)	Burlington GP9 "2328," *99*	—	295	—[1]
(18897)	Christmas GP7 "1999," *99*	—	210	—[1]
(18900)	PRR Diesel Switcher "8900," *88 u, 89*	26	34	—[1]
(18901)/(18902)	PRR Alco AA set "8901" and "8902," *88*	110	130	—[1]
(18903)/(18904)	Amtrak Alco AA set "8903" and "8904," *88-89*	90	130	—[1]
(18903)	Amtrak "Mopar Express," *99*	—	500	—[1]
(18905)	PRR 44-tonner "9312," *92*	90	105	—[1]
(18906)	Erie-Lackawanna RS-3 "8906," *91 u*	100	135	—[1]
(18907)	Rock Island 44-tonner "371," *93*	80	90	—[1]
(18908)/(18909)	NYC Alco AA set "8908" and "8909," *93*	105	115	—[1]
(18910)	CSX Diesel Switcher "8910," *93*	35	40	—[1]
(18911)	UP Diesel Switcher "8911," *93*	30	33	—[1]
(18912)	Amtrak Diesel Switcher "8912," *93*	31	35	—[1]
(18913)	Santa Fe Alco A Unit "8913," *93-94*	55	65	—[1]
(18915)	WM Alco A Unit "8915," *93*	60	75	—[1]
(18916)	WM Alco A Unit Dummy "8916," *93*	34	38	—[1]
18917	Soo Line NW-2, *93*	65	75	—[1]
(18918)	B&M NW-2 "8918," *93*	70	85	—[1]
(18919)	Santa Fe Alco A Unit Dummy "8919," *93-94*	33	50	—[1]
(18920)	Frisco NW-2 "254," *94*	65	75	—[1]
(18921)	C&NW NW-2 "1017," *94*	80	110	—[1]
(18922)	New Haven Alco A Unit "8922," *94*	75	105	—[1]
(18923)	New Haven Alco A Unit Dummy "8923," *94*	50	55	—[1]
(18924)	Illinois Central Diesel Switcher "8924," *94-95*	31	35	—[1]
(18925)	D&RGW Diesel Switcher "8925," *94-95*	32	35	—[1]
(18926)	Reading Diesel Switcher "8926," *94-95*	27	34	—[1]
(18927)	U.S. Navy NW-2 "65-00637," *94-95*	75	95	—[1]
(18928)	C&NW NW-2 Calf, *95*	42	45	—[1]
(18929)	B&M NW-2 Calf, *95*	44	49	—[1]
(18930)	Crayola Diesel Switcher, *94 u, 95*	27	30	—[1]
(18931)	Chrysler Mopar NW-2 "1818," *94 u*	70	85	—[1]
(18932)	Jersey Central NW-2 "8932," *96*	—	65	—[1]
(18933)	Jersey Central NW-2 Calf "8933," *96*	—	55	—[1]
(18934)/(18935)	Reading Alco AA set "300" and "304," *95*	75	95	—
(18936)	Amtrak Alco A Unit "8936," *95*	—	65	—
(18937)	Non-powered Amtrak FA-2 ALCO, *95-97*	—	49	—
(18938)	U.S.Navy NW-2 Calf, *95*	55	65	—
(18939)	Union Pacific NW-2 Diesel Switcher set, *96*	—	130	—
(18943)	Georgia Power NW-2 "1960," *95 u*	—	170	—
(18946)	U.S.C.G. NW-2 Switcher "8946," *96*	—	80	—
(18947)	Port of Lionel City Alco FA-2 "2030," *97*	—	70	—

		Exc	New	Cond/$
(18948)	Port of Lionel City Alco FB-2 "2030B," 97	—	55	__1
(18949)	NYC NW-2 "622," black, 97		NM	__1
(18951)	Erie NW-2 "6220," black, 97		NM	__1
(18952)	AT&SF Alco PA-1 "2000," 97	—	235	__2
(18953)	NYC Alco PA-1 "2000," 97	—	245	__2
(18954)	AT&SF Alco FA-2 "212" Powered, 97-99	—	80	__1
(18955)	NJ Transit NW-2 Switcher "500," 96 u	—	110	__1
(18956)	Dodge Motorsports "8956" NW-2, 96 u	—	150	__1
(18959)	NYC NW-2 Switcher "622," 97	—	450	__1
(18961)	Erie Alco PA-1"850," 98	—	335	__1
(18965)	Santa Fe Alco PB1, 98	—	255	__1
(18966)	New York Central Alco BP1 "20008," 98	—	250	__1
(18971)	Alco A-Unit (Non-Powered), 98	—	65	__1
(18972)	Rock Island Alco FA AA, 98		NM	__1
(18973)	RI Alco FA-2 "2031" Powered, 98-99		NRS	__1
(18974)	RI Alco FA-2 Dummy, 98-99		NRS	__1
(18975)	Southern 44-Ton Switcher "1955," 99	—	190	__1
(18978)	C&O NW-2 Switcher "624," 99-00	—	375	__1
18981	Pennsylvania Railroad Speeder "16," 04		CP	__1
18982	Santa Fe Railroad Speeder "122," 04		CP	__1
19000	Blue Comet Dining Car, 87 u	65	85	__1
19001	Southern Dining Car, 87 u	70	90	__1
19002	Pennsylvania Dining Car, 88 u	29	45	__1
19003	Milwaukee Road Dining Car, 88 u	29	44	__1
19010	B&O Dining Car, 89 u	30	45	__1
(19011)	Lionel Lines Baggage Car "9011," 93	250	355	__1
(19015)	Lionel Lines Passenger Car "9015," 91	110	140	__1
(19016)	Lionel Lines Passenger Car "9016," 91	90	120	__1
(19017)	Lionel Lines Passenger Car "9017," 91	95	125	__1
(19018)	Lionel Lines Observation Car "9018," 91	90	115	__1
(19019)	SP Baggage Car "9019," 93	110	150	__1
(19023)	SP Passenger Car "9023," 92	115	140	__1
(19024)	SP Passenger Car "9024," 92	85	100	__1
(19025)	SP Passenger Car "9025," 92	100	115	__1
(19026)	SP Observation Car "9026," 92	85	100	__1
(19027)	Reading Baggage Car "9027," 92		NM	__1
(19031)	Reading Passenger Car "9031," 92		NM	__1
(19032)	Reading Passenger Car "9032," 92		NM	__1
(19033)	Reading Observation Car "9033," 92		NM	__1
(19038)	Adolphus Busch Observation Car, 92-93 u	—	80	__1
(19039)	Pere Marquette Baggage Car, 93	—	75	__1
(19040)	Pere Marquette Passenger Car "1115," 93	—	75	__1
(19041)	Pere Marquette Passenger Car "1116," 93	—	75	__1
(19042)	Pere Marquette Observation Car "36," 93	—	75	__1
(19047)	Baltimore & Ohio Combination Car "9047," 96	—	42	__1
(19048)	Baltimore & Ohio Passenger Car "9048," 96	—	50	__1

		Exc	New	Cond/$
(19049)	Baltimore & Ohio Dining Car "9049," *96*	—	42	—1
(19050)	Baltimore & Ohio Observation Car "9050," *96*	—	42	—1
(19056)	NYC Heavyweight Baggage Car, *96*	—	105	—1
(19057)	NYC Heavyweight "Willow Run" Coach, *96*	—	100	—1
(19058)	NYC Heavyweight "Willow Trail" Coach, *96*	—	75	—1
(19059)	NYC Heavyweight "Seneca Valley" Observation, *96*	—	100	—1
(19060)	Pullman Heavyweight set, *96*	—	315	—2
(19061)	Wabash Railway Passenger set, *97*	—	240	—1
(19062)	Wabash Railway City of Columbia Coach "2361," *97*	—	90	—1
(19063)	Wabash Railway City of Danville Coach "2362," *97*	—	75	—1
(19064)	Wabash REA Baggage Car "2360," *97*	—	75	—1
(19065)	Wabash Windy City Observation "2363," *97*	—	90	—1
(19066)	Commodore Vanderbilt Pullman Heavyweight 2-pack, *97*	—	190	—1
(19067)	Comm. Vanderbilt Willow River Pullman "2543," *97*	—	100	—1
(19068)	Comm. Vanderbilt Willow Valley Pullman "2544," *97*	—	100	—1
(19069)	Pullman Baby Madison set "9500-02," *97*	—	155	—1
(19070)	Baby Madison REA/Combo "9501," *97*	—	40	—1
(19071)	Baby Madison Laurel Gap Coach "9500," *97*	—	40	—1
(19072)	Baby Madison Laurel Summit Coach "9500," *97*	—	40	—1
(19073)	Baby Madison Catskill Valley Observation "9502," *97*	—	40	—1
(19074)	Legends of Lionel Madison set, *97*	—	395	—1
(19075)	Lionel Legends Mazzone Coach "2621," *97*	—	90	—1
(19076)	Lionel Legends Caruso Coach "2624," *97*	—	90	—1
(19077)	Lionel Legends Raphael Coach "2652," *97*	—	90	—1
(19078)	Lionel Legends Cowen Observation "2600," *97*	—	90	—1
(19079)	NYC Heavyweight Passenger Car set, *97*	—	345	—1
(19080)	NYC Heavyweight REA Baggage Car "2564," *97*	—	100	—1
(19081)	NYC Heavyweight Park Place Coach "2565," *97*	—	100	—1
(19082)	NYC Heavyweight Star Beam Coach "2566," *97*	—	100	—1
(19083)	NYC Heavyweight Hudson Valley Observation "2566," *97*	—	100	—1
(19087)	C&O Heavyweight Passenger Car 4-pack "2571-74," *97*	—	300	—1
(19088)	C&O Heavyweight Baggage Car "2571," *97*	—	100	—1

		Exc	New	Cond/$
(19089)	C&O Heavyweight Sleeper Car "2572," 97	—	100	—[1]
(19090)	C&O Heavyweight Diner Car "2573," 97	—	110	—[1]
(19091)	C&O Heavyweight Observation Car "2574," 97	—	100	—[1]
(19093)	Commodore Vanderbilt Heavyweight Sleeper Cars 2-pack, 98	—	170	—[1]
(19094)	Comm. Vanderbilt Niagara Falls Sleeper, 98	—	75	—[1]
(19095)	Comm. Vanderbilt Highland Falls Sleeper, 98	—	75	—[1]
(19096)	Legends of Lionel Madison Cars 2-pack, 98	—	175	—[1]
(19097)	Lionel Legends "Bonnano" Coach "2653," 98	—	80	—[1]
(19098)	Lionel Legends "Pagano" Coach "2654," 98	—	105	—[1]
(19099)	Pennsylvania "Liberty Gap" Baggage Car "2623," 99	—	85	—[1]
(19100)	Amtrak Baggage Car "9100," 89	115	145	—[1]
(19101)	Amtrak Combination Car "9101," 89	75	85	—[1]
(19102)	Amtrak Passenger Car "9102," 89	75	85	—[1]
(19103)	Amtrak Vista Dome Car "9103," 89	70	90	—[1]
(19104)	Amtrak Dining Car "9104," 89	65	80	—[1]
(19105)	Amtrak Full Vista Dome Car "9105," 89 u	70	80	—[2]
(19106)	Amtrak Observation Car "9106," 89	75	90	—[1]
(19107)	SP Full Vista Dome Car, 90 u	70	75	—[3]
(19108)	N&W Full Vista Dome Car "576," 91 u	90	100	—[1]
(19109)	Santa Fe Baggage Car "3400," 91	150	195	—[1]
(19110)	Santa Fe Combination Car "3500," 91	115	165	—[1]
(19111)	Santa Fe Dining Car "601," 91	110	155	—[1]
(19112)	Santa Fe Passenger Car, 91	120	165	—[1]
(19113)	Santa Fe Vista Dome Observation Car, 91	120	170	—[1]
(19116)	Great Northern Baggage Car "1200," 92	95	110	—[1]
(19117)	Great Northern Combination Car "1240," 92	75	95	—[1]
(19118)	Great Northern Passenger Car "1212," 92	75	95	—[1]
(19119)	Great Northern Vista Dome Car "1322," 92	75	95	—[1]
(19120)	Great Northern Observation Car "1192," 92	75	95	—[1]
(19121)	Union Pacific Vista Dome Car "9121," 92 u	105	120	—[1]
(19122)	D&RGW California Zephyr Baggage Car, 93	120	140	—[2]
(19123)	D&RGW California Zephyr "Silver Bronco" Vista Dome Car, 93	95	115	—[1]
(19124)	D&RGW California Zephyr "Silver Colt" Vista Dome Car, 93	95	115	—[1]
(19125)	D&RGW California Zephyr "Silver Mustang" Vista Dome Car, 93	100	125	—[1]
(19126)	D&RGW California Zephyr "Silver Pony" Vista Dome Car, 93	95	115	—[1]
(19127)	D&RGW California Zephyr Vista Dome Observation Car, 93	95	115	—[1]
(19128)	Santa Fe Full Vista Dome Car "507," 92 u	175	185	—[1]
(19129)	Illinois Central Full Vista Dome Car			

		Exc	New	Cond/$
	"9129," *93*	75	85	—¹
(19130)	Lackawanna Passenger Cars, set of 4, *94*	295	365	—¹
(19131)	Lackawanna Baggage Car "2000" (See 19130)	—	115	—¹
(19132)	Lackawanna Dining Car "469" (See 19130)	—	100	—¹
(19133)	Lackawanna Passenger Car "260" (See 19130)	—	100	—¹
(19134)	Lackawanna Observation Car "789" (See 19130)	—	85	—¹
(19135)	Lackawanna Combination Car "425," *94*	85	100	—¹
(19136)	Lackawanna Passenger Car "211," *94*	70	80	—¹
(19137)	New York Central Roomette Car, *95*	85	100	—¹
(19138)	Santa Fe Roomette Car, *95*	85	105	—²
(19139)	Norfolk & Western Baggage Car "577," *95*	105	135	—¹
(19140)	Norfolk & Western Combination Car "494," *95*	75	90	—¹
(19141)	Norfolk & Western Dining Car "495," *95*	105	135	—¹
(19142)	Norfolk & Western Passenger Car "538," *95*	75	95	—¹
(19143)	Norfolk & Western Passenger Car "537," *95*	75	95	—¹
(19144)	Norfolk & Western Observation Car "582," *95*	75	90	—¹
(19145)	Chesapeake & Ohio Combination Car "1403," *96*	—	85	—²
(19146)	Chesapeake & Ohio Passenger Car "1623," *96*	—	85	—¹
(19147)	Chesapeake & Ohio Passenger Car "1803," *96*	—	75	—¹
(19148)	C&O Chessie Club Coach "1903," *96*	—	75	—¹
(19149)	C&O Gadsby Kitchen Pass./Diner "1950," *96*	—	75	—¹
(19150)	Chesapeake & Ohio Observation Car "2504," *96*	—	65	—¹
(19151)	Norfolk & Western Duplex Roomette car, *96*	—	95	—²
(19152)	Union Pacific Duplex Roomette Car, *96*	—	70	—¹
(19153)	Chesapeake & Ohio Passenger Cars, set of 4, *96*	—	325	—²
(19154)	Atlantic Coast Line Passenger Cars set, *96*	—	310	—¹
(19155)	ACL Passenger/Combo "101," *96*	—	90	—¹
(19156)	ACL "Talladega" Diner, *96*	—	90	—¹
(19157)	ACL "Moultrie" Coach, *96*	—	90	—¹
(19158)	ACL Observation "256," *96*	—	90	—¹
(19159)	Norfolk & Western Passenger Cars, set of 4, *95 u*	300	385	—
(19160)	AT&SF Super Chief REA Baggage Car, *96*	—	75	—
(19161)	AT&SF Super Chief Silver Sky Coach, *96*	—	80	—
(19162)	AT&SF Super Chief "Silver Mesa"			

		Exc	New	Cond/$
	Vista Dome, *96*	—	75	—¹
(19163)	AT&SF Super Chief "Silver Rail" Observation, *96*	—	75	—¹
(19164)	Chesapeake & Ohio Passenger Cars, *96*	—	145	—¹
(19165)	AT&SF Super Chief set, *96*	—	295	—¹
(19166)	NP Vista Dome set, *97*	—	320	—¹
(19167)	NP Pullman "2571," *97*	—	105	—¹
(19168)	NP Pullman "2571," *97*	—	105	—¹
(19169)	NP Pullman "2570," *97*	—	95	—¹
(19170)	NP Pullman "2571," *97*	—	100	—¹
(19171)	NYC Streamlined Passenger set "2570-75," *97*	—	365	—¹
(19172)	NYC Aluminum Passenger Baggage "2570," *97*	—	85	—¹
(19173)	NYC Aluminum Passenger Diner "Manhattan Island," *97*	—	100	—¹
(19174)	NYC Aluminum Passenger Coach "Queensboro Bridge," *97*	—	100	—¹
(19175)	NYC Aluminum Passenger Observation "Windgate Brook," *97*	—	90	—¹
(19176)	AT&SF "Indian Arrow" Diner "2572," *97*	—	90	—¹
(19177)	AT&SF "Grass Valley" Coach "2573," *97*	—	90	—¹
(19178)	AT&SF "Citrus Valley" Coach "2574," *97*	—	90	—¹
(19179)	AT&SF "Vista Heights" "2575," *97*	—	90	—¹
(19180)	AT&SF Surfliner Passenger set "2572-75," *97*	—	325	—¹
(19181)	GN Empire Builder "Prairie View" Full Vista Dome, *98*	—	75	—¹
(19182)	GN Empire Builder "River View" Full Vista Dome, *98*	—	75	—¹
(19183)	Great Northern Empire Builder Vista Dome Cars 2-pack, *98*	—	150	—¹
(19184)	Milwaukee Passenger Set 4-pack, *99*	—	440	—¹
(19185)	Milwaukee Road Aluminum Passenger Coach "194 Red River Valle, *99*	—	125	—¹
(19186)	Milwaukee Road Aluminum Passenger Diner "170," *99*	—	110	—¹
(19187)	Milwaukee Road Aluminum Pass. Observation "186 Cedar Rapids," *99*	—	120	—¹
(19188)	Milwaukee Road Aluminum Passenger Baggage "1336," REA, *99*	—	110	—¹
(19194)	KCS Alum Passenger Car 4-pack, *00*	—	380	—¹
19200	Tidewater Southern Boxcar, *87*	11	19	—¹
19201	Lancaster & Chester Boxcar, *87*	34	55	—¹
19202	PRR Boxcar, *87*	28	34	—¹
19203	D&TS Boxcar, *87*	11	19	—¹

		Exc	New	Cond/$
19204	Milwaukee Road Boxcar (FF #2), *87*	24	33	—1
19205	Great Northern DD Boxcar (FF #3), *88*	22	28	—1
19206	Seaboard System Boxcar, *88*	17	22	—1
19207	CP Rail DD Boxcar, *88*	14	18	—1
19208	Southern DD Boxcar, *88*	14	18	—1
19209	Florida East Coast Boxcar, *88*	15	19	—1
19210	Soo Line Boxcar, *89*	17	20	—1
19211	Vermont Railway Boxcar, *89*	20	23	—1
19212	PRR Boxcar, *89*	22	26	—2
19213	SP&S DD Boxcar, *89*	18	21	—1
19214	Western Maryland Boxcar (FF #4), *89*	24	28	—1
19215	Union Pacific DD Boxcar, *90*	13	14	—1
19216	Santa Fe Boxcar, *90*	15	19	—1
19217	Burlington Boxcar, *90*	14	17	—1
19218	New Haven Boxcar, *90*	16	19	—1
19219	Lionel Lines 1900-1906 Boxcar w/ Diesel RailSounds, *90*	120	145	—1
19220	Lionel Lines 1926-1934 Boxcar, *90*	27	30	—1
19221	Lionel Lines 1935-1937 Boxcar, *90*	27	30	—1
19222	Lionel Lines 1948-1950 Boxcar, *90*	27	30	—1
19223	Lionel Lines 1979-1989 Boxcar, *90*	26	29	—1
19228	Cotton Belt Boxcar, *91*	16	17	—1
19229	Frisco Boxcar w/ Diesel RailSounds (FF #5), *91*	75	90	—1
19230	Frisco DD Boxcar (FF #5), *91*	25	30	—1
19231	TA&G DD Boxcar, *91*	17	20	—1
19232	Rock Island DD Boxcar, *91*	17	19	—1
19233	Southern Pacific Boxcar, *91*	17	22	—1
19234	NYC Boxcar, *91*	65	75	—1
19235	MKT Boxcar, *91*	55	65	—1
19236	NKP DD Boxcar (FF #6), *92*	19	26	—1
19237	C&IM Boxcar, *92*	14	19	—1
19238	Kansas City Southern Boxcar, *92*	18	23	—1
19239	Toronto, Hamilton & Buffalo DD Boxcar, *92*	14	19	—1
19240	Great Northern DD Boxcar, *92*	14	18	—1
19241	Mickey Mouse 60th Anniversary Hi-cube Boxcar, *91 u*	135	190	—1
19242	Donald Duck 50th Anniversary Hi-cube Boxcar, *91 u*	125	160	—1
(19243)	Clinchfield Boxcar "9790," *91 u*	32	37	—1
(19244)	L&N Boxcar "9791," *92*	29	31	—1
19245	Mickey's World Tour Hi-cube Boxcar, *92 u*	39	47	—2
19246	Disney World 20th Anniversary Hi-cube Boxcar, *92 u*	39	47	—1
(19247)	6464 Series Boxcars, 1st Edition, set of 3, *93*	350	405	—2

		Exc	New	Cond/$
(19248)	Western Pacific Boxcar "6464," *93*	75	85	—1
(19249)	Great Northern Boxcar "6464," *93*	75	85	—1
(19250)	M&St L Boxcar "6464," *93*	80	90	—1
(19251)	Montana Rail Link DD Boxcar "10001," *93*	21	27	—1
19254	Erie Boxcar (FF #7), *93*	21	25	—1
19255	Erie DD Boxcar (FF #7), *93*	23	27	—1
19256	Goofy Hi-cube Boxcar, *93*	27	34	—1
(19257)	6464 Series Boxcars, 2nd Edition, set of 3, *94*	135	150	—2
(19258)	Rock Island Boxcar "6464," *94*	28	38	—1
(19259)	Western Pacific Boxcar "6464100," *94*	34	49	—1
(19260)	Western Pacific Boxcar "6464100," *94*	39	55	—1
19261	Perils of Mickey Hi-cube Boxcar I, *93*	31	33	—1
19262	Perils of Mickey Hi-cube Boxcar II, *93*	31	33	—1
19263	NYC DD Boxcar (SSS), *94*	36	42	—1
19264	Perils of Mickey Hi-cube Boxcar III, *94*	31	35	—1
19265	Mickey Mouse 65th Anniversary Hi-cube Boxcar, *94*	37	40	—1
(19266)	6464 Series Boxcars, 3rd Edition, set of 3, *95*	90	100	—3
(19267)	NYC "Pacemaker" Boxcar "6464125," *95*	43	49	—1
(19268)	Missouri Pacific Boxcar "6464150," *95*	37	41	—1
(19269)	Rock Island Boxcar "6464," *95*	34	39	—1
19270	Donald Duck 60th Anniversary Hi-cube Boxcar, *95*	36	40	—1
19271	Minnie Mouse Hi-cube Boxcar, *95*	44	46	—1
(19272)	6464 Series Boxcars, 4th edition, set of 3, *96*	90	115	—2
(19273)	BAR "State of Maine" Boxcar "6464275," *96*	—	35	—1
(19274)	Southern Pacific "Overnight" Boxcar "6464225," *96*	—	32	—1
(19275)	Pennsylvania Boxcar "6464," *96*	—	40	—1
(19276)	6464 Boxcar Series V "19277-79," *96*	—	95	—3
19277	Rutland Boxcar "6464-300" (Series V), *96*	—	34	—1
19278	B&O Boxcar "6464-325" (Series V), *96*	—	34	—1
19279	Central of Georgia "6464-375" (Series V), *96*	—	32	—1
19280	Mickey's Wheat Hi-cube Boxcar, *96*	—	32	—1
19281	Mickey's Carrots Hi-cube Boxcar, *96*	—	45	—1
19282	Santa Fe "Super Chief" Boxcar "6464-196," *96*	—	27	—1
19283	Erie Boxcar "6464-296," *96*	—	29	—1
19284	Northern Pacific Boxcar "6464-396," *96*	—	32	—1
19285	Bangor and Aroostook "State of Maine" Boxcar "6464-275," *96*	—	30	—1
19286	Warner Bros. "All Abirrrrd" Boxcar, *96*	—	46	—1
19287	NYC/PC Merger Boxcar "6464-125X" (SSS), *97*	60	85	—1

		Exc	New	Cond/$
(19288)	PRR/CR Merger Boxcar "6464-200X" (SSS), *97*	50	80	—¹
(19289)	Monon "Hoosier Line" Boxcar "6464," *97*	—	27	—¹
(19290)	Seaboard "Silver Meteor" Boxcar "6464," *97*	—	35	—¹
(19291)	GN Boxcar "6464-397," dark green, *97*	—	35	—¹
(19292)	6464 Boxcar Series VI "19293-95," *97*	—	105	—¹
(19293)	MKT Boxcar "6464-350" (Series VI), *97*	28	33	—¹
(19294)	B&O Boxcar "6464-400" (Series VI), *97*	33	43	—¹
(19295)	NH Boxcar "6464-425" (Series VI), *97*	31	43	—¹
19300	PRR Ore Car, *87*	16	24	—¹
19301	Milwaukee Road Ore Car, *87*	24	30	—¹
19302	Milwaukee Road Quad Hopper w/ coal load (FF #2), *87*	21	29	—¹
19303	Lionel Lines Quad Hopper w/ coal load, *87 u*	20	28	—²
19304	GN Covered Quad Hopper (FF #3), *88*	27	29	—¹
19305	Chessie System Ore Car, *88*	19	24	—¹
19307	B&LE Ore Car w/ load, *89*	19	24	—¹
19308	GN Ore Car w/ load, *89*	17	22	—¹
19309	Seaboard Covered Quad Hopper, *89*	17	22	—¹
19310	L&C Quad Hopper w/ coal load, *89*	22	31	—¹
19311	SP Covered Quad Hopper, *90*	14	19	—¹
19312	Reading Quad Hopper w/ coal load, *90*	22	33	—¹
19313	B&O Ore Car w/ load, *90-91*	20	25	—¹
19315	Amtrak Ore Car w/ load, *91*	25	35	—¹
19316	Wabash Covered Quad Hopper, *91*	21	29	—¹
19317	Lehigh Valley Quad Hopper w/ coal load, *91*	55	65	—¹
19318	NKP Quad Hopper w/ coal load (FF #6), *92*	29	33	—¹
19319	Union Pacific Covered Quad Hopper, *92*	19	23	—¹
19320	PRR Ore Car w/ load, *92*	21	30	—¹
19321	B&LE Ore Car w/ load, *92*	21	30	—¹
19322	C&NW Ore Car w/ load, *93*	27	34	—¹
19323	Detroit & Mackinac Ore Car w/ load, *93*	20	29	—¹
19324	Erie Quad Hopper w/ coal load (FF #7), *93*	23	30	—¹
(19325)	N&W 4-Bay Hopper w/ coal "6446-1," *97*	—	80	—¹
(19326)	N&W 4-Bay Hopper w/ coal "6446-2," *96*	—	65	—¹
(19327)	N&W 4-Bay Hopper w/ coal "6446-3," *96*	—	55	—¹
(19328)	N&W 4-Bay Hopper w/ coal "6446-4," *96*	—	55	—¹
(19329)	N&W 4-Bay Hopper w/ coal "6436," *97*	—	55	—
(19330)	Cotton Belt 4-bay Hopper w/ Coal "64661," *98*	—	45	—
(19331)	Cotton Belt 4-bay Hopper w/ Coal "64662," *98*	—	45	—
(19332)	Cotton Belt 4-bay Hopper w/ Coal "64663," *98*	—	45	—
(19333)	Cotton Belt 4-bay Hopper w/ Coal "64664," *98*	—	45	—

		Exc	New	Cond/$
(19338)	Cotton Belt 4-Bay Hopper 2-pack, *99*	—	120	—¹
(19339)	Cotton Belt 4-Bay Hopper "64469," *99*		NRS	—¹
(19340)	Cotton Belt 4-Bay Hopper "64470," *99*		NRS	—¹
(19341)	LV 2-Bay Hopper "6456," *99*	—	30	—¹
(19344)	D&RGW 3-Bay Cylindrical Hopper "15990," *99-00*	—	49	—¹
(19345)	CN 3-Bay Cylindrical Hopper "370708," *99-00*	—	85	—¹
(19346)	PRR 4-Bay Hopper w/Coal Load "744433," *01*	—	40	—¹
(19347)	LV 2-Bay Hopper "643657," *01*	—	40	—¹
(19348)	Duluth, Missabe & Iron Range Ore Car "28000," *03*	—	25	—¹
(19349)	US Steel Ore Car "19349," *03*	—	25	—¹
(19350)	Postwar Alaska Quad Hopper "6636," *03*	—	35	—¹
19400	Milwaukee Road Gondola w/ cable reels (FF #2), *87*	22	30	—¹
19401	GN Gondola w/ coal load (FF #3), *88*	21	25	—¹
19402	GN Crane Car (FF #3), *88*	41	55	—¹
19403	WM Gondola w/ coal load (FF #4), *89*	19	23	—¹
19404	Trailer Train Flatcar w/ WM trailers (FF #4), *89*	32	36	—¹
19405	Southern Crane Car, *91*	50	80	—¹
19406	West Point Mint Car, *91 u*	55	85	—¹
19408	Frisco Gondola w/ coil covers (FF #5), *91*	28	32	—¹
19409	Southern Flatcar w/ stakes, *91*	18	22	—¹
19410	NYC Gondola w/ canisters, *91*	47	55	—¹
19411	NKP Flatcar w/ Sears trailer (FF #6), *92*	47	60	—²
19412	Frisco Crane Car, *92*	49	65	—¹
19413	Frisco Flatcar w/ stakes, *92*	19	25	—¹
19414	Union Pacific Flatcar w/ stakes (SSS), *92*	19	26	—¹
(19415)	Erie Flatcar w/ trailer "7200" (FF #7), *93*	28	39	—¹
(19416)	ICG TTUX Flatcar set w/ trailers "19417" and "19418" (SSS), *93*	70	85	—¹
19417/19418	ICG TTUX Flatcars w/ trailers (See 19416)			
19419	Charlotte Mint Car, *93*	32	39	—²
19420	Lionel Lines Vat Car, *94*	23	27	—¹
19421	Hirsch Brothers Vat Car, *95*	24	29	—¹
(19423)	Circle-L Racing Flatcar w/ stock cars "6424," *96*	—	29	—¹
(19424)	Edison Electric Dep. Center Flatcar w/ Transformer "6461," *97*	—	38	—¹
(19425)	Artrain CSX Flatcar w/ Trailer, *96 u*	—	80	—¹
(19427)	Evans Auto Loader "6414," *99*	—	65	—¹
(19428)	Evans Boat Loader "6414," *99*	—	70	—²
(19429)	Culvert Gondola "35621," *98-99*	—	55	—¹
(19430)	AT&SF Flatcar w/Beechcraft Bonanza "6411," *98*	—	37	—¹

		Exc	New	Cond/$
(19437)	LRRC Flatcar w/ trailer, *97 u*	—	55	—¹
(19438)	Standard O Christmas Gondola, *98*	—	44	—¹
(19439)	Flatcar with Safes, *98*	—	35	—¹
(19440)	Flatcar with FedEx Trailer, *98*	—	37	—¹
(19441)	Lobster Vat Car, *98*	—	32	—¹
(19442)	Water Supply Flatcar w/ tank (SSS), *98*	—	31	—¹
(19444)	Flatcar with VW Bug, *98*	—	45	—¹
(19445)	Borden Milk Tank Car "520," *99*	—	39	—¹
(19446)	Pittsburg Paint Vat Car, *99*	—	43	—¹
(19447)	Mama's Baked Beans Vat Car, *99*	—	35	—¹
(19448)	Easter Gondola w/ Candy "6462," *99*	—	30	—¹
(19449)	Liquified Gas Tank Car "6469," *99*	—	32	—¹
(19450)	Barrel Ramp Car "6343," *99*	—	36	—¹
(19451)	Wheel Car "6262," *99*	—	32	—¹
(19454)	PRR Flat Car with Gondola "6424," *99*	—	25	—¹
(19455)	Lionel Lines Flatcar with Cooper-Jarrett Trailers "6430," *99*		NRS	—¹
(19457)	Lionel Lines Extension Searchlight Car, *99*	—	40	—¹
(19459)	Valentine Gondola w/ Candy "6462," *99*	—	50	—¹
(19471)	Mobil Flatcar w/ 2 trailers, *00 u*	—	95	—¹
(19472)	Mobil Bulkhead Flatcar w/ Tank, *00 u*	—	55	—¹
(19473)	LRRC Log Dump Car, *99 u*	—	35	—¹
(19474)	L&N Flatcar w/ Die-Cast Trailer Frames 6424, *99*	—	30	—¹
(19474)	L&N Flatcar w/ Die-Cast Trailer Frames 6424, *99*	—	30	—¹
(19476)	Lionel Zoo Gondola with Animals "6462," *99-00*	—	43	—¹
(19477)	Monday Night Football Flatcar with Trailer, *01*	—	30	—¹
(19478)	Culvert Gondola "6342," *99*	—	48	—¹
(19479)	Borden's Milk Car "521," *00*	—	41	—¹
(19480)	Valentine's Vat Car "6475," *99-00*	—	35	—¹
(19481)	Easter Vat Car "2000," *99-00*	—	38	—¹
(19482)	NYC Flat w/ 2 trailers "6424," *00*	—	60	—¹
(19483)	VW Beetle Flatcar "2000," *00*	—	47	—¹
(19484)	Lionel Flatcar w/Timbers "6264," *00*	—	30	—¹
(19485)	PRR Culvert Gondola "347004," *01*	—	46	—¹
19486	NYC Lumber Flatcar, *01*	—	40	—¹
(19487)	Flatcar w/ Airplane "6800," *00*	—	37	—¹
19489	Evans Auto Loader "500085," *00*	—	50	—¹
(19490)	Postwar Libby's Vat Car "6475," *01-02*	—	37	—¹
(19491)	Christmas Vat Car, *01*	—	30	—¹
(19492)	WM Skeleton Log Car 3-pack, *01*	—	95	—¹
(19496)	Westside Lumber Skeleton Log Car 3-pack, *01*	—	105	—¹
19500	Milwaukee Road Reefer (FF #2), *87*	34	44	—¹

		Exc	New	Cond/$
19502	C&NW Reefer, *87*	31	37	—1
19503	Bangor & Aroostook Reefer, *87*	25	28	—1
19504	Northern Pacific Reefer, *87*	17	20	—1
19505	Great Northern Reefer (FF #3), *88*	30	36	—1
19506	Thomas Newcomen Reefer, *88*	17	21	—1
19507	Thomas Edison Reefer, *88*	19	24	—1
19508	Leonardo da Vinci Reefer, *89*	19	24	—1
19509	Alexander Graham Bell Reefer, *89*	17	20	—1
19510	PRR Stockcar (FARR #5), *89 u*	25	26	—1
19511	WM Reefer (FF #4), *89*	25	29	—1
19512	Wright Brothers Reefer, *90*	17	21	—1
19513	Ben Franklin Reefer, *90*	18	21	—1
19515	Milwaukee Road Stock Car (FF #2), *90 u*	27	33	—1
19516	George Washington Reefer, *89 u, 91*	14	19	—1
19517	Civil War Reefer, *89 u, 91*	14	19	—1
19518	Man on the Moon Reefer, *89 u, 91*	13	17	—1
19519	Frisco Stock Car (FF #5), *91*	22	26	—1
19520	CSX Reefer, *91*	15	19	—1
19522	Guglielmo Marconi Reefer, *91*	19	23	—1
19523	Dr. Robert Goddard Reefer, *91*	19	23	—1
19524	Delaware & Hudson Reefer (SSS), *91*	28	31	—1
19525	Speedy Alka Seltzer Reefer, *91 u*	31	39	—1
19526	Jolly Green Giant Reefer, *91 u*	22	34	—1
19527	Nickel Plate Road Reefer (FF #6), *92*	24	33	—1
19528	Joshua L. Cowen Reefer, *92*	24	30	—1
19529	A.C. Gilbert Reefer, *92*	21	25	—1
19530	Rock Island Stock Car, *92 u*	34	39	—1
19531	Rice Krispies Reefer, *92 u*	23	33	—1
(19532)	Hormel Reefer "901," *92 u*	20	27	—1
19535	Erie Reefer (FF #7), *93*	26	29	—1
19536	Soo Line REA Reefer (SSS), *93*	26	31	—1
19537	Kellogg's Corn Flakes Reefer, *93*		NM	—1
(19538)	Hormel Reefer "102," *94*	24	28	—1
19539	Heinz Reefer, *94*	26	31	—1
19540)	Broken Arrow Ranch Stock Car "3356," *97*	—	34	—1
19552)	Rutland Reefer "395" (Std O), *00*	—	37	—1
19553)	AT&SF Stock Car "23003," *00*	—	39	—1
19554)	Milk Car "36621," *00*	—	135	—1
19555)	Swift Reefer "5837" Red, *01*	—	33	—1
19556)	Swift Reefer "1020" Silver, *01*	—	32	—1
19557)	Circus Stock Car "6376," *00*	—	34	—1
19558)	Postwar MKT Stock Car "6556," *02*	—	27	—1
19560)	Lionel Archives NP 2-Door Stock Car "6356," *02*	—	33	—1
19564)	Postwar Santa Fe Refrigerator Car "6672," *03*	—	35	—1

		Exc	New	Cond/$
(19565)	Archive Burlington Refrigerator Car "6672," *03*	—	35	—[1]
(19599)	Old Glory Reefers, set of 3, *89 u, 91*	43	50	—[1]
19600	Milwaukee Road 1-D Tank Car (FF # 2), *87*	40	48	—[1]
19601	North American 1-D Tank Car (FF #4), *89*	30	32	—[1]
19602	Johnson 1-D Tank Car (FF #5), *91*	24	31	—[1]
19603	GATX 1-D Tank Car (FF #6), *92*	36	47	—[1]
19604	Goodyear 1-D Tank Car (SSS), *93*	32	35	—[1]
19605	Hudson's Bay 1-D Tank Car (SSS), *94*	30	34	—[1]
(19607)	Sunoco 1-D Tank Car "6315," *96*	—	31	—[1]
(19608)	Sunoco Aviation Services 1-Dome Tank Car "6315" (SSS), *97*	—	38	—[1]
(19611)	Gulf Oil Single-Dome Tank Car "6315," *98*	—	32	—[1]
(19612)	Gulf Oil 3-Dome Tank Car "6425," *98*	—	31	—[1]
(19614)	BASF SD Tank Car "UTLX 78252," *99-00*	—	25	—[1]
(19615)	Vulcan Chemicals SD Tank Car, *99-00*	—	25	—[1]
(19621)	Centennial SD Tank Car "6015-1," *99*	—	44	—[1]
(19622)	Centennial SD Tank Car "6015-2," *99*	—	48	—[1]
(19623)	Centennial SD Tank Car "6015-3," *99*	—	46	—[1]
(19624)	Centennial SD Tank Car "6015-4," *99*	—	44	—[1]
(19625)	Ethyl Tank Car "6236," *01*	—	31	—[1]
(19626)	Diamond Chemical Tank Car "19419," *01*	—	27	—[1]
(19627)	Shell SD Tank Car "1227," *01*	—	48	—[1]
(19628)	Lion Oil SD Tank Car "2256," *01*	—	35	—[1]
(19629)	Lifesaver SD Tank Car, *01*		NM	—[1]
(19634)	General American Tank Car Corp. 1-Dome Tank Car, *01*	—	30	—[1]
(19635)	U.S. Army 1-Dome Tank Car "10936," *01*	—	31	—[1]
(19636)	Hooker Chemicals 1-Dome Tank Car "6180," *01*	—	40	—[1]
(19637)	GATX TankTrain Tank Car "44589," (Std. O) , *02*	—	60	—[1]
(19638)	CN TankTrain Tank Car "75571," (Std. O) , *02*	—	65	—[1]
(19639)	GATX TankTrain Tank Car 3-pack, (Std. O) , *02*	—	140	—[1]
(19644)	Union Texas 1-Dome Tank Car "9922," *02*	—	33	—[1]
(19645)	Penn Salt 1-Dome Tank Car "4730," *02*	—	33	—[1]
(19646)	CN Intermediate TankTrain Tank Car "75571" (Std. O), *03*	—	45	—[1]
(19647)	GATX Intermediate TankTrain Tank Car "44589" (Std. O), *03*	—	45	—[1]
19651	Santa Fe Tool Car, *87*	26	31	—
19652	Jersey Central Bunk Car, *88*	18	23	—
19653	Jersey Central Tool Car, *88*	20	25	—
19654	Amtrak Bunk Car, *89*	20	23	—

		Exc	New	Cond/$
19655	Amtrak Tool Car, *90-91*	19	24	—1
19656	Milwaukee Road Bunk Car w/ smoke, *90*	40	50	—1
19657	Wabash Bunk Car w/ smoke, *91-92*	36	41	—1
19658	Norfolk & Western Tool Car, *91*	25	30	—1
(19660)	Lionel Mint Car, *98*	—	55	—1
(19663)	Pratt's Hollow Bunk Car "5717," *99*	—	43	—1
(19664)	Ambassador Award Bunk Car "1998" (Bronze), *99 u*	—	405	—1
(19665)	Ambassador Engineer Bunk Car "1998" (Silver), *99 u*	—	560	—1
(19666)	Ambassador Cowen Bunk Car "1998" (Gold), *99 u*	—	375	—1
(19667)	Wellspring Gold Bullion Car, *99*	—	48	—1
(19669)	King Tut Museum Car "9660," *99*	—	65	—1
(19670)	NY Federal Reserve Bullion Car "6445," *00*	—	47	—1
(19671)	Lionel Model Shop Display Car "6445-01," *99-00*	—	55	—1
(19672)	Lionel Mines Mint Car, *00u*	—	250	—1
19673	Wellspring Capital Management Mint Car, *99 u*	—	200	—1
19674	Lionel Lines Platinum Car, *00*	—	43	—1
19675	Lionel Model Shop Display "6445-2," *01*	—	42	—1
19676	Philadelphia Mint Car, *01*	—	40	—1
19677	Ft. Knox Mint Car "6445," *00*	—	50	—1
(19678)	U.S. Army Bunk Car, *02*	—	45	—1
(19679)	St. Louis Federal Reserve Mint Car, *02*	—	36	—1
(19681)	Area 51 Alien Suspension Car, *02*	—	47	—1
(19682)	Alaska Klondike Mining Co. Mint Car, *02*	—	40	—1
19683	Pony Express Mint Car, *02*		CP	—1
(19686)	Chicago Federal Reserve Mint Car "6445," *03-04*	—	45	—1
(19687)	UP Bunk Car w/ smoke "3887," *03*		CP	—1
(19688)	Postwar Fort Knox Mint Car "6445," *02-03*		35	—1
(19689)	CIBRO TankTrain Tank Car 3-Pack (Std. 0), *03*		100	—1
(19696)	U.S. Savings Bond Mint Car, *0*		150	—1
19697	U.S. Bureau of Engraving and Printing Mint Car "19697," *04*		CP	—1
19698	San Francisco Federal Reserve Mint Car, *04*		CP	—1
19700	Chessie System E/V Caboose, *88*	55	65	—1
19701	Milwaukee Road N5c Caboose (FF #2), *88*	44	55	—1
19702	PRR N5c Caboose, *87*	40	49	—1
19703	Great Northern E/V Caboose (FF #3), *88*	55	65	—1
19704	WM E/V Caboose w/ smoke (FF #4), *89*	43	50	—1
19705	CP Rail E/V Caboose w/ smoke, *89*	46	50	—1
19706)	UP E/V Caboose w/ smoke "9706," *89*	45	50	—2

		Exc	New	Cond/$
19707	SP Work Caboose w/ searchlight and smoke, *90*	70	85	—[1]
(19708)	Lionel Lines B/W Caboose "1990," *90*	47	50	—[1]
19709	PRR Work Caboose w/ smoke, *89, 91*	70	80	—[1]
19710	Frisco E/V Caboose w/ smoke (FF #5), *91*	50	55	—[1]
19711	Norfolk Southern E/V Caboose w/ smoke, *92*	47	65	—[1]
19712	PRR N5c Caboose, *91*	47	55	—[1]
19714	NYC Work Caboose w/ searchlight and smoke, *92*	85	110	—[1]
(19715)	DM&IR E/V Caboose "C-217," *92 u*	55	65	—[1]
(19716)	Illinois Central E/V Caboose w/ smoke "9405," *93*	75	90	—[1]
(19717)	Susquehanna B/W Caboose "0121," *93*	44	55	—[1]
(19718)	Chicago & Illinois Midland E/V Caboose "74," *92 u*	38	45	—[1]
(19719)	Erie B/W Caboose "C-300" (FF #7), *93*	47	55	—[1]
19720	Soo Line E/V Caboose (SSS), *93*	46	55	—[1]
(19721)	GM&O E/V Caboose "2956," *93 u*	47	50	—[1]
19723	Disney E/V Caboose, *94*	50	65	—[1]
(19724)	JC Penney/MKT E/V Caboose "125," *94 u*	50	60	—[1]
19726	NYC B/W Caboose (SSS), *95*	43	50	—[1]
(19727)	Pennsylvania N5c Caboose "477938," *96*	—	32	—[1]
(19728)	N&W Bay Window Caboose, *96*	—	75	—[1]
(19732)	AT&SF B/W Caboose "6517," *96*	—	46	—[1]
(19733)	New York Central Caboose "6357," *96*	—	29	—[1]
(19734)	Southern Pacific Caboose "6357," *96*	—	27	—[1]
(19736)	PRR N5c Caboose "6417" "Buffalo Zone," Tuscan, *97*	—	32	—[1]
(19737)	Lackawanna Searchlight Caboose "2420," *97*	—	85	—[1]
(19738)	Conrail N5c Caboose "6417" (SSS), *97*	—	50	—[1]
(19739)	NYC Woodside Caboose "6907," *97*	—	70	—[1]
(19740)	Virginian N5c Caboose "6427," *97 u*	—	65	—[1]
(19741)	Pennsylvania N5c Caboose "6417," *98*	—	55	—[1]
(19742)	Erie Bay Window Caboose w/ Caboose Talk "C301," *98*	—	85	—[2]
(19748)	SP&S B/W Caboose "6517," *97 u*	—	50	—[1]
(19749)	SP Bay Window Caboose "6517," *98*	—	100	—[1]
(19750)	1998 Holiday Music Bay Window Caboose, *98*	—	160	—[1]
(19751)	PRR N5c Caboose PRR "492418," *98*	—	39	—[1]
(19752)	NP Bay Window Caboose "407," *98*	—	55	—[1]
(19753)	UP EV Caboose "25641," *98*	—	55	—[1]
(19754)	NYC Caboose "20112," *98*	—	55	—[1]
(19755)	Centennial Porthole Caboose, *99*	—	55	—[1]
(19756)	Lionel Lines Bay Window Caboose, *99*	—	50	—[1]
(19758)	DL&W Work Caboose "6419," *99*	—	55	—

		Exc	New	Cond/$
(19759)	Corvette N5c Caboose, *99*	—	60	—1
(19772)	Lionel Visitor's Center Vat Car, *99 u*	—	43	—1
(19773)	Lionel Kids Club Barrel Ramp Car "6343," *96 u*—		50	—1
(19774)	LRRC Porthole Caboose "1999," *99 u*	—	55	—2
19775	LRRC Stock Car, *99*		NRS	—1
(19778)	Southern/Case Cutlery Woodside Caboose 1889 (Std. O), *99u*		NRS	—1
(19779)	SP Bay Window Caboose "1908," *99*	—	55	—1
(19780)	LV Porthole Caboose "641751," *99-00*	—	55	—1
(19781)	Vapor Records Holiday Porthole Caboose "6417," *99-00*	—	42	—1
(19782)	NYC B/W Caboose "21719," *00*	—	75	—1
(19783)	Ford Mustang Extended Vision Caboose, *01*	—	50	—1
(19785)	SP Bay Window Caboose "6517," *00*	—	60	—1
(19786)	Pennsylvania RR Extended Vision Caboose, *00u*	—	40	—1
(19787)	Pennsylvania RR Extended Vision Caboose "477927," *01*	—	40	—1
(19790)	Postwar Lehigh Valley Caboose "6417," *02*	—	40	—1
(19792)	Postwar Erie Bay Window Caboose "C301," *03*	—	45	—1
19800	Circle L Ranch Operating Cattle Car, *88*	95	135	—1
19801	Poultry Dispatch Chicken Car, *87*	31	45	—1
19802	Carnation Milk Car, *87*	95	115	—1
19803	Reading Ice Car, *87*	42	50	—2
19804	Wabash Operating Hopper, *87*	27	35	—1
19805	Santa Fe Operating Boxcar, *87*	25	33	—1
19806	PRR Operating Hopper, *88*	35	42	—1
19807	PRR E/V Caboose w/ smoke, *88*	40	47	—3
19808	NYC Ice Car, *88*	43	55	—1
19809	Erie-Lackawanna Operating Boxcar, *88*	27	35	—1
19810	Bosco Milk Car, *88*	110	135	—2
19811	Monon Brakeman Car, *90*	55	60	—1
19813	Northern Pacific Ice Car, *89 u*	42	50	—1
19815	Delaware & Hudson Brakeman Car, *92*	45	55	—1
(19816)	Madison Hardware Operating Boxcar "190991," *91 u*	170	210	—2
19817	Virginian Ice Car, *94*	37	50	—1
(19818)	Dairymen's League Milk Car "788," *94*	85	105	—1
19819	Poultry Dispatch Car (SSS), *94*	36	43	—1
(19820)	Diecast Metal Tender w/ RailSounds II, *95-96*	—	175	—1
(19821)	UP Opera, *95*	35	41	—1
19822	Pork Dispatch Car, *95*	32	41	—1
19823	Burlington Ice Car, *94 u, 95*	40	50	—1
(19824)	US Army Target Launcher, *96*	—	29	—2
19825	EMD Generator Car, *96*	—	50	—2

		Exc	New	Cond/$
(19827)	NYC Operating Boxcar, 97	—	38	—1
(19828)	C&NW Animated Stock Car and Stockyard "3356," 96-97	—	130	—1
(19830)	US Mail Operating Boxcar "3428," 97	—	42	—1
(19831)	GM Generator Car w/ Power Pole and Wire "3530," 97	—	55	—1
(19832)	Lionel Cola Ice Car "6352," 97	—	43	—1
(19833)	Railsounds II Tender "2426RS," 97	—	240	—1
(19834)	LL 6-Wheel Crane Car "2460," 97	—	60	—1
(19835)	FedEx Animated Boxcar "3464X," 97	—	42	—1
(19837)	Bucyrus 6-Wheel Crane Car "2460," 99	—	60	—1
(19845)	Command Control Aquarium Car "3435," 98	—	165	—1
(19846)	Animated Giraffe Car "3376C," 98	—	160	—1
(19850)	Lionel RailSounds Stock Car "33760," 00	—	130	—1
(19853)	Firefighting Instruction Generator Car (SSS), 98	—	60	—1
(19854)	Lionelville Fire Car #1 (SSS), 98	—	55	—1
(19855)	Christmas "Aquarium" Car, 98	—	60	—1
(19856)	Mermaid Transport, 98	—	65	—1
(19857)	NYC Fire Instruction Car "19853," 98-99	—	175	—1
(19858)	Lionelville Operational Searchlight Car "19854," 99	—	55	—1
(19859)	REA Steam R/S Boxcar "6267," 99	—	165	—1
(19860)	Conrail Diesel R/S Boxcar "169671," 99	—	145	—1
(19864)	Animated Ostrich Boxcar "9700," 99	—	37	—1
(19867)	Operational Poultry Dispatch Car "3434," 99	—	48	—1
(19868)	Shark Aquarium Car "3435," 99	—	190	—1
(19869)	Alien Aquarium Car "3435," 99	—	49	—1
(19877)	AT&SF Operating Barrel Car, 99	—	55	—1
(19878)	Operating Helium Tank Flatcar "3362," 99	—	34	—1
19880	Lionel Lines Ext Searchlight Car, 00	—	50	—1
(19882)	Sanderson Farms Poultry Car "3434," 99	—	45	—1
(19883)	Lionel Lines Bucyrus Erie Crane Car "64608," 99		NRS	—1
19884	Atlantis Travel Aquarium Car, 00 u	—	85	—1
(19885)	3456 N&W Operating Hopper Car "22000," 00	—	41	—1
(19886)	Seaboard Boxcar w/ Steam Railsounds "16126," 00	—	140	—1
(19887)	SP Boxcar w/ Diesel RailSounds "651663," 00	—	140	—1
(19888)	Christmas Music Boxcar, 01	—	85	—1
(19889)	PRR B/W Caboose w/ Crewtalk "477719," 00	—	155	—1
(19890)	Santa Fe B/W Caboose w/ Crewtalk "999211," 00	—	160	—1
19894	Pony Express Mint Car, 03		CP	—1

		Exc	New	Cond/$
(19894)	Hood's Milk Car w/Platform, *03-04*	—	95	—1
19895	3356 Santa Fe Horse Car w/Corral, *04*		CP	—1
(19896)	US Marines Missile Launch Sound Car "45," *03-04*	—	150	—1
19897	NYC Crane Car w/TMCC "X-13," *04*		CP	—1
19898	Nestle Nesquik Operating MilkCar, *04*		CP	—1
(19899)	Pennsylvania Command Control Crane Car "19899," *03-04*	—	300	—1
19900	Toy Fair Boxcar, *87 u*	65	80	—1
19901	"I Love Virginia" Boxcar, *87*	25	35	—1
19902	Toy Fair Boxcar, *88 u*	60	90	—1
19903	Christmas Boxcar, *87 u*	40	49	—1
19904	Christmas Boxcar, *88 u*	36	49	—1
19905	"I Love California" Boxcar, *88*	22	28	—1
19906	"I Love Pennsylvania" Boxcar, *89*	22	27	—1
19907	Toy Fair Boxcar, *89 u*	55	85	—1
19908	Christmas Boxcar, *89 u*	39	50	—2
19909	"I Love New Jersey" Boxcar, *90*	21	27	—1
19910	Christmas Boxcar, *90 u*	28	33	—2
19911	Toy Fair Boxcar, *90 u*	75	95	—1
19912	"I Love Ohio" Boxcar, *91*	21	28	—1
(19913)	Christmas Boxcar, regular issue, *91*	40	50	—1
19913	Christmas Boxcar for Lionel Employees, *91 u*	165	220	—1
19914	Toy Fair Boxcar, *91 u*	55	80	—1
19915	"I Love Texas" Boxcar, *92*	35	60	—1
19916	Christmas Boxcar for Lionel Employees, *92 u*	255	315	—1
19917	Toy Fair Boxcar, *92 u*	75	95	—1
19918	Christmas Boxcar, *92 u*	65	95	—1
19919	"I Love Minnesota" Boxcar, *93*	40	60	—1
(19920)	Lionel Visitor's Center Boxcar, *92 u*	28	36	—1
19921	Christmas Boxcar for Lionel Employees, *93 u*	160	220	•—1
19922	Christmas Boxcar, *93*	31	38	—1
19923	Toy Fair Boxcar, *93 u*	60	90	—1
19924	Lionel Railroader Club Boxcar, *93 u*	22	27	—2
19925	Learning Center Boxcar for Lionel Employees, *93 u*	125	135	—1
19926	"I Love Nevada" Boxcar, *94*	21	26	—1
(19927)	Lionel Visitor's Center Boxcar "1993," *93 u*	26	33	—1
19928	Christmas Boxcar for Lionel Employees, *94 u*	300	350	—1
19929	Christmas Boxcar, *94*	30	40	—1
19930	Lionel Railroader Club Quad Hopper w/ coal load, *94 u*	26	28	—2

		Exc	New	Cond/$
19931	Toy Fair Boxcar, *94 u*	70	100	__2
19932	Lionel Visitor's Center Boxcar, *94 u*	28	36	__1
19933	"I Love Illinois" Boxcar, *95*	21	27	__1
(19934)	Lionel Visitor's Center Boxcar "1995," *95 u*	25	33	__1
(19935)	Lionel Railroader Club 1-D Tank Car "1995," *95 u*	25	32	__1
19937	Toy Fair Boxcar, *95 u*	47	65	__1
19938	Christmas Boxcar, *95*	29	37	__1
19939	Christmas Boxcar for Lionel Employees, *95 u*	320	380	__1
(19940)	Lionel Railroad Vat Car, *96 u*	—	33	__1
19941	"I Love Colorado" Boxcar, *95*	23	30	__1
19942	"I Love Florida" Boxcar, *96*	19	27	__1
(19943)	"I Love Arizona" Boxcar, *96*	19	24	__1
(19944)	Lionel Visitor's Center Tank Car, *96 u*	—	38	__1
(19945)	Holiday Boxcar, *96*	—	31	__2
(19946)	Christmas Boxcar for Lionel Employees, *96 u*	—	230	__1
(19947)	Lionel Corporation Toy Fair Boxcar "9700," *96 u*	—	170	__1
(19948)	Visitors Center Flatcar w/ Trailer, *96 u*	—	41	__1
(19949)	"I Love Ny" Boxcar "9700," *97*	—	45	__1
(19950)	"I Love Montana" Boxcar "9700," *97*	—	31	__1
(19951)	"I Love Massachusetts" Boxcar "9700," *98*	—	29	__1
(19952)	"I Love Indiana" Boxcar, "9700," *98*	—	33	__1
(19953)	LRRC Boxcar, 97 *u*; covers, 98 *u*	—	45	__1
(19955)	Lionel Visitor's Center Gondola ˆ w/ coil covers, *98 u*	—	31	__1
(19956)	Toy Fair Boxcar "777," *98 u*	—	65	__1
(19957)	Ambassador Caboose "1997," *97 u*	—	400	__1
(19958)	Ambassador Silver Caboose, "1998" (Std O), *98 u*	—	500	__1
(19959)	Ambassador Gold Caboose, "1998" (Std O), *98 u*	—	700	__1
(19960)	LOTS Western Pacific Boxcar "1952" (Std. O), *92 u*	60	75	__1
19961	Gadsden Pacific Inspiration Consolidated Copper Company Ore Car w/ load, *92 u*	36	40	__1
(19962)	TTOS Southwest SP 3-bay ACF Hopper "496035" (Std. O), *92 u*	50	65	__1
(19963)	TTOS Union Equity 3-bay ACF Hopper "86892" (Std. O), *92 u*	38	44	__1
(19964)	U.S. JCI Senate Boxcar, *92 u*	70	95	__1
(19965)	LRRC Aquarium Car "3435," *99 u*	—	80	__1
(19966)	LRRC Gondola "9820" (Std O), *98 u*	20	32	__2
(19967)	Kids Club Animated Gondola, *98 u*	—	44	__1
(19968)	"I Love Maine" Boxcar "9700," *99*	—	40	__1

		Exc	New	Cond/$
(19969)	"I Love Vermont" Boxcar "9700," *99*	—	40	—[1]
(19970)	"I Love New Hampshire" Boxcar "9700," *99*	—	34	—[1]
(19971)	"I Love Rhode Island" Boxcar "9700," *99*	—	34	—[1]
(19976)	Lionel Employee Holiday Boxcar "1999," *99 u*	—	180	—[1]
(19977)	Toy Fair Boxcar "9700," *99 u*	—	70	—[2]
(19978)	"Gold" Boxcar "1900-2000," *99-00*	—	60	—[1]
(19981)	Lionel Centennial Boxcar "1998-1," *99*	—	30	—[1]
(19982)	Lionel Centennial Boxcar "1998-2," *99*	—	30	—[1]
(19983)	Lionel Centennial Boxcar "1998-3," *99*	—	30	—[1]
(19984)	Lionel Centennial Boxcar "1998-4," *99*	—	30	—[1]
(19985)	"I Love Georgia" Boxcar 9700, *99-00*	—	45	—[1]
(19986)	"I Love North Carolina" Boxcar 9700, *99-00*	—	40	—[1]
(19987)	"I Love South Carolina" Boxcar 9700, *99-00*	—	40	—[1]
(19988)	"I Love Tennessee" Boxcar 9700, *99-00*	—	65	—[1]
(19989)	Toy Fair Boxcar, *00 u*	—	70	—[1]
(19991)	LRRC Gold Club Boxcar, *00 u*	—	65	—[1]
(19992)	LRRC Western Union Tel. Tool Car "3550," *00 u*	—	55	—[1]
(19994)	LRRC Western Union Camp Car "1307," *01 u*	—	60	—[1]
19995	LRRC 25th Anniversary Boxcar (Std. O), *01*	—	60	—[1]
(19996)	Toy Fair 2001 Boxcar, *01u*	—	50	—[1]
(19997)	Lionel Employee 2001 Boxcar, *01u*	—	115	—[1]
(19998)	Christmas Boxcar, *01*	—	41	—[1]
19999	Lionel Visitor's Center 4-bay Hopper "19999," *02 u*		NRS	—[1]
(21029)	World of Little Choo Choo set, *94 u, 95*	36	43	—[1]
21596	(See 17898)			
(21719)	NYC Bay Window Caboose, *99*	—	70	—[1]
(21750)	Nickel Plate Rolling Stock 4-pack, *98*	—	160	—[1]
(21751)	PRR Rolling Stock 4-pack, *98*	—	170	—[1]
(21752)	Conrail Unit Trailer Train Set, *98*	—	390	—[1]
(21753)	1998 Service Station Fire Rescue Train Set, *98*	455	500	—[1]
(21754)	BNSF 3-Bay Covered Hopper 2-pack (Std. O), *98*	—	65	—[1]
(21755)	4-Bay Covered Hoppers 2-pack, *98*	—	65	—[1]
(21756)	Overstamped 6464 Style Boxcars 2-pack, *98*	—	55	—[1]
(21757)	UP Freight Car Set, *98*	—	190	—[1]
(21758)	Bethlehem Steel Service Station Exclusive "44," *99*	—	375	—[1]
(21759)	Canadian Pacific F3 Passenger Set, *99*	—	1200	—[2]
(21761)	B&M Boxcar Set 4-pack, *99*	—	180	—[1]
(21763)	New Haven Freight Set, *99*	—	230	—[1]
(21766)	ACL Passenger Car Set 2-pack, *99*	—	275	—[1]
(21769)	Centennial SD Tank Car Set 4-pack, *99*	—	190	—[1]

		Exc	New	Cond/$
(21770)	NYC Reefer Set 4-pack, *99*	—	200	—1
(21771)	D&RGW Stock Car Set 4-pack, *99*	—	275	—1
(21774)	Custom Series Consist I 3-pack "6424," *99*	—	150	—1
(21775)	Lionel Train Wreck Recovery Set, *99*	—	190	—1
(21778)	AT&SF Trainmaster Freight Set, *99*		NRS	—1
(21779)	Seaboard Freight Car Set, *99*	—	235	—1
(21780)	NYC Aluminum Pass Car Set 2-pack, *99*	—	170	—1
(21781)	Case Cutlery Freight Set, *99u*	—	1000	—1
(21782)	PRR Congressional Set, *00*	—	910	—1
(21783)	Monday Night Football 2-pack, *01-02*	—	50	—1
(21784)	QVC PRR Coal Freight Steam Set, *00 u*	—	340	—1
(21785)	QVC Gold Mine Freight Steam Set, *00 u*	—	340	—1
(21786)	Santa Fe F3 ABBA Passenger Set "200," *00*	—	1750	—1
(21787)	Blue Comet Steam Passenger Set, *01-02*	—	900	—1
(21788)	Postwar Missile Launch Freight Set, *02-03*	—	350	—1
(21789)	NS GP9 Flatcar Set "102," SSS, CC, *01*	—	500	—1
(21790)	CN TankTrain Dash 9 Diesel Freight Set, *02*	—	570	—1
(21791)	Freedom Train Diesel Passenger Set w/RailSounds, *03*	—	620	—1
(21792)	C&O Coal Hopper 6-pack #2 (Std. O), *01*	—	145	—1
(21793)	Virginian Coal Hopper 6-pack #2 (Std. O), *01*	—	160	—1
(21794)	Pioneer Seed GP7 Freight Set, *01 u*	—	825	—1
(21795)	Case Farmall Freight Set, *01u*	—	860	—1
(21796)	Lionel Centennial Freight Set, *01 u*	—	490	—1
(21797)	SP Daylight Passenger Set, *01*	—	690	—1
(21900)	Union Civil War Train Set, *99*	—	355	—1
(21901)	Confederate Civil War Train Set, *99*	—	355	—1
(21902)	Construction Zone Set, *99 u*	—	87	—1
(21904)	Safari Adventure Set, *99 u*	—	90	—1
(21905)	NYC Flyer for Mass Merchants Set, *99u*	—	100	—1
(21909)	AGFA Film Steam Freight Set, *98 u*	—	1050	—1
(21914)	Lionel Lines Freight Set, *99*	—	120	—1
(21916)	Lionel Village Trolley, *99*	—	75	—1
(21917)	N&W Freight Set, *99*	—	70	—1
(21918)	Thomas Circus Play Set, *00*	—	100	—1
(21920)	Amtrak "Talgo" Passenger Set, *99*		NM	—1
(21922)	Erie Lackawanna Phoebe Snow Passenger Set, *99*	—	1300	—1
(21924)	Holiday Trolley Set, *99*	—	75	—1
(21925)	Thomas Tank Engine Island of Sodor Train Set, *99-00*	—	150	—1
(21932)	JC Penney NYC Freight Flyer Steam Set, *00 u*	—	170	—1
(21934)	Custom Series Consist II 3-pack "6424," *99*	—	150	—1
(21936)	WB Looney Tunes Set, *00 u*	—	330	—1
(21944)	"Celebrate a Lionel Christmas" Steam Set, *00-01*	—	145	—1

		Exc	New	Cond/$
(21945)	Christmas Trolley Set, *00*	—	100	—¹
(21948)	NYC Freight Flyer Set w/Air Whistle, *00*	—	240	—¹
(21950)	Maersk SD70 Maxi-stack set, *00*	425	530	—¹
(21951)	World War II Troop Train Set, *00*	—	425	—¹
(21952)	2000 Lionel Lines Service Station Special Set, *00*	—	325	—¹
(21953)	Ford Mustang GP7 CC Set, *01*	—	340	—¹
(21955)	D&RGW F3 AA Passenger Set "5521," CC, *01*	—	1000	—¹
(21956)	New York Central Freight Set "5412," *99-00*	—	430	—¹
(21969)	Lionel Village Trolley Set, *00*	—	85	—¹
(21970)	SP RS-3 Diesel Freight Set w/Horn, *00-01*	—	110	—¹
(21971)	Pennsylvania Flyer Steam Set, *00*	—	150	—¹
(21972)	Frisco GP7 Diesel Freight Set w/Horn, *00*	—	150	—¹
(21973)	AT&SF Passenger Set w/RailSounds, *00-01*	—	375	—¹
(21974)	AT&SF Passenger Set w/SignalSounds, *00-01*	—	240	—¹
(21975)	Burlington Steam Freight Set w/SignalSounds, *00*	—	275	—¹
(21976)	Centennial Steam Freight Starter Set, *00*	—	575	—¹
(21977)	NYC Trainmaster Freight Set, *99-00*	—	640	—¹
(21978)	AT&SF Trainmaster Freight Set, *99-00*	—	450	—¹
(21981)	Pennsy NYC Flyer Set, *00u*	—	150	—¹
(21988)	NYC Freight Set w/RailSounds, *00*	—	380	—¹
(21989)	Burlington Steam Freight Set w/RailSounds, *00*	—	300	—¹
(21990)	NYC Flyer Freight Set w/RailSounds, *00*	—	175	—¹
(21999)	Whirlpool Steam Freight Set, *00 u*	—	720	—¹
(22902)	Quonset Hut, *98-99*	—	22	—¹
(22907)	Die-cast Girder Bridge, *98-01*	—	10	—¹
(22910)	Gilbert Tractor-Trailer, *98*	—	23	—¹
(22914)	PowerHouse Lockon, *98-01*	—	21	—¹
(22915)	Municipal Building, *98-99*	—	30	—¹
(22916)	190-Watt Power Accessory System, *98*	—	425	—¹
(22918)	The Lionel Locomotive Backshop, *98*	275	380	—²
(22919)	ElectroCouplers kit for GP9, *98-00*	—	20	—¹
(22920)	Steam Service Siding, *98*		NM	—¹
(22922)	Intermodal Crane, *98*	—	195	—¹
(22929)	Lionel Factory, *98*		NM	—¹
(22931)	Die-Cast Cantilever Signal Bridge, *98-03*	25	32	—¹
(22932)	High Tension Metal Wire Tower, *98*		NM	—¹
(22933)	Section Gang House, *98*		NM	—¹
(22934)	Walkout Cantilever Signal, *98-03*	—	38	—¹
(22935)	Hot Box Detector, *98*		NM	—¹
(22936)	3-Piece Coaling Tower, *98*	—	65	—¹
(22938)	High Tension Plastic Tower, *98*		NM	—¹

		Exc	New	Cond/$
(22939)	Transformer Substation, 98		NM	—1
(22940)	Mast Signal, 98-00	—	37	—1
(22942)	Accessories Box, 98-01	—	20	—1
(22944)	Automatic Operating Semaphore, 98-03	—	25	—1
(22945)	Block Target Signal, 98-00	—	39	—1
(22946)	Automatic Crossing Gate and Railroad Crossing Signal, 98-99	—	45	—1
(22947)	Auto Crossing Gate, 98-00	—	36	—1
(22948)	Gooseneck Street Lamps set of 2, 98-00	—	195	—1
(22949)	Highway Lights set of 4, 98-99	—	20	—1
(22950)	Classic Street Lamps set of 3, 98-02	—	20	—1
(22951)	Dwarf Signal, 98-00	—	24	—1
(22952)	Classic Billboard set of 3, 98-00	—	15	—1
(22953)	Linex Gasoline Tall Oil Tank, 98-99	—	6	—1
(22954)	Linex Gasoline Wide Oil Tank, 98-99	—	6	—1
(22955)	ElectroCouplers Kit for J class Tender and B&A Tender, 98-00	—	20	—1
(22956)	ElectroCouplers Kit for Switcher/NW2, 98	—	20	—1
(22957)	ElectroCouplers Kit for F3, 98-01	—	20	—1
(22958)	ElectroCouplers Kit for Dash 9, 98-01	—	20	—1
(22959)	ElectroCoupler Conversion Kit for Atlantic Steamer, 98-01	—	13	—1
(22960)	TrainMaster Command Basic Upgrade Kit, 98-01	—	34	—1
(22961)	Standard GP9 B Unit Upgrade Kit, 98-01	—	30	—1
(22962)	Deluxe GP9 B Unit Upgrade Kit (with Black Trucks), 98-01		48	—1
(22963)	RailSounds Upgrade Kit w/ Steam Railsounds, 98-01	—	55	—1
(22964)	RailSounds Upgrade Kit w/ Diesel Railsounds, 98-01	—	55	—1
(22965)	Command Control Culvert Loader, 98-01	—	265	—1
(22966)	Figure-8 Add-On Track Pack (O-27), 98-03		CP	—1
(22967)	Double-Loop Add-On Track Pack (O-27), 98-03		CP	—1
(22968)	Double-Loop Complete Track Pack (O-27), 98-03		65	—1
(22969)	Deluxe Complete Track Pack (O gauge), 98-03		CP	—1
(22972)	Bascule Bridge, 98-99	—	280	—1
(22973)	Lionel Corp Tractor-Trailer, 98	—	16	—1
(22975)	Culvert Unloader CC, 99-00	—	205	—1
(22979)	GP9 B-Unit Deluxe Upgrade Kit (w/ Silver Trucks), 98-01	—	34	—1
(22980)	TMCC SC-2 Switch Controller, 99-03	—	39	—1
(22982)	ZW Postwar Celebration Series Controller			

		Exc	New	Cond/$
	& Transformer Set, *98*	—	260	—¹
(22983)	180-Watt PowerHouse Power Supply, *99-03*	—	65	—¹
(22990)	Route 66 Autos on Flatcar 4-pack, *99*	—	32	—¹
(22991)	Christmas Tree w/Blue Comet Train, *99-00*	—	60	—¹
(22993)	Route 66 Sinclair/Dino Cafe, *99-00*	—	285	—¹
(22997)	Oil Drum Loader, *99-00*	—	115	—¹
(22998)	Triple Action Magnetic Crane, *99*	—	200	—¹
(22999)	Sound Dispatching Station, *99-00*	—	90	—¹
(23000)	Operating Base Smithsonian NYC Dreyfuss Hudson (2-rail), *92 u*	—	190	—¹
(23001)	Operating Base NYC Dreyfuss Hudson (3-rail), *93 u*	—	190	—¹
(23002)	Operating Base NYC Hudson, *92 u, 93-94*	—	190	—¹
(23003)	Operating Base PRR B-6 Switcher, *92 u, 93-94*	—	190	—¹
(23004)	Operating Base NP 4-8-4, *92 u, 93-94*	—	190	—¹
(23005)	Operating Base Reading T-1, *92 u, 93-94*	—	190	—¹
(23006)	Operating Base Chessie System T-1, *92 u, 93-94*	—	190	—¹
(23007)	Operating Base SP Daylight, *92 u, 93-94*	—	190	—¹
(23008)	Operating Base NYC L-3 Mohawk, *92 u, 93-94*	—	190	—¹
(23009)	Operating Base PRR S-2 Turbine, *92 u, 93-94*	—	190	—¹
(23010)	Left Remote Switch 31" "3010" (O), *95-99*	—	37	—¹
(23011)	Right Remote Switch 31" "3011" (O), *95-99*	—	37	—¹
(23012)	Operating Base F3 ABA Diesels, *92 u, 93-94*	—	190	—¹
24101	Mainline Color Position Signal, *04*		CP	—¹
(24102)	Industrial Water Tower, *03*		CP	—¹
(24103)	Double Floodlight Tower, *03*		CP	—¹
(24104)	Hobo Tower, *03*		CP	—¹
(24105)	Track Gang, *03*	—	70	—¹
(24106)	Exploding Ammunition Dump, *02*	—	22	—¹
(24107)	Missile Firing Range Set, *02*	—	60	—¹
(24108)	World War II Pylon, *03*	—	90	—¹
(24109)	Santa Fe Railroad Tugboat, *03*	—	145	—¹
(24110)	Pennsylvania Railroad Tugboat, *03*	—	145	—¹
(24111)	Swing Bridge, *03*		CP	—¹
(24112)	Oil Field w/Bubble Tubes, *03*		CP	—¹
(24113)	Lionelville Ford Auto Dealership, *03*		CP	—¹
(24114)	AMC/ARC Gantry Crane, CC, *03*		CP	—¹
(24115)	AMC/ARC Log Loader, CC, *03*		CP	—¹
(24117)	Covered Bridge, *02-03*		CP	—¹
24119	Big Bay Lighthouse, *04*		CP	—¹
(24122)	Lionelville People Pack, *03*	—	15	—¹
(24123)	Passenger Station People Pack, *03*	—	15	—¹

		Exc	New	Cond/$
(24124)	Carnival People Pack, 03	—	15	—1
24130	TMCC 135/180 PowerMaster, 04		CP	—1
(24131)	Dumbo Pylon, 03		CP	—1
(24134)	Bethlehem Steel Gantry Crane, 02	—	165	—1
(24135)	Lionel Lighthouse, 02-03	—	70	—1
(24137)	Mr. Spiff and Puddles Historic Layout, 03	—	50	—1
(24138)	Playtime Playground Historic Layout, 03	—	60	—1
(24139)	Duck Shooting Gallery Historic Layout, 03		CP	—1
(24140)	Charles Bowdish Homestead Historic Layout, 03	—	80	—1
(24147)	Lionel Sawmill, 03		CP	—1
(24148)	Coal Tipple Coal Pack, 02		CP	—1
(24149)	NYC Hobo Hotel, 02	—	42	—1
(24152)	Conveyor Lumber Loader, 03		CP	—1
(24153)	Railroad Control Tower, 03		CP	—1
(24154)	Maiden Rescue, 03	—	35	—1
24155	Blinking Light Billboard, 04		CP	—1
24156	Lionelville Street Lamps, 04		CP	—1
24159	Illuminated Station Platform, 04		CP	—1
24160	Rub-a-Dub-Dub Historic Layout, 04		CP	—1
24161	Test-O-Strength Historic Layout, 04		CP	—1
24164	Summer Vacation, 04		CP	—1
24168	Tire Swing Historic Layout, 04		CP	—1
24170	Rover's Revenge, 04		CP	—1
24171	Campbell's Soup Water Tower, 04		CP	—1
24172	Balancing Man Historic Layout, 04		CP	—1
(24173)	Derrick Platform "462," 03		CP	—1
24197	City Accessory Pack, 04		CP	—1
24500	D&RGW Alco PA A-A Set "601," 04		CP	—1
24503	D&RGW Alco PB Unit, 04		CP	—1
24174	Icing Station, 04		CP	—1
24177	Hot Air Balloon Ride, 04		CP	—1
24179	Scrambler Amusement Ride Historic Layout, 04		CP	—1
24180	Choo Choo Barn Lionelville Zoo, 04		CP	—1
24182	Lionelville Firehouse, 04		CP	—1
24183	Lionelville Gas Station, 04		CP	—1
24187	Classic Billboard Set, 04		CP	—1
24191	Park People Pack, 04		CP	—1
24192	Park Benches People Pack, 04		CP	—1
24193	Railroad Yard People Pack, 04		CP	—1
24194	Civil Servants People Pack, 04		CP	—1
24196	Farm People Pack, 04		CP	—1
(24504)	Santa Fe E6 A-A "14-15," CC, 03	—	530	—1
(24507)	Milwaukee Road E6 A-A "15-16," CC, 03	—	530	—1
(24511)	Burlington FT A-A Set "113-A/d" w/RailSounds, 03	—	245	—1

		Exc	New	Cond/$
(24516)	Santa Fe F3 B Unit, *03*	—	275	—1
(24517)	NYC F3 B Unit, *03*	—	250	—1
(24518)	WP F3 B Unit, *03*	—	300	—1
(24519)	B&O F3 B Unit, *03*	—	300	—1
(24520)	Alaska F3 A-A Set, *03*	—	650	—1
(24521)	Alaska F3 B Unit (Non-powered), *03*	—	200	—1
(24522)	Alaska F3 B Unit, *03*	—	300	—1
24528	Postwar Rio Grande Non-Powered F3 A Unit "2379T," *04*		CP	—1
24529	Santa Fe F3 A-A Set "18," CC, *04*		CP	—1
24532	Santa Fe F3 B Unit (non-powered) "18A," *04*		CP	—1
24533	Santa Fe F3 B Unit "18B," *04*		CP	—1
24562	Santa Fe Powered EMD F3 B Unit, *04*		CP	—1
24563	PRR Powered EMD F3 B Unit, *04*		CP	—1
25404	FEC "The Champion" Aluminum Passenger Car 2-pack, *04*		CP	—1
25407	FEC "The Champion" Aluminum Diner w/StationSounds, *04*		CP	—1
25416	SP "Daylight" Aluminum Passenger Car 2-pack, *04*		CP	—1
25419	SP "Daylight" Aluminum Diner w/StationSounds, *04*		CP	—1
25420	PRR "The Trail Blazer" Aluminum Passenger Car 2-pack, *04*		CP	—1
25423	PRR "The Trail Blazer" Aluminum Diner w/StationSounds, *04*		CP	—1
(26000)	C&O Flatcar with Pipes, *01*	—	20	—1
(26001)	BP Flatcar with Trailers "6424," *01u*	—	150	—1
(26002)	Monopoly Flatcar with Airplane, *00u*		NRS	—1
(26003)	Lackawanna Flatcar with NH Trailer, *01*	—	60	—1
(26004)	Conrail Flatcar with Trailer "71693," *01*	—	50	—1
(26005)	Nickel Plate Flatcar with Trailer, *01*	—	50	—1
(26006)	Southern Flatcar with Trailer "50126," *01*	—	50	—1
(26007)	NW Flatcar with Trailer "203029," *01*	—	50	—1
(26008)	Farmall Flatcar, *01u*		NRS	—1
(26011)	B&M Flatcar with Bulkheads, *01u*		NRS	—1
26013	CN Flatcar w/ Zamboni "26013," *01*	—	44	—1
(26014)	JC Penney Flatcar, *01u*	—	135	—1
(26016)	Soo Line Flatcar with Trucks, *01u*		NRS	—1
(26017)	Soo Line Flatcar with Trailer, *01u*		NRS	—1
(26018)	Soo Line Flatcar with Trailer, *01u*		NRS	—1
(26019)	Alaska Gondola "13801," *02*	—	30	—1
(26020)	Postwar Flatcar with Submarine "3830," *02*	—	38	—1
(26021)	CN Flatcar with Trailer Features "685965," *02*	—	37	—1
(26022)	PFE Flatcar with Trailers Features "26022," *02*	—	32	—1
(26023)	Postwar Flatcar with Bulldozer "6816," *02*	—	44	—1

		Exc	New	Cond/$
(26024)	Postwar Flatcar with Scraper "6817," *02*	—	44	__1
(26025)	Postwar Flatcar with Rocket "6407," *02*	—	34	__1
(26026)	Postwar Flatcar with Mercury Capsules "6413," *02*	—	75	__1
(26027)	Flatcar with U.S. Army Boat "6425," *02*	—	30	__1
(26028)	Conrail Well Car "768121," *02*	—	40	__1
(26033)	NYC Gondola "6462," *01*	—	30	__1
(26035)	Lionel Lines Flatcar with Traffic Helicopter, *01*	—	50	__1
(26039)	Lionel Lions Flatcar w/ Zamboni Ice Machines, *02*	—	39	__1
(26042)	B&O Gondola with Canisters "601272," *03*	—	20	__1
(26043)	Seaboard Flatcar with Trailer "48109," *03*	—	30	__1
(26044)	NYC Flatcar with Trailers "506089," *03*	—	35	__1
(26045)	Postwar Flatcar with Big Inch Pipes "2411," *03*	—	40	__1
(26046)	Postwar Flatcar with Cable Reels "6561," *03*	—	30	__1
(26047)	Postwar Flatcar with Transformer "2461," *03*	—	25	__1
(26048)	Postwar Flatcar w/ Boat "6801," *02*	—	32	__1
(26049)	Steamboat Willie Flatcar with Boat, *03*	—	25	__1
(26056)	Southern Flatcar w/ Bulkheads "50125," *02*	—	19	__1
(26057)	SP Flatcar w/ Tractors "599365," *02*	—	37	__1
(26058)	SP Flatcar w/ Trailer Frames "599366," *02*	—	35	__1
(26061)	Lionelville Tree Transport Gondola, *03*	—	40	__1
(26062)	NYC Gondola with Cable Reels "26062," *03*	—	20	__1
(26063)	Pennsylvania Flatcar w/Bulkheads "26063," *03*	—	19	__1
26064	Rock Island Flatcar w/Trailer "90088," *04*		CP	__1
26065	Railway Express Agency Flatcar w/Piggyback Trailers "TLCX2," *04*		CP	__1
26066	Great Northern Flatcar w/Bulkheads "26066," *04*		CP	__1
26067	Southern Gondola w/Cable Reels "60141," *04*		CP	__1
(26070)	Nestle Nesquik Flatcar w/Trailer "26070," *03*	—	40	__1
(26077)	Girl's Lionel Lines Flatcar w/Autos "6424," *03*	—	40	__1
(26078)	Boy's Lionel Lines Flatcar w/Boat "6801," *03*	—	40	__1
26082	Frisco Two-tier Auto Carrier "26082," *04*		CP	__1
(26100)	PRR 1-D Tank Car, *00*	—	25	__1
(26101)	Lenoil 1-D Tank Car "6015," *00*	—	32	__1
(26102)	AEC Glow-in-Dark 1-D Tank Car, *00*	—	35	__1
(26103)	GATX Tank Train 1-D Tank Car "44588," *00*	—	34	__1
(26107)	BP Petroleum 3-D Tank Car, *00 u*	—	95	__1
(26108)	Lionel Visitor's Center Reefer "206482," *00 u*	—	30	__1
(26109)	NYC/P&LE SD Tank Car, *00*	—	42	__1
(26110)	SP 3-Dome Tank Car "6415," *00-01*	—	15	__1

		Exc	New	Cond/$
(26111)	Frisco Tank Car, *00*	—	29	—¹
(26112)	Gulf Oil Tank Car, *00*	—	40	—¹
(26113)	U.S. Army Tank Car, *00*	—	35	—¹
(26114)	Service Station Ltd. 1-Dome Tank Car (SSS), *00*	—	30	—¹
(26115)	Lionel Celebrate SD Tank Car, *00 u*	—	75	—¹
(26116)	Pepe La Pew SD Tank Car, *00 u*	—	90	—¹
(26118)	NYC Tank Car "101900," *01*	—	25	—¹
26119	Protex 3D Tank Car "1054," *00*	—	29	—¹
26120	KCS Tank Car "1229," *00*	—	32	—¹
(26122)	Pioneer Seed Tank Car, *00u*	NRS		—¹
(26123)	Santa Fe Stock Car "23002," *01*	—	35	—¹
(26124)	C&O 1-Dome Tank Car "X1019," *01*	—	30	—¹
(26126)	Cheerios Boxcar, *98*	—	46	—¹
26127	Wellspring Capital Management Clear 1-dome Tank Car w/Confetti, *00 u*	—	200	—¹
(26131)	Santa Fe 1-Dome Tank Car "335268," *02*	—	22	—¹
(26132)	UP 1-Dome Tank Car "69015," *02*	—	35	—¹
(26133)	Tootsie Roll 1-Dome Tank Car "26133," *02*	—	35	—¹
26135	Whirlpool Tank car, *01*	NRS		—¹
(26136)	Southern 1-Dome Tank Car "8790011," *03*	—	20	—¹
(26137)	Jack Frost 1-Dome Tank Car "106," *03*	—	30	—¹
(26138)	Nestle Nesquik 1-Dome Tank Car "26138," *03*	CP		—¹
(26139)	Lionel Lines Stockcar with Horses "26139," *03*	—	35	—¹
(26141)	Whirlpool 1-Dome Tank Car, *03 u*	—	75	—¹
26144)	Chessie System 1-Dome Tank Car "2233," *02*	—	22	—¹
26145)	Do It Best 1-Dome Tank Car, *03 u*	—	95	—¹
26146)	Do It Best 1-Dome Tank Car, *03 u*	—	95	—¹
26147)	Lionel Archives Diamond Chemicals 1-Dome Tank Car "6315," *02*	—	33	—¹
26149)	Egg Nog 1-Dome Tank Car, *03*	—	40	—¹
26150)	Alaska 3-Dome Tank Car "26150," *03*	—	20	—¹
26151)	NP Wood-sided Refrigerator Car "26151," *03*	—	19	—¹
6152	Morton Salt 1-Dome Tank car "26152," *04*	CP		—¹
6153	Pillsbury 1-Dome Tank Car "26153," *04*	CP		—¹
6154	NYC 3-Dome Tank Car "26154," *04*	CP		—¹
6155	Pennsylvania 1-Dome Tank Car "26155," *04*	CP		—¹
6156	North Western Wood-sided Refrigerator Car "15356," *04*	CP		—¹
6157	Ballyhoo Brothers Circus Stockcar "26157," *04*	CP		—¹
6158	Campbell's Soup 1-Dome Tank Car, *04*	CP		—¹
26164)	Girl's Lionel Lines I-Dome Tank Car "6315," *03*—		40	—¹
26200)	NP Boxcar "18211," *98*	—	37	—¹

Exc New Cond/\$

		Exc	New	Cond/\$
(26201)	Operation Lifesaver Boxcar, *98*	—	30	—¹
(26203)	D&H Boxcar "1829," *98*	—	25	—¹
(26204)	Alaska Boxcar "10806," *98-99*	—	35	—¹
(26205)	Rocky & Bullwinkle Boxcar "9700," *99*	—	36	—¹
(26206)	Curious George Boxcar "9700," *99*	—	40	—¹
(26208)	Vapor Records Boxcar #2, *98*	—	31	—¹
(26214)	Celebrate the Century Stamp Boxcar, *98 u*	—	100	—¹
(26215)	AEC Glow-in-the-Dark Boxcar, *98*	—	90	—¹
(26216)	Cheerios Boxcar "9700," *98 u*	—	90	—²
(26218)	Quaker Oats Boxcar, *98 u*	—	375	—¹
(26219)	Ace Hardware Boxcar, *98 u*	NRS		—¹
(26220)	Smuckers Boxcar "9700," *98 u*	—	85	—²
(26222)	Penn Central Boxcar "125962," *99*	—	31	—¹
(26223)	FEC Boxcar "5027," *99*	—	31	—¹
(26224)	D&H Boxcar "9700," *99*	—	24	—¹
(26228)	Vapor Records Holiday Boxcar "9700," *99 u*	—	80	—¹
(26230)	AEC Glow-in-the-Dark Boxcar II "9700," *99*	—	37	—¹
(26232)	Martin Guitar Lumber Boxcar "9823," *99*	—	35	—¹
(26234)	NYC Boxcar "9700," *99*	—	25	—¹
(26235)	Valentine Boxcar "9700," *99*	—	40	—¹
(26236)	Aircraft Boxcar "9700," *99*	—	31	—¹
(26237)	Boy Scout Boxcar "9700," *99*	—	90	—¹
(26238)	Detroit Historical Museum Boxcar "9700," *99*	—	32	—¹
(26239)	M.A.D.D Boxcar "9700," *99*	—	24	—¹
(26240)	Starter Set RailBox Boxcar "9700," *99-00*	—	28	—¹
(26241)	Starter Set Norfolk & Western "9700," *99-00*	—	15	—¹
(26242)	D.A.R.E Boxcar "9700," *99*	—	30	—
(26243)	Lionel Christmas Boxcar "9700," *99*	—	39	—
(26244)	Woody Woodpecker Box Car "9700," *99*	—	44	—
(26247)	Lionel Lines Boxcar "9700," *99*	—	38	—
(26253)	Acme Explosives Boxcar "9700," *99u*	NRS		—
(26254)	Keebler Boxcar "9700," *99u*	NRS		—
(26255)	NYC Boxcar "200495," *99u*	—	30	—
(26256)	Salvation Army Charity Boxcar "9700," *99*	—	29	—
(26257)	Wheaties Boxcar "9700," *99*	—	75	—
(26264)	Lionel Station Boxcar, *99*	—	45	—
(26265)	NYC Pacemaker Boxcar "9700," *00*	—	30	—
(26271)	AEC Glow-in-the-Dark Boxcar "9700-glo," *99*	—	39	—
(26272)	Christmas Boxcar, *00*	—	47	—
(26275)	Boy Scout Boxcar "9700," *00*	—	55	—
(26276)	C&O 9700 Boxcar "23296," *99-00*	—	23	—
(26277)	UP Boxcar "491050," *00*	—	20	—
(26278)	Cap'n Crunch Christmas Boxcar, *99*	—	550	—
(26280)	Tinsel Town Express Boxcar w/Music, *00*	—	50	—
(26284)	NY Toy Fair Preview Boxcar, *99 u*	—	725	—
(26285)	NYC Pacemaker Boxcar "9700," *00*	—	40	—

Exc New Cond/$

		Exc	New	Cond/$
(26288)	AEC Glow-in-Dark "9700" Boxcar, 99	—	33	—1
(26290)	SP Boxcar, 00	—	20	—1
(26291)	Pennsylvania Boxcar "47158," 00	—	20	—1
(26292)	Frisco Boxcar "22015," 00	—	20	—1
(26293)	Burlington Boxcar, 00	—	30	—1
(26294)	Centennial Express Boxcar, 00		NRS	—1
(26295)	TrainMaster Boxcar, 99 u	—	55	—1
(26296)	Service Station Ltd. Boxcar Set (SSS), 00	—	115	—1
(26298)	Taz Bobbing Boxcar, 00	—	50	—1
26300	UPSFlatcar w/Trailers, 04		CP	—1
(26502)	UP Bay Window Caboose "6517," 97	—	50	—1
(26503)	AT&SF High-Cupola Caboose "7606R," 97	—	85	—1
(26504)	Mobil Oil Square Window Caboose "6257," 97u	—	30	—1
(26505)	Lionelville Fire Co. Work Caboose, 98	—	50	—1
(26506)	N&W Square Window Caboose "562748," 98	—	15	—1
(26507)	D&H Square Window Caboose "35707," 98	—	20	—1
(26508)	Alaska RR Square Window Caboose "1081," 98	—	28	—1
(26511)	Quaker Oats NP Square Window Caboose, 98u	—	43	—1
(26513)	NYC Emergency Caboose "26505," 99	—	43	—1
(26515)	Lionel Lines Bobber Caboose, 99	—	10	—1
(26516)	Safari RR Bobber Caboose, 99u	—	10	—1
(26519)	Christmas Work Caboose "6496," 99	—	41	—1
(26520)	Bethlehem Steel Work Caboose "6130" SSS, 99	—	55	—1
(26523)	Keebler Cheezit S/W Caboose, 99u		NRS	—1
(26524)	NYC Square Window Caboose "295," 99u	—	20	—1
(26526)	Santa Fe S/W Caboose "999471," 01	—	28	—1
(26527)	Christmas Work Caboose w/ Presents, 02	—	32	—1
(26528)	PRR Square Window Caboose "6257," 99	—	21	—1
(26530)	LL Square Window Caboose "6257," 99	—	22	—1
(26532)	NYC Square Window Caboose "296," 00	—	20	—1
(26533)	SP Square Window Caboose, 00	—	20	—1
(26534)	PRR Square Window Caboose "6257," 00	—	20	—1
(26535)	Frisco Square Window Caboose "1700," 00	—	20	—1
(26536)	Centennial Express S/W Caboose, 00		NRS	—1
(26537)	Lionel Mines Square Window Caboose, 00u	—	45	—1
(26539)	Whirlpool Square Window Caboose, 00u		NRS	—1
(26542)	ACL S/W Caboose "069," 01	—	31	—1
(26543)	GN Square Window Caboose "X66," 00-01	—	28	—1
(26544)	Alaska S/W Caboose "1084," 01	—	25	—1
(26545)	Snap-On Square Window Caboose, 00u		NRS	—1
(26548)	Pioneer Seed Square Window Caboose, 00u		NRS	—1
(26549)	PRR Square Window Caboose "4977947," 01	—	20	—1
(26550)	NYC Square Window Caboose "19293," 01	—	20	—1
(26551)	Chessie System Center Cupola Caboose, 01	—	25	—1

		Exc	New	Cond/$
(26552)	Santa Fe S/W Caboose "999472," *01*	—	25	—¹
(26553)	C&O Center Cupola Caboose "A918," *01*	—	30	—¹
(26554)	Monopoly Short Line S/W Caboose, *00u*		NRS	—¹
(26556)	NH Center Cupola Caboose, *01*	—	35	—¹
(26557)	Farmall Square Window Caboose, *01u*		NRS	—¹
(26559)	N&W Center Cupola Caboose "518408," *01*	—	20	—¹
(26560)	B&M Square Window Caboose, *01u*	—	20	—¹
(26564)	Soo Line Center Cupola Caboose, *01u*	—	20	—¹
(26565)	Lionel Employee S/W Caboose "2001," *01u*	—	200	—¹
(26566)	WP Square Window Caboose "731," *02*	—	25	—¹
(26568)	Nickel Plate S/W Caboose "1155," *02*	—	25	—¹
(26569)	Southern Square Window Caboose "252," *02*	—	25	—¹
(26570)	B&O Square Window Caboose "295," *02*	—	25	—¹
26572	Lionel 20th Century Square Window Caboose, *00 u*	—	25	—¹
(26580)	Wabash Square-Window Caboose "2805," *03*	—	20	—¹
(26581)	C&O Square-Window Caboose "C-1831," *03*	—	20	—¹
(26582)	L&N Square-Window Caboose "318," *03*	—	20	—¹
(26583)	Pennsylvania Square-Window Caboose "477814," *03*	—	25	—¹
(26594)	Ontario Northland Work Caboose "26594," *03*	—	25	—¹
(26595)	UP Caboose "26595," *03*	—	18	—¹
26596	NYC Caboose "17716," *04*		CP	—¹
26597	Great Northern Caboose "X295," *04*		CP	—¹
26598	UP Caboose "26598," *04*		CP	—¹
26599	Duluth, Missabe & Iron Range Work Caboose "26599," *04*		CP	—¹
(26706)	Lighted Christmas Boxcar, *00*	—	47	—¹
(26707)	Lionel Steel Operating Welding Flatcar "1108," *00*	—	90	—¹
(26709)	Flatcar w/ Psychedelic Psubmarine "6511," *99*	—	32	—¹
(26710)	Southern Railroad Carsounds Stockcar, *99*	—	95	—¹
(26712)	Churchill Downs Horse Car "6473," *99-00*	—	40	—
(26713)	Shay Log Car 3-pack "9823," *99*	—	110	—
(26714)	Westside Lumber Flatcar w/ Logs (Std O), *99*	—	45	—
(26715)	Westside Lumber Flatcar w/ Logs (Std O), *99*	—	45	—
(26716)	Westside Lumber Flatcar w/ Logs (Std O), *99*	—	45	—
(26717)	Orion Star Boxcar 9600, *00*	—	30	—
(26718)	Christmas RailSounds Boxcar, *00*	—	160	—
(26719)	Bobbing Ghost Halloween Boxcar "9700," *00*	—	40	—
(26721)	Lionel Lines Coal Dump Car "3379," *00*	—	31	—
(26722)	Lionel Lines Log Dump Car "3351," *00*	—	31	—
(26723)	Lion Chasing Trainer Gondola "3444," *00*	—	49	—
(26724)	Veterans Day Boxcar "9700," *00*	—	70	—

		Exc	New	Cond/$
(26725)	NYC Jumping Hobo Boxcar "88160," 00	—	50	__1
(26726)	T. Rex Bobbing Boxcar "9700," 00	—	41	__1
(26727)	San Francisco City Lights Boxcar, 00	—	55	__1
(26736)	Lionel Birthday Boxcar, 02 u	—	43	__1
(26737)	Chasing Santa Operating Gondola "6462," 00 u	—	65	__1
(26738)	Lionel Mines Gondola, 00u		NRS	__1
(26739)	Santa & Snowman Boxcar, 00	—	46	__1
(26740)	Reindeer Car, 00	—	49	__1
(26741)	Operating Santa Boxcar, 00	—	49	__1
(26743)	Christmas Reindeer Car, 01	—	55	__1
26745	Lionel Traveling Aquarium Car "506," 01	—	70	__1
26746	Bobbing Vampire Boxcar, 01	—	46	__1
26747	Halloween Bats Aquarium Car, 01	—	50	__1
(26748)	T & P Operating Hopper Car "9699," 01	—	38	__1
26749	Alaska Log Dump Car, 01	—	29	__1
(26750)	Carnegie Science Center Boxcar "9200," 99	—	90	__1
26751	Chessie Coal Dump Car, 01	—	27	__1
(26752)	Christmas Aquarium Car, 01	—	55	__1
(26753)	Christmas Operating Dump Car, 01	—	45	__1
(26757)	Operating Barrel Car "35621," 00	—	55	__1
(26758)	AEC Nuclear Gondola "719766," 01	—	70	__1
(26759)	Lionel Postwar Coal Dump Car "3459," 02	—	55	__1
(26760)	Lionel Postwar Log Dump Car "3461," 02	—	55	__1
(26761)	AEC Security Caboose "3535," 01	—	60	__1
(26762)	Postwar Minuteman Car "3665," 01	—	60	__1
(26763)	Postwar Exploding Boxcar "6448," 01	—	40	__1
(26764)	Bethlehem Steel Operating Welding Car, 01	—	55	__1
(26765)	Postwar Sheriff and Outlaw Car "3370," 01-02	—	47	__1
(26766)	Priority Mail Operating Boxcar, 01-02	—	43	__1
(26768)	Postwar Searchlight Car "6520," 02	—	50	__1
(26769)	Santa Fe Command Control Crane Car "199793," 03	—	300	__1
(26770)	Wabash Brakeman Car "3424," 01	—	65	__1
(26773)	Chessie Searchlight Car, 01	—	20	__1
(26774)	Santa Fe Log Dump Car, 01	—	25	__1
26775	US Army Searchlight Car, 00	—	50	__1
26776	US Army Operating Boxcar "26413," 00	—	55	__1
26777	United States Flag Boxcar, 01u	—	250	__1
26779	Burlington Operating Hopper "189312," 02	—	40	__1
26780	Postwar Bronx Zoo Giraffe Car "3376," 02	—	36	__1
26781	Postwar Operating Radar Car "3540," 02	—	32	__1
26782	Lenny the Lion Bobbing Head Car, 02	—	38	__1
26784	Stingray Express Aquarium Car, 02	—	40	__1
26785	Flatcar with Power Boat, 02	—	25	__1
26786)	Lionelville Operating Parade Car, 02	—	40	__1

		Exc	New	Cond/$
(26787)	Erie Jumping Hobo Boxcar, *01-02*	—	50	—¹
(26788)	Christmas Music Boxcar, *02*	—	44	—¹
(26789)	Kiss Kringle Chase Gondola, *02*	—	40	—¹
(26790)	Christmas Lighted Boxcar, *02*	—	38	—¹
(26791)	UP Animated Gondola, *02*	—	40	—¹
(26792)	REA Operating Boxcar "6299," *03*	—	39	—¹
(26793)	Alaska Extension Searchlight Car, *01*	—	44	—¹
(26794)	Postwar PFE Ice Car "6352," *01-02*	—	60	—¹
(26795)	NYC Stock Car w/ Cattle Sounds "3121," *02*	—	47	—¹
(26796)	Lionel Farms Poultry Dispatch Car "26796," *01*	—	49	—¹
(26797)	GN Log Dump Car "60011," *02*	—	50	—¹
(26798)	Bethlehem Steel Coal Dump Car "26798," *02*	—	60	—¹
26801	Jumping Bart Simpson Boxcar, *04*		CP	—¹
26802	Simpsons Animated Gondola, *04*		CP	—¹
26803	Santa Fe Derrick Car "26803," *04*		CP	—¹
26804	NYC Coal Dump Car "26804," *04*		CP	—¹
26805	Pennsylvania Log Dump Car "26805," *04*		CP	—¹
26806	Archive Pillsbury Operating Boxcar "3428," *04*		CP	—¹
26807	Blue Chip Line Motorized Animated Gondola, *04*		CP	—¹
26808	Egg Nog Barrel Car, *04*		CP	—¹
26809	Santa's Mobile Lighting Service Extension Searchlight Car, *04*		CP	—¹
(26905)	Bethlehem Steel Gondola w/ Canisters "6462," *98*	—	34	—¹
(26906)	Southern Pacific Flatcar w/ Corgi '57 Chevy "9823," *98*	—	36	—¹
(26908)	T.T.U.X. w/Apple trailers "6300," *98*	—	70	—¹
(26913)	E. St. Louis Gondola "9820," *98*	—	30	—¹
(26920)	UP Die Cast Ore Car "64861," *97*	—	55	—¹
(26921)	UP Die Cast Ore Car "64862," *97*	—	55	—¹
(26922)	UP Die Cast Ore Car "64863," *97*	—	55	—
(26923)	UP Die Cast Ore Car "64864," *97*	—	55	—
(26924)	UP Die Cast Ore Car "64865," *97*	—	55	—
DX26925	(See 12810)			
(26925)	UP Die Cast Ore Car "64866," *97*		60	—
(26926)	Union Pacific Die Cast Ore Car, *98*	—	55	—
(26927)	Union Pacific Die Cast Ore Car, *98*	—	55	—
(26928)	Union Pacific Die Cast Ore Car, *98*	—	55	—
(26929)	Union Pacific Die Cast Ore Car, *98*	—	50	—
(26936)	Die-cast Tank Car 4-pack, *98*	—	355	—
(26937)	Die-cast Hopper 4-pack, *98*	—	350	—
(26938)	NYC Reefer, *99*	—	80	—
(26940)	Rio Grande Stock Car "37710," *99*	—	80	—
(26946)	D&H Semi-scale Hopper "9642"	—	100	—

		Exc	New	Cond/$
(26947)	Gulf Die-cast Tank Car, *98*	—	105	—1
(26948)	P&LE Die-cast Hopper, *98*	—	75	—1
(26949)	NP Flatcar w/ Trailer "6424-2017," *98*	—	47	—1
(26950)	NP Flatcar w/ Trailer "6424-2016," *98*	—	47	—1
(26951)	TTX Flatcar w/ PRR Trailer "475185," *98*	—	65	—1
(26952)	J.B. Hunt Flatcar w/ trailer, *98*	—	40	—1
(26953)	J.B. Hunt Flatcar w/ trailer, *98*	—	40	—1
(26954)	J.B. Hunt Flatcar w/ trailer, *98*	—	40	—1
(26955)	J.B. Hunt Flatcar w/ trailer, *98*	—	40	—1
(26956)	C&O Gondola (O27), *98-99*	—	15	—1
(26957)	Delaware & Hudson Flatcar w/ stakes, *98*	—	20	—1
(26961)	Lionellville Fire Co. Flatcar, w/ ladder (SSS) load "6418-1," 98, *98*	—	50	—1
(26961)	Lionellville Fire Co. Flatcar, w/ ladder (SSS) load "6418-1," 98, *98*	—	50	—1
(26971)	Lionel Steel 16-wheel Depressed Flatcar, *98*	—	140	—1
(26972)	Animated Pony Express Gondola, *98*	—	36	—1
(26973)	Getty Die-cast Tank Cars 3-pack, *98*	—	270	—1
(26974)	Getty Die-cast SD Tank Car "4003," *98*	—	80	—1
(26975)	Getty Die-cast SD Tank Car "4004," *98*	—	90	—1
(26976)	Getty Die-cast SD Tank Car "4005," *98*	—	80	—1
(26977)	Sinclair Die-cast Tank Cars 3-pack, *98*	—	280	—1
(26978)	Sinclair Tank Car UTLX "64026," *98*	—	105	—1
(26979)	Sinclair Tank Car UTLX "64027," *98*	—	85	—1
(26980)	Sinclair Tank UTLX "64028," *98*	—	90	—1
(26981)	Gulf Die-cast Tank Car 2-pack, *99*	—	140	—1
(26985)	B&O Die-Cast Hoppers 2-pack "235154," *99*	—	160	—1
(26987)	Chessie System B&O Die-cast 4-Bay Hopper "235154," *99*	—	90	—1
(26991)	Lionelville Ladder Firecar, Dept #2, *99*	—	47	—1
(26992)	NYC Reefer, *99*	—	85	—1
(26993)	NYC Reefer, *99*	—	85	—1
(26994)	NYC Reefer, *99*	—	110	—1
(26995)	Rio Grande Stock Car "37714," *99*	—	80	—1
(26996)	Rio Grande Stock Car "37715," *99*	—	80	—1
(26997)	Rio Grande Stock Car "37716," *99*	—	80	—1
27100	C&NW PS-2CD 4427 Hopper "450669" (Std. O), *04*		CP	—1
7101	Morton Salt PS-2CD 4427 Hopper "504" (Std. O), *04*		CP	—1
27102	Pillsbury PS-2CD 4427 Hopper "3980" (Std. O), *04*		CP	—1
27103	Soo Line PS-2CD 4427 Hopper "70207" (Std. O), *04*		CP	—1
(27104)	Wabash Cylindrical Hopper "33007" (Std. O), *03*	—	42	—1

		Exc	New	Cond/$
(27105)	PC Cylindrical Hopper "884312" (Std. O), *03*	—	42	—[1]
(28000)	C&NW Hudson 4-6-4 "3005," *99*	—	205	—[1]
(28004)	B&O E6 4-4-2 Atlantic Steam Loco, Traditional, *99-00*	—	410	—[1]
(28005)	PRR E6 4-4-2 Atlantic Steam Loco, Traditional, *99-00*	—	345	—[1]
(28006)	AT&SF E6 4-4-2 Atlantic Steam Loco, Traditional, *99-00*	—	265	—[1]
(28007)	NYC Hudson 4-6-4 "5406," *99*	—	380	—[1]
(28008)	C&O Hudson 4-6-4 "306," *99*	—	345	—[1]
(28009)	Santa Fe Hudson 4-6-4 "3463," *99*	—	330	—[1]
(28011)	C&O 2-6-6-6 Allegheny Steam "1601," *99*	—	2000	—[2]
(28012)	Commodore Vanderbilt 4-6-4 Hudson Steam Locomotive, red, *00 u*	—	1700	—[1]
(28013)	NH Pacific 4-6-2 "1335," *99*	—	325	—[1]
(28014)	NYC Pacific 4-6-2 "4930," *99*	—	305	—[1]
(28015)	Santa Fe Pacific 4-6-2 "3449," *99*	—	340	—[1]
(28016)	Southern Pacific 4-6-2 "1408," *99*	—	345	—[1]
(28017)	Case Cutlery 4-6-2 Steamer, *99 u*	—	295	—[1]
(28018)	Reading Camelback "571," CC, *01*	—	440	—[1]
(28020)	Lionel Lines Pacific 4-6-2 "3344," *99*	—	250	—[1]
(28022)	West Side Lumber Shay "800," *99*	—	1200	—[1]
(28023)	PRR K4 4-6-2 Pacific Steam Loco, "1361," Command Control, *99*	—	390	—[1]
(28024)	Commodore Vanderbilt 4-6-4 Hudson Steam Locomotive, blue, *00 u*	—	2000	—[1]
(28025)	PRR K4 4-6-2 Pacific Steam Locomotive, Traditional, *99*	—	330	—[1]
(28026)	LL 4-6-2 Pacific Steam Locomotive, "1999," Command Control, *99*	—	325	—[1]
(28027)	NYC 4-6-4 Hudson Steam Loco "5413," *00*	—	590	—[1]
(28028)	Virginian 2-6-6-6 Allegheny Steam "1601," *99*	—	1350	—[2]
(28029)	UP Big Boy 4-8-8-4 Articulated Steam Locomotive "4006," *99-00*	—	1350	—[4]
(28030)	NYC 4-6-4 Hudson "5450," Gray, CC, *00*	—	315	—[1]
(28031)	NYC 4-6-4 Hudson "5451" gray, *00*		NM	—[1]
(28032)	B&O 4-6-2 Pacific Steam Loco, Command Control, *00*	—	315	—[1]
(28033)	B&O 4-6-2 Pacific Steam Loco, Traditional, *00*	—	195	—[1]
(28034)	UP 4-6-2 Pacific Steam Loco, Command Control, *00*	—	310	—[1]
(28035)	UP 4-6-2 Pacific Steam Loco, Traditional, *00*	—	210	—[1]
(28036)	SP 2-8-0 Consolidation "2685" Steam Locomotive, CC, *00-01*	—	400	—[1]

		Exc	New	Cond/$
(28037)	SP 2-8-0 Consolidation "2686" Steam Locomotive, Traditional, *00-01*	—	295	—[1]
(28038)	UP 2-8-0 Consolidation "324" Steam Locomotive, CC, *00-01*	—	385	—[1]
(28039)	UP 2-8-0 Consolidation "326" Steam Locomotive, Traditional, *00-01*	—	250	—[1]
(28051)	B&O EM-1 2-8-8-4 Articulated Steam Loco "7617," *00*	—	980	—[1]
(28052)	N&W Class A 2-6-6-4 Articulated Steam Locomotive "1218," *00*	—	1100	—[5]
(28055)	GN 4-6-4 Hudson "1725" Steam Locomotive, Traditional, *00-01*	—	158	—[1]
(28057)	SRR 4-8-2 Mountain "1491," CC, *00*	—	810	—[1]
(28058)	NH 4-8-2 Mountain "3310," CC, *00*	—	740	—[1]
(28059)	WP 4-8-2 Mountain "179," CC, *00*	—	860	—[1]
(28062)	Lionel Lines Gold-plated 700E J-1E 4-6-4 Hudson"1900" w/case, *00*	—	1350	—[1]
(28063)	PRR T-1 4-4-4-4 Duplex "5511," CC, *00*	—	860	—[1]
(28064)	UP Challenger Coal Tender "3985," CC, *00 u*	1350	1800	—[1]
(28065)	NYC 4-6-4 Hudson w/ Railsounds "5412," *00*	—	290	—[1]
(28066)	B&O 4-6-2 President Polk, CC, *01*	—	710	—[1]
(28067)	Erie 4-6-2 "2934," CC, *01*	—	630	—[1]
(28068)	D&RG 4-6-4 Hudson "2001" Steam Locomotive, Traditional, *01u*	—	300	—[1]
(28069)	Lionel Century Club NYC Niagara "6024," *00 u*	—	1000	—[1]
(28070)	SP Daylight 4-4-2 Atlantic "3000," CC, *01*	—	475	—[1]
(28071)	NP 4-4-2 Atlantic "604," CC, *01*	—	350	—[1]
(28072)	NYC 4-6-4 Hudson J3a "5444," CC, *01*	—	940	—[1]
(28074)	NP Berkshire "759," CC, *01*	—	980	—[1]
(28075)	C&O 2-6-6-2 "1521," CC, *01*	—	860	—[1]
(28076)	NP 2-6-6-2 "921," CC, *01*	—	900	—[1]
(28077)	UP Lionmaster Challenger 4-6-6-4 "3983," CC, *01*	—	710	—[1]
(28078)	PRR J1a 2-10-4 "6465," CC, *01*	—	930	—[1]
(28079)	C&O Class T 2-10-4 "3004," CC, *01*	—	880	—[1]
(28080)	NYC 0-8-0 Yard Goat "7745" Steam Locomotive, CC, *01-02*	—	540	—[1]
(28081)	C&O 0-8-0 Yard Goat "75" Steam Locomotive, CC, *01-02*	—	520	—[1]
(28084)	NYC Dreyfuss 4-6-4 Hudson "5452" Steam Locomotive, CC, *01-02*	—	850	—[1]
(28085)	N&W 2-8-8-2 Class Y6b Articulated "2200" Steam Locomotive, CC, *03*	—	1300	—[1]
(28086)	PRR H9 Consolidation "1111," CC, *01*	—	480	—[1]

		Exc	New	Cond/$
(28087)	UP Auxiliary Tender Yellow, CC, *01*	—	225	__1
(28088)	N&W Auxiliary Water Tender, CC, *01-02*	—	210	__1
(28089)	PRR T-1 4-4-4-4 Duplex "5511," 2-Rail, *00*	—	1150	__1
(28090)	UP Challenger Oil Tender "3977," 2-Rail, *00 u*	—	1800	__1
(28098)	NYC 4-6-0 Ten-Wheeler "1916" Steam Locomotive, CC, *01-02*	—	520	__1
(28099)	UP Challenger Oil Tender "3977," CC, *00 u*	—	1700	__1
(28200)	D&H U30C "702," CC, *02*	—	375	__1
(28201)	UP SD90MAC "8049," *03*	—	300	__1
(28202)	Conrail SD80MAC "7203," *03*	—	300	__1
(28203)	CSX SD80MAC "803," *03*	—	300	__1
(28204)	NS SD80MAC "7201," *03*	—	300	__1
(28205)	Chessie System SD9 "1833," CC, *03*	—	200	__1
(28207)	Erie Lackawanna U33C Diesel "3304," CC, *02*	—	355	__1
(28208)	BN U33C Diesel "5734," CC, *02*	—	355	__1
(28211)	CP SD90MAC "9107," *03*	—	300	__1
(28213)	Amtrak GE Dash 8 Diesel "516," CC, *02*	—	300	__1
(28214)	BNSF GE Dash 8 Diesel "582," CC, *02*	—	325	__1
(28215)	B&O EMD GP30 Diesel "6939," CC, *02*	—	315	__1
(28216)	Reading EMD GP30 Diesel "5513," CC, *02*	—	315	__1
(28217)	Rio Grande EMD GP30 Diesel "3013," CC, *02*	—	315	__1
28218	Lehigh Valley C-420 "407," CC, *04*		CP	__1
28219	Seaboard C-420 "136," CC, *04*		CP	__1
28220	Smuckers Box Car, *N/A*		NRS	__1
28224	Jersey Central SD40-2 "3067," CC, *04*		CP	__1
28225	SPSF SD40T-2 "8521," CC, *04*		CP	__1
28226	NS SD80MAC "7204," CC, *04*		CP	__1
28227	UP SD70MAC "4979," CC, *04*		CP	__1
(28228)	C&NW Dash 9-44CW "8669," CC, *03*	—	350	__1
(28229)	SP Dash 9-44CW "8132," CC, *03*	—	350	__1
28230	Amtrak Dash 8 "505," CC, *04*		CP	__1
(28292)	Chessie System U30C "3312," CC, *02*	—	300	__1
(28293)	Santa Fe U28CG "354," CC, *02*	—	375	__1
(28500)	Mopac GP20 "2274," *99-00*	—	145	__1
(28501)	AT&SF Merger GP9 "2924," Traditional, *99*	—	180	__1
(28502)	AT&SF Merger GP9 "2925," Command Control, *99-00*	—	255	__1
(28503)	ACL GP7, Command Control, *00*	—	250	__1
(28504)	ACL GP7, Traditional, *00*	—	170	__1
(28505)	Monon C-420 "505," CC, *00-01*	—	230	__1
(28506)	Monon C-420 "506," Traditional, *00-01*	—	165	__1
(28507)	NH C-420 "2556," CC, *00-01*	—	310	__1
(28508)	NH C-420 "2557," Traditional, *00-01*	—	290	__1
(28509)	FEC GP7 Triple Lashup "607/608/609," *99*	—	560	__1
(28514)	B&O GP9 "6590," *00*	—	85	__1
28515	Lionel Service Station C-420, CC, *00*	—	145	__1

		Exc	New	Cond/$
(28517)	C&NW GP7 "1518," CC, *00-01*	—	295	—1
(28518)	PRR EP5 Electric "2352," CC, *00*	—	405	—1
(28519)	NP GP9 "2349," CC, *01*	—	295	—1
(28521)	SP RS-11"5725," CC, *01-02*	—	305	—1
(28522)	MP RS-11 "4611," CC, *01-02*	—	305	—1
(28523)	SOO SD-40-2 "6622," CC, *01*	—	375	—1
(28524)	Chessie SD-40-2 "7616," CC, *01*	—	355	—1
(28527)	AEC GP-9 "2001," CC, *01*	—	340	—1
(28529)	Norfolk Southern GP9, CC, *02*	—	200	—1
(28530)	NP Alco S-4 Diesel "722," CC, *02*	—	285	—1
(28531)	Santa Fe Alco S-2 Diesel "2337," CC, *02*	—	285	—1
(28532)	LV Alco S-2 Diesel "150," CC, *02*	—	305	—1
(28533)	SAL Alco S-4 Diesel "1489," CC, *02*	—	285	—1
(28534)	Archive GTW GP9 "4134," CC, *01*		NM	—1
(28535)	U.S. Army Transportation Corps GP9m, *02*		NM	—1
(28536)	Rock Island GP7 "1274," CC, *02-03*	—	230	—1
(28538)	WP S-2 "553," CC, *03*	—	320	—1
(28539)	B&O S-2 "9045," CC, *03*	—	320	—1
(28540)	UP SD40T-2 "4455," CC, *03*	—	390	—1
(28541)	SP SD40T-2 "8239," CC, *03*	—	400	—1
(28542)	Rio Grande SD40T-2 "5350," CC, *03*	—	400	—1
(28543)	Ontario Northland RS-3 "1308," *03*	—	70	—1
28544	Pennsylvania RS-11 "8618," CC, *04*		CP	—1
(28545)	NP RS-11 "900," CC, *03*	—	325	—1
(28612)	WP 4-4-2 Atlantic Steam Locomotive, Traditional, *02*	—	80	—1
28613	Reading 0-6-0 Docksider "1251," Traditional, *04*		CP	—1
(28615)	B&O 4-6-4 Hudson Steam Locomotive, Traditional, *02*	—	225	—1
(28616)	Nickel Plate 2-8-4 Berkshire Steam Locomotive, Traditional, *02*	—	190	—1
(28617)	Southern 2-8-4 Berkshire Steam Locomotive, Traditional, *02*	—	235	—1
28624	Santa Fe 0-6-0 Docksider "2174," Traditional, *04*		CP	—1
(28625)	Wabash 4-4-2 Atlantic Steam Locomotive "8625," Traditional, *03*	—	85	—1
(28626)	Pennsylvania 4-6-4 Hudson Steam Locomotive "626," Traditional, *03*	—	175	—1
(28627)	C&O 2-8-4 Berkshire Steam Locomotive "2755" Traditional, *03*	—	200	—1
(28628)	L&N 2-8-4 Berkshire Steam Locomotive "1970" Traditional, *03*	—	200	—1
28636	D&RGW 4-4-2 Atlantic "8636," Traditional, *04*		CP	—1
28637	UP 4-6-4 Hudson "673," Traditional, *04*		CP	—1

		Exc	New	Cond/$
28638	Great Northern 2-8-4 Berkshire "3414," Traditional, *04*		CP	—[1]
28639	NYC 2-8-4 Berkshire "9401," Traditional, *04*		CP	—[1]
28646	North Pole Central Lines 2-8-4 Berkshire "1900," Traditional, *04*		CP	—[1]
28646	North Pole Central Lines 2-8-4 Berkshire "1900," Traditional, *04*		CP	—[1]
(28742)	B&O 4-6-0 Camelback "1630" Steam Locomotive, CC, *03*	CP	375	—[1]
(28743)	B&O 4-6-0 Camelback "1632" Steam Locomotive, Traditional, *03*	—	300	—[1]
(28744)	D&H 4-6-0 Camelback "548" Steam Locomotive, CC, *03*	—	375	—[1]
(28745)	D&H 4-6-0 Camelback "555" Steam Locomotive, Traditional, *03*	—	300	—[1]
(28746)	Erie 4-6-0 Camelback "860" Steam Locomotive, CC, *03*	—	375	—[1]
(28747)	Erie 4-6-0 Camelback "878" Steam Locomotive, Traditional, *03*	—	300	—[1]
(28748)	Jersey Central 4-6-0 Camelback "772" Steam Locomotive, CC, *03*	—	375	—[1]
(28749)	Jersey Central 4-6-0 Camelback "773" Steam Locomotive, Traditional, *03*	—	300	—[1]
(28750)	Lackawanna 4-6-0 Camelback "690" Steam Locomotive, CC, *03*	—	375	—[1]
(28751)	Lackawanna 4-6-0 Camelback "1031" Steam Locomotive, Traditional, *03*	—	300	—[1]
(28752)	LIRR 4-6-0 Camelback "126" Steam Locomotive, CC, *03*	—	375	—[1]
(28753)	LIRR 4-6-0 Camelback "127" Steam Locomotive, Traditional, *03*	—	300	—[1]
(28754)	NYO&W 4-6-0 Camelback "249" Steam Locomotive, CC, *03*	—	375	—[1]
(28755)	NYO&W 4-6-0 Camelback "253" Steam Locomotive, Traditional, *03*	—	300	—[1]
(28756)	Pennsylvania-Reading 4-6-0 Camelback "6000" Steam Locomotive, CC, *03*	—	375	—[1]
(28757)	Pennsylvania-Reading 4-6-0 Camelback "6001" Steam Locomotive, Traditional, *03*	—	300	—[1]
(28758)	Susquehanna 4-6-0 Camelback "30" Steam Locomotive, CC, *03*	—	375	—[1]
(28759)	Susquehanna 4-6-0 Camelback "36" Steam Locomotive, Traditional, *03*	—	300	—[1]
(28800)	N&W GP7 "507," *99-00*	—	70	—[1]
(28801)	Lionel Lines 44-ton Switcher, *99*	—	135	—[1]
(28806)	Jersey Central Baby Train Master "1516,"			

		Exc	New	Cond/$
	CC, *01*	—	375	—¹
(28811)	Santa Fe Baby Train Master "3003," CC, *01*	—	315	—¹
(28813)	Milwaukee Road Baby Train Master "406," CC, *01*	—	310	—¹
(28815)	B&O GP30 "6935," CC, *02*	—	310	—¹
(28817)	Reading GP30 "5513," CC, *02*	—	310	—¹
(28819)	Rio Grande GP30 "3013," CC, *02*	—	310	—¹
(28821)	GT GP-7 "4438," *01*	—	100	—¹
(28822)	SRR RS-3 "2127," *01*	—	70	—¹
(28823)	Virginian Rectifier "234," *01*	—	170	—¹
(28824)	Santa Fe FT Non-Powered "172," *00*	NM		—¹
(28826)	Pioneer Seed GP7 "2001," Traditional, *00u*	NRS		—¹
(28827)	Chessie GP38, Traditional, *01*	—	100	—¹
(28830)	Soo Line GP9, Traditional, *01u*	NRS		—¹
(28831)	Conrail U36B "2971," Traditional, *02*	—	100	—¹
(28832)	Santa Fe RS-3 "2099," Traditional, *02*	—	70	—¹
(28836)	NYC F-M H-16-44 Diesel "7000," CC, *02*	—	330	—¹
(28837)	NH F-M H-16-44 Diesel "591," CC, *02*	—	325	—¹
(28838)	UP F-M H-16-44 Diesel "1340," CC, *02*	—	325	—¹
28839	Alaska RS-11 "2000," CC, *04*	CP		—¹
(28840)	Burlington GP30 "945," CC, *03*	—	325	—¹
(28841)	Seaboard GP30 "1315," CC, *03*	—	325	—¹
(28845)	Amtrak RS-3 "106," *03*	—	70	—¹
28846	Western Pacific U36B "3067," Traditional, *04*	CP		—¹
28847	Duluth, Missabe & Iron Range GP38 "203," Traditional, *04*	CP		—¹
28850	NYC GP30 "6115" CC, *04*	CP		—¹
(29000)	PRR Madison Coach "2622 Caleb Strong," *99*	—	80	—¹
(29001)	PRR Madison Coach "2621 Villa Royal," *99*	—	80	—¹
(29002)	PRR Madison Coach "2624 Philadelphia," *99*	—	80	—¹
(29003)	PRR Madison Cars 4-pack, *98*	—	235	—¹
(29004)	NYC Heavyweight Passenger Set 2-pack, *99*	—	170	—¹
(29007)	NYC Pullman Passenger Car 2-pack, *98u*	—	95	—¹
(29008)	NYC Heavyweight Diner "383," *98*	—	90	—¹
(29009)	NYC Heavyweight Combo Car "Van Twiller," *98*	—	90	—¹
(29010)	C&O Heavyweight Passenger Set 2-pack, *99*	—	130	—¹
(29011)	C&O Heavyweight Passenger Car (See 29010), *99*			
(29012)	C&O Heavyweight Passenger Car (See 29010), *99*			
(29039)	Lionel Lines Recovery Combo Car "9501," *99*	NRS		—¹
(29041)	Alaska Streamline Passenger (4-pack), *99-00*	—	230	—¹
(29042)	Alaska Streamline Baggage "6310," *99-00*	NRS		—¹
(29043)	Alaska Streamline Coach "5408," *99-00*	NRS		—¹

Exc New Cond/$

		Exc	New	Cond/$
(29044)	Alaska Streamline Vista Dome "7014," 99-00		NRS	—1
(29046)	B&O Streamline Passenger (4-pack), 99-00	—	165	—1
(29047)	B&O Streamline Baggage, 99-00		NRS	—1
(29048)	B&O Streamline Coach, 99-00		NRS	—1
(29049)	B&O Streamline Vista Dome, 99-00		NRS	—1
(29050)	B&O Streamline Observation, 99-00		NRS	—1
(29051)	AT&SF Streamline Passenger (4-pack), 99-00	—	200	—1
(29052)	AT&SF Streamline Baggage, 99-00		NRS	—1
(29053)	AT&SF Streamline Coach, 99-00		NRS	—1
(29054)	AT&SF Streamline Vista Dome, 99-00		NRS	—1
(29055)	AT&SF Streamline Obsevation, 99-00		NRS	—1
(29056)	NYC Streamline Passenger (4-pack), 99-00	—	185	—1
(29057)	NYC Streamline Baggage, 99-00		NRS	—1
(29058)	NYC Streamline Coach, 99-00		NRS	—1
(29059)	NYC Streamline Vista Dome, 99-00		NRS	—1
(29060)	NYC Streamline Observation, 99-00		NRS	—1
(29061)	PRR Madison Passenger (4-pack), 99-00	—	190	—1
(29062)	PRR Madison Baggage "Indian Point," 99-00	—	50	—1
(29063)	PRR Madison Coach "Christopher Columbus," 99-00	—	50	—1
(29064)	PRR Madison Coach "Andrew Jackson," 99-00	—	50	—1
(29065)	PRR Madison Obsevation "Broussard," 99-00	—	50	—1
(29066)	CNJ Madison Passenger (4-pack), 99-00	—	195	—1
(29067)	CNJ Madison Baggage "420," 99-00	—	50	—1
(29068)	CNJ Madison Coach "Beachcomber," 99-00	—	50	—1
(29069)	CNJ Madison Coach "Echo Lake," 99-00	—	50	—1
(29070)	CNJ Madison Observation "1178," 99-00	—	50	—1
(29071)	NYC Baby Madison (4-pack), 00	—	155	—1
(29072)	NYC Baby Madison Baggage "1001," 00		NRS	—1
(29073)	NYC Baby Madison Coach "1005," 00		NRS	—1
(29074)	NYC Baby Madison Coach "1006," 00		NRS	—1
(29075)	NYC Baby Madison Observation "1019 Detroit," 00		NRS	—1
(29076)	SR Baby Madison (4-pack), 00	—	155	—1
(29077)	SR Baby Madison Baggage "702 Deleware," 00		NRS	—1
(29078)	SR Baby Madison Coach "800 North Carolina," 00		NRS	—1
(29079)	SR Baby Madison Coach "801 Maryland," 00		NRS	—1
(29080)	SR Baby Madison Observation "1100," 00		NRS	—1
(29081)	AT&SF Baby Madison (4-pack), 00	—	160	—1
(29082)	AT&SF Baby Madison Baggage/RPO "1765," 00		NRS	—1
(29083)	AT&SF Baby Madison Coach "3040" Chair, 00		NRS	—1

		Exc	New	Cond/$
(29084)	AT&SF Baby Madison Coach "1535 Coach Club," *00*		NRS	—¹
(29085)	AT&SF Baby Madison Observation "10," *00*		NRS	—¹
(29086)	Madison Set 3-pack, *99*	—	325	—¹
(29090)	Lionel Liontech Madison Car "2656," *99*	—	75	—¹
(29091)	Cowen Legends Madison Passenger "2657," *99-00*	—	70	—¹
29105	PRR "The Trail Blazer" Aluminum Passenger Car 4-pack, *04*		CP	—¹
29108	Searchlight Car, *00*	—	30	—¹
29110	B&O "The Columbian" Aluminum Passenger Car 4-pack, *04*		CP	—¹
29115	SP "Daylight" Aluminum Passenger Car 4-pack, *04*		CP	—¹
(29122)	Erie-Lackawanna F3 A-B Passenger Set, *99*	—	860	—²
(29123)	Erie-Lackawanna Aluminum Passenger Baggage "203," *99*	—	100	—¹
(29124)	Erie-Lackawanna Aluminum Passenger Diner "770," *99*	—	100	—¹
(29125)	Erie-Lackawanna Aluminum Passenger Coach "Eleanor Lord," *99*	—	100	—¹
(29126)	Erie-Lackawanna Aluminum Passenger Obs. "789 Tavern Lounge," *99*	—	125	—¹
(29127)	ACL Aluminum Baggage "152," *99*		NRS	—¹
(29128)	ACL Aluminum Coach "North Hampton," *99*		NRS	—¹
(29129)	Texas Special Passenger Set 4-pack, *99*	650	700	—¹
(29130)	Texas Special Aluminum "1200 Edward Burleson," *99*	—	115	—¹
(29131)	Texas Special Aluminum "1201 David G. Burnett," *99*	—	115	—¹
(29132)	Texas Special Aluminum "1202 J. Pinckney Henderson," *99*	—	115	—¹
(29133)	Texas Special Aluminum "1203," *99*	—	100	—¹
(29134)	WP Passenger Set 4-pack, *99*	—	485	—¹
(29135)	Calif. Zephyr Aluminum Vista "Silver Poplar," *99*	—	150	—¹
(29136)	Calif. Zephyr Aluminum Vista "Silver Palm," *99*	—	150	—¹
(29137)	Calif. Zephyr Aluminum Vista "Silver Tavern," *99*	—	150	—¹
(29138)	Calif. Zephyr Aluminum Vista "Silver Planet," *99*	—	150	—¹
(29139)	Lionel Kughn Madison Car "2655," *99*	—	105	—¹
(29140)	NYC Aluminum Sleeper "Castleton Bridge," *99*	—	120	—¹
(29141)	NYC Aluminum Combine			

		Exc	New	Cond/\$
	"Martin Van Buren," *99*	—	120	—1
(29142)	CP Aluminum Vista "Skyline 596," *99*		125	—1
(29143)	CP Aluminum Observation "Banff Park," *99*		125	—1
29144	Santa Fe "El Capitan" Aluminum Passenger Car 4-pack, *04*		CP	—1
(29149)	CB&Q California Zephyr Aluminum Passenger Car 2-Pack, *03*	—	350	—1
(29152)	Santa Fe Super Chief Aluminum Passenger Car 2-Pack, *03*		CP	—1
(29155)	D&H Aluminum Passenger Car 2-Pack, *03*		CP	—1
(29158)	Southern The Southerner Aluminum Passenger Car 2-Pack, *03*		CP	—1
29165	Amtrak "Phase IV" Superliner Passenger Car 2-pack, *04*		CP	—1
29168	Amtrak "Phase IV" Superliner Diner w/StationSounds, *04*		CP	—1
29169	Alaska Superliner Passenger Car 2-pack, *04*		CP	—1
29172	Alaska Superliner Diner w/StationSounds, *04*		CP	—1
(29200)	LRRC Boxcar "9700," *98 u*	—	44	—2
(29202)	Santa Fe Map Boxcar "6464," *97 u*	—	75	—1
(29203)	Maine Central Boxcar "6464-597," *97 u*	—	30	—2
(29204)	Century Club Boxcar "1900-2000," *97 u*	—	550	—1
(29205)	MM Railroad Hi-cube Boxcar "9555," *97*	—	45	—1
(29206)	Vapor Records Boxcar (1st), *97*		NRS	
(29209)	6464 Boxcar Series VII 3-pack, *98*	—	105	—1
(29210)	GN Boxcar "6464-50," *98*	—	39	—1
(29211)	B&M Boxcar "6464-450," *98*	—	33	—1
(29212)	Timken Boxcar "6464-500," *98*	—	35	—1
(29213)	AT&SF Grand Canyon Route 6464 Boxcar "6464-198," *98*	—	25	—1
(29214)	Southern Railway 6464 Boxcar "6464-298," *98*	—	31	—1
(29215)	Canadian Pacific 6464 Boxcar "6464-398," *98*	—	30	—1
(29217)	Airex Boxcar, *97 u*	—	80	—1
(29218)	Vapor Records Boxcar "6464-496," *97 u*	—	145	—2
(29220)	1997 Lionel Centennial Series High-Cube Boxcar 4-Car Set, *98*	—	120	—1
(29220)	GN Boxcar "6464-450," *98*	—	95	—1
(29221)	1997 Centennial Series High-Cube Boxcar "9697-1," *98*	—	50	—1
(29222)	1997 Centennial Series High-Cube Boxcar "9697-2," *98*	—	50	—1
(29223)	1997 Centennial Series High-Cube Boxcar "9697-3," *98*	—	50	—1
(29224)	1997 Centennial Series High-Cube Boxcar			

		Exc	New	Cond/$
	"9697-4," 98	—	50	—1
(29225)	H.O.R.D.E. Music Festival Boxcar, 97	47	55	—3
(29226)	Century Club Berkshire Boxcar, 97 u	160	250	—2
(29227)	Century Club GG-1 Boxcar, 98 u	—	75	—2
(29228)	Century Club Turbine Boxcar "671," 99 u	—	70	—2
(29229)	Vapor Records Holiday Car, 98	—	125	—1
(29231)	Animated Halloween Boxcar, 98	—	39	—1
(29232)	Lenny the Lion Hi-Cube, 98	—	65	—2
(29233)	CR Overstamp PC Boxcar "6464-598," 98	—	50	—1
(29234)	CR Overstamp Erie Boxcar "6464-698," 98	—	50	—1
(29235)	NYC Boxcar "6464-510," 99	—	41	—1
(29236)	Katy Boxcar "6464-515," 99	—	41	—1
(29237)	M&StL Boxcar "6464-525," 99	—	33	—1
(29248)	Century Club F3 Boxcar "2333," 99 u	—	75	—1
(29250)	Phoebe Snow boxcar "6464-199," 99	—	55	—1
(29251)	BN Boxcar "6464-299," 99	—	42	—1
(29252)	CP Boxcar "6464-399," 99	—	43	—1
(29253)	B&M Boxcar 6565 "76032," 99	—	50	—1
(29254)	B&M Boxcar 6565 "76033," 99	—	50	—1
(29255)	B&M Boxcar 6565 "76034," 99	—	50	—1
(29256)	B&M Boxcar 6565 "76035," 99	—	50	—1
(29257)	Southern Boxcar "9464-199," 99	—	40	—1
(29258)	Reading Boxcar "9464-299," 99	—	37	—1
(29259)	NP Bicentennial Boxcar "9464-399," 99	—	40	—1
(29265)	Maine Central Boxcar 6565 "8661," 99	—	39	—1
(29266)	Frisco Boxcar 6565 "8722," 99	—	38	—1
(29267)	6464 Boxcar Series VIII 3-pack, 99	—	105	—1
(29268)	Rio Grande Boxcar 6565 "63067," 99	—	40	—1
(29271)	Lionel Cola Tractor-Trailer, 98	—	11	—1
(29279)	JC/CR Boxcar "6464-28X," 99	—	47	—1
(29280)	LV/CR Boxcar "6464-31X," 99	—	47	—1
(29281)	Post-Merger Boxcar Conrail Overstamped CNJ & LV 2-pack Set, 99	—	70	—1
(29282)	Archive 3-pack "6464," 99	—	105	—1
(29283)	NYC Boxcar "6464-900," 99	—	55	—1
(29284)	GN Boxcar "6464/0000," 99	—	40	—1
(29285)	Seaboard Boxcar, 99	—	36	—1
(29286)	Overstamp Boxcars (2-pack), 99	—	70	—1
(29287)	NH/PC Boxcar "6464-29X," 99	20	38	—1
(29288)	RDG/CR Boxcar "6464-32X," 99	—	41	—1
(29289)	6464- Boxcar Series IX (3-pack), 99-00	—	85	—1
(29290)	D&RGW Boxcar "6464-650," 00	—	48	—1
(29291)	AT&SF Boxcar "6464-700," 00	—	45	—1
(29292)	NH Boxcar "6464-725," 00	—	46	—1
(29293)	NH Boxcar "6464-425," 99	—	95	—1
(29294)	Hellgate Bridge Boxcar "1900-2000," 99 u	—	90	—4

		Exc	New	Cond/$
(29295)	PRR 6565 "Don't Stand Me Still" Boxcar "24018," *99-00*	—	44	—¹
(29296)	PRR 6565 "Merchandise" Boxcar "29296," *99-00*	—	40	—¹
(29297)	PRR 6565 "No Damage" Boxcar "47158," *99-00*	—	45	—¹
(29298)	Lionel Boxcar "6464-2000," *00*	—	44	—¹
(29400)	Bethlehem Steel Slag Car 3-Pack (Std. O), *03*	—	160	—¹
(29404)	Bethlehem Steel Hot Metal Car 3-Pack (Std. O), *03*	—	190	—¹
(29408)	PRR Coil Car, *01*	—	40	—¹
(29411)	Sherwin-Williams Vat Car, *02*	—	35	—¹
(29412)	Tabasco Brand Vat Car, *02*	—	27	—¹
(29413)	Airex Boat Loader Car "29413," *02*	—	34	—¹
(29414)	PRR Evans Auto Loader "480123," *01*	—	50	—¹
(29415)	WM Skeleton Log Car 3-pack #2 (Std. O), *02*	—	90	—¹
(29419)	West Side Lumber Skeleton Log Car 3-pack #2 (Std. O), *02*	—	90	—¹
(29423)	Wellspring Capital Management Happy Holidays Vat Car, *03 u*	—	245	—¹
(29424)	Meadow River Lumber Skeleton Log Car 3-Pack (Std. O), *03*	—	90	—¹
(29429)	Campbell's Soup Vat Car "29429," *03*	—	35	—¹
(29430)	Meadow River Lumber Skeleton Log Car 3-Pack, 2 (Std. O), *03*	—	90	—¹
(29438)	UP TTUX Car, *03*	—	60	—¹
(29439)	Lionel Postwar Evans Auto Loader "6414," *02*	—	43	—¹
(29441)	UP Flatcar w/ Grader "53471," *02*	—	43	—¹
(29442)	CSX Flatcar w/ Backhoe "600513," *02*	—	43	—¹
(29453)	"Elk River" Lumber Skeleton Log Car 3-Pack, 2 (Std. O), *03*	—	90	—¹
(29457)	NS Flatcar w/Caterpillar Load "157590," *03*	—	42	—¹
(29458)	BNSF Flatcar w/Caterpillar Load "922268," *03*	—	42	—¹
(29459)	Archive Water Barrel Car "1878," *03*	—	35	—¹
(29460)	Archive Lionel Lines Flatcar w/Piggyback Trailers "3460," *03*	—	35	—¹
(29461)	Postwar Flatcar w/Red-and-White Airplane "6500," *03*	—	32	—¹
(29462)	Postwar Flatcar w/White-and-Red Airplane "6500," *03*	—	32	—¹
(29463)	Postwar Evans Auto Loader "6414," *03*	—	39	—¹
29464	U.S. Army Vat Car "29464," *04*		CP	—¹
29465	U.S. Steel Slag Car 3-pack (Std. O), *04*		CP	—¹
29469	U.S. Steel Hot Metal Car 3-pack (Std. O), *04*		CP	—¹
(29473)	Youngstown Sheet & Tube Slag Car 3-Pack (Std. O), *03*	—	150	—¹

		Exc	New	Cond/$
(29477)	Youngstown Sheet & Tube Hot Metal Car 3-Pack (Std. O), *03*	—	170	—[1]
(29481)	Cass Scenic Railroad Skeleton Log Car 3-Pack (Std. O), *03*	—	90	—[1]
29488	Cass Scenic Railroad Skeleton Log Car 3-pack #2 (Std. O), *04*		CP	—[1]
29492	Pickering Lumber Skeleton Log Car 3-pack #1 (Std. O), *04*		CP	—[1]
29496	Pickering Lumber Skeleton Log Car 3-pack #2 (Std. O), *04*		CP	—[1]
(29703)	PRR Porthole Caboose, *01*	—	45	—[1]
29708	C&O BW Caboose "8315," *04*		CP	—[1]
29709	Pennsylvania Porthole Caboose "477951," *04*		CP	—[1]
29800	M.O.W. Crane Car w/TMCC "X-800," *04*		CP	—[1]
(29900)	"I Love Wisconsin" Boxcar "9700," *01*	—	34	—[1]
(29901)	"I Love Kentucky" Boxcar "9700," *01*	—	26	—[1]
(29902)	"I Love Iowa" Boxcar "9700," *01*	—	31	—[1]
(29903)	"I Love Missouri" Boxcar "9700," *01*	—	31	—[1]
(29906)	"I Love Connecticut" Boxcar "9700," *02*	—	31	—[1]
(29907)	"I Love West Virginia" Boxcar "9700," *02*	—	31	—[1]
(29908)	"I Love Delaware Boxcar "9700," *02*	—	31	—[1]
(29909)	"I Love Maryland" Boxcar "9700," *02*	—	46	—[1]
(29910)	Toy Fair Centennial Boxcar "9700," *03*	—	35	—[1]
(29912)	"I Love Alabama" Boxcar "9700," *03*	—	35	—[1]
(29913)	"I Love Mississippi" Boxcar "9700," *03*	—	35	—[1]
(29914)	"I Love Louisiana" Boxcar "9700," *03*	—	35	—[1]
(29915)	"I Love Arkansas" Boxcar "9700," *03*	—	35	—[1]
(29920)	"I Love North Dakota" Boxcar "9700," *03*	—	35	—[1]
(29921)	"I Love South Dakota" Boxcar "9700," *03*	—	35	—[1]
(29922)	"I Love Nebraska" Boxcar "9700," *03*	—	35	—[1]
(29923)	"I Love Kansas" Boxcar "9700," *03*	—	35	—[1]
(29949)	Weyerhaeuser Timber Skeleton Log Car 3-Pack, 2 (Std. O), *03*	—	90	—[1]
30002	Neil Young's Greendale Diesel Freight Set, *04*		CP	—[1]
(31700)	Postwar Girl's Train Freight Set, *01*	—	500	—[1]
(31701)	Postwar Boy's Train Freight Set, *02*	—	325	—[1]
(31704)	Alton Limited Steam Passenger Set, *02*	—	700	—[1]
(31705)	50th Anniversary Hudson passenger Set, *02*	—	1050	—[1]
(31706)	UP Burro Crane Set, *02*	—	210	—[1]
(31707)	C&O Diesel Freight Set, *03*	—	285	—[1]
(31708)	Postwar #1805 Land-Sea-Air Marines Missile Launch Set, *03*	—	350	—[1]
(31710)	BN Coal Train Diesel Freight Set w/RailSounds, *03*	—	600	—[1]

		Exc	New	Cond/$
(31711)	Postwar #1563W Wabash Diesel Freight Set w/RailSounds, *03*	—	580	—¹
(31712)	UP Alco PA Diesel Passenger Set w/RailSounds, *03*	—	400	—¹
(31713)	Southern Crescent Limited Steam Passenger Set w/RailSounds, *03*	—	150	—¹
31714	Amtrak Acela Diesel Passenger set w/RailSounds, *04*		CP	—¹
(31715)	Fire Rescue Steam Freight Set, *02*	—	285	—¹
31716	Century Club 2 Niagrara Milk Train Set, *N/A*	—	850	—¹
(31716)	Fire Rescue Steam Freight Set, *03*		CP	—¹
(31717)	CP Rail Snow Removal Train Set, *03*	—	250	—¹
(31718)	SP "Oil Can" TankTrain Freight Set, *03*	—	100	—¹
31719	Western Maryland Fireball Diesel Freight set, *04*		CP	—¹
31720	FEC "The Champion" Diesel Passenger set w/RailSounds, *04*		CP	—¹
31721	Postwar #13138 "Majestic" Electric Freight set w/RailSounds, *04*		CP	—¹
31727	Postwar #2291W Rio Grande Diesel Freight Set w/RailSounds, *04*		CP	—¹
31728	Elvis "He Dared to Rock" Steam Freight Set, *04*		CP	—¹
(31901)	Christmas Steam Freight Set, *02*	—	145	—¹
(31902)	PRR K4 Freight Set, *01-02*	—	560	—¹
(31904)	C&O Steam Freight Set w/ RailSounds, *01*	—	400	—¹
(31905)	NH RS-11 Freight Set, CC, *01*	—	630	—¹
(31907)	PRR Atlantic Freight Set, *01u*	—	400	—¹
(31908)	Reading Hobo Express Freight Set, *01u*	—	350	—¹
(31909)	Santa Fe Shell Tank Car Freight Set, *01u*	—	350	—¹
(31910)	Soo Line Diesel Freight Set, *01u*	—	350	—¹
(31911)	Snap-On Anniversary Steam Freight Set, *00 u*	—	450	—¹
(31913)	PRR Steam Freight Flyer Set, *01*	—	125	—¹
(31914)	NYC Steam Freight Flyer Set w/ Railsounds, *01-02*	—	170	—¹
(31915)	Chessie GP-38 Freight Set, *01-02*	—	155	—¹
(31916)	Santa Fe Steam Freight Set, *01*	—	300	—¹
(31918)	C&O Steam Freight Set w/ Signalsounds, *01*	—	315	—¹
(31919)	T&P Steam Passenger Set w/ RailSounds, *01*	—	210	—¹
(31920)	LL Bean Freight Set, *01u*	—	225	—¹
(31923)	PRR Flyer Freight Set, *01u*	—	130	—¹
(31924)	UP RS-3 Freight Set, *02*	—	95	—¹
(31926)	Area 51 FA Freight Set, *02*	—	145	—¹
(31928)	Great Train Robbery Steam, *02*	—	160	—¹
(31928)	Great Train Robbery Steam, *02*	—	160	—¹
(31931)	Ballyhoo Circus Freight Set, *02*	—	205	—¹

		Exc	New	Cond/$
(31932)	NYC FT Passenger Set w/RailSounds, *02*	—	285	—1
(31933)	Santa Fe Steam Freight Set w/RailSounds, *02*	—	320	—1
(31934)	Lionel 20th Century Express Steam Freight Set, *00 u*	—	315	—1
(31936)	Pennsylvania Flyer Steam Freight Set, *03-04*		CP	—1
(31938)	Southern Diesel Freight Set, *03-04*		CP	—1
(31939)	Great Train Robbery Steam Freight Set, *03*		CP	—1
(31940)	NYC Flyer Steam Freight Set w/RailSounds, *03*		CP	—1
(31941)	Winter Wonderland Railroad Christmas Train Steam Freight Set, *03*	—	145	—1
(31942)	Norman Rockwell Christmas Train, *03*	—	330	—1
(31944)	NYC Limited Diesel Passenger Set w/RailSounds, *03*	—	285	—1
(31945)	Santa Fe Super Steam Freight Set w/RailSounds, *03*	—	350	—1
31946	Disney Christmas Steam Train Set, *04*		CP	—1
(31947)	World of Disney Steam Freight Set, *03*	—	215	—1
(31950)	Kraft Holiday UP RS-3 Freight Set, *02 u*	—	140	—1
(31952)	Great Northern Glacier Route Diesel Freight Set, *03-04*		CP	—1
(31953)	"Riding the Rails" Hobo Train Steam Freight Set, *03-04*		CP	—1
31956	Thomas the Tank Engine set, *04*		CP	—1
31958	Santa Fe Flyer Steam Freight set w/RailSounds, *04*		CP	—1
31960	Polar Express Steam Passenger set, *04*		CP	—1
(31961)	Bloomingdales Pennsylvania Flyer Steam Freight Set, *02 u*	—	150	—1
31962	Nickel Plate Road Super Freight set w/RailSounds, *04*		CP	—1
(31962)	GN Glacier Route Freight Set, *03*		CP	—1
31963	Southern Pacific Overnight Steam Freight set, *04*		CP	—1
(31963)	Riding the Rails Hobo Steam Freight Set, *03*		CP	—1
31966	Holiday Tradition Steam Freight Set, *04*		CP	—1
31969	NYC Flyer Steam Freight set w/RailSounds, *04*		CP	—1
31989	Overland Freight Express UP Set, *04*		CP	—1
(32900)	DC Billboard Lionel, *99*	—	24	—1
(32902)	Construction Zone Signs (6), *99-03*		CP	—1
(32904)	Lionel Hellgate Bridge, *99*	275	485	—2
(32905)	Lionel Irvington Factory, *99-00*	—	345	—2
(32910)	Rotary Coal Dumper w/ Rotary Bathtub Gondola, *02*	—	385	—1
(32919)	Animated Maiden Rescue, *99*	—	65	—1
(32920)	Animated Pylon w/ Airplane, *99*	—	130	—1
(32921)	Electric Coaling Station "97," *99-01*	—	145	—1
(32922)	Highway Barrels (6), *99-03*		CP	—1

		Exc	New	Cond/$
(32923)	36-Watt Accessory Transformer, *99-03*		CP	__1
(32923)	Accessory Transformer, 36-watt, *99-02*	—	22	__1
(32929)	Icing Station with Santa, *99*	—	95	__1
(32930)	ZW Controller w/two 180-Watt Transformers, *99-02*	—	325	__1
(32933)	Christmas Stocking Hanger Set (4-pc.), *99-00*	—	50	__1
(32934)	Stocking Hanger, Gondola, *99-00*	—	15	__1
(32935)	Stocking Hanger, Boxcar, *99-00*	—	15	__1
(32960)	Hindenburger Cafe, *99*	—	175	__1
(32961)	Route 66 U.F.O. Cafe, *99*	—	165	__1
(32987)	Hobo Campfire, *99-00*	—	55	__1
(32988)	#192 Railroad Control Tower, *99-00*	—	75	__1
(32989)	#464 Sawmill, *99-00*	—	75	__1
(32990)	Linex Oil Derrick, *99-00*	—	60	__1
(32991)	WLLC Radio Station, *99*	—	55	__1
(32996)	362 AT&SF Barrel Loader, "3562-25," *00*	—	115	__1
(32997)	Aluminum Rico Station, *00*	—	260	__1
(32998)	Lionel Hobby Shop, *99-00*	—	325	__1
(32999)	Hellgate Bridge, *99-00*	—	315	__3
(33000)	Lionel Lines RailScope GP-9 "3000," *88-90*	165	230	__1
(33002)	RailScope B&W TV, *88-90*	50	80	__1
(33004)	NYC RailScope GP-9 "3004," *90*		NM	__1
(33005)	Union Pacific RailScope GP-9 "3005," *90*		NM	__1
34102	Amtrak Shelter, *04*		CP	__1
(34108)	Lionelville Suburban House, *03*		CP	__1
(34109)	Lionelville Large Suburban House, *03*		CP	__1
(34110)	Lionelville Estate House, *03*		CP	__1
(34111)	Lionelville Deluxe Fieldstone House, *03*		CP	__1
(34112)	Lionelville Fieldstone House, *03*		CP	__1
(34113)	"Lionelville Large Suburban House, 2," *03*		CP	__1
(34114)	Late Illuminated Station and Terrace "128," *03*		CP	__1
(34117)	Early Illuminated Station and Terrace "128," *03*		CP	__1
34120	TMCC Direct Lockon, *04*		CP	__1
34121	Lionelville Bungalow, *04*		CP	__1
34122	Lionelville Bungalow w/Garage, *04*		CP	__1
34123	Lionelville Bungalow w/Addition, *04*		CP	__1
34124	Lionelville Anastasia's Bakery, *04*		CP	__1
34125	Lionelville Cotton's Candy, *04*		CP	__1
34126	Lionelville Market, *04*		CP	__1
34127	Lionelville O'Grady's Tavern, *04*		CP	__1
34128	Lionelville Pharmacy, *04*		CP	__1
34129	Lionelville Kiddie City Toy Store, *04*		CP	__1
34130	Lionelville Jim's 5 and 10, *04*		CP	__1
34131	Lionelville Al's Hardware, *04*		CP	__1
34162	Operating Oil Pump, *04*		CP	__1

		Exc	New	Cond/$
34163	Speeder Shed, *04*		CP	__1
34190	Carousel, *04*		CP	__1
34191	Hobo Depot, *04*		CP	__1
34192	Operating Lumberjacks, *04*		CP	__1
34192	Operating Lumberjacks, *04*		CP	__1
34193	UPS Animated Billboard, *04*		CP	__1
(36000)	Route 66 Flatcar with 2 Red Sedans, *98*	—	44	__1
(36001)	Route 66 Flatcar with 2 Wagons, *98*	—	47	__1
(36002)	Pratt's Hollow Passenger Cars 4-pack, *98*	—	455	__1
(36006)	Uranium Flatcar "6508," *99*	—	60	__1
(36016)	Flatcar with Propellers, *98*	—	55	__1
(36020)	Flatcar "TT-6424" w/ Auto Frames, *99*	—	37	__1
(36021)	Alaska Flatcar w/ Airplane "6424," *99*	—	38	__1
(36024)	J.B. Hunt Flatcar w/ trailer "64245," *99*	—	44	__1
(36025)	J.B. Hunt Flatcar w/ trailer "64246," *99*	—	50	__1
(36026)	Flatcars w/ J.B. Hunt Trailers 2-pack, *99*	—	90	__1
(36027)	Tredegar Iron Works Flatcar w/ cannon, *99*	—	45	__1
(36028)	Heavy Artillery Flatcar w/ cannon, *99*	—	45	__1
(36029)	SP Auto Carrier "516712," *99*	—	44	__1
(36030)	Troublesome Truck "1," *99*	—	35	__1
(36031)	Troublesome Truck "2," *99*	—	35	__1
(36032)	Christmas Gondola w/Presents "6462," *99*	—	44	__1
(36036)	C&O Gondola, *99*	—	20	__1
(36038)	Construction Zone Gondola, *99u*		NRS	__1
(36040)	Bethlehem Flatcar w/ block (SSS), *99*	—	75	__1
(36041)	Bethlehem Ore Car (SSS), *99*	—	40	__1
(36043)	Custom Consist Flatcar w/ pickup truck, *99*	—	40	__1
(36044)	Custom Consist Flatcar w/ dragster, *99*	—	40	__1
(36047)	Construction Zone Gondola, *99u*		NRS	__1
(36048)	Construction Zone Gondola, *99u*		NRS	__1
(36054)	Archaeological Exp Gondola w/ Eggs, *00 u*	—	55	__1
(36055)	Flatcar with Dragster, *01u*	—	30	__1
(36056)	Flatcar with Roadster, *01u*	—	30	__1
(36059)	Season's Greetings Gondola, *99u*	—	50	__1
(36062)	NYC 6462 Gondola, *99-00*	—	19	__1
(36063)	Conrail Gondola "604768," *99-00*	—	20	__1
(36064)	Billboard Flatcar "6424," *00*	—	40	__1
(36065)	Wabash Flat "25536" w/ Trailer, *00*	—	31	__1
(36066)	Christmas Gondola w/Presents Load, *00*	—	36	__1
(36067)	King Auto Sales Flat w/ 1 pink caddy "6424," *00*	—	41	__1
(36068)	Pine Peak Tree Transport Gondola, *00*		NRS	__1
(36079)	Service Station Ltd. Flatcar with Trailer, *00*	—	35	__1
(36082)	Whirlpool Flatcar with Trailer, *00u*		NRS	__1
(36083)	Santa Fe "168998" Gondola, *01*	—	17	__1
36084	Grand Trunk Coil Car, *00*	—	37	__1

		Exc	New	Cond/$
36085	FEC Coil Car, 00	—	33	—1
36086	SP Flatcar w/ Trailer, 01	—	34	—1
(36087)	Flatcar w/ Wood Whistle "6424," 01	—	25	—1
(36088)	Allis Chalmers Condenser Car "6519," 00	—	39	—1
36089	Frisco Flatcar w/ Airplane, 00	—	40	—1
(36090)	TT Flat w/ Pepsi Truck "6424," 01	—	49	—1
36091	Maersk Flat w/ Diecast Tractors "250129," 00	—	55	—1
36092	Maersk Flat w/ Diecast Frames "250130," 00	—	50	—1
36093	Soo TT Auto Carrier "906760," 00	—	49	—1
(36094)	PC F-9 Well Car "768122," 01	—	41	—1
(36095)	Christmas Chase Gondola, 01	—	49	—1
(36098)	PRR Gondola "385186," 01	—	20	—1
(36200)	Quaker Life Cereal Boxcar, 00	440	485	—1
(36202)	Miniature Railroad & Village 80th Anniversary Boxcar, 00u	—	115	—1
(36203)	Whirlpool Boxcar, 00u	—	100	—1
(36205)	eBay Boxcar, 00	—	190	—1
(36206)	REA Boxcar, 01	—	25	—1
(36207)	Vapor Records Christmas Boxcar, 01	—	34	—1
(36208)	Father's Day Boxcar, 00	—	33	—1
(36210)	Burlington Hi-Cube Boxcar "19825," 01	—	40	—1
(36211)	NP "659999" Hi-Cube Boxcar, 01	—	33	—1
(36212)	Lionel Employee Christmas Boxcar, 00u	—	390	—1
(36213)	Vapor Records Christmas Boxcar, 00	—	35	—1
(36215)	Train Station 25th Anniversary Boxcar, 00 u	—	65	—1
(36218)	Snap-On Boxcar, 00u	—	100	—1
(36220)	Pioneer Seed Boxcar, 00u		NRS	—1
(36221)	PRR Boxcar "569356," 01	—	20	—1
(36222)	NYC Boxcar "162440," 01	—	20	—1
(36223)	Chessie System Boxcar, 01	—	20	—1
(36224)	Santa Fe Boxcar "16263," 01	—	20	—1
(36225)	C&O Boxcar "250549," 01	—	20	—1
(36226)	E-Hobbies Boxcar, 01u	—	150	—1
(36227)	Monopoly Community Chest Boxcar, 00u	—	50	—1
(36228)	Lionel Visitor Center Boxcar, 01u	—	40	—1
(36229)	Island Trains 20th Anniversary Boxcar, 01u	—	25	—1
(36232)	Farmall Boxcar, 01u		NRS	—1
(36234)	Carnegie Science Center Boxcar "9700," 01u	—	100	—1
(36236)	TM Books & Video "I Love Lionel" Boxcar "7474-1," 01u	—	50	—1
(36239)	LL Bean Boxcar, 01u	—	100	—1
(36240)	Do It Best Boxcar, 01u	—	100	—1
(36242)	Erie Lackawanna Boxcar "73113," 02	—	22	—1
(36243)	Christmas Boxcar "2002," 02	—	31	—1
(36244)	Teddy Bear Centennial Boxcar, 02	—	35	—1
(36245)	Lionel 20th Century Boxcar "L900-1925," 00 u	—	30	—1

		Exc	New	Cond/$
(36246)	Lionel 20th Century Boxcar "1926-1950," *00 u*—		30	__1
(36247)	Lionel 20th Century Boxcar "1951-1975," *00 u*—		30	__1
(36248)	Lionel 20th Century Boxcar "1976-2000," *00 u*—		30	__1
(36253)	2003 O Gauge Christmas Boxcar, *03*	—	32	__1
(36254)	Goofy Hi-Cube Boxcar, *03*	—	40	__1
(36255)	Donald Duck Hi-Cube Boxcar, *03*	—	40	__1
(36256)	GN Boxcar "6341," *03*	—	20	__1
(36264)	Santa Fe Boxcar "600196, *02*	—	18	__1
(36265)	Angela Trotta Thomas "Window Wishing" Boxcar, *02*	—	34	__1
(36267)	Mickey Mouse Hi-Cube Boxcar, *03*	—	50	__1
36270	Angela Trotta Thomas 10th Ann. Boxcar "Holidays," *02-03*	—	30	__1
36272	New Haven Boxcar "6501," *04*		CP	__1
36273	Railbox Hi-Cube Boxcar "15000," *04*		CP	__1
36275	2004 Christmas Boxcar, *04*		CP	__1
36276	Angela Trotta Thomas "Tis the Season" Boxcar, *04*		CP	__1
36277	Pluto Hi-Cube Boxcar, *04*		CP	__1
36278	Winnie the Pooh Hi-Cube Boxcar, *04*		CP	__1
36291	Simpsons Boxcar, *04*		CP	__1
(36305)	eBay Boxcar "9700," *00u*	—	100	__1
36500	Western Pacific Caboose "36500," *04*		CP	__1
36501	D&RGW Caboose "36501," *04*		CP	__1
36502	Reading Caboose "36502," *04*		CP	__1
36515	North Pole Central Lines Caboose "36515," *04*		CP	__1
36519	Lionel Lines Caboose "36519," *04*		CP	__1
36520	Santa Fe Caboose "36520," *04*		CP	__1
(36701)	Baldwin Locomotive Works Operating Welding Car "36701," *02*	—	60	__1
(36702)	Postwar Bosco Milk Car with Platform "3672," *02*	—	115	__1
(36703)	Lionel Postwar Circus Horse Car and Corral, 3366	—	110	__1
(36704)	Animated Reindeer Stockcar and Corral, *02*	—	125	__1
(36718)	AEC Security Caboose, *02*	—	42	__1
(36720)	Aladdin Aquarium Car, *03*	—	45	__1
(36721)	101 Dalmatians Animated Gondola, *03*	—	45	__1
(36722)	Peter Pan Bobbing Head Boxcar, *03*	—	45	__1
(36726)	Santa Fe Searchlight Car "36726," *03*	—	50	__1
(36727)	Weyerhaeuser Moe & Joe Flatcar, *03*	—	60	__1
(36728)	SP Walking Brakeman Boxcar 163143," *03*	—	42	__1
36729	Lionel Lines Animated Caboose "36729," *04*		CP	__1
(36730)	U.S. Army Missile Launch Sound Car "44," *03*—		175	__1
(36731)	Motorized Aquarium Car "3435," *03*	—	75	__1
(36732)	C&NW Jumping Hobo Car, *03*	—	40	__1

		Exc	New	Cond/$
(36733)	Christmas Music Boxcar, *03*	—	40	__1
(36734)	Santa Fe Operating Searchlight Car "20611," *02*—		25	__1
(36735)	WP Ice Car "7045," *02*	—	55	__1
36736	D&RGW Stockcar w/RailSounds "39268," *04*		CP	__1
(36738)	T&P Poultry Dispatch Car "36738," *02*	—	50	__1
(36739)	Postwar Lionel Lines Log Dump Car "3461," *03*—		50	__1
(36740)	Postwar Lionel Lines Coal Dump Car "3469," *03*—		50	__1
(36743)	Santa Claus Bobbing Head Boxcar, *03*	—	40	__1
(36744)	Little Mermaid Aquarium Car, *03*	—	60	__1
(36745)	Toy Story Animated Gondola, *03*	—	60	__1
(36758)	Patriotic Lighted Boxcar, *02*	—	45	__1
(36760)	Lionel Archives B&O Sentinel Operating Brakeman Boxcar, "3424," *02*	—	65	__1
(36761)	Wellspring Capital Management Illuminated Boxcar, *02 u*	—	240	__1
(36764)	West Side Lumber Log Dump Car "36764," *03*—		50	__1
(36765)	Alaska Coal Dump Car "401" Steam Locomotive, CC, *03*	—	50	__1
(36767)	Santa's Radar Tracking Car, *03*	—	40	__1
36769	Fourth of July Lighted Boxcar, *03*	—	70	__1
36770	American Refrigerator Transit Ice Car "23701," *04*		CP	__1
36771	CN Barrel Car "74208," *04*		CP	__1
36772	Spokane, Portland & Seattle Log Dump Car "36772," *04*		CP	__1
36773	Jersey Central Coal Dump Car "92926," *04*		CP	__1
36774	Pennsylvania "Moe & Joe" Lumber Flatcar "36774," *04*		CP	__1
36776	Santa Fe Walking Brakeman Car "19938," *04*		CP	__1
36778	C&O Searchlight Car "216614," *04*		CP	__1
36780	Sea-Monkeys Motorized Aquarium Car, *04*		CP	__1
36781	Finding Nemo Aquarium Car, *04*		CP	__1
36783	Disney Operating Boxcar, *04*		CP	__1
36784	Monsters Inc. Bobbing Head Boxcar, *04*		CP	__1
(36786)	Postwar MP Operating Boxcar "3494-150," *03*	—	40	__1
36787	M.O.W. Remote Control Searchlight Car "36787," *04*		CP	__1
36788	Lionel Lines Steam Tender w/TrainSounds, *04*		CP	__1
36789	Railbox Boxcar w/TrainSounds, *04*		CP	__1
36790	Christmas Music Boxcar, *04*		CP	__1
(36793)	Pennsylvania Derrick Car "36793," *03*	—	22	__1
(36794)	NYC Log Dump Car "36794," *03*	—	25	__1
(36795)	Southern Coal Dump Car "36795," *03*	—	25	__1
(36796)	GN Searchlight Car "36796," *03*	—	25	__1
(36797)	Operation Iraqi Freedom Minuteman Car			

		Exc	New	Cond/$
	"36797," *03*	—	45	—1
(36900)	Depressed Center Flatcar w/ Backshop Load, *99*	100	110	—1
(36913)	Allied Chemical 1-D Tank Car (2-pack), *00*	—	150	—1
(36914)	Allied Chemical 1-D Tank Car Die-Cast White "ACDX 68075," *00*	—	90	—1
(36915)	Allied Chemical 1-D Tank Car Die-Cast White "ACDX 68076," *00*	—	90	—1
(36916)	Allied Chemical 1-D Tank Car (2-pack), *00*	—	165	—1
(36917)	Allied Chemical 1-D Tank Car Die-Cast Black "ACDX 65124," *00*	—	90	—1
(36918)	Allied Chemical 1-D Tank Car Die-Cast Black "ACDX 65125," *00*	—	90	—1
(36927)	B&O DC Hopper 6-pack "435040/45," *01*	—	520	—1
(36935)	Maersk Maxi-Stack 2-pack "250131/2," *00*	—	105	—1
(36937)	SP Maxi-Stack "513957," *02*	—	75	—1
(38000)	Lionel Century Club II NYC Hudson 4-6-4 Empire State, *02 u*	—	990	—1
(38004)	Virginian 4-6-0 Ten-Wheeler "203" Steam Locomotive, CC, *01-02*	—	570	—1
(38005)	Long Island 4-6-0 Ten-Wheeler "138" Steam Locomotive, CC, *01-02*	—	530	—1
(38007)	UP Auxilary Tender, Black, CC, *01*	—	205	—1
(38008)	UP Auxilary Tender Gray, CC, *01*	—	215	—1
(38009)	DRG 4-6-6-4 Challenger "3803," CC, *01*	—	1800	—1
(38010)	Clinchfield 4-6-6-4 Challenger "673," CC, *01*	—	1650	—1
(38012)	Wheeling & Lake Erie 2-6-6-2 "8005," CC, *01*	—	850	—1
(38013)	D&H 4-6-6-4 Lionmaster Challenger "1527," CC, *01*	—	760	—1
(38014)	DRG 4-6-6-4 Lionmaster Challenger "3800," CC, *01*	—	710	—1
(38016)	Southern 0-8-0 Yard Goat "6536" Steam Locomotive, CC, *01-02*	—	530	—1
(38017)	CN 2-6-0 Mogul "86" Steam Locomotive, CC, *03*		CP	—1
(38018)	Wabash 2-6-0 Mogul "826" Steam Locomotive, CC, *03*		CP	—1
(38019)	B&M 2-6-0 Mogul "1455" Steam Locomotive, CC, *03*		CP	—1
38020)	PRR 4-4-4-4 Lionmaster Duplex T1 "5514" Steam Locomotive, CC, *02-03*	—	630	—1
38021)	WP 4-6-6-4 Challenger Steam Locomotive "402," CC, *02*	—	650	—1
38022)	WM 4-6-6-4 Challenger Steam Locomotive "1206," CC, *02*	—	690	—1
38023)	UP 4-6-6-4 Challenger Steam Locomotive			

		Exc	New	Cond/$
	"3976," CC, *02*	—	690	—1
(38025)	PRR 4-6-2 K4 Pacific "1361" Steam Locomotive CC, *02*	—	900	—1
(38026)	N&W 4-8-4 J Class Northern "606" Steam Locomotive, CC, *02*	—	1450	—1
(38027)	Meadow River Lumber Co. Heisler Geared "6" Steam Locomotive, CC, *03*	—	950	—1
(38028)	PRR 6-8-6 S2 Class "6200" Steam Turbine, *01*	—	650	—1
(38029)	UP 4-12-2 "9000" Steam Locomotive, CC, *03*	—	500	—1
(38030)	Santa Fe 2-8-8-2 "1795" Steam Locomotive, CC, *03*	—	900	—1
38031	SP 2-8-8-4 AC-9 "3809," CC, *04*		CP	—1
(38032)	Virginian 2-8-8-2 "741" Steam Locomotive, CC, *03*	—	900	—1
(38036)	Long Island 2-8-0 Consolidation, *01*	—	390	—1
(38037)	PRR-Reading Seashore 2-8-0 Consolidation "6072" Steam Locomotive, CC, *01*	—	495	—1
(38038)	D&RG Auxilary Water Tender, *01*	—	230	—1
(38039)	Clinchfield Auxilary Water Tender, *01*	—	220	—1
(38040)	LV 4-6-0 Camelback, *01*	—	450	—1
(38042)	C&NW 4-6-0 Ten-Wheeler "361" Steam Locomotive, CC, *02*	—	450	—1
(38043)	Frisco 4-6-0 Ten-Wheeler "719" Steam Locomotive, CC, *02*	—	425	—1
(38044)	PRR 4-6-2 K4 Pacific "5385" Steam Locomotive, CC, *02*	—	920	—1
(38045)	NYC 4-6-4 Lionmaster Hudson J-3a "5418" Steam Locomotive, CC, *03*	—	495	—1
(38046)	GN 0-8-0 Steam Locomotive "815," CC, *02*	—	530	—1
(38047)	N&W 0-8-0 Steam Locomotive "266," CC, *02*	—	530	—
(38048)	Nickel Plate Road 0-8-0 Steam Locomotive "303," CC, *02*	—	530	—
(38049)	N&W 2-6-6-4 Articulated Steam Locomotive "1234," CC, *02*	—	690	—
(38050)	Nickel Plate 2-8-4 Berkshire "779" Steam Locomotive, CC, *03*	—	900	—
(38051)	Erie 2-8-4 Berkshire "3315" Steam Locomotive, CC, *03*	—	900	—
(38052)	Pere Marquette 2-8-4 Berkshire "1225" Steam Locomotive, CC, *03*	—	100	—
(38053)	NYC 4-8-2 Mohawk L-2a "2793" Steam Locomotive, CC, *03*		CP	—
38055	Santa Fe 4-8-4 Northern "3751" CC, *04*		CP	—
(38056)	Pennsylvania 4-8-2 Mountain M 1 a "6759" Steam Locomotive, CC, *03*	—	750	—

MODERN ERA 1970–2005

Exc New Cond/$

		Exc	New	Cond/$
(38057)	Weyerhaeuser Timber Co. Shay Steam Locomotive, CC, 03	—	1000	—¹
38058	C&O 2-8-8-2 H7 "1580," CC, 04		CP	—¹
38060	UP 2-8-8-2 H7 "3590," CC, 04		CP	—¹
(38061)	Cass Scenic RR Heisler Geared "6" Steam Locomotive, CC, 03	—	1050	—¹
(38062)	Lionel Lines 4-6-2 Pacific "8062" Steam Locomotive, CC, 02-03	—	275	—¹
(38065)	UP 2-8-8-2 Mallet Steam Locomotive "3672," CC, 02	—	980	—¹
(38066)	"Elk River Coal & Lumber Co." Shay Steam Locomotive, CC, 03	—	1000	—¹
(38067)	Milwaukee Road 4-6-2 Pacific "6316" Steam Locomotive, CC, 03	—	300	—¹
(38068)	WM 4-6-2 Pacific "204" Steam Locomotive, CC, 03	—	300	—¹
38070	C&O 4-6-2 Pacific "489," CC, 04		CP	—¹
(38075)	UP 4-8-8-4 Lionmaster Big Boy "4024" Steam Locomotive, CC, 03		CP	—¹
38076	C&O 2-8-4 Berkshire "2699," CC, 04		CP	—¹
38077	Virginian 2-8-4 Berkshire "508," CC, 04		CP	—¹
38079	SP 4-8-4 Northern GS-2 "4410" CC, 04		CP	—¹
38080	WP 4-8-4 Northern GS-64 "485" CC, 04		CP	—¹
38082	Pennsylvania 2-8-8-2 Y3 "374," CC, 04		CP	—¹
38083	N&W 2-8-8-2 Y3 "2009," CC, 04		CP	—¹
(38085)	NYC 4-6-4 Lionmaster Hudson J-3a "5422" Steam Locomotive, CC, 03	—	495	—¹
(38086)	B&A 4-6-4 Lionmaster Hudson "607" Steam Locomotive, CC, 03	—	495	—¹
(38088)	NYC 2-6-0 Mogul "1924" Steam Locomotive, CC, 03		CP	—¹
38089	Pennsylvania 4-6-2 Pacific "3678," CC, 04		CP	—¹
38090	Clinchfield 4-6-6-4 Lionmaster Challenger "672" CC, 04		CP	—¹
38091	NP 4-6-6-4 Lionmaster Challenger "5121" CC, 04		CP	—¹
38092	Pickering Lumber Heisler "5," CC, 04		CP	—¹
38092	Pickering Lumber Heisler "5," CC, 04		CP	—¹
38093	UP 4-6-6-4 Lionmaster Challenger "3980" CC, 04		CP	—¹
(38100)	Texas Special F3 AB Set "2245," 99	750	810	—¹
(38103)	Texas Special F3 "2245," 99	380	445	—¹
38114)	AT&SF FT B Unit, 99-00	—	170	—¹
38115)	NYC FT B Unit, 99-00	—	130	—¹
38116)	B&O FT B Unit, 99-00	—	130	—¹
38144)	C&O F3 AA "7019/7021," 00	—	700	—¹

		Exc	New	Cond/$
(38147)	GN Alco FA-2 AA Diesel Set, CC, *02*	—	405	—1
(38150)	Platinum Ghost "2333," *99*	—	540	—3
(38153)	Spirit of the Century "2333," *99*	—	1100	—1
(38160)	Pennsylvania Alco FB-2 Unit, *02*	—	125	—1
(38161)	MKT Alco FB-2 Unit, *02*	—	125	—1
(38162)	Burlington FT B Unit, *01*		NRS	—1
(38167)	Burlington FT AA, *01*		NRS	—1
(38176)	Pennsylvania Alco FA-2 AA Diesel Set, CC, *02*	—	405	—1
(38182)	MKT Alco FA-2 AA Diesel Set, CC, *02*	—	405	—1
(38188)	Southern F3 ABA "2356," *00*	—	740	—1
(38194)	GN Alco FB-2 Unit, *02*	—	125	—1
(38196)	Santa Fe FT A Unit "171," *00*		NRS	—1
(38197)	SP F3 ABA "2387," *00*	—	640	—1
[38356]	LOTS Dow Chemical 3-D Tank Car, *87*	75	110	—1
(39008)	PRR Heavyweight Passenger Set (4-pack), *00*	—	220	—1
(39009)	PRR Heavyweight Passenger Set Combo "Indian Rock," *00*		NRS	—1
(39010)	PRR Heavyweight Passenger Set Coach "Andrew Carnegie," *00*		NRS	—1
(39011)	PRR Heavyweight Passenger Set Coach "Salmon P. Chase," *00*		NRS	—1
(39012)	PRR Heavyweight Passenger Set Observation "Skyline View," *00*		NRS	—1
(39013)	B&O Heavyweight Passenger Set (4-pack), *00*	—	400	—1
(39016)	B&O Heavyweight Passenger Set (4-pack), *00*	—	200	—1
(39017)	B&O Heavyweight Passenger Set Combo "Harper's Ferry," *00*		NRS	—1
(39018)	B&O Heavyweight Passenger Set Coach "Youngstown," *00*		NRS	—1
(39019)	B&O Heavyweight Passenger Set Coach "New Castle," *00*		NRS	—1
(39020)	B&O Heavyweight Passenger Set Observation "Chicago," *00*		NRS	—1
(39028)	LL Madison Passenger Set (3-pack), *00*	—	180	—1
(39029)	Lionel Lines Madison Passenger Set Coach "Irvington 2625," *00*		NRS	—1
(39030)	LL Madison Passenger Set Coach "Madison 2627," *00*		NRS	—
(39031)	LL Madison Passenger Set Coach "Manhattan 2628," *00*		NRS	—
(39032)	UP Madison Passenger Car 4-pack, *00*	—	244	—
(39042)	N&W Heavyweight Passenger Car 4-pack, *00*	—	325	—
(39047)	B&O Heavyweight Passenger Car 2-pack, *01*	—	200	—
(39050)	PRR Heavyweight Passenger Car 2-pack, *01*	—	200	—

		Exc	New	Cond/$
(39053)	Alaska Streamliner Pass Car 2-pack, *01*	—	90	__1
(39056)	NYC Streamliner Pass Car 2-pack, *01*	—	75	__1
(39059)	Santa Fe Streamliner Pass Car 2-pack, *01*	—	100	__1
(39062)	B&O Streamliner Pass Car 2-pack, *01*	—	75	__1
(39065)	PRR Streamliner Pass 4-pack, *01*	—	165	__1
(39079)	SP Heavyweight Passenger Car 2-pack, *01*	NM		__1
(39082)	Blue Comet Heavyweight Passenger Car 2-pack, *02*	—	250	__1
(39085)	Freedom Train Heavyweight Passenger Car 3-Pack, *03*	—	225	__1
(39092)	PRR 027 Streamline Passenger Car 2-pack, *01*	—	70	__1
(39099)	Alton Limited Heavyweight Passenger Car 2-Pack, *03*	—	200	__1
(39100)	Congressional set "William Penn" Coach, *00*	—	100	__1
(39101)	Congressional set "Molly Pitcher" Coach, *00*	—	100	__1
(39102)	Congressional set "Betsy Ross" Vista Dome, *00*	—	100	__1
(39103)	Congressional set "Alexander Hamilton" Observation, *00*	—	100	__1
(39104)	Phoebe Snow Stationsounds Car, *99*	—	245	__1
(39105)	Milwaukee Road Hiawatha Stationsounds Car, *99*	—	195	__1
(39106)	CP Aluminum Passenger Car Set (2-pack), *00*	—	190	__1
(39107)	CP Aluminum Passenger Coach "Blair Manor 2553," *00*	NRS		__1
(39108)	CP Aluminum Passenger Coach "Craig Manor 2554," *00*	NRS		__1
(39109)	Spirit of Century Aluminum Passenger Car (4-pack), *99*	—	425	__1
(39110)	Spirit of the Century Full Vista Dome Car, *99-00*	—	100	__1
(39111)	Spirit of the Century Full Vista Dome Car, *99-00*	—	100	__1
(39112)	Spirit of the Century Full Vista Dome Car, *99-00*	—	100	__1
(39113)	Spirit of the Century Skytop Observation Car, *99-00*	—	100	__1
(39118)	Texas Special Station Sounds Aluminum Pass "1203" "Garland," *99-00*	—	280	__1
(39119)	Southern Aluminum Pass Car Set (4-pack), *00*	—	350	__1
(39120)	Southern Aluminum Passenger Baggage "Grand Junction 1701," *00*	NRS		__1
(39121)	Southern Aluminum Passenger Coach "Charlottsville 812," *00*	NRS		__1
(39122)	Southern Aluminum Passenger Coach "Roanoke 814," *00*	—	250	__1
(39123)	Southern Aluminum Passenger Observation "Memphis 1152," *00*	NRS		__1
(39124)	Amtrak Superliner Aluminum Passenger Car			

		Exc	New	Cond/$
	4-pack, *02*	—	355	—[1]
(39129)	Santa Fe Superliner Aluminum Passenger Car 4-pack, *02*	—	355	—[1]
(39141)	Rock Island Aluminum Passenger Car 4-pack, *01*	—	400	—[1]
(39146)	UP Aluminum Passenger Cars, 4-pack, *01*	—	285	—[1]
(39151)	CP Aluminum Passenger Car 2-pack, *01*	—	330	—[1]
(39154)	PRR Congressional Aluminum Passenger Car 2-pack, *02*	—	170	—[1]
(39155)	PRR Congressional Baggage Car, *02*		CP	—[1]
(39156)	PRR Congressional Coach "Robert Morris," *02*		CP	—[1]
(39157)	Southern Aluminum Passenger Car 2-pack, *01*	—	230	—[1]
(39160)	KCS Aluminum Passenger Car 2-pack, *01*	200	220	—[1]
(39163)	E-L Aluminum Passenger Car 2-pack, *01*	—	185	—[1]
(39166)	Texas Special Aluminum Passenger Car 2-pack, *01*	300	430	—[1]
(39169)	ACL Aluminum Passenger Car 4-pack, *01*	—	275	—[1]
(39179)	NP Aluminum Passenger Car 2-pack, *02*	—	230	—[1]
(39182)	WP Aluminum Passenger Car 2-pack, *02*	—	230	—[1]
(39185)	Rio Grande Aluminum Passenger Car 2-pack, *02*	—	230	—[1]
(39194)	UP Aluminum Passenger Car 2-pack, *02*	—	190	—[1]
(39197)	CP Aluminum StationSounds Car, *02*	—	210	—[1]
(39198)	PRR Aluminum StationSounds Car, *02*	—	220	—[1]
(39200)	Hellgate Bridge Boxcar II "1900-2000," *00 u*	—	75	—[3]
(39201)	Century Club Hudson Boxcar "773," *00 u*	—	55	—[1]
(39202)	Lionel Centennial Boxcar "1900-2000," *00*	—	47	—[1]
(39203)	6464 Boxcar Series X 3-pack, *01*	—	95	—[1]
(39204)	New Haven Boxcar "6464-725," *01*	—	40	—[1]
(39205)	Alaska Boxcar "6464-825," *01*	—	50	—[1]
(39206)	NYC Boxcar "6464-900," *01*	—	40	—[1]
39207	UP Boxcar 6565 "508500" Red, *00*	—	50	—[1]
39208	UP Boxcar 6565 "903658" Silver, *00*	—	45	—[1]
39209	UP Boxcar 6565 "500200" Yellow, *00*	—	42	—[1]
(39210)	6530 Fire Fighting Car, *00*	—	40	—[1]
(39211)	6464 Archive 2 Boxcar 3-pack, *00*	—	85	—[1]
(39215)	LCC II Niagara Boxcar, *01u*	—	75	—[1]
(39216)	PRR 2-Door Boxcar "47211," *01*	—	40	—[1]
(39217)	LCC II Member Boxcar, *00u*	—	75	—[1]
(39218)	LCC II Member Boxcar, gold, *01u*	—	100	—[1]
(39220)	B&LE Heavyweight Boxcar 6565 "82101," *01*	—	41	—[1]
(39221)	L&N Heavyweight Boxcar 6565 "109829," *01*	—	42	—[1]
(39222)	Conrail Heavyweight Boxcar 6565 "269198," *01*	—	42	—[1]
(39223)	Postwar 6464 Boxcar Series 3-pack, *02*	—	110	—[1]
(39227)	Postwar 6468 Automobile Boxcar 3-pack, *01*	—	95	—[1]

		Exc	New	Cond/$
(39236)	Postwar WP Boxcar "6464-250," 01	—	50	—1
39237	LCC II M-10000 Boxcar, 02 u	—	40	—1
(39238)	Elvis Boxcar, 03	—	40	—1
(39239)	P&LE Boxcar "22300," 02	—	35	—1
(39240)	Pennsylvania Boxcar "118747," 02	—	35	—1
(39241)	PC Boxcar "252455," 02	—	35	—1
(39242)	Archive 6464 Boxcar Series 3-Pack, 03-04	—	95	—1
39246	LCC II Sharknose Boxcar, 03 u	—	40	—1
(39247)	Postwar NYC Double-Door Boxcar "6468," 02-03	—	32	—1
39249	Christmas Boxcar, 03		NRS	—1
(39250)	Campbell's Kids Centennial Boxcar, 03-04	—	45	—1
39252	Lenny Dean 60th Anniversary Boxcar, 04		CP	—1
39253	Archive 6464 Boxcar Series 3-pack #2, 04		CP	—1
(39257)	Boy's WP Boxcar "6464-100," 03	—	45	—1
(39258)	Elvis Presley Boxcar, 2, 03-04	—	40	—1
(39259)	Buick Centennial Boxcar, 03	—	35	—1
39262	Elvis Presley Boxcar #3, 04		CP	—1
39400	Republic Steel Slag Car 3-pack (Std. O), 04		CP	—1
39404	Republic Steel Hot Metal Car 3-pack (Std. O), 04		CP	—1
(51007)	LCC II UP M-10000 Set, 00u	600	970	—1
51008	Burlington "Pioneer Zephyr" Diesel Passenger set w/RailSounds, 04		CP	—1
51200	(See 17510)			
(51201)	Lionel Lines Rail Chief Passenger Set, 90	—	480	—1
(51220)	NYC "Imperial Castle" Passenger Car, 93 u	—	500	—1
(51221)	NYC "Niagara County" Passenger Car, 93 u	—	500	—1
(51222)	NYC "Cascade Glory" Passenger Car, 93 u	—	500	—1
(51223)	NYC "City of Detroit" Passenger Car, 93 u	—	500	—1
(51224)	NYC "Imperial Falls" Passenger Car, 93 u	—	500	—1
(51225)	NYC "Westchester County" Passenger Car, 93 u	—	500	—1
(51226)	NYC "Cascade Grotto" Passenger Car, 93 u	—	500	—1
(51227)	NYC "City of Indianapolis" Passenger Car, 93 u	—	500	—1
(51228)	NYC "Manhattan Island" Observation Car, 93 u	—	500	—1
(51229)	NYC Dining Car "680," 93 u	—	500	—1
(51230)	NYC Baggage Car "5017," 93 u	—	500	—1
(51231)	NYC "Century Club" Passenger Car, 93 u	—	500	—1
(51232)	NYC "Thousand Islands" Observation Car, 93 u	—	500	—1
(51233)	NYC Dining Car "684," 93 u	—	500	—1
(51234)	NYC Baggage Car "5020," 93 u	—	500	—1
(51235)	NYC "Century Tavern" Passenger Car, 93 u	—	500	—1

		Exc	New	Cond/$
(51236)	NYC "City of Toledo" Passenger Car, *93 u*	—	500	—1
(51237)	NYC "Imperial Mansion" Passenger Car, *93 u*	—	500	—1
(51238)	NYC "Imperial Palace" Passenger Car, *93 u*	—	500	—1
(51239)	NYC "Cascade Spirit" Passenger Car, *93 u*	—	500	—1
(51240)	NYC Dining Car "681," *93 u*	—	500	—1
(51241)	NYC "City of Chicago" Passenger Car, *93 u*	—	500	—1
(51242)	NYC "Imperial Garden" Passenger Car, *93 u*	—	500	—1
(51243)	NYC "Imperial Fountain" Passenger Car, *93 u*	—	500	—1
(51244)	NYC "Cascade Valley" Passenger Car, *93 u*	—	500	—1
(51245)	NYC Dining Car "685," *93 u*	—	500	—1
51249	UP Overland Sleeper, *N/A*	—	120	—1
51300	Shell Semi-Scale 1-D Tank Car "8124," *91*	—	155	—2
(51301)	Lackawanna Semi-Scale Reefer "7000," *92*	250	310	—1
(51401)	PRR Semi-Scale Boxcar "100800," *91*	145	165	—1
(51402)	C&O Semi-Scale Stock Car "95250," *92*	190	205	—1
51501	B&O Semi-Scale Hopper "532000," *91*	105	120	—1
(51502)	Lionel Lines Steel Die-cast Ore Car "6486-3" (SSS), *96*	—	80	—1
(51503)	Lionel Lines Steel Die-cast Ore Car "6486-1" (SSS), *96*	—	80	—1
(51504)	Lionel Lines Steel Die-cast Ore Car "6486-2" (SSS), *96*	—	80	—1
(51600)	NYC Depressed Center Flatcar w/ transformer "6418," *96*	—	125	—1
51701	NYC Semi-Scale Caboose "19400," *91*	150	155	—1
(51702)	PRR N-8 Caboose "478039," *91-92*	250	355	—1
52000	Detroit-Toledo TCA Flatcar w/ trailer, *92 u*	80	95	—1
52001	NETCA B&M Quad Hopper w/ coal load, *92 u*	50	75	—1
[52002]	VTC Passenger Cars (See 7692)			
52003	Ozark TCA "Meet Me in St. Louis" Flatcar w/ trailer, *92 u*	—	450	—1
[52004]	LCAC Algoma Central Gondola w/ coil covers "9215," *92 u*	75	95	—1
[52005]	LCAC Canadian National F-3 B Unit "9517," *93 u*	—	30	—1
[52006]	LCAC CP Boxcar "930016" (Std. O), *93 u*	—	145	—1
[52007]	NLOE Long Island RS-3 "1552," *92 u*	120	250	—1
(52008)	TCA Bucyrus Erie Crane Car "1993X," *93 u*	55	60	—1
(52009)	Sacramento Valley TTOS Western Pacific Boxcar "64641993," *93 u*	41	45	—2
(52010)	TTOS Weyerhaeuser DD Boxcar "838593" (Std. O), *93 u*	49	59	—1
52011	Gadsden Pacific Tucson, Cornelia & Gila Bend Ore Car w/ load, *93 u*	31	40	—
52013	Artrain Norfolk Southern Flatcar w/ trailer (Std. O), *92 u*	175	275	—

		Exc	New	Cond/$
(52014)	LOTS BN TTUX Flatcar set w/ N&W trailers "637500a" and "637500B," *93 u*	155	185	—¹
52016	NETCA B&M Gondola w/ coil covers, *93 u*	55	65	—¹
52018	Lakes & Pines TCA 3M Boxcar, *93 u*	—	450	—¹
[52019]	NLOE Long Island Boxcar "8393," *93 u*	30	47	—¹
[52020]	NLOE Long Island B/W Caboose "8393," *93 u*	60	85	—¹
(52021)	TTOS Weyerhaeuser Tractor and Trailer, *93 u*	24	31	—¹
52022	TTOS Union Pacific Boxcar, *93 u*	—	400	—¹
(52023)	LCCA D&TS 2-bay ACF Hopper "2601" (Std. 0), *93 u*	38	42	—³
52024	Artrain Conrail Auto Carrier, *93 u*	95	105	—¹
(52025)	LCCA Madison Hardware Tractor and Trailer, *93 u*	21	29	—²
[52026]	NLOE Long Island Flatcar w/ Grumman trailer "8394," *94 u*	230	380	—¹
52027	Gadsden Pacific Pinto Valley Mine Ore Car w/ load, *94 u*	29	32	—¹
(52028)	TTOS Ford Cars, set of 3, *94 u*	65	85	—¹
(52029)	TTOS Ford 1-D Tank Car "12" (O27), *94 u*	30	35	—¹
(52030)	TTOS Ford Gondola "4023," *94 u*	23	29	—¹
(52031)	TTOS Ford Hopper "1458" (O27), *94 u*	28	33	—¹
(52032)	TTOS Ford 1-D Tank Car "14" w/ Kughn inscription (O27), *94 u*	75	105	—¹
(52033)	Wolverine TTOS Lionel Lines Tractor and Trailer (See 52040)	—	55	—¹
(52034)	Wolverine TTOS Grand Trunk Flatcar "52040" (See 52040)			
(52035)	TCA Yorkrail GP-9 "1750," shell only, *94 u*	44	55	—¹
52036	TCA 40th Anniversary B/W Caboose, *94 u*	46	55	—¹
52037	TCA Yorkrail GP9 "1754," *94 u*	155	190	—¹
52038	LCCA Southern Hopper w/ coal load "360794" (Std. 0), *94 u*	38	42	—¹
52039	LCCA "Track 29" Bumper, *94 u*	—	17	—¹
52040	Wolverine TTOS GTW Flatcar w/ Lionel Lines Tractor and Trailer, *94 u*	55	60	—²
52041)	LOTS BN TTUX Flatcar set w/ Conrail trailers "637500d" and "637500E," *94 u*	75	105	—²
52042)	LOTS BN TTUX Flatcar w/ CN trailer "637500C," *94 u*	55	65	—¹
52043]	NETCA LL Bean Boxcar "1994," *94 u*	90	130	—¹
52044)	Eastwood Vat Car, *95 u*	—	45	—¹
52045]	TCA Penn Dutch Milk Car "61052," *94 u*	—	90	—¹
52046)	TTOS ACL Boxcar "16247," *94 u*	—	110	—¹
52047)	Southwest TTOS Cotton Belt Woodside Caboose w/ smoke "1921" (Std. 0), *93-94 u*	70	75	—¹

		Exc	New	Cond/$
(52048)	LOTS CN Tractor and Trailer "197993," *94 u*	32	35	—¹
52049	Artrain BN Gondola w/ coil covers, *94 u*	55	70	—¹
[52050]	Schuylkill Haven Borough Day SP-type Caboose "1994," *94 u*	—	37	—¹
(52051)	TCA Baltimore & Ohio "Sentinel" Boxcar "6464095," *95 u*	45	49	—²
[52052]	TCA 40th Anniversary Boxcar, *94 u*	—	90	—¹
52053	TTOS Carail Boxcar, *94 u*	50	55	—¹
52054	Carail Boxcar, *94 u*		NRS	—¹
(52055)	LCCA Sovex Tractor and Trailer, *94 u*	22	32	—¹
(52056)	LCCA Southern Tractor and Trailer "206502," *94 u*	22	31	—¹
(52057)	TTOS Western Pacific Boxcar "64641995," *95 u*	47	50	—²
(52058)	Central California TTOS Santa Fe Boxcar "64641895," *95 u*	39	55	—¹
(52059)	Eastern TCA Clinchfield Quad Hopper w/ coal load "16413," *94 u*	85	110	—¹
[52060]	VTC Tender w/ whistle "7694," *94 u*	—	70	—¹
[52061]	NLOE Long Island Stern's Pickle Products Vat Car "8395," *95 u*	—	155	—¹
(52062)	TCA "Skytop" Observation Car "1995," *95 u*	225	370	—³
(52063)	TCA New York Central "Pacemaker" Boxcar "6464125," *95 u*	—	375	—¹
(52064)	TCA Missouri Pacific Boxcar "6464150," *95 u*	—	360	—¹
(52065)	Penn-Dutch Grain Operating Boxcar "9028," *96u*	—	100	—¹
(52066)	Trainmaster Tractor and Trailer, *94 u*	—	130	—¹
(52067)	LOTS Burlington Ice Car "50240," *95 u*	—	55	—²
(52068)	Toy Train Parade TTOS Contadina Boxcar "16245," *94 u*	—	50	—¹
52069	Carail Tractor and Trailer, *94 u*	—	75	—¹
52070	Knoebel's Boxcar, *95 u*	—	60	—¹
52071	Gadsden Pacific Copper Basin Railway Ore Car w/ load, *95 u*	—	32	—¹
[52072]	NLOE Grumman Tractor, *94 u*	—	70	—¹
(52073)	Southwest TTOS Pacific Fruit Express Reefer "459402" (Std. O), *95 u*	—	60	—¹
(52074)	LCCA Iowa Beef Packers Reefer "197095" (Std. O), *95 u*	—	37	—²
52075	United Auto Workers Boxcar, *95 u*	—	85	—
[52076]	NLOE Long Island Observation Car "8396," *96 u*	—	350	—
(52077)	Pacific Northwest TCA Great Northern Hi-cube Boxcar "9695," *95 u*	—	460	—
(52078)	TTOS Southern Pacific SD-9 "5366," *96 u*	—	250	—

		Exc	New	Cond/$
(52079)	TTOS SP B/W Caboose "1996," *96 u*	—	55	—1
[52080]	NETCA Boston & Maine Flatcar w/ trailer "91095," *95 u*	—	250	—1
(52081)	C&NW Boxcar "6464555," *96u*	—	75	—1
52082	Steamtown Lackawanna Boxcar, *95 u*	—	100	—1
(52083)	Eastwood Chemicals Flatcar w/ Tanker "16380," *95 u*	—	45	—1
(52084)	TTOS Union Pacific I-Beam Flatcar w/ load "16380," *95 u*	—	170	—1
(52085)	TCA Full Vista Dome Car "1996," *96 u*	—	130	—2
(52086)	Canadian TTOS Pacific Great Eastern Boxcar "64641972," *96 u*	—	55	—1
(52087)	TTOS New Mexico Central Boxcar "64641996," *96 u*	—	55	—1
[52088]	Desert TCA 25th Anniversary On-Track Step Van, *96 u*	—	125	—1
52089	Gadsden Pacific SMARRCO Ore Car w/ load, *96 u*	—	30	—1
(52090)	LCCA Pere Marquette DD Boxcar (Std. O), *96 u*	—	39	—1
(52091)	LCCA Lenox Tractor and Trailer, *95 u*	—	21	—1
(52092)	LCCA Iowa Interstate Tractor and Trailer, *95 u*	—	23	—1
(52093)	Lone Star TCA Boxcar "6464696," *96 u*	—	65	—1
(52096)	Dept. 56 Snow Village Boxcar "9756," *95u*	—	80	—1
52097	Artrain Chessie System Reefer, *95 u*	—	75	—1
(52098)	National Bureau of Standards Boxcar (Std. O), *96u*	—	70	—1
(52099)	MP TOFC Flatcar, *96 u*	—	70	—1
52100	Grand Rapids Station Platform, *96*		NRS	—1
52100	LCCA Station Platform, *98*	—	20	—1
(52101)	Chicagoland RR Club Maxistack Flatcar "64287," *97 u*	—	80	—1
(52102)	Chicagoland RR Club AT&SF E/V Caboose "999758," *96 u*	—	75	—1
(52103)	Chicagoland RR Club AT&SF E/V Caboose "999556," *96 u*		75	—1
52104	St. Louis LRRC Tractor & Trailer, *96 u*		NRS	—1
(52105)	Superstition Mountain Operating Gondola "61997," *97 u*	—	80	—1
(52106)	TCA "City of Phoenix" Dining Car "1997," *97u*	—	100	—1
(52107)	LCCA Pickup Truck, *96 u*	—	50	—1
(52108)	LCCA Step Van, *96 u*	—	50	—1
(52110)	CSPM&O Boxcar, *97 u*	22	60	—1
52111	NETCA Ben & Jerry's Flatcar w/ tractor, *94*	—	350	—1
(52112)	NLOE LIRR Aluminum Passenger Car "9733," *97 u*	—	300	—1

(52113)	NDG&W 3-bay Hopper, *97 u*	—	55	—¹
(52114)	NYC Flatcar w/ trailer, *97 u*	—	70	—¹
(52115)	LCAC Wabash Lake Auto Carrier "9519," *98 u*	—	100	—¹
(52116)	Milwaukee Road Flatcar w/Tractor and Trailer "194797," *97 u*	—	60	—¹
(52117)	St. Louis LRRC Wabash Flatcar w/ trailer, *97 u*	—	65	—¹
(52118)	TCA D&RGW Boxcar "5477097," *97 u*	—	65	—¹
(52119)	TCA Museum 20th Anniversary Boxcar, *97 u*		NRS	—¹
(52120)	Shedd Aquarium Car "3435-557," *98 u*	—	85	—¹
(52121)	Mobilgas 1-Dome Tank Car "238" (Std. O), *97u*	—	75	—¹
(52122)	NLOE Meenan Oil 1-D Tank Car, "8397," 97 u; "9883," 98 u	—	60	—¹
(52123)	Long Island RR "Ronkonkoma" Full Vista Dome "9783," *97u*	—	300	—¹
(52123)	Long Island RR "Hicksville" Dining Car "9883," *98u*	—	300	—¹
(52124)	El Paso & South Western Ore Car w/Load, *97u*	—	40	—¹
(52125)	(See 2346)			
(52126)	MILW Boxcar w/ CTT logo "21027," *97 u*	—	60	—¹
(52127)	Southern TCA Hopper (Std. O) "360997," *98 u*	—	70	—¹
(52128)	TCA Pennsylvania Dutch Boxcar "91653," *97 u*	—	80	—¹
52129	LOTS Lighted Billboard, *97*		NRS	—¹
(52130)	Hot Wheels TOFC Flatcar "21697," *97 u*	—	60	—¹
52131	LCCA Airplane Blue, *98*	—	40	—¹
(52132)	Knoebel's #2, *99 u*	—	75	—¹
(52133)	Knoebel's Boxcar, *98 u*	—	75	—¹
(52134)	Knoebel Phoenix #4 Boxcar, *00 u*	—	75	—¹
(52135)	Santa Fe Refrigerator Car "22739," *98u*	—	60	—¹
52136A	Christmas Special Tractor and Trailor, *97*		NRS	—¹
52136B	Frisco Special Tractor and Trailer, *98*		NRS	—¹
(52137)	Red Wing Shoes Boot Oil Tank Car, *98*	—	50	—¹
52138	LCCA Airplane Orange, *98*	—	35	—¹
(52139)	Dept. 56 Square Window Caboose "6256," *97u*	—	70	—¹
(52140)	Artrain UP Bunk Car, *97 u*	—	100	—¹
(52141)	Zep Boxcar, *96*	—	75	—¹
52142	Mass Central Maxi-Stack Flatcar, *98u*	—	120	—¹
(52143)	TCA "City of Providence" Coach "1998," *98u*	—	140	—¹
(52144)	NLOE LIRR/Grumman TOFC Flatcar "8398," *98 u*	—	110	—¹
(52145)	Long Island RR "Jamaica" Coach "99831," *99u*	—	300	—¹
(52145)	Long Island RR "Penn Station" Coach "99832," *99u*	—	300	—¹
(52146)	Ocean Spray Plug Door Refrigerator Car "OSCX 1998," *98u*	—	130	—¹

(52147)	Frisco/Campbell 66 TOFC Flatcar, 98 _u_; "52148-558," 99 _u_	—	75	—1
(52148)	REA/Santa Fe Operating Boxcar "52148-558," 99_u_	—	70	—1
(52149)	TTOS Conrail Flatcar w/ Shovel, 98 _u_	—	45	—1
(52150)	Frisco/Campbell 66 TOFC Flatcar, 98 _u_	—	130	—1
(52151)	Amtrak Express Baggage Boxcar "71998" (Std. O), 98_u_	—	60	—1
(52152)	Ben Franklin Philadelphia Woodside Refrigerator Car, 98_u_	—	120	—1
52153	6414 Auto set (4-pack), 98		NRS	—1
(52154)	Pacific Fruit Express Refrigerator Car "459403" (Std. O), 98_u_	—	70	—1
(52155)	TCA "City of San Francisco" Baggage Car "1999," 99_u_	—	140	—1
(52157)	Holly Bros. 3-D Tank Car "6156," 98 _u_	—	75	—1
(52158)	Monopoly Mint Car "M-0539," 98	—	205	—1
(52159)	Monopoly Depressed Center Flatcar w/Transformer, 98	—	95	—1
(52160)	Monopoly Water Works Tank Car, 98	—	95	—1
(52161)	Monopoly SP-type Caboose "M-1006," 98	—	55	—1
(52162)	LOTS GM&O DD Boxcar "24580," 99 _u_	—	65	—1
(52163)	Milwaukee LRC Milwaukee Road DD Boxcar "194798," 99 _u_	—	60	—1
(52164)	SP Ore Car with Load, 98_u_	—	40	—1
(52165)	Artrain Square Window Caboose, "6256," 97_u_	—	75	—1
(52166)	NLOE LIRR/Northrop TOFC Flatcar "8399," 99 _u_	—	110	—1
(52167)	AT&SF Flatcar w/ Navajo trailer "83199," 99 _u_	—	70	—1
(52168)	Carail Flatcar with Trailer "17455," 99_u_	—	85	—1
(52169)	Zep Manufacturing Co. Flatcar with Trailer "62734," 99_u_		NRS	—1
(52170)	CLRC SP Operating Boxcar, 99 _u_	—	65	—1
(52171)	CLRC UP Operating Boxcar, 99 _u_	—	65	—1
(52172)	L&N Boxcar, 99 _u_	—	65	—1
52173	Long Island RR F3 AA Shells, 00		NRS	—1
(52174)	REA Baggage Car "0083," 00_u_		NRS	—1
(52175)	Dept. 56 4-6-4 Hudson, 99 _u_	—	440	—1
(52176)	Fort Worth & Denver Boxcar "8277," 99_u_	—	55	—1
(52177)	Arizona Southern RR Ore Car with Load, 99_u_	—	40	—1
(52178)	CLRC Burlington Route Operating Boxcar, 00 _u_	—	65	—1
(52179)	CLRC ACL Operating Boxcar, 00 _u_	—	65	—1
(52180)	Milwaukee Road Flatcar w/ trailer "194799," 99 _u_	—	70	—1
(52181)	Monopoly Set 2 (4-pack), 99	—	345	—1
(52182)	Monopoly Railroads Boxcar "M0636," 99 _u_	—	80	—1

		Exc	New	Cond/$
(52183)	Monopoly Jail Car "M-1131," 99	—	70	—1
(52184)	Monopoly Free Parking Flat w/2 Autos, 99	—	75	—1
(52185)	Monopoly Chance Gondola "M-0893," 99	—	60	—1
(52186)	Grucci Fireworks Boxcar "2000," 00u	—	75	—1
(52187)	Madison Hardware Flatcar w/2 Trailers "1909-1999," 99	—	80	—1
(52188)	Carail Aquarium w/2 Autos, 25th Anniversary, 99	—	70	—1
(52189)	Monopoly 4-6-4 Hudson Steam Locomotive "1999," 99	—	430	—1
(52190)	St. Louis LRC IC TOFC Flatcar, 00 u	—	80	—1
(52191)	TCA "City of Grand Rapids" Sleeper/Roomete "2000," 00u	—	135	—1
(52192)	TTOS SP Crane & Gondola 2-pack, 00 u	—	75	—1
(52193)	TTOS SP Crane, 00 u	—	50	—1
(52194)	TTOS SP Gondola, 00 u	—	35	—1
(52195)	LCCA CP Maxistack Flatcar "200030," 00 u	—	100	—1
(52196)	LOTS CP Maxistack Flatcar "524115," 00 u	—	90	—1
(52197)	Artrain GP38 "2380," 00 u	—	250	—1
(52198)	Frisco Boxcar "5477000," 00u	—	40	—1
52199	Real Plastic Snow 4-bay Hopper "6756," 00	NRS		—1
(52205)	SP Overnight Merchandise Service Boxcar 5-pack "6464-2000," 00u	—	200	—1
52206	LCCA SD40 w/ E/V Caboose "2000," 00 u	NRS		—1
52207	Lionel Lines SD40, Traditional, 00	—	600	—1
(52208)	Lionel Lines Extended Vision Caboose, 00u	—	200	—1
(52209)	World's Fair Sleeper/Roomette Car "0183," 01u	—	150	—1
52210	Rico Station, 00	—	30	—1
(52212)	Berkshire Brewing Reefer, 00 u	—	180	—1
(52213)	BHP Copper Ore Car, 00u	—	40	—1
(52215)	C&NW Cylindrical Hopper (Std. O), 01u	—	60	—1
(52216)	C&NW Cylindrical Hopper (Std. O), 02u	—	60	—1
52217	LCCA/LOTS 2000 Convention Billboard, 00	—	10	—1
(52218)	Monopoly 4-4-2 Steam Freight set, 00 u	—	325	—1
(52219)	Monopoly 4-6-4 Bronze Hudson "2000," 00 u	—	530	—1
(52220)	TCA "City of Chattanooga" Vista Dome "2001," 01u	—	140	—1
(52221)	Norfolk Southern Boxcar "2001," 01u	—	50	—1
(52222)	SP Daylight Flatcar with Trailer, 01u	—	50	—1
52223	CLRC Santa Fe REA Operating Boxcar, 00 u	—	50	—1
52224B	SP Flatcar w/Trailer Flatcar Service tractor and Trailer, 01	—	25	—1
52224A	SP Flatcar w/ Navajo Tractor and Trailer, 01	—	25	—1
(52225)	Monopoly 4-6-4 Pewter Hudson "2001," 01 u	—	400	—1
(52226)	Angela Trotta Thomas Boxcar "2000," 01u	—	100	—1

		Exc	New	Cond/$
52227	Artrain Space Boxcar, *01 u*		NRS	—¹
(52228)	Milwaukee Road 1-Dome Tank Car, *00u*		NRS	—¹
(52229)	Milwaukee Road 1-Dome Tank Car, *00u*		NRS	—¹
(52230)	Milwaukee Road 1-Dome Tank Car 2-pack, *00u*		NRS	—¹
(52231)	British Columbia RR 1-Dome Tank Car, *00u*		NRS	—¹
(52232)	Central RR of Long Island Boxcar, *01u*		NRS	—¹
(52234)	WM F9 Well Car w/Transformer, *01u*	—	60	—¹
(52235)	World's Fair Vista-Dome Car "0283," *02u*		CP	—¹
(52236)	Moxie Boxcar, *01u*	—	180	—¹
52237	Lionel Gondola "2002" yellow, *01*	—	110	—¹
52238	Lionel Gondola "2002" red, *01*	—	110	—¹
52239	Lionel Gondola "2002" silver, *01*	—	110	—¹
52240	Lionel Gondola 3-pack "2002," *01*	—	110	—¹
52241	Lionel Gondola "2002" black, *02*		NRS	—¹
52242	Lionel Gondola "2002" blue, *02*	—	35	—¹
(52243)	National Toy Train Museum 1-Dome Tank Car "1954" (Std. O), *01u*	—	50	—¹
52244	Louisville & Nashville Horse Car, *01*		NRS	—¹
(52246)	Milwaukee Road 2-Door Boxcar "194701," *01u*		NRS	—¹
(52248)	Tombstone & Southern RR Ore Car, *01u*	—	40	—¹
(52249)	Knoebels Amusement Park 75th Anniversary Boxcar "9700," *01u*	—	80	—¹
(52250)	TCA "City of Chicago" Combo Car "2002," *02u*	—	130	—¹
(52251)	PRR Customized Mail/Cargo Car, *01u*	—	50	—¹
52253	San Pedro Boxcar, *02*		NRS	—¹
52254	Happy Holidays Gondola "6462-56," *01*		NRS	—¹
(52255)	Lionel Lines Artrain 30th Anniversary Flatcar with Billboard, *01*	—	100	—¹
(52256)	New York & Atlantic Ry. Boxcar "8302," *02u*	—	60	—¹
52257	Season's Greetings Gondola "4002," *01*		NRS	—¹
52258	UP Flatcar with UP tractor and trailer, *02*		NRS	—¹
(52259)	MP GP20 "28500," Traditional, *01u*		NRS	—¹
(52260)	LOTS Baltimore Aquarium Car, *01 u*	—	110	—¹
(52261)	Schlitz Beer/URT Refrigerator Car "92132," *02u*	—	60	—¹
52263	World's Fair Combine Car "0383," *02*		NRS	—¹
(52264)	Durango & Silverton Operating Hopper "9325," *02u*		CP	—¹
52265	Milwaukee Road/Zoological Society of Milwaukee Aquarium Car "4701," *02*	—	55	—¹
52266	PRR "Coal Goes to War" Hopper "707025," *02*	—	115	—¹
52267	PRR "Coal Goes to War" Hopper "707026," *02*	—	115	—¹
(52270)	Jenney Mfg. Co. Tank Car, *02u*	—	150	—¹
(52271)	National Toy Train Museum Wheel Car "1957," *02u*		CP	—¹
52272	Lionel Gondola "2002" Gold, *02*	—	80	—¹

		Exc	New	Cond/$
52273	LCCA Subcar, *02*	—	150	__1
52274	TCA "City of Los Angeles" RPO Car "2003" orange, *03*		NRS	__1
52276	California Gold Mint Car "2003," *03*	—	80	__1
52277	Carnegie Science Center 10th Anniversary Boxcar "9700," *02*	—	60	__1
52279	D&N Ore Care, *02*		NRS	__1
52280	LOTS Product Mint Car, *02*		NRS	__1
52281	LOTS PRR Operating Boxcar, *03*	—	60	__1
52282	Western Pacific Feather Boxcar (red) "2003," *03*		NRS	__1
52287	Minute Man Operating Boxcar, *03*		NRS	__1
52295	National Toy Train Museum Gondola w/ pipes, *03*		NRS	__1
52296	Flatcar w/tractor and tanker, *03*		NRS	__1
(52299)	UP Las Vegas Jackpot Security Transport "2003," *03 u*	—	100	__1
52306	NE Trans TOFC, *03*		NRS	__1
(62162)	Automatic Crossing Gate and Signal "262," *99-04*	—	34	__1
(62180)	Railroad Signs (14), *99-04*	—	4	__1
(62181)	Telephone Pole set "150," *99-04*	—	5	__1
(62283)	Die-cast illuminated bumpers "260," *99-04*	—	15	__1
(62709)	Rico Station kit, *99-00*	—	40	__1
(62716)	Short Extension Bridge, *99-03*	—	7	__1
(62900)	Lock-on, *99-04*		CP	__1
(62901)	Ives Track Clips (O-27) (12), *99-04*	—	5	__1
(62905)	Lock-on with Wires, *99-04*		CP	__1
(62909)	Smoke Fluid, *99-04*		CP	__1
(62927)	Lubrication/Maintenance Set, *99-04*	—	10	__1
(62985)	The Lionel Train Book, *99-03*	—	12	__1
(65014)	Half-Curved Track 27" (O27), *99-04*		CP	__1
(65019)	Half-Straight Track (O27), *99-04*		CP	__1
(65020)	90° Crossover (O27), *99-04*		CP	__1
(65021)	Left Manual Switch 27" (O27), *99-04*		CP	__1
(65022)	Right Manual Switch 27" (O27), *99-04*		CP	__1
(65023)	45° Crossover (O27), *99-04*		CP	__1
(65024)	Straight Track 35" (O27), *99-04*		CP	__1
(65033)	Curved Track 27" (O27), *99-04*		CP	__1
(65038)	Straight Track 9" (O27), *99-04*		CP	__1
(65041)	Insulator Pins (12) (O27), *99-04*		CP	__1
(65042)	Steel Pins (12) (O27), *99-04*		CP	__1
(65049)	Curved Track 42" (O27), *99-04*		CP	__1
(65113)	Curved Track 54" (O27), *99-04*		CP	__1
(65121)	Left Remote Switch 27" (O27), *99-04*		CP	__1
(65122)	Right Remote Switch 27" (O27), *99-04*		CP	__1

		Exc	New	Cond/$
(65149)	Remote Uncoupling Section (O27), *99-04*		CP	__1
(65165)	Right Remote Switch 72" (O), *99-04*		CP	__1
(65166)	Left Remote Switch 72" (O), *99-04*		CP	__1
(65167)	Right Remote Switch 72" (O27), *99-04*	—	15	__1
(65168)	Left Remote Switch 42" (O27), *99-04*	—	15	__1
(65500)	Straight Track 10" (O), *99-04*		CP	__1
(65501)	Curved Track 31" (O), *99-04*		CP	__1
(65504)	Half-Curved Track 31" (O), *99-04*		CP	__1
(65505)	Half-Straight Track (O), *99-04*		CP	__1
65514	Half Curved Track (O-27), *99-03*		CP	__1
(65523)	Straight Track 40" (O), *99-04*		CP	__1
(65530)	Remote Uncoupling Section (O), *99-04*		CP	__1
(65540)	90° Crossover (O), *99-04*		CP	__1
(65543)	Insulator Pins (12) (O), *99-04*		CP	__1
(65545)	45° Crossover (O), *99-04*		CP	__1
(65551)	Steel Pins (12) (O), *99-04*		CP	__1
(65554)	Curved Track 54" (O), *99-04*		CP	__1
(65572)	Curved Track 72" (O), *99-04*		CP	__1
[80948]	LOTS Michigan Central Boxcar, *82 u*	125	200	__1
(81024)	Christmas Train Set, *02-04*	—	150	__1
(81027)	Thomas the Tank Engine Set, *01-04*	—	120	__1
[86009]	LCAC CN Bunk Car, *86 u*	—	100	__1
[87010]	LCAC CN Express Reefer, *87 u*	—	100	__1
[88011]	LCAC CN Woodside Caboose (Std. O), *88 u*	—	440	__1
(99000)	Keebler Elf in Express Steam Freight, *99 u*	—	930	__1
(99001)	Mickey's Holiday Express Freight Set, *99u*	—	200	__1
(99002)	Looney Tunes Square Window Caboose, *99u*		NRS	__1
(99006)	Keebler Flatcar with Bulkheads, *99u*		NRS	__1
(99007)	Smuckers Fudge 1-D Tank Car, *99 u*	—	80	__1
(99008)	Mickey's Merry Christmas Boxcar "9700," *99u*		NRS	__1
(99009)	Mickey's Holiday Express S/W Caboose, *99u*		NRS	__1
(99013)	Case Cutlery Tank Car "1889," *00u*		NRS	__1
(99014)	Case Cutlery Gondola "1889," *00u*		NRS	__1
(99015)	Case Cutlery Boxcar "1889," *00u*		NRS	__1
(99018)	Case Cutlery Rolling Stock 3-pack, *00u*	—	200	__1
[121315]	LOTS PRR Hi-cube Boxcar, *84 u*	95	195	__1
[830005]	LCAC CN Boxcar, *83 u*		300	__1
[840006]	LCAC Canadian Wheat Board Covered Quad Hopper, *84 u*	—	125	__1
[900013]	LCAC CN Flatcar w/ trailers, *90 u*	—	205	__1
Not Assigned	Disney Mickey Millennium Steam Freight Set, *00 u*	—	375	__1
Not Assigned	NY Toy Fair Boxcar, *01 u*	—	70	__1
Not Assigned	NY Toy Fair Loco Puzzle, *01 u*		NRS	__1
Not Assigned	Pacific Fruit Express Reefer "459403," *98*		NRS	__1
Not Assigned	FEC Flatcar w/ Ertl dump truck "6434," *98*		NRS	__1

	Exc	New	Cond/$
Not Assigned Lionel Const. Depressed Flatcar w/ Ertl Uniloader "6461," *98*		NRS	—¹
Not Assigned Plasticville U.S.A. Boxcar "9741," *01u*	—	75	—¹
UCS Remote Control Track (O), *70*	4	7	—¹
[No Number] Pacific Northwest TCA F-3 AA, shells only, *74 u*	—	60	—¹
[No Number] LCCA Lionel Lines Tender only, *76-77 u*	22	26	—¹
[No Number] TCA Lone Star Texas Special F-3 A Unit, shell only, *81 u*		NRS	—¹
No Number L.A.S.E.R. Playmat, *81-82*	—	8	—¹
No Number Cannonball Freight Playmat, *81-82*	—	8	—¹
No Number Black Cave Flyer Playmat, *82*	—	8	—¹
[No Number] TCA Lone Star Texas Special F-3 B Unit, shell only, *82 u*		NRS	—¹
No Number Station Platform, *83-84*	—	8	—¹
No Number Rocky Mountain Platform, *83-84*	—	8	—¹
No Number Commando Assault Train Playmat, *83-84*	—	8	—¹
[No Number] TCA Sacramento-Sierra Lionel Lines Tender, shell only, *84 u*		NRS	—¹
No Number B&A Hudson and Standard O cars set, *86 u*	1500	1700	—¹
No Number The Blue Comet set, *78-80, 87 u*	560	620	—¹
No Number Burlington "Texas Zephyr" set, *80, 80 u*	980	1150	—¹
No Number Jersey Central set, *86*	345	370	—¹
No Number Chessie System Special set, *80, 86 u*	560	620	—¹
No Number Chicago & Alton Limited set, *81, 86 u*	560	620	—¹
No Number Favorite Food Freight set, *81-82*	245	325	—¹
No Number The General set, *77-80*	240	285	—¹
No Number Great Northern set (FARR #3), *81, 81 u*	620	690	—¹
No Number Illinois Central "City of New Orleans" set, *85, 87, 93*	790	940	—¹
No Number Joshua Lionel Cowen set, *80, 80 u, 82*	540	580	—¹
No Number Lionel Lines set, *82-84 u, 86, 86-87 u, 94-95*	530	620	—¹
No Number Mickey Mouse Express set, *77-78, 78 u*	980	1600	—¹
No Number The Mint set, *79 u, 80-83, 84 u, 86 u, 87, 91 u, 93*	—	900	—¹
No Number NYC "20th Century Limited" set, *83, 83 u, 95*	980	1150	—¹
No Number N&W "Powhatan Arrow" set, *81, 81 u, 82 u, 91 u*	1450	1700	—¹
No Number PRR set, *79-80, 79-80 u, 81 u, 83 u*	1200	1350	—¹
No Number PRR set (FARR #5), *84-85, 89 u*	600	660	—¹
No Number Rock Island & Peoria set, *80-82*	240	315	—¹
No Number Santa Fe set (FARR #1), *79, 79 u*	460	580	—¹
No Number Southern set (FARR #4), *83, 83 u*	620	690	—¹

	Exc	New	Cond/$
No Number Southern Crescent Limited set, *77-78, 87 u*	540	650	—1
No Number Southern Pacific Daylight Diesel set, *82-83, 82-83 u, 90 u*	2150	2300	—1
No Number The Spirit of '76 set, *74-76*	570	690	—1
No Number Toys "R" Us Thunderball Freight set, *75 u*		NRS	—1
No Number Union Pacific set (FARR #2), *80, 80 u*	540	580	—1
No Number Union Pacific "Overland Route" set, *84, 92 u*	770	840	—1
No Number Wabash set (FF #1), *86, 87*	720	870	—1
No Number Amtrak Passenger set, *89, 89 u*	640	770	—1
No Number Baltimore & Ohio set, *94, 96*		NRS	—1
No Number C&NW Passenger set, *93*	385	460	—1
No Number Chesapeake & Ohio set, *95-96*		NRS	—1
No Number D&RGW "California Zephyr" set, *92, 93*	—	900	—1
No Number Erie-Lackawanna Passenger set, *93, 94*	940	980	—1
No Number Erie set (FF #7), *93*	385	460	—1
No Number Frisco set (FF #5), *91*	405	425	—1
No Number Great Northern "Empire Builder" set, *92, 93*	620	730	—1
No Number Illinois Central "City of New Orleans" set, *85, 87, 93*	980	1150	—1
No Number Illinois Central set, *91-92, 95*	255	285	—1
No Number Lionel Lines Madison Car set, *91, 93*	560	620	—1
No Number The Mint set, *79 u, 80-83, 84 u, 86 u, 87, 91 u, 93*	940	1050	—1
No Number Milwaukee Road set (FF #2), *87, 90 u*	380	405	—1
No Number Missouri Pacific set, *95*	—	390	—1
No Number Norfolk & Western "Powhatan Arrow" Passenger set, *95*	370	445	—1
No Number Nickel Plate Road set (FF #6), *92*	385	460	—1
No Number New Haven set, *94-95*	—	400	—1
No Number Northern Pacific set, *90-92*	190	250	—1
No Number New York Central set, *89, 91*	240	270	—1
No Number Pennsylvania set, *87-90, 95*	240	270	—1
No Number Pere Marquette set, *93*	720	770	—1
No Number SP Daylight Steam set, *90, 92, 93*	790	940	—1
No Number Santa Fe "Super Chief" set, *91, 91 u, 92 u, 93, 95*	1400	1700	—1
No Number Union Pacific set, *94*	430	500	—1
No Number Wabash set (FF #1), *86, 87*	790	940	—1
No Number Western Maryland set (FF #4), *89*	345	405	—1

Section 4
MODERN TINPLATE

O GAUGE CLASSICS

1-263E	Lionel Lines "Blue Comet" 2-4-2 (See 51004)		
44E	(See 51100)		
350E	Lionel Lines "Hiawatha" 4-4-2 (See 51000)		
882	Lionel Lines Combition Car (See 51000)		
883	Lionel Lines Passenger Car (See 51000)		
884	Lionel Lines Observation Car (See 51000)		
892	(See 51202)		
893	(See 51203)		
894	(See 51204)		
895	(See 51205)		
1612	Lionel Lines Passenger Car (See 51004)		
1613	Lionel Lines Passenger Car (See 51004)		
1614	Lionel Lines Baggage Car (See 51004)		
1615	Lionel Lines Observation Car (See 51004)		
8814	(See 51400)		
8816	(See 51500)		
8817	(See 51700)		
8820	(See 51800)		
(51000)	Milwaukee Road "Hiawatha" set, *88 u*	900	__2
(51001)	Lionel #44 Freight Special set, *89*	770	__1
(51004)	Blue Comet set, *91*	1500	__1
(51100)	Lionel Lines Electric "44E" (See 51001), *89*		
(51201)	Rail Chief Passenger Cars, set of 4, *90*	500	__2
(51202)	Lionel Lines Combition Car "892" (See 51201)		
(51203)	Lionel Lines Passenger Car "893" (See 51201)		
(51204)	Lionel Lines Passenger Car "894" (See 51201)		
(51205)	Lionel Lines Observation Car "895" (See 51201)		
(51400)	Lionel Lines Boxcar "8814" (See 51001), *89*		
(51500)	Lionel Lines Hopper "8816" (See 51001), *89*		
(51700)	Lionel Lines Caboose "8817" (See 51001), *89*		
(51800)	Lionel Lines Searchlight Car "8820" (See 51001), *89*		

STANDARD GAUGE CLASSICS

1-44	(See 13805)
1-214	(See 13605)
1-215	(See 13303,
1-318E	Lionel Lines Electric (See 13001)
1-381E	(See 13102)

1-384E	(See 13101)
1-390E	(See 13100)
1-400E	(See 13103)
1-408E	(See 13107)
1-4390	American Flyer "West Point" Baggage Car (See 13003)
1-4391	American Flyer "Academy" Passenger Car (See 13003)
1-4392	American Flyer "Army/vy" Observation Car (See 13003)
1-4689	(See 13109)
2-390E	(See 13106)
2-400E	(See 13108)
7E	(See 13104)
8	(See 13803)
9	(See 13803)
126	(See 13801)
183	(See 13413)
184	(See 13414)
185	(See 13415)
200	(See 13900)
201	(See 13901)
323	(See 13400)
324	(See 13401)
325	(See 13402)
326	(See 13416)
327	(See 13417)
328	(See 13418)
437	(See 13804)
1115	(See 13800)
1217	(See 13702)
1412	(See 13404)
1413	(See 13405)
1414	(See 13407)
1416	(See 13406)
1420	(See 13409)
1421	(See 13410)
1422	(See 13411)
1423	(See 13425)
1512	(See 13300)
1513	(See 13600)
1517	(See 13700)
1520	(See 13200)
2412	(See 13421)
2413	(See 13422)
2414	(See 13423)
2416	(See 13424)

4400C	(See 51900)		
5130	Lionel Lines Flatcar w/ lumber (See 13001)		
5140	Lionel Lines Reefer (See 13001)		
5150	Lionel Lines "Shell" Tank Car (See 13001)		
5160	Lionel Lines Caboose (See 13001)		
(13001)	1-318E Freight Express Train set, *90-91*	960	—1
(13002)	Fireball Express set, *90 u*	1600	—1
(13003)	American Flyer "Mayflower" Passenger Car set, *92*	2000	—1
(13004)	Milwaukee Road Hiawatha Passenger Set, *01-02*	1900	—
(13008)	NYC CommodoreVanderbilt Passenger Set, *02*	1500	—
(13100)	Lionel Lines 2-4-2 "1-390E," *88 u*	610	—1
(13101)	Lionel Lines 2-4-0 "1-384E," *89 u*	650	—1
(13102)	Lionel Lines Electric "1-381E," *89 u*	880	—1
(13103)	Lionel Lines "Blue Comet" 4-4-4 "1-400E," *90*	1200	—1
(13104)	Lionel Lines "Old #7" 4-4-0 "7E," *90*	850	—1
(13106)	Lionel Lines "Fireball Express" 2-4-2 "2-390E" (See 13002)		
(13107)	Lionel Lines Electric "1-408E," *91*	880	—1
(13108)	Lionel Lines 4-4-4 "2-400E," *91*	1100	—1
(13109)	American Flyer "Mayflower" Elec. "1-4689," *92*	2500	—1
(13200)	Lionel Lines Searchlight Car "1520," *89 u*	110	—1
(13300)	Lionel Lines Gondola "1512," *89 u*	75	—1
(13303)	Lionel Lines Sunoco Tank Car "1-215," *92*	135	—1
(13400)	Lionel Lines Baggage Car "323," *88 u*	155	—1
(13401)	Lionel Lines Passenger Car "324," *88 u*	135	—1
(13402)	Lionel Lines Observation Car "325," *88 u*	135	—1
(13403)	Lionel Lines State Passenger Car set, *89 u*	1100	—1
(13404)	Lionel Lines "California" Passenger Car "1412" (See 13403)		
(13405)	Lionel Lines "Colorado" Passenger Car "1413" (See 13403)		
(13406)	Lionel Lines "New York" Observation Car "1416" (See 13403)		
(13407)	Lionel Lines "Illinois" Passenger Car "1414," *90*	450	—1
(13408)	Lionel Lines "Blue Comet" Passenger Car set, *90*	1500	—1
(13409)	Lionel Lines "Faye" Passenger Car "1420" (See 13408),		
(13410)	Lionel Lines "Westphal" Passenger Car "1421" (See 13408),		
(13411)	Lionel Lines "Tempel" Observation Car "1422" (See 13408)		
(13412)	Lionel Lines "Old #7" Passenger Car set, *90*	800	—1
(13413)	Lionel Lines Combition Car "183" (See 13412)		

		Exc	New Cond/\$
(13414)	Lionel Lines Passenger Car "184" (See 13412)		
(13415)	Lionel Lines Observation Car "185" (See 13412)		
(13416)	Lionel Lines "New Jersey" Baggage Car "326"" (See 13002)		
(13417)	Lionel Lines "Connecticut" Passenger Car "327" (See 13002)		
(13418)	Lionel Lines "New York" Observation Car "328" (See 13002)		
(13420)	Lionel Lines State Passenger Car set, *91*	1300	—[1]
(13421)	Lionel Lines "California" Passenger Car "2412" (See 13420)		
(13422)	Lionel Lines "Colorado" Passenger Car "2413" (See 13420)		
(13423)	Lionel Lines "Illinois" Passenger Car "2414," *92 u*	450	—[1]
(13424)	Lionel Lines "New York" Observation Car "2416" (See 13420)		
(13425)	Lionel Lines "Barrd" Passenger Car "1423," *91 u*	1500	—[1]
(13600)	Lionel Lines Cattle Car "1513," *89 u*	90	—[1]
13601	Season's Greetings Boxcar, *89 u*	105	—[1]
13602	Season's Greetings Boxcar, *90 u*	100	—[1]
13604	Season's Greetings Boxcar, *91 u*	110	—[1]
(13605)	Lionel Lines Boxcar "1-214," *92*	155	—[1]
(13700)	Lionel Lines Caboose "1517," *89 u*	105	—[1]
(13702)	Lionel Lines Caboose "1217," *91*	115	—[1]
(13800)	Lionelville Passenger Station "1115," *88 u*	390	—[1]
(13801)	Lionelville Station "126," *89 u*	290	—[1]
(13802)	Lionel Rubout Boat, *90*	400	—[1]
13803	Lionel Racing Automobiles "8" and "9," *91*	770	—[1]
(13804)	Lionelville Switch Tower "437," *91*	400	—[1]
(13805)	Lionel Racing Boat "1-44," *91*	410	—[1]
13807	Racing Automobiles Straight Track, *91 u*	NRS	
(13808)	Racing Automobiles Inner Radius Curve Track, *91 u*	NRS	
(13809)	Racing Automobiles Outer Radius Curve Track, *91 u*	NRS	
13900	Electric Rapid Transit Trolley "200," *89 u*	290	—[1]
13901	Electric Rapid Transit Trolley Trailer "201," *89 u*	150	—[1]
(51900)	Sigl Bridge and Control Panel "4400C," *89 u*	399	—[1]

Section 5
LARGE SCALE

(See 85120)
(See 85115)
(See 85117)
(See 85121)
(See 85122)
(See 85100)
(See 85101, 85124)
(See 85112)
(See 87400)
(See 87401)
(See 87404)
(See 85006)
(See 85007)
(See 87700)
(See 87701, 87724)
(See 87709)
(See 85008, 87712)
(See 85013)
(See 85003)
(See 85005)
(See 55000, 85000)
(See 85001)
(See 85102)
(See 85103)
(See 85104)
(See 85105)
(See 85106)
(See 85107)
(See 85108)
(See 85109)
(See 85110)
(See 85111)
(See 85113)
(See 85114)
(See 86000)
(See 86001)
(See 86002)
(See 86003)
(See 86004)
(See 86005)
(See 87402)

		Exc	New	Cond/$
(See 87403)				
(See 87405)				
(See 87406)				
(See 87407)				
(See 87500)				
(See 87501)				
(See 87502)				
(See 87503)				
(See 87504)				
(See 87508)				
(See 87702)				
(See 87703)				
(See 87704)				
(See 87705)				
(See 87706)				
(See 87707)				
(See 87708)				
(See 87711)				
(See 87713)				
(See 87716)				
(See 87800)				
(See 87806)				
(See 87808)				
(55000)	Lionel Lines RailScope 0-4-0T "5000," *88-90*	150	230	___
(81000)	Gold Rush Special set, *87-90*		160	___
(81001)	Thunder Mountain Express set, *88-89*		200	___
(81002)	Frontier Freight set, *88-89*		175	___
(81003)	Great Northern set, *90*		NM	___
(81004)	North Pole Railroad set, *89-91*		165	___
(81006)	Union Pacific Limited set, *90-91*	100	220	___
(81007)	Disney Magic Express set, *90*		250	___
(81008)	Walt Disney World set, *92*		NM	___
(81011)	Thomas the Tank Engine set, *93 u*	110	130	___
(81014)	James and Troublesome Trucks set, *94-95*	85	130	___
(81016)	Thomas the Tank Engine Deluxe set, *94-95*		180	___
(81017)	Ornament Express set, *94-95*		150	___
(81019)	Christmas Train Set, *98-01*		150	___
(81024)	Silver Bell Express Christmas Train Set, *02-04*		150	___
(81027)	Thomas the Tank Engine Set, *01-03*		120	___
(81050)	Gold Rush Special set w/ mailer, *87 u*		NRS	___
(81051)	Spiegel PRR set, *87 u*		NRS	___
(81054)	Gold Rush Special set w/o transformer, *90 u*		NRS	___
(81057)	North Pole Railroad set w/ mailer, *90 u*		NRS	___
(81059)	JCPenney Thomas the Tank Engine set, *94 u*	125	150	___

(81061)	Thomas the Tank Engine set, *95*	130	___
(81064)	Gold Rush Set, *99*	NM	___
(82000)	Straight Track, *87-96, 02-04*	CP	___
(82001)	Curved Track (4.3' diameter), *87-96, 02-04*	CP	___
(82002)	Straight Track, box of 4, *87-96*	9	___
(82003)	Curved Track 4.3', box of 4, *87-96*	9	___
(82004)	Curved Track, (5.3'), *88-04*	CP	___
(82006)	35" Straight Track, *88-96*	12	___
(82007)	Right-hand Remote Switch, *89-03*	CP	___
(82008)	Left-hand Remote Switch, *89-03*	CP	___
(82010)	Thomas Track Pack, *94-95*	40	___
(82011)	Thomas Left Manual Switch, *94-95*	18	___
(82012)	Thomas Right Manual Switch, *94-95*	18	___
(82013)	Thomas Curved Track 4.3', box of 4, *94-95*	9	___
(82014)	Thomas Straight Track, box of 4, *94-95*	9	___
(82015)	Right Manual Switch, *95-96*	18	___
(82016)	Left Manual Switch, *95-96*	18	___
(82101)	Lockon w/ wires, *88-96, 02-04*	CP	___
(82102)	Conversion Rail Joiners (6), *88-96*	3	___
(82103)	Conversion Knuckle Couplers (2), *88-91*	5	___
(82104)	Water Tower kit, *88-89*	50	___
(82105)	Engine House kit, *88-89*	125	___
(82106)	Watchman Shanty kit, *88-89*	65	___
(82107)	Passenger and Freight Station kit, *88-89*	100	___
(82108)	Manual Uncoupler, *88-96*	5	___
(82109)	Brass Pins (12), *88-96*	5	___
(82110)	Lumber Shed kit, *89*	65	___
(82111)	Freight Platform kit, *89*	90	___
(82112)	Figure set (6), *89-96*	9	___
(82115)	RailSounds Control Box, *90-95*	20	___
(82115)	Wooden Vehicle Assortment, *89*	NM	___
(82116)	DC Converter Box, *91 u, 92-96*	40	___
(82116)	1936 Ford Pickup, *89*	NM	___
(82117)	Crossing Gate and Signal, *91*	NM	___
(82117)	1928 Ford Model A Coupe, *89*	NM	___
(82118)	1936 Ford "Woody" Station Wagon, *89*	NM	___
(82120)	Thomas Sound System, *94-95*	5	___
(82121)	Thomas Play Pack, *94-95*	60	___
(82121)	Thomas Play Pack, *94-95*	60	___
(82122)	Thomas Building Pack, *94-95*	27	___
(82122)	Thomas Building Pack, *94-95*	27	___
(85000)	Seaboard System GP-9 "5000," *90-91*	315	___
(85000)	Seaboard System GP-9 "5000," *90-91*	315	___
(85001)	Conrail GP-7 "5001," *90-91*	315	___

		Exc	New	Cond/$
(85001)	Conrail GP-7 "5001," *90-91*		315	___
(85003)	BN GP-20 "2003," *91 u, 92-94*		365	___
(85003)	BN GP-20 "2003," *91 u, 92-94*		365	___
(85005)	BN GP-20 Dummy "2004," *92-94*		225	___
(85006)	Union Pacific GP-20 "485," *93-95*		265	___
(85007)	Union Pacific GP-20 Dummy "486," *93-95*		235	___
(85008)	Santa Fe GP-9 "712," *95*		NM	___
(85013)	Santa Fe GP-9 Dummy "722," *95*		NM	___
(85014)	Pennsylvania GP-9 Diesel, "7151," *98*		375	___
(85015)	Milwaukee Road GP-20 Diesel, "971," *98*		375	___
(85100)	Pennsylvania 0-6-0T "100," *87*		110	___
(85101)	D&RG 0-6-0T "101," *87-90*		100	___
(85102)	New York Central 4-4-2 "5102," *88*	150	200	___
(85103)	Santa Fe 4-4-2 "5103," *88*		200	___
(85104)	Santa Fe 0-4-0T "5104," *88-89*		90	___
(85105)	Pennsylvania 0-4-0T "5105," *88-89*		90	___
(85106)	Chessie System 4-4-2 "5106," *89*		190	___
(85107)	Great Northern 4-4-2 "5107," *89*		200	___
(85108)	B&O 0-4-0T "5108," *89*		95	___
(85109)	Canadian Pacific 0-6-0T "5109," *89*		100	___
(85110)	PRR 4-4-2 "5110," *90, 94-95*	160	350	___
(85111)	Great Northern 0-4-0T "5111," *90*		NM	___
(85112)	RI&P 0-6-0T "112," *90*		NM	___
(85113)	Union Pacific 0-4-0T "5113," *90-91*		100	___
(85114)	North Pole Railroad 0-4-0T "5114," *89-91*		105	___
(85115)	Disneyland 0-6-0T "3," *90*		110	___
(85117)	Disney World 0-6-0T "4," *91*		NM	___
(85120)	Thomas the Tank Engine 0-6-0T "1," *93 u, 94-95*		65	___
(85121)	James the Red Engine 2-6-0 "5," *94-95*		80	___
(85122)	Ornament Express 0-6-0T "8," *94-95*		75	___
(85124)	D&RG 0-6-0T "101," *95*		40	___
(86000)	PRR Passenger Car "6000," *88-89*		65	___
(86001)	PRR Observation Car "6001," *88-89*		65	___
(86002)	Union Pacific Passenger Car "6002," *90-91*		65	___
(86003)	Union Pacific Observation Car "6003," *90-91*		65	___
(86004)	Disney World Passenger Car "6004," *91*		NM	___
(86005)	Disney World Observation Car "6005," *91*		NM	___
(86006)	"Annie" Passenger Car, *93 u, 94-95*		55	___
(86007)	"Clarabel" Passenger Car, *93 u, 94-95*		55	___
87000	New York Central Boxcar, *89*		45	___
87001	Pennsylvania Boxcar, *88*		45	___
87002	Santa Fe Boxcar, *88*		45	___
87003	Great Northern Boxcar, *89*		45	___
87004	Southern Boxcar, *90*		50	___

		Exc New	Cond/$
87005	Northern Pacific Boxcar, *90*	50	__
87006	Christmas Boxcar, *89 u*	75	__
87007	Christmas Boxcar, *90 u*	80	__
87009	Western Pacific Boxcar, *91*	50	__
87013	Christmas Boxcar, *95*	35	__
(87015)	Christmas Boxcar, *96*	45	__
(87016)	Union Pacific Boxcar, "507406," *98*	45	__
(87017)	Large Scale Christmas Boxcar, "9700," *98*	45	__
(87018)	Large Scale Christmas Boxcar "7001," *00*	40	__
(87021)	Happy Holidays 1999 Boxcar "7001," *99*	40	__
(87022)	Christmas Boxcar, *01*	40	__
(87023)	2002 Large Scale Christmas Boxcar, *02*	40	__
87024	2003 Large Scale Christmas Boxcar, *03*	40	__
87025	2004 Christmas Boxcar, *04*	CP	__
87100	Union Pacific PFE Reefer, *88*	50	__
87101	Pennsylvania Reefer, *88*	50	__
87102	Chesapeake & Ohio Reefer, *89*	50	__
87103	Tropicana Reefer, *90*	55	__
87104	Gerber Reefer, *90*	55	__
87105	Seaboard Reefer, *89*	50	__
87107	A&P Reefer, *91*	60	__
87108	Pacific Fruit Express Reefer, *95*	35	__
87018	Large Scale Christmas Boxcar, *00*	40	__
87109	Santa Fe Reefer, *95*	35	__
(87110)	Pennsylvania Reefer, "91910," *98*	40	__
(87111)	NYC Refrigerator Car "78903," *99*	44	__
87200	Buford and Roscoe Handcar, *89-90*	70	__
87201	Milwaukee Road Ore Car, *89*	35	__
87202	Chessie System Ore Car, *89*	35	__
87203	Santa and Snowman Handcar, *90*	85	__
87204	Northern Pacific Ore Car, *90*	40	__
87205	Pennsylvania Ore Car, *90*	40	__
87207	Mickey & Donald Handcar, *91, 95*	75	__
87208	Wile E. Coyote & Roadrunner Handcar, *92*	100	__
87210	Santa Fe Ore Car, *95*	40	__
(87212)	Santa and Snowman Handcar, "Tinsel Town," *99*	50	__
(87214)	Ontario Northland Ore Car "6071," *99*	44	__
87216	Mickey Mouse and Goofy Handcar, *03*	75	__
(87400)	PRR Gondola "400," *87*	35	__
(87401)	D&RG Gondola "401," *87-90*	30	__
(87402)	Santa Fe Gondola "7402," *88*	35	__
(87403)	New York Central Gondola "7403," *88*	35	__
(87404)	Disneyland Gondola "404," *90*	40	__
(87405)	Chessie System Gondola "7405," *89*	35	__

		Exc New	Cond/$
(87406)	Southern Gondola "7406," *89*	35	
(87407)	MKT Gondola "7407," *90*	40	
(87410)	Ornament Express Gondola w/ ornaments, *94-95*	NRS	
(87411)	"Troublesome Trucks" Gondola, *94-95*	23	
(87500)	D&RG Flatcar "7500," *88*	35	
(87501)	Pennsylvania Flatcar "7501," *88*	35	
(87502)	Santa Fe Flatcar "7502," *88-89*	30	
(87503)	ICG Flatcar "7503," *89*	30	
(87504)	Union Pacific Flatcar "7504," *89*	30	
87505	Soo Line Flatcar w/ logs, *90*	45	
87507	Great Northern Flatcar, *90*	NM	
(87508)	Merry Christmas Lines Flatcar, *89-91*	35	
87600	Alaska Tank Car, *89*	55	
87601	Santa Fe Tank Car, *89*	50	
87602	Gulf Tank Car, *90*	55	
87603	Borden Tank Car, *90*	55	
87604	Shell Tank Car, *91*	65	
87612	Santa Fe Tank Car, *95*	40	
(87614)	GATX Tank Train SD Tank Car "44589," *99*	44	
(87700)	Pennsylvania Caboose "700," *87*	50	
(87701)	D&RG Caboose "701," *87-90*	50	
(87702)	Santa Fe Caboose "7702," *88*	45	
(87703)	New York Central Caboose "7703," *88*	45	
(87704)	Santa Fe Bobber Caboose "7704," *88-89*	40	
(87705)	Great Northern Caboose "7705," *89*	50	
(87706)	Chessie System Caboose "7706," *89*	50	
(87707)	B&O Bobber Caboose "7707," *89*	40	
(87708)	Canadian Pacific Bobber Caboose "7708," *89*	45	
(87709)	Disneyland Caboose "709," *90*	50	
(87010)	CN LCAC Reefer, *96*	150	
(87711)	Great Northern Bobber Caboose "7711," *90*	NM	
(87712)	RI&P Caboose "712," *90*	NM	
(87713)	Pennsylvania Caboose "7713," *90*	50	
(87716)	North Pole Railroad Bobber Caboose "7716," *89-91*	45	
(87722)	Ornament Express Bobber Caboose, *94-95*	NRS	
(87724)	D&RG Caboose "701," *95*	20	
(87800)	NYC Searchlight Car "7800," *89-90*	85	
87802	Conrail Boxcar w/ ETD, *90-91*	70	
87803	Seaboard Boxcar w/ ETD, *90-91*	70	
(87806)	REA Boxcar w/ Steam RailSounds, *91*	NM	
87808	Union Pacific Searchlight Car "7808," *95*	70	
87809	Railbox Boxcar, *95*	45	

Section 6
UNCATALOGED CLUB CARS AND SPECIAL PRODUCTION

ARTRAIN

___	**9486**	GTW "I Love Michigan" Boxcar, *87*
___	**17885**	Artrain 1-D Tank Car, *90*
___	**17891**	Grand Trunk Boxcar, *91*
___	**19425**	Artrain 25th Anniversary CSX Flatcar w/ trailer, *97*
___	**52013**	Norfolk Southern Flatcar w/ trailer (Std O), *92*
___	**52024**	Conrail Auto Carrier, *93*
___	**52049**	Burlington Northern Gondola w/ coil covers, *94*
___	**52097**	Chessie System Reefer, *95*
___	**52140**	Union Pacific Bunk Car, *97*
___	**(52165)**	SP Caboose "6256," *97*
___	**(52197)**	Santa Fe GP38 Diesel Locomotive, *00*
___	**(52227)**	Artrain Space Boxcar, *01 u*
___	**(52255)**	Lionel Lines Artrain USA 30th Anniversary Flatcar w/ Billboard, *01*

CARNEGIE SCIENCE CENTER

___	**(26750)**	Great Miniature Railroad and Village Boxcar "9700," *99*
___	**(36202)**	Great Miniature Railroad and Village 80th Anniversary Boxcar "9700," *00*
___	**(36234)**	Great Miniature Railroad and Village Boxcar "9700," *01*
___	**(52277)**	Carnegie Science Center 10th Anniversary Boxcar "9700," *02*

CHICAGOLAND RAILROAD CLUB

___	**(52081)**	C&NW Boxcar "6464555," *96*
___	**(52101)**	BN Maxi-Stack Flatcar w/ containers "64287," *97*
___	**(52102)**	Santa Fe E/V Caboose "999556" w/ black roof, *96*
___	**(52103)**	Santa Fe E/V Caboose "999758" w/ red roof, *96*
___	**(52120)**	Shedd Aquarium Car "3435-557," *98*
___	**(52148)**	REA/Santa Fe Boxcar "52148-558," *99*
___	**(52170)**	SP Operating Boxcar "52170-561," *99*
___	**(52171)**	UP Operating Boxcar "52171-561," *99*
___	**(52171)**	UP Operating Boxcar "52171-561," *99*

UNCATALOGED CLUB CARS AND SPECIAL PRODUCTION

___	**(52178)**	Burlington Operating Boxcar "52178-559," *00*
___	**(52178)**	Burlington Operating Boxcar "52178-559," *00*
___	**(52179)**	ACL Operating Boxcar "52179-500," *00*
___	**(52179)**	ACL Operating Boxcar "52179-500," *00*
___	**(52215)**	CLRC CNW 3-Bay Cyl. Hopper, *01 u*
___	**(52215)**	CLRC CNW 3-Bay Cyl. Hopper, *01 u*
___	**(52216)**	C&NW Cylindrical Hopper (Std. O), *02*
___	**(52216)**	C&NW Cylindrical Hopper (Std. O), *02*
___	**(52223)**	CLRC Santa Fe REA Operating Boxcar, *00 u*
___	**(52223)**	CLRC Santa Fe REA Operating Boxcar, *00 u*
___	**(52251)**	PRR Customized Mail/Cargo Car, *01*
___	**(52259)**	MP GP20 "28500," Traditional, *01*
___	**52282**	Western Pacific Feather Boxcar (red) "2003," *03*
___	**(52287)**	Minute Man Operating Boxcar, *03*
___	**(52299)**	UP Las Vegas Jackpot Security Transport "2003," *03*
___	**52309**	Patriotic Tank Car, *03*
___	**52352**	Poland Spring Boxcar, *04*
___	**Not Assigned** CLRC MILW Fuel SD Tank Car "907797," *01 u*	
___	**Not Assigned** CLRC MILW Water SD Tank Car "908309," *01 u*	

CLASSIC TOY TRAINS

___	**(52126)**	MILW Boxcar w/ CTT Logo "21027," *97*

DEPT. 56

___	**(16270)**	Heritage Village Boxcar, *98*
___	**(52096)**	Snow Village Boxcar "9756," *95*
___	**(52139)**	Dept. 56 Square Window Caboose "6256," *97*
___	**(52157)**	Dept. 56 Holly Brothers 3D Tank Car, *98 u*
___	**(52175)**	4-6-4 Hudson "NO. 56" Steam Locomotive, CC, *99*
___	**(52199)**	Real Plastic Snow 4-Bay Hopper "6756," *00*
___	**(52273)**	LCCA Flatcar w/ Sub, *02*

EASTWOOD AUTOMOBILIA

___	**(16275)**	Eastwood Radio Flyer Boxcar "16275," *96*
___	**(16757)**	Johnny Lightning Auto Carrier "3435," *96*
___	**[16985]**	Eastwood Flatcar w/ 2 Ford Vans, *97*
___	**(26002)**	Monopoly Flatcar with Airplane, *00*
___	**(26554)**	Monopoly Short Line Square Window Caboose, *00*
___	**(36227)**	Monopoly Community Chest Boxcar, *00*
___	**(52044)**	Eastwood Vat Car, *95*
___	**(52083)**	Eastwood PRR Flat w/ tanker, "21697," *95 u*

UNCATALOGED CLUB CARS AND SPECIAL PRODUCTION

___	**(52130)**	Eastwood Hot Wheels TOFC w/Tank Trailer, *97*
___	**(52158)**	Monopoly Mint Car "M0539," *98*
___	**(52181)**	Monopoly Rolling Stock 4-pack, *99*
___	**(52182)**	Monopoly Railroads Boxcar "M0636," *99*
___	**(52183)**	Monopoly Railroads Jail Car "M1131," *99*
___	**(52184)**	Monopoly Railroads Flatcar with Autos, *99*
___	**(52185)**	Monopoly Railroads Gondola "M0893," *99*
___	**(52218)**	Monopoly Railroads Steam Freight Set, *00*

HOUSTON TINPLATE OPERATORS SOCIETY (HTOS)

___	**(8901)**	Miracle Petroleum 1-Dome Tank Car, *01*
___	**(8999)**	Lone Star Aquarium Car, *99*
___	**Not Assigned**	Sam Houston Mint Car "8901," *00*

INLAND EMPIRE TRAIN COLLECTORS ASSOC. (IETCA)

___	**[1979]**	IETCA Boxcar, *79*
___	**[1980]**	IETCA SP-type Caboose, *80*
___	**[1981]**	IETCA Quad Hopper, *81*
___	**[1982]**	IETCA 3-D Tank Car, *82*
___	**[1983]**	IETCA Reefer, *83*
___	**[1986]**	IETCA Bunk Car, *86*
___	**[7518]**	IETCA Carson City Mint Car, *84*

LIONEL CENTRAL OPERATING LINES (LCOL)

___	**[1981]**	LCOL Boxcar, *81*
___	**[1986]**	LCOL Work Caboose, shell only, *86*
___	**[5724]**	Pennsylvania Bunk Car, *84*
___	**[6508]**	Canadian Pacific Crane Car, *83*
___	**[9184]**	Erie B/W Caboose, *82*
___	**[9475]**	D&H "I Love NY" Boxcar, *85*

LIONEL COLLECTORS ASSOCIATION OF CANADA (LCAC)

___	**[5710]**	Canadian Pacific Reefer, *83*
___	**[5714]**	Michigan Central Reefer, *85*
___	**[6100]**	Ontario Northland Covered Quad Hopper, *82*
___	**[8103]**	Toronto, Hamilton & Buffalo Boxcar, *81*
___	**[8204]**	Algoma Central Boxcar, *82*
___	**[8507]/[8508]**	Canadian National F3 AA, shells only, *85*
___	**[8912]**	Canada Southern Operating Hopper, *89*
___	**[9413]**	Napierville Junction Boxcar, *80*
___	**[9718]**	Canadian National Boxcar, *79*

UNCATALOGED CLUB CARS AND SPECIAL PRODUCTION

___	**[17893]**	BAOC 1-D Tank Car "914," *91*
___	**[52004]**	Algoma Central Gondola w/ coil covers "9215," *92*
___	**[52005]**	Canadian National F3 B Unit "9517," *93*
___	**[52006]**	Canadian Pacific Boxcar "930016" (Std O), *93*
___	**(52115)**	Wabash Lake Railway 2-Tier Auto Carrier "WL 9519," *98*
___	**(52125)**	Toronto, Hamilton & Buffalo Gondola 2-pack "2346-2354," *99*
___	**[86009]**	Canadian National Bunk Car, *86*
___	**[87010]**	Canadian National Express Reefer, *87*
___	**[88011]**	Canadian National Woodside Caboose (Std O), *88*
___	**[830005]**	Canadian National Boxcar, *83*
___	**[840006]**	Canadian Wheat Board Covered Quad Hopper, *84*
___	**[900013]**	Canadian National Flatcar w/ trailers, *90*

LIONEL COLLECTORS CLUB OF AMERICA (LCCA)

LCCA National Convention Cars

___	**6112**	Commonwealth Edison Quad Hopper w/ coal load, *83*
___	**6323**	Virginia Chemicals 1-D Tank Car, *86*
___	**(6567)**	Illinois Central Gulf Crane Car "100408," *85*
___	**7403**	LNAC Boxcar, *84*
___	**(8068)**	Rock Island GP20 "1980," *80*
___	**9118**	Corning Covered Quad Hopper, *74*
___	**9155**	Monsanto 1-D Tank Car, *75*
___	**9212**	Seaboard Coast Line Flatcar w/ trailers, *76*
___	**X9259**	Southern B/W Caboose, *77*
___	**9358**	Sands of Iowa Covered Quad Hopper, *80*
___	**9435**	Central of Georgia Boxcar, *81*
___	**9460**	D&TS DD Boxcar, *82*
___	**[9701]**	Baltimore & Ohio DD Boxcar, *72*
___	**9727**	TA&G Boxcar, *73*
___	**9728**	Union Pacific Stock Car, *78*
___	**9733**	Airco Boxcar w/ tank, *79*
___	**17870**	East Camden & Highland Boxcar (Std O), *87*
___	**17873**	Ashland Oil 3-D Tank Car, *88*
___	**17876**	Columbia, Newberry & Laurens Boxcar (Std O), *89*
___	**17880**	D&RGW Woodside Caboose (Std O), *90*
___	**17887**	Conrail Flatcar w/ Armstrong Tile trailer (Std O), *91*
___	**17888**	Conrail Flatcar w/ Ford New Holland trailer (Std O), *91*
___	**(17899)**	NASA Uni-body Tank Car "190" (Std O), *92*
___	**(18090)**	D&RGW 4-6-2 "1990," *90*
___	**(52023)**	D&TS 2-bay ACF Hopper "2601" (Std O), *93*
___	**(52038)**	Southern Hopper w/ coal load "360794" (Std O), *94*

UNCATALOGED CLUB CARS AND SPECIAL PRODUCTION

___	**(52074)**	Iowa Beef Packers Reefer "197095" (Std O), *95*
___	**(52090)**	Pere Marquette DD Boxcar "71996" (Std O), *96*
___	**(52107)**	LCCA On-Track Pick-Up Orange, *96 u*
___	**(52108)**	LCCA On-Track Van Blue, *96 u*
___	**(52110)**	CStPM&O Boxcar "71997" (Std O), *97*
___	**(52151)**	Amtrak Express Baggage Boxcar "71998" (Std O), *98*
___	**(52176)**	Fort Worth & Denver Boxcar "8277" (Std O), *99*
___	**(52195)**	CP Maxi-stack Flatcar "200030," *00 u*
___	**(52206)**	LCCA SD40 w/ E/V Caboose "2000," *00 u*
___	**(52244)**	Louisville & Nashville Horse Car "2001," *01*
___	**(52266)**	PRR "Coal Goes To War" Hopper "707025," *02*
___	**(52267)**	PRR "Coal Goes To War" Hopper "707026," *02*

LCCA Meet Specials

___	**[6014-900]**	Frisco Boxcar (O27), *75-76*
___	**6483**	Jersey Central SP-type Caboose, *82*
___	**[9016]**	Chessie System Hopper (O27), *79-80*
___	**[9036]**	Mobilgas 1-D Tank Car (O27), *78-79*
___	**[9142]**	Republic Steel Gondola w/ canisters, *77-78*
___	**[No Number]**	Lionel Lines Tender only, *76-77*

Other LCCA Production

___	**[9739]**	D&RGW Boxcar, *78*
___	**[9771]**	Norfolk & Western Boxcar, *77*
___	**(17895)**	LCCA Tractor, *91*
___	**(17896)**	Lancaster Lines Tractor, *91*
___	**(29232)**	Lenny the Lion Hi-Cube, signed by Lenny Dean, *99*
___	**(52025)**	Madison Hardware Tractor and Trailer, *93*
___	**(52039)**	"Track 29" Bumper, *94*
___	**(52055)**	SOVEX Tractor and Trailer, *94*
___	**(52056)**	Southern Tractor and Trailer "206502," *94*
___	**(52091)**	Lenox Tractor and Trailer, *95*
___	**(52092)**	Iowa Interstate Tractor and Trailer, *95*
___	**(52100)**	LCCA Station Platform, *98*
___	**(52100)**	Grand Rapids Station Platform, *96*
___	**(52152)**	Philadelphia Reefer, *98*
___	**(52153)**	6414 Auto Set (4-pack), *98*
___	**(52207)**	Lionel Lines SD40, Traditional, *00*
___	**(52257)**	Season's Greetings Gondola, *01*
___	**Not Assigned**	RJ Corman RR Boxcar "4002," *01*
___	**6464-2002**	Maddox Retirement Boxcar "02," *02*

UNCATALOGED CLUB CARS AND SPECIAL PRODUCTION

LIONEL KIDS CLUB (LKC)

___	**(19695)**	Western Union 1-Dome Tank Car, *03*
___	**(19773)**	LKC Barrel Ramp Car "6343," *99*
___	**(36769)**	Fourth of July Lighted Boxcar, *03*

LIONEL OPERATING TRAIN SOCIETY (LOTS)

LOTS National Convention Cars

___	**[303]**	Stauffer Chemical 1-D Tank Car, *85*
___	**[3764]**	Kahn Boxcar, *81*
___	**[6111]**	L&N Covered Quad Hopper, *83*
___	**[6211]**	C&O Gondola w/ canisters, *86*
___	**[9414]**	Cotton Belt Boxcar, *80*
___	**(16812)**	Grand Trunk 2-bay ACF Hopper "16812" (Std O), *96*
___	**(16813)**	Pennsylvania Power & Light Co. Hopper w/ coal load (Std O), *97*
___	**(17874)**	Milwaukee Road Log Dump Car "59629," *88*
___	**(17875)**	PHD Boxcar "1289," *89*
___	**(17882)**	B&O DD Boxcar w/ ETD "298011," *90*
___	**(17890)**	CSX Auto Carrier "151161," *91*
___	**(18890)**	Union Pacific RS-3 "8805," *90*
___	**(19960)**	Western Pacific Boxcar "1952" (Std O), *92*
___	**[38356]**	Dow Chemical 3-D Tank Car, *87*
___	**(52014)**	BN TTUX Flatcar set w/ N&W trailers "637500A/B," *93*
___	**(52041)**	BN TTUX Flatcar set w/ Conrail trailers "637500D/E," *94*
___	**(52067)**	Burlington Ice Car "50240," *95*
___	**(52135)**	AT&SF Reefer "22739," *98*
___	**(52162)**	GM&O DD Boxcar "24580," *99*
___	**[52196]**	CP Maxi-stack Flatcar w/2 Containers "524115," *00*
___	**(52234)**	WM F9 Well Car with Transformer, *01*
___	**(52261)**	Schlitz Beer/URT Refrigerator Car "92132," *02*
___	**[80948]**	Michigan Central Boxcar, *82*
___	**[121315]**	Pennsylvania Hi-cube Boxcar, *84*

Other LOTS Production

___	**[1223]**	Seattle & North Coast Hi-cube Boxcar, *86*
___	**(12958)**	LCCA/LOTS Banquet Water Tower, *00*
___	**(52042)**	BN TTUX Flatcar w/ Canadian National trailer "637500C," *94*
___	**(52048)**	Canadian National Tractor and Trailer "197993," *94*
___	**(52129)**	Lighted Billboard (Scranton), *97*
___	**(52217)**	LCCA/LOTS 2000 Convention Billboard, *00*
___	**(52260)**	National Aquarium in Baltimore Car "2001," *01*

UNCATALOGED CLUB CARS AND SPECIAL PRODUCTION

LIONEL CENTURY CLUB (LCC)

___	**(14532)**	LCC II PRR Sharknose AA Set, *00*
___	**(18053)**	Lionel Century Club Berkshire Steam Locomotive 2-8-4 "726," *97*
___	**(18057)**	Lionel Century Club Steam Locomotive 6-8-6 "671," *98*
___	**(18058)**	Lionel Century Club Hudson Steam Locomotive 4-6-4 "773," *97*
___	**(18135)**	Lionel Century Club NYC F-3 AA Diesel "2333," *97*
___	**(18178)**	Lionel Century Club NYC F-3 B-Unit, *99*
___	**(18314)**	Lionel Century Club PRR GG-1 "2332," *97*
___	**(18340)**	LCC II FM Demo Train Master Set, "TM-1," "TM-2" 00, *00*
___	**(28069)**	LCC II NYC 4-8-6 Niagara "6024" Steam Locomotive, CC, *00*
___	**(29204)**	Lionel Century Club Boxcar "1900-2000," *96*
___	**(29226)**	Lionel Century Club Berkshire Boxcar, *97*
___	**(29227)**	Lionel Century Club GG-1 Boxcar, *98*
___	**(29228)**	Lionel Century Club Turbine Boxcar "671," *99*
___	**(29248)**	Lionel Century Club F3 Boxcar "2333," *99*
___	**(38000)**	Lionel Century Club II NYC 4-6-4 Hudson Empire State Express Steam Locomotive, *00*
___	**(39215)**	Lionel Century Club II Niagara Boxcar, *01*
___	**(39217)**	Lionel Century Club 2 Boxcar, *00 u*
___	**(39218)**	Lionel Century Club 2 Gold Boxcar, *00 u*
___	**(39249)**	Christmas Boxcar, *03*
___	**(51007)**	Lionel Century Club 2 UP M-10000 Passenger Set, *00 u*

LIONEL RAILROADER CLUB (LRRC)

___	**0780**	LRRC Boxcar, *82*
___	**0781**	LRRC Flatcar w/ trailers, *83*
___	**0782**	LRRC 1-D Tank Car, *85*
___	**0784**	LRRC Covered Quad Hopper, *84*
___	**(12875)**	LRRC Tractor and Trailer, *94*
___	**(12921)**	LRRC Illuminated Station Platform, *95*
___	**16800**	LRRC Ore Car, *86*
___	**16801**	LRRC Bunk Car, *88*
___	**16802**	LRRC Tool Car, *89*
___	**16803**	LRRC Searchlight Car, *90*

UNCATALOGED CLUB CARS AND SPECIAL PRODUCTION

___	**16804**	LRRC B/W Caboose, *91*
___	**(18680)**	LRRC Countdown Hudson 4-6-4 "2000," *00*
___	**(18684)**	LRRC Pacific 4-6-2 "1999," *99*
___	**(18818)**	LRRC GP38-2 "1992," *92*
___	**(19437)**	LRRC Flatcar w/ Inside Track Trailer "1997," *97*
___	**(19473)**	LRRC Operating Log Dump Car "3351," *99*
___	**(19774)**	LRRC Caboose Porthole "1999," *99*
___	**(19775)**	LRRC Stock Car, *99*
___	**19924**	LRRC Boxcar, *93*
___	**19930**	LRRC Quad Hopper w/ coal load, *94*
___	**(19935)**	LRRC 1-D Tank Car "1995," *95*
___	**(19940)**	LRRC Vat Car, *96*
___	**(19953)**	LRRC Lionel Corporation Boxcar "6464-97," *97*
___	**(19965)**	LRRC Aquarium Car "3435," *99*
___	**(19966)**	LRRC Gondola "9820" (Std O), *98*
___	**(19978)**	LRRC Membership Kit, *99-00*
___	**(19991)**	LRRC Gold Member Boxcar, *00*
___	**(19992)**	LRRC Western Union Tool Car "3550," *00*
___	**(19994)**	Western Union Sleeping Car "1307," *01*
___	**(19995)**	LRRC 25th Anniversary Boxcar (Std. O), *01*
___	**(28062)**	LRRC Century 4-6-4 Hudson "2000," *00*
___	**(29200)**	LRRC Lionel Corporation Boxcar "9700," *96*

LIONEL RAILROAD CLUB—MILWAUKEE

___	**[52116]**	Milwaukee Road Flatcar w/ Tractor and Trailer "194797," *97*
___	**(52163)**	Milwaukee Road DD Boxcar "194798," *98*
___	**(52180)**	Milwaukee Road Flatcar w/Trailer "194799," *00*
___	**(52230)**	Milwaukee Road 1-Dome Tank Car 2-pack, *00*
___	**(52246)**	Milwaukee Road 2-Door Boxcar "194701," *01*
___	**(52265)**	Milwaukee Road/Zoological Society of Milwaukee Aquarium Car "4701," *02*

NASSAU LIONEL OPERATING ENGINEERS (NLOE)

___	**[8389]**	Long Island Boxcar, *89*
___	**[8390]**	Long Island Covered Quad Hopper, *90*
___	**[8391A]**	Long Island Bunk Car, *91*
___	**[8391B]**	Long Island Tool Car, *91*
___	**[8392]**	Long Island 1-D Tank Car, *92*
___	**[52007]**	Long Island RS-3 "1552," *93*

UNCATALOGED CLUB CARS AND SPECIAL PRODUCTION

___	**[52019]**	Long Island Boxcar "8393," *93*
___	**[52020]**	Long Island B/W Caboose "8393," *93*
___	**[52026]**	Long Island Flatcar w/ Grumman trailer "8394," *94*
___	**[52061]**	Long Island Stern's Pickle Products Vat Car "8395," *95*
___	**[52072]**	Grumman Tractor, *94*
___	**[52076]**	Long Island Observation Car "8396," *96*
___	**(52112)**	Long Island Full Vista Dome Aluminum Passenger Car "9783," *97*
___	**(52122)**	Meenan Oil 1-D Tank Car "8397" (Std O.), *97*
___	**(52123)**	Long Island Aluminum Diner Car, "9883," *98*
___	**(52144)**	LIRR Flatcar w/Grumman Van (TT), *99*
___	**(52145)**	Long Island Aluminum Passenger Coaches, "9983-1/9983-2," *99*
___	**(52166)**	Long Island Flatcar w/ Grumman Trailer "8398," *98*
___	**(52173)**	Long Island RR F3 AA Shells, *00*
___	**(52174)**	REA Baggage Car "0083," *00*
___	**[52186]**	Grucci Fireworks Boxcar, *00*
___	**(52209)**	World's Fair Sleeper/Roomette Car "0183," *01*
___	**(52232)**	Central RR of Long Island Boxcar, *01*
___	**(52235)**	World's Fair Vista-Dome Car "0283," *02*
___	**(52256)**	New York & Atlantic Ry. Boxcar "8302," *02*
___	**(52263)**	World's Fair Combine Car "0383," *02*
___	**(52296)**	Republic TOFC, *03*

ST. LOUIS LIONEL RAILROAD CLUB (ST. LOUIS LRRC)

___	**(52099)**	MP Flatcar w/ St. Louis LRRC trailer, *96*
___	**(52104)**	St. Louis LRRC T&T, *96 u*
___	**(52117)**	Wabash Flatcar w/ REA Tractor and Trailer, *97*
___	**(52136A)**	Christmas Special Tractor and Trailer, *97*
___	**(52136B)**	Frisco Special Tractor and Trailer, *98*
___	**(52147)**	Frisco Campbell TOFC Flatcar (TT), *98*
___	**(52150)**	Frisco Campbell TOFC Flatcar (TT), *98*
___	**(52167)**	AT&SF Flatcar w/Navajo Trailers "831999," *99*
___	**(52190)**	IC Flatcar w/Trailers, *00*
___	**(52222)**	SSW (Cotton Belt) Flatcar w/SP Tractor and Trailer, *01*
___	**(52224A)**	SP Flatcar with Navajo Tractor and Trailer, *01*
___	**(52224B)**	SP Flatcar with Trailer Flatcar Service Tractor and Trailer, *01*
___	**(52258)**	UP Flatcar with UP Tractor and Trailer, *02*

TRAIN COLLECTORS ASSOCIATION (TCA)

TCA National Convention Cars

___	**(0511)**	TCA St. Louis Baggage Car "1981," *81*
___	**5734**	TCA REA Reefer, *85*
___	**6315**	TCA Pittsburgh 1-D Tank Car, *72*
___	**6464-1970**	TCA Chicago Boxcar, *70*
___	**6464-1971**	TCA Disneyland Boxcar, *71*
___	**6926**	TCA New Orleans E/V Caboose, *86*
___	**(7205)**	TCA Denver Combination Car "1982," *82*
___	**(7206)**	TCA Louisville Passenger Car "1983," *83*
___	**(7212)**	TCA Pittsburgh Passenger Car "1984," *84*
___	**7812**	TCA Houston Stock Car, *77*
___	**(8476)**	TCA 4-6-4 "5484," *85*
___	**(9123)**	TCA Dearborn Auto Carrier "1973" (3-tier), *73*
___	**9319**	TCA Silver Jubilee Mint Car, *79*
___	**(9544)**	TCA Chicago Observation Car "1980," *80*
___	**9611**	TCA Boston Hi-cube Boxcar, *78*
___	**9774**	TCA Orlando Southern Belle Boxcar, *75*
___	**(9779)**	TCA Philadelphia Boxcar "9700-1976," *76*
___	**9864**	TCA Seattle Reefer, *74*
___	**(11737)**	TCA 40th Anniversary F3 ABA set "40," *93*
___	**(17879)**	TCA Valley Forge Dining Car "1989," *89*
___	**(17883)**	New Georgia Railroad Passenger Car "1990," *90*
___	**(17898)**	Wabash Reefer "21596," *92*
___	**(52008)**	Bucyrus Erie Crane Car "1993X," *93*
___	**(52035)**	Yorkrail GP9 "1750," shell only, *94*
___	**(52036)**	TCA 40th Anniversary B/W Caboose, *94*
___	**(52037)**	Yorkrail GP9 "1754," *94*
___	**(52062)**	TCA "Skytop" Observation Car "1995," *95*
___	**(52085)**	TCA Full Vista Dome Car "1996," *96*
___	**(52106)**	TCA City of Phoenix Diner "1997," *97*
___	**(52142)**	TCA Mass. Central Maxi-stack "5100-01," *98*
___	**(52143)**	TCA City of Providence Passenger Car "1998," *98*
___	**(52155)**	TCA City of San Francisco Baggage Car "1999," *99*
___	**(52191)**	TCA "City of Grand Rapids" Duplex Aluminum Passenger, *00 u*
___	**(52198)**	TCA Frisco Boxcar "5477000," *00 u*
___	**(52210)**	TCA Rico Station, *00 u*
___	**(52220)**	City of Chattanooga Vista Dome Car "2001," *01*
___	**(52221)**	TCA Norfolk Southern Boxcar "2001," *01*
___	**(52250)**	City of Chicago Combo Car "2002," *02*

UNCATALOGED CLUB CARS AND SPECIAL PRODUCTION

TCA Museum-Related Cars

___	[1018-1979]	Mortgage Burning Hi-cube Boxcar, *79*
___	[5731]	L&N Reefer, *90*
___	[7780]	TCA Museum Boxcar, *80*
___	[7781]	Hafner Boxcar, *81*
___	[7782]	Carlisle & Finch Boxcar, *82*
___	[7783]	Ives Boxcar, *83*
___	[7784]	Voltamp Boxcar, *84*
___	[7785]	Hoge Boxcar, *85*
___	[9771]	Norfolk & Western Boxcar, *77*
___	(16811)	Rutland Boxcar "5477096," *96*
___	[52045]	Penn Dutch Milk Car "61052," *94*
___	(52051)	Baltimore & Ohio "Sentinel" Boxcar "6464095," *95*
___	[52052]	TCA 40th Anniversary Boxcar, *94*
___	(52063)	NYC "Pacemaker" Boxcar "6464125," *95*
___	(52064)	Missouri Pacific Boxcar "6464150," *95*
___	(52065)	Penn-Dutch Grain Operating Boxcar "9208," *01*
___	(52118)	Rio Grande Boxcar "5477097," *97*
___	(52119)	TCA Museum 20th Anniversary Boxcar, *97*
___	(52128)	Pennsylvania Dutch Pretzels Boxcar, *99*
___	(52172)	L&N Share the Freedom Boxcar "5477099," *99*
___	(52198)	Frisco Boxcar "5477000," *00*
___	(52226)	Angela Trotta Thomas Boxcar "2000," *01*
___	(52242)	Lionel Gondola "2002" Blue, *02*
___	(52243)	National Toy Train Museum 1-Dome Tank Car 1954, *01*
___	(52271)	National Toy Train Museum Wheel Car "1957," *02*

TCA Bicentennial Special Set

___	1973	TCA Bicentennial Observation Car, *76*
___	1974	TCA Bicentennial Passenger Car, *76*
___	1975	TCA Bicentennial Passenger Car, *76*
___	1976	TCA Bicentennial U36B, *76*

Atlantic Division TCA

___	[1980]	Atlantic Division Flatcar w/ trailers, *80*
___	[6101]	Burlington Northern Covered Quad Hopper, *82*
___	[9186]	Conrail N5C Caboose, *79*
___	[9193]	Budweiser Vat Car, *84*
___	[9466]	Wanamaker Boxcar, *83*
___	[9788]	Lehigh Valley Boxcar, *78*

UNCATALOGED CLUB CARS AND SPECIAL PRODUCTION

___ **[No Number]** Pennsylvania Reading Seashore Bunk Car, *85*

Desert Division TCA
___ **[52088]** Desert Division 25th Anniversary On-Track Step Van, *96*
___ **(52105)** TCA Superstition Mountain Operating Gondola "61997," *97*

Dixie Division TCA
___ **(52127)** TCA Dixie Division 10th Anniversary Southern 3-bay Hopper "360997," *98*

Eastern Division TCA
___ **(52059)** Clinchfield Quad Hopper w/ coal load "16413," *94*

Eastern Division TCA—Washington, Baltimore and Annapolis
___ **[9412]** Richmond, Fredericksburg & Potomac Boxcar, *79*
___ **[9740]** Chessie System Boxcar, *76*
___ **[9771]** Norfolk & Western Boxcar, *78*
___ **[9783]** B&O "Time-Saver" Boxcar, *77*

Ft. Pitt Division TCA
___ **[1984-30X]** Heinz Ketchup Boxcar, *84*

Great Lakes Division TCA
___ **[9740]** Chessie System Boxcar, *76*
___ **[1983]** Churchill Downs Boxcar, *83*
___ **[1983]** Churchill Downs Reefer, *83*

Great Lakes Division TCA—Detroit-Toledo Chapter
___ **[8957]** Burlington Northern GP20, *80*
___ **[8958]** Burlington Northern GP20 Dummy, *80*
___ **[9119]** Detroit & Mackinac Covered Quad Hopper, *77*
___ **[9272]** New Haven B/W Caboose, *79*
___ **[9401]** Great Northern Boxcar, *78*
___ **[9730]** CP Rail Boxcar, *76*
___ **52000** Detroit-Toledo Division Flatcar w/ trailer, *92*

Great Lakes Division TCA—Three Rivers Chapter
___ **[9113]** Norfolk & Western Quad Hopper, *76*

Great Lakes Division TCA Western Michigan Chapter
___ **[9730]** CP Rail Boxcar, *74*

UNCATALOGED CLUB CARS AND SPECIAL PRODUCTION

Lake & Pines Division TCA
___ **52018**   3-M Boxcar, *93*

Lone Star Division TCA
___ **[7522]**   New Orleans Mint Car w/ coin, *86*
___ **(52093)**   Lone Star Division Boxcar "6464696," *96*

Lone Star Division TCA—North Texas Chapter
___ **[9739]**   D&RGW Boxcar, *76*
___ **[No Number]**Texas Special F3 A Unit, shell only, *81*
___ **[No Number]**Texas Special F3 B Unit, shell only, *82*

METCA
___ **[10]**   Jersey Central F3 A Unit, shell only, *71*
___ **[9272]**   New Haven B/W Caboose, *79*
___ **[9754]**   New York Central "Pacemaker" Boxcar, *76*

Midwest Division TCA
___ **[4]**   C&NW F3 A Unit, shell only, *77*
___ **[00005]**   Midwest Division Covered Quad Hopper, *78*
___ **[1287]**   C&NW Reefer, *84*
___ **[1988]**   Illinois Central Boxcar, *88*
___ **[7600]**   Frisco "Spirit of '76" N5C Caboose "00003," *76*
___ **[9725]**   Midwest Division Stock Car "00002," *75*
___ **[9872]**   PFE Reefer "00006," *79*
___ **(52237)**   Lionel Gondola "2002," Yellow, *01*
___ **(52238)**   Lionel Gondola "2002," Red, *01*
___ **(52239)**   Lionel Gondola "2002," Silver, *01*
___ **(52240)**   Lionel Gondola 3-pack "2002," *01*
___ **(52241)**   Lionel Gondola "2002," Black, *02*
___ **Not Assigned** Lionel Gondola "2002," Blue, *02*
___ **Not Assigned** Lionel Gondola "2002," Gold, *02*

Midwest Division TCA Museum Express
___ **[9264]**   Illinois Central Gulf Covered Quad Hopper, *78*
___ **[9289]**   Chicago & North Western N5C Caboose, *80*
___ **[9785]**   Conrail Boxcar, *77*
___ **[9786]**   Chicago & North Western Boxcar, *79*

NETCA
___ **[1203]**   Boston & Maine NW-2, shell only, *72*
___ **[5710]**   Canadian Pacific Reefer, *82*
___ **[5716]**   Vermont Central Reefer, *83*
___ **[6124]**   Delaware & Hudson Covered Quad Hopper, *84*

UNCATALOGED CLUB CARS AND SPECIAL PRODUCTION

___	**[8051]**	Hood's Milk Boxcar, *86*
___	**[9181]**	Boston & Maine N5C Caboose, *77*
___	**[9400]**	Conrail Boxcar, *78*
___	**[9415]**	Providence & Worcester Boxcar, *79*
___	**[9423]**	NYNH&H Boxcar, *80*
___	**[9445]**	Vermont Northern Boxcar, *81*
___	**[9753]**	Maine Central Boxcar, *75*
___	**[9768]**	Boston & Maine Boxcar, *76*
___	**[9785]**	Conrail Boxcar, *78*
___	**52001**	Boston & Maine Quad Hopper w/ coal load, *92*
___	**52016**	Boston & Maine Gondola w/ coil covers, *93*
___	**[52043]**	L.L. Bean Boxcar "1994," *94*
___	**[52080]**	B&M Flatcar w/ trailer "91095," *95*
___	**(52111)**	Ben & Jerry's NETCA Flatcar w/Trailer, *96*
___	**(52146)**	Ocean Spray Plug Door Reefer "OSCX 1998," *98*
___	**(52212)**	Berkshire Brewing Refrigerator Car, *00*
___	**(52236)**	Moxie Boxcar, *01*
___	**(52270)**	Jenney Mfg. Co. Tank Car, *02*
___	**(52306)**	NE Trans TOFC, *03*

Ozark Division TCA—Gateway Chapter

___	**[5700]**	Oppenheimer Reefer, *81*
___	**[9068]**	Reading Bobber Caboose, *76*
___	**[9601]**	Illinois Central Gulf Hi-cube Boxcar, *77*
___	**[9767]**	Railbox Boxcar, *78*
___	**52003**	"Meet Me In St. Louis" Flatcar w/ trailer, *92*

Pacific Northwest Division TCA

___	**(52077)**	Great Northern Hi-cube Boxcar "9695," *95*
___	**[No Number]**	Pacific Northwest Division F3 AA, shells only, *74*

Rocky Mountain Division TCA

___	**1971-1976**	Rocky Mountain Division Reefer, *76*

Sacramento—Sierra Chapter TCA

___	**[6401]**	Virginian B/W Caboose, *84*
___	**[9301]**	US Mail Operating Boxcar, *76*
___	**[9414]**	Cotton Belt Boxcar, *80*
___	**[9427]**	Bay Line Boxcar, *81*
___	**[9444]**	Louisiana Midland Boxcar, *82*
___	**[9452]**	Western Pacific Boxcar, *83*
___	**[9705]**	D&RGW Boxcar, *75*
___	**[9723]**	Western Pacific Boxcar, *73*

UNCATALOGED CLUB CARS AND SPECIAL PRODUCTION

___	[9726]	Erie-Lackawanna Boxcar, *79*
___	[9730]	CP Rail Boxcar, *77*
___	[9785]	Conrail Boxcar, *78*
___	[No Number]	Lionel Lines Tender, shell only, *84*

Southern Division TCA

___	[1976]	Florida East Coast F-3 ABA, shells only, *76*
___	[1986]	Southern Division Bunk Car, *86*
___	[6111]	L&N Covered Quad Hopper, *83*
___	[9287]	Southern N5C Caboose, *77*
___	[9352]	Trailer Train Flatcar w/ Circus trailers, *80*
___	[9403]	Seaboard Coast Line Boxcar, *78*
___	[9405]	Chattahoochie Boxcar, *79*
___	[9443]	Florida East Coast Boxcar, *81*
___	[9471]	ACL Boxcar, *84*
___	[9482]	Norfolk & Southern Boxcar, *85*
___	[16606]	Southern Searchlight Car, *88*

TOY TRAIN OPERATING SOCIETY (TTOS)

TTOS National Convention Cars

___	[1984]	TTOS Sacramento Northern Boxcar, *84*
___	[1985]	TTOS Snowbird Covered Quad Hopper, *85*
___	6076	Santa Fe Hopper (O27), *70*
___	6582	TTOS Portland Flatcar w/ wood load, *86*
___	[9326]	Burlington Northern B/W Caboose, *82*
___	9347	TTOS Niagara Falls 3-D Tank Car, *79*
___	[9355]	Delaware & Hudson B/W Caboose, *82*
___	[9361]	Chicago & North Western B/W Caboose, *82*
___	[9382]	Florida East Coast B/W Caboose, *82*
___	9512	TTOS Summerdale Junction Passenger Car, *74*
___	9520	TTOS Phoenix Combination Car, *75*
___	9526	TTOS Snowbird Observation Car, *76*
___	9535	TTOS Columbus Baggage Car, *77*
___	9678	TTOS Hollywood Hi-cube Boxcar, *78*
___	9868	TTOS Oklahoma City Reefer, *80*
___	[9883]	TTOS Phoenix Reefer, *83*
___	(17871)	NYC Flatcar w/ Kodak and Xerox trailers "81487," *87*
___	(17872)	Anaconda Ore Car "81988," *88*
___	(17877)	MKT 1-D Tank Car "3739469," *89*
___	17884	Columbus & Dayton Terminal Boxcar (Std O), *90*
___	(17889)	Southern Pacific Flatcar w/ trailer "15791" (Std O), *91*

UNCATALOGED CLUB CARS AND SPECIAL PRODUCTION

___	**(19963)**	Union Equity 3-bay ACF Hopper "86892" (Std O), *92*
___	**(52010)**	Weyerhaeuser DD Boxcar "838593" (Std O), *93*
___	**(52029)**	Ford 1-D Tank Car "12" (O27), *94*
___	**(52030)**	Ford Gondola "4023," *94*
___	**(52031)**	Ford Hopper "1458" (O27), *94*
___	**(52057)**	Western Pacific Boxcar "64641995," *95*
___	**(52087)**	New Mexico Central Boxcar "64641996," *96*
___	**(52114)**	NYC Flatcar w/ Gleason & SASIB Trailers, *97*
___	**(52149)**	Conrail Flatcar w/Blum Coal Shovel, *98*
___	**(52192)**	TTOS SP Crane & Gondola 2-pack, *00 u*
___	**(52193)**	SP Crane Car "SPMW 6060," *00*
___	**(52194)**	SP Gondola "7111," *00*
___	**(52231)**	British Columbia RR 1-D Tank Car, *01*

TTOS Division Cars

___	**(52009)**	Sacramento Valley Division Western Pacfic Boxcar "64641993," *93*
___	**52040**	Wolverine Division GTW Flatcar w/ LL Tractor and Trailer, "52033," *94*
___	**(52058)**	Central California Division Santa Fe Boxcar "64641895," *95*
___	**(52086)**	Canadian Division Pacific Great Eastern Boxcar "64641972," *96*

Southwest Division TTOS Cal-Stewart

___	**(19962)**	Southern Pacific 3-bay ACF Hopper "496035" (Std O), *92*
___	**(52047)**	Cotton Belt Woodside Caboose w/ smoke "1921" (Std O), *93-94*
___	**(52073)**	Pacific Fruit Express Reefer "459402" (Std O), *95*
___	**(52098)**	National Bureau of Standards Boxcar (Std O), *96*
___	**(52121)**	Mobilgas Tank Car "238" (Std O), *97*
___	**(52154)**	Pacific Fruit Express Reefer "459403" (Std O), *98*
___	**(52205)**	SP Overnight Merchandise Service Boxcar 5-pack, *00*

TTOS New Mexico Division Cars

___	**(52264)**	Durango & Silverton Operating Hopper "9325," *02*

Other TTOS Production

___	**[1983]**	TTOS Phoenix 3-D Tank Car, *83*
___	**(17894)**	Southern Pacific Tractor, *91*
___	**(52021)**	Weyerhaeuser Tractor and Trailer, *93*
___	**52022**	Union Pacific Boxcar, *93*

UNCATALOGED CLUB CARS AND SPECIAL PRODUCTION

	(52032)	Ford 1-D Tank Car "14" w/ Kughn inscription (O27), *94*
___	(52046)	ACL Boxcar "16247," *94*
___	52053	TTOS Carail Boxcar, *94*
___	(52068)	Toy Train Parade TTOS Contadina Boxcar "16245," *94*
___	(52078)	Southern Pacific SD9 "5366," *96*
___	(52079)	Southern Pacific B/W Caboose "1996," *96*
___	(52084)	Union Pacific I-Beam Flatcar w/ load "16380," *95*
___	(52113)	Northeastern Division Genesee & Wyoming RR 3-Bay ACF Hopper "10000" (Std O), *97*

TTOS Gadsden Pacific Ore Cars

___	17878	Magma Ore Car w/ load, *89*
___	17881	Phelps-Dodge Ore Car w/ load, *90*
___	17886	Cyprus Ore Car w/ load, *91*
___	19961	Inspiration Consolidated Copper Co. Ore Car w/ load, *92*
___	52011	Tucson, Cornelia & Gila Bend Ore Car w/ load, *93*
___	52027	Pinto Valley Mine Ore Car w/ load, *94*
___	52071	Copper Basin Railway Ore Car w/ load, *95*
___	52089	SMARRCO Ore Car w/ load, *96*
___	(52124)	EPSW Ore Car w/ load, *97*
___	(52164)	SP Ore Car w/ load, *98*
___	(52177)	Arizona Southern Ore Car w/ load, *99*
___	(52213)	TTOS GPD Ore Car BHP Copper, *00 u*
___	(52248)	Tombstone & Southern RR Ore Car, *01*

VIRGINIA TRAIN COLLECTORS (VTC)

___	[7679]	VTC Boxcar, *79*
___	[7681]	VTC N5C Caboose, *81*
___	[7682]	VTC Covered Quad Hopper, *82*
___	[7683]	Virginia Fruit Express Reefer, *83*
___	[7684]	Vitraco 3-D Tank Car, *84*
___	[7685]	VTC Boxcar, *85*
___	[7686]	VTC GP7, *86*
___	[7692-1]	VTC Baggage Car (O27), *92*
___	[7692-2]	VTC Combination Car (O27), *92*
___	[7692-3]	VTC Dining Car (O27), *92*
___	[7692-4]	VTC Passenger Car (O27), *92*
___	[7692-5]	VTC Vista Dome Car (O27), *92*
___	[7692-6]	VTC Passenger Car (O27), *92*
___	[7692-7]	VTC Observation Car (O27), *92*
___	[52060]	VTC Tender w/ whistle "7694," *94*

Section 7
LIONEL CATALOGS 1945–2005

	Year	Description	Size	Pages	Exc	New
___	**1945**	Consumer Catalog	8½" x 11"	4 pages		NRS
___	**1946**	Consumer Catalog	8⅜" x ¼"	20 pages	50	85
___	**1947**	Consumer Catalog	11¼" x 7⅝"	32 pages	30	45
___	**1948**	Consumer Catalog	11¼" x 8"	36 pages	30	50
___	**1949**	Consumer Catalog	11¼" x 8"	40 pages	75	100
___	**1950**	Consumer Catalog	11¼" x 8"	44 pages	45	75
___	**1951**	Consumer Catalog	11¼" x 7¾"	36 pages	25	45
___	**1952**	Consumer Catalog	11¼" x 7¾"	36 pages	20	35
___	**1953**	Consumer Catalog	11¼" x 7⅝"	40 pages	20	30
___	**1954**	Consumer Catalog	11¼" x 7⅝"	44 pages	20	30
___	**1955**	Consumer Catalog	11¼" x 7⅝"	44 pages	20	30
___	**1956**	Consumer Catalog	11¼" x 7⅝"	40 pages	12	24
___	**1956**	Consumer Catalog	11¼" x 7⅝"	40 pages	12	24
___	**1957**	Consumer Catalog	11¼" x 7½"	52 pages	11	22
___	**1958**	Consumer Catalog	11¼" x 7⅝"	56 pages	10	17
___	**1959**	Consumer Catalog	11" x 8½"	56 pages	11	17
___	**1960**	Consumer Catalog	11" x 8⅜"	56 pages	6	10
___	**1961**	Consumer Catalog	8½" x 11"	72 pages	6	10
___	**1962**	Consumer Catalog	8½" x 11"	100 pages	8	12
___	**1963**	Consumer Catalog	8⅜" x 10⅞"	56 pages	4	6
___	**1964**	Consumer Catalog	8⅜" x 10⅞"	24 pages	4	6
___	**1965**	Consumer Catalog	8½" x 10⅞"	40 pages	4	6
___	**1966**	Consumer Catalog	10⅞" x 8⅜"	40 pages	4	7
___	**1967**	Same Catalog as 1966			4	6
___	**1968**	Consumer Catalog	8½" x 11"	8 pages	4	6
___	**1969**	Consumer Catalog	11" x 8½"	8 pages	3	5
___	**1970**	Consumer Catalog w/ foldout poster	8½" x 11"	8 pages	3	5
___	**1971**	Consumer Catalog	8½" x 11"	12 pages	3	5
___	**1972**	Consumer Catalog	8½" x 11"	16 pages	3	5
___	**1973**	Consumer Catalog	8½" x 11"	16 pages	2	4
___	**1974**	Consumer Catalog	8½" x 11"	20 pages	2	4
___	**1975**	Consumer Catalog	8½" x 11"	24 pages	2	4
___	**1976**	Consumer Catalog	8½" x 11"	24 pages	2	4
___	**1977**	Consumer Catalog	8½" x 11"	24 pages	2	4
___	**1978**	Consumer Catalog	8½" x 11"	24 pages	2	4
___	**1979**	Consumer Catalog	8½" x 11"	24 pages	2	4
___	**1980**	Consumer Catalog	8½" x 11"	28 pages	2	4

	Year	Description	Size	Pages	Exc	New
___	**1981**	Consumer Catalog	5½" x 7"	32 pages	1	2
___	**1982**	Traditional Series Consumer Catalog	8½" x 11"	20 pages	2	4
___	**1982**	Collector Series Consumer Catalog	8½" x 11"	12 pages	2	4
___	**1983**	Traditional Series Consumer Catalog	8½" x 11"	20 pages	2	3
___	**1983**	Collector Series Consumer Catalog	8½" x 11"	16 pages	2	3
___	**1984**	Traditional Series Consumer Catalog	8½" x 11"	20 pages	2	3
___	**1984**	Collector Series Consumer Catalog	8½" x 11"	16 pages	2	3
___	**1985**	Traditional Series Consumer Catalog	8½" x 11"	20 pages	2	3
___	**1985**	Collector Series Consumer Catalog	8½" x 11"	12 pages	2	3
___	**1986**	Traditional Series Consumer Catalog	8½" x 11"	16 pages	2	3
___	**1986**	Collector Series Consumer Catalog	8½" x 11"	16 pages	2	3
___	**1986**	Stocking Stuffers Brochure	8½" x 11"	4 pages	2	3
___	**1987**	Consumer Catalog	8½" x 11"	40 pages	3	4
___	**1987**	Large Scale Brochure	11" x 8½"	6 pages	1	2
___	**1987**	Stocking Stuffers Brochure	8½" x 11"	4 pages	2	3
___	**1988**	Consumer Catalog	8½" x 11"	40 pages	2	3
___	**1988**	Large Scale Catalog	8½" x 11"	16 pages	1	2
___	**1988**	Classics Brochure	8½" x 11"	4 pages	1	2
___	**1988**	Hiawatha Brochure	8½" x 11"	4 pages	2	3
___	**1988**	Stocking Stuffers Flyer	8½" x 11"	1 page	2	3
___	**1989**	Pre-Toy Fair Consumer Catalog	8½" x 11"	20 pages	2	3
___	**1989**	Toy Fair Consumer Catalog	8½" x 11"	28 pages	2	3
___	**1989**	Pre-Toy Fair Classics Brochure	8½" x 11"	4 pages	1	2
___	**1989**	Toy Fair Classics Brochure	8½" x 11"	4 pages	1	2
___	**1989**	Large Scale Catalog	8½" x 11"	20 pages	1	2
___	**1989**	Stocking Stuffers	8½" x 11"	4 pages	2	3

	Year	Description	Size	Pages	Exc	New
___	1990	Brochure Book 1 Consumer Catalog	8½" x 11"	20 pages	2	4
___	1990	Book 2 Consumer Catalog	8½" x 11"	36 pages	2	3
___	1990	Large Scale Catalog	8½" x 11"	16 pages	1	2
___	1990	Stocking Stuffers Brochure	8½" x 11"	6 pages	2	3
___	1991	Book 1 Consumer Catalog	8½" x 11"	24 pages	2	4
___	1991	Book 2 Consumer Catalog	8½" x 11"	60 pages	2	3
___	1991	Stocking Stuffers Brochure	8½" x 11"	6 pages	2	3
___	1992	Book 1 Consumer Catalog	8½" x 11"	32 pages	2	4
___	1992	Book 2 Consumer Catalog	8½" x 11"	48 pages	2	3
___	1992	Stocking Stuffers Brochure	8½" x 11"	8 pages	2	3
___	1993	Book 1 Consumer Catalog	8½" x 11"	32 pages	2	4
___	1993	Book 2 Consumer Catalog	8½" x 11"	52 pages	2	3
___	1993	Stocking Stuffers/ 1994 Spring Releases Catalog	8½" x 11"	28 pages	2 3	
___	1994	Consumer Catalog	8½" x 11"	64 pages	3	4
___	1994	Thomas the Tank Engine Catalog	8½" x 11"	8 pages	1	2
___	1994	Trainmaster Transformer Catalog	8½" x 11"	8 pages	1	2
___	1994	Stocking Stuffers/ 1995 Spring Releases Catalog	8½" x 11"	32 pages	2	3
___	1994	Preschool Brochure	8½" x 11"	4 pages	1	2
___	1994	Crayola Brochure	8½" x 11"	4 pages	1	2
___	1994	Gift Collection Catalog	8½" x 11"	12 pages	1	2
___	1995	Consumer Catalog	8½" x 11"	88 pages	3	4
___	1995	Stocking Stuffers/ 1996 Spring Releases Catalog	8½" x 11"	32 pages	2	3
___	1996	Consumer Catalog	8½" x 11"	24 pages	2	3
___	1996	Consumer Catalog illustrated	10" x 8"	24 pages	2	3
___	1996	Accessories Catalog	10" x 8"	32 pages	2	3

	Year	Catalog	Size	Pages	Exc	New
___	**1997**	Heritage Catalog	10" x 8"	12 pages	2	3
___	**1997**	Century Club Catalog	10" x 8"	16 pages	2	3
___	**1997**	Classic I Catalog	10" x 8"	24 pages	2	3
___	**1997**	Classic II Catalog	10" x 8"	36 pages	2	3
___	**1997**	Lionel Brochure	10" x 8"	4 pages	2	3
___	**1997**	Fall '97 Heritage II Catalog	10" x 8"	12 pages	2	3
___	**1998**	Classic Catalog	8½" x 9"	76 pages	2	3
___	**1998**	Heritage Catalog	11" x 8½"	24 pages	2	3
___	**1998**	Legendary Trains Catalog	10⅞" x 8½"	64 pages	2	3
___	**1998**	Gilbert American Flyer Trains Brochure	8½" x 11"	4 pages	1	2
___	**1999**	Classic Trains Catalog Volume 1	8¼" x 10½"	63 pages	2	3
___	**1999**	Classic Trains Catalog Volume 2	8¼" x 10½"	45 pages	2	3
___	**1999**	Heritage Catalog	11" x 8½"	26 pages	2	3
___	**1999**	Classic Trains Catalog Volume 3	8¼" x 10¾"	58 pages	2	3
___	**2000**	Classic Trains Catalog Volume 1	8" x 10¾"	110 pages	2	3
___	**2000**	Classic Trains Catalog, Volume 2	8" x 10¾"	85 pages	2	3
___	**2001**	Classic Trains Catalog, Volume 1	8" x 10¾"	122 pages	2	3
___	**2001**	Classic Trains Catalog Volume 2	8" x 10¾"	122 pages	2	3
___	**2001**	Challenger Brochure,	8½" x 11"	4 pages	1	2
___	**2001**	Hiawatha Brochure,	11" x 8½"	4 pages	1	2
___	**2002**	Classic Trains Catalog Volume 1	8" x 10¾"	122 pages	2	3
___	**2002**	Classic Trains Catalog, Volume 2	8" x 10¾"	110 pages	2	3
___	**2003**	Classic Trains Catalog, Volume 1	8" x 10¾"	132 pages	2	3
___	**2003**	Classic Trains Catalog, Volume 2	8" x 10¾"	152 pages	2	3
___	**2004**	Train Catalog, Volume 1, "The Polar Express"	8" x 10¾"	164 pages		CP
___	**2004**	Train Catalog, Volume 2	8" x 10¾"	188 pages		CP

ABBREVIATIONS
Pocket Guide Descriptions

A	diesel A unit
AA	two diesel A units
AAR	Association of American Railroads (truck type)
AC	alternating current
acc.	accessory
ACF	hopper type
Alco	diesel type
Alco A	diesel type
Alco FA-2A	diesel type
Alco FA-2B	diesel type
Anniv.	Anniversary
appro.	approaches
auto.	automatic
B	diesel B unit
Bag.	baggage
Bldg.	building
Blvd.	boulevard
Box.	boxcar
b/w	black and white
B/W	bay window
bump.	bumper(s)
Cab.	caboose
cata.	catalog
CC	command control
cent.	central
chem.	chemical
con.	connection
cont.	control
Conv.	conversion
CP	current production
C.V.	Commodore Vanderbilt
Dash 8	diesel type
Dash 9	diesel type
DC	direct current
DD	double-door
dep.	depressed
d.p.d.t.	double-pole, double-throw switches
dir.	direct
dum.	dummy
dz.	dozen
elec.	electric
electr.	electronic
EP-5	electric type locomotive
ETD	end-of-train device
Exp.	express
ext.	extended
E/V	extended vision
F-3	diesel type
F.A.O.S.	F A O Schwarz
FARR	Famous American Railroad Series
FF	Fallen Flag Series
Flat.	flatcar
FM	Fairbanks-Morse
GG-1	electric type locomotive
GE	switcher type
Gen.	General, steam type
Gon.	gondola
GP-7	diesel type
GP-9	diesel type
GP-20	diesel type
GP-35	diesel type
GP-38-2	diesel type
Hi-cube	boxcar type
Hop.	hopper
HS	heat-stamped
illum.	illuminated
ins.	insulated, insulator
lett.	lettering
litho.	lithographed
low-cup.	low-cupola
maint.	maintenance
man.	manual
MB	multi-block door
mech.	mechanical
merch.	merchandise
MU	multiple unit (commuter cars)
N5C	caboose type
N8	caboose type
NBA	National Basketball Assoc.

NHL	National Hockey League		**St.**	state
NM	not manufactured		**Sta.**	station
NW-2	diesel type		**Std.**	Standard gauge (2⅛" between outside rails)
O	Lionel gauge (1¼" between outside rails)		**Std. O**	Standard O (scale length and dimension)
OO	Lionel Gauge (¾" between outside rails)		**Steam**	steam engine
Obs.	observation		**str.**	straight
oper.	operating		**Sup.**	super
or.	orange		**S/W**	square window
pass.	passenger		**Switch.**	switcher
pc(s).	piece(s)		**Tdr.**	tender
port.	porthole		**TOFC**	flatcar type
pow.	power, powered		**TT**	TruTrack
pr.	pair		**TTUX**	flatcar type
Pull.	Pullman		**Trk.**	track
Quad	quad hopper		**Trans.**	transformer
Rad.	radius		***u* or uncat.**	uncataloged
R.C.	remote control		**U36B**	diesel type
RDC	diesel-powered passenger unit		**U36C**	diesel type
rect.	rectifier		**V. D.**	Vista Dome
rectifier	electric type locomotive		**w/**	with
Reefer	refrigerator car		**w/o**	without
Refrig.	refrigerator		**whl.**	wheel
rem.	remote		**1-D**	one dome
rnd.	round		**2-D**	two dome
RS	rubber-stamped		**3-D**	three dome
RS-3	diesel type			
RSC-3	diesel type			
RSD-4	diesel type			
SB	single-block door			
SD-9	diesel type			
SD-18	diesel type			
SD-24	diesel type			
SD-28	diesel type			
SD-38	diesel type			
SD-40	diesel type			
SD-50	diesel type			
SD-60M	diesel type			
sec.	section			
SP	caboose type			
spec.	special			
SSS	Service Station Special			

Railroad Name Abbreviations

ACL	Atlantic Coast Line
ACY	Akron, Canton, and Youngstown
ALASK	Alaska Railroad
AT&SF (ATSF)	Atchison, Topeka, and Santa Fe
B&A	Boston and Albany
BAOC	British American Oil Co.
BAR	Bangor and Aroostook
B&LE	Bessemer and Lake Erie
B&M	Boston and Maine
BN	Burlington Northern
B&O	Baltimore and Ohio
C&A	Chicago and Alton
C&IM	Chicago and Illinois Midland
CB&Q (CBQ)	Chicago, Burlington, and Quincy
CCC&StL	Cleveland, Cincinnati, Chicago, and St. Louis
CN	Canadian National
CNJ	Central of New Jersey
C&NW (CNW)	Chicago and North Western
C&O	Chesapeake and Ohio
CP	Canadian Pacific
CRI&P	Chicago, Rock Island, and Peoria
CSt PM&O	Chicago, St. Paul, Minneapolis, and Omaha
D&H	Delaware and Hudson
DL&W	Delaware, Lackawanna, and Western
DM&IR	Duluth, Missabe, and Iron Range
D&RG	Denver and Rio Grande
D&RGW	Denver and Rio Grande Western
DT&I	Detroit, Toledo, and Ironton
D&TS	Detroit and Toledo Shore Line
EJ&E	Elgin, Joliet, and Eastern
EMD	Electro-Motive Division
Erie-Lack.	Erie-Lackawanna
FEC	Florida East Coast
GM&O	Gulf, Mobile, and Ohio
GN	Great Northern
GTW	Grand Trunk Western
IC	Illinois Central
ICG	Illinois Central Gulf
IETCA	Inland Empire Train Collectors Association
L&C	Lancaster and Chester
Lack	Lackawanna
LCAC	Lionel Collectors Association of Canada
LCCA	Lionel Collectors Club of America
LCOL	Lionel Central Operating Lines
LL	Lionel Lines
L&N	Louisville and Nashville
LNAC	Louisville, New Albany, and Corydon
LOTS	Lionel Operating Train Society
LRRC	Lionel Railroader Club

LV	Lehigh Valley
MD&W	Minnesota, Dakota, and Western
METCA	New York Metropolitan Division TCA
MKT	Missouri, Kansas, Texas (KATY)
MNS (MN&S)	Minneapolis, Northfield, and Southern
MP (MoPac)	Missouri Pacific
MPA	Maryland and Pennsylvania (Ma and Pa)
MILW	Milwaukee Road
M&StL	Minneapolis and St. Louis
NC&StL	Nashville, Chattanooga, and St. Louis
NdeM	Nacionales de Mexico Railway
NETCA	New England Division Train Collectors Association
NH	New Haven
NKP	Nickel Plate Road
NLOE	Nassau Lionel Operating Engineers
NP	Northern Pacific
N&W	Norfolk and Western
NYC	New York Central
NYNH&H	New York, New Haven, and Hartford
ON	Ontario Northland
PC	Penn Central
P&E	Peoria and Eastern
PFE	Pacific Fruit Express
PHD	Port Huron and Detroit
P&LE	Pittsburgh and Lake Erie
PRR	Pennsylvania Railroad
REA	Railway Express Agency
RF&P	Richmond, Fredericksburg, and Potomac
RI	Rock Island
RI&P	Rock Island and Peoria
SCL	Seaboard Coast Line
SMARRCO	San Manuel Arizona Railroad Company
SP	Southern Pacific
SP&S	Spokane, Portland, and Seattle
SUNX	Sunoco
TA&G	Tennessee, Alabama, and Georgia
TCA	Train Collectors Association
T&P	Texas and Pacific
TP&W	Toledo, Peoria, and Western
TTOS	Toy Train Operating Society
UP	Union Pacific
USMC	United States Marine Corps
VTC	Virginia Train Collectors
V&TRR	Virginia and Truckee Railroad
Wab.	Wabash
W&ARR (W&A)	Western and Atlantic Railroad
WB&A	Washington, Baltimore, and Annapolis Chapter TCA
WM	Western Maryland
WP	Western Pacific

NOTES

NOTES